taste of home
casseroles
slow cooker
& soups

taste of home
B O O K S

REIMAN MEDIA GROUP, INC. · GREENDALE, WISCONSIN

taste of home

A TASTE OF HOME/READER'S DIGEST BOOK

Editor: Janet Briggs
Art Director: Lori Arndt
Associate Art Directors: Edwin Robles, Jr., Rudy Krochalk
Layout Designers: Kathy Crawford, Catherine Fletcher
Proofreaders: Linne Bruskewitz, Jean Duerst
Editorial Assistant: Barb Czysz
Food Director: Diane Werner RD
Recipe Testing and Editing: Taste of Home Test Kitchen
Food Photography: Reiman Photo Studio
Cover Photo Photographers: Jim Wieland, Lori Foy
Cover Food Stylists: Jennifer Janz, Suzanne Breckenridge, Tamara Kaufman
Cover Set Stylists: Grace Natoli Sheldon, Melissa Haberman, Stephanie Marchese (Senior)

Vice President, Executive Editor/Books: Heidi Reuter Lloyd
Senior Editor, Retail & Direct Marketing Books: Mark Hagen
Creative Director: Ardyth Cope
Vice President, Book Marketing: Robert Graham Botta
Chief Marketing Officer: Lisa Karpinski
Senior Vice President, Editor in Chief: Catherine Cassidy
President, Consumer Marketing: Dawn Zier
President, Food & Entertaining: Suzanne M. Grimes
President and Chief Executive Officer: Mary G. Berner

Pictured on front cover: Meaty Spinach Manicotti (p. 62), Sweet 'n' Tangy Chicken (p. 180)
and Chunky Chicken Soup (p. 262).
Pictured on back cover: Leftover-Turkey Bake (p. 16), Slow-Cooked Stew (p. 186) and Chicken Noodle Soup (p. 248).

International Standard Book Number (10): 0-89821-614-1
International Standard Book Number (13): 978-0-89821-614-1
Library of Congress Control Number: 2008926167

For other Taste of Home books and products, visit www.tasteofhome.com.
For more Reader's Digest products and information, visit
www.rd.com (in the United States)
www.rd.ca (in Canada)

Printed in U.S.A.
3 5 7 9 10 8 6 4 2

Table of Contents

Introduction 4

Casserole Recipes 5

Slow Cooker Recipes 125

Soup Recipes 247

Indexes 371

One-Dish Meals
CLASSIC COMFORT FOOD TO SERVE UP 3 TASTY WAYS

When your family craves home-style foods, and you're looking for delicious meal-in-one options, turn to this ultimate collection. **Casseroles, Slow Cooker & Soups** is bursting with 536 taste-tempting foods your family will love.

You'll cook every meal with confidence knowing that each delicious recipe in this 3-in-1 collection was tested by the kitchen staff and readers of *Taste of Home*, America's #1 cooking magazine.

Each section of this book showcases a down-home cooking style—from oven-baked casseroles, to fix-and-forget slow cooking and simmering good soups. Inside you'll find:

Savory Casseroles—Sample tasty dinnertime bakes, breakfast creations and saucy sides. All of these enticing recipes are perfect for family dinners or potlucks.

Slow Cooker Classics—Discover the magic of slow-cooked dishes from appetizers, soups, entrees, sides and desserts. With a little prep, these fuss-free meals cook while you're at work or play.

Simmering Soups—Dish up savory soups, hearty chili, cream soups and cozy chowders. For lighter fare, especially in the summer, try the luscious chilled and fruity soups. Some recipes slowly simmer for hours and others are ready in just minutes.

All of the recipes in this book list prep and cook time and use readily available ingredients to help in meal planning. And, you'll cook like a pro with the easy-to-follow directions. Plus, each collection is packed with tantalizing full-color photos—393 in all—to take the guesswork out of cooking.

With this 3-in-1 collection of family-pleasing favorites, you can't help but serve up homemade goodness and mouth-watering flavor.

Casseroles

Chicken & Turkey 6

Beef & Ground Beef 24

Pork & Lamb 46

Seafood 66

Meatless 80

Breakfast & Brunch 90

Side Dishes 102

Indexes 371

Chicken & Turkey

Turkey Shepherd's Pie

PREP: 10 MIN. **BAKE:** 45 MIN.

We live way out in the country, and the nearest grocery store is 25 miles away. So I've become quite skilled at turning leftovers into second-time-around successes like this.
—Linda Howe, Jackman, Maine

- 2 cups cubed cooked turkey
- 3/4 cup turkey gravy
- 1 cup shredded carrots
- 2 cups prepared stuffing
- 1 can (15-1/4 ounces) whole kernel corn, drained
- 2 cups warm mashed potatoes

In a greased 2-qt. baking dish, layer the turkey, gravy, carrots, stuffing and corn. Top with the potatoes. Bake, uncovered, at 325° for 45-50 minutes or until edges of potatoes are browned. Yield: 4-5 servings.

Hearty Pasta Casserole

PREP: 45 MIN. **BAKE:** 35 MIN.

- 2 cups cubed peeled butternut squash
- 1/2 pound fresh brussels sprouts, halved
- 1 medium onion, cut into wedges
- 2 teaspoons olive oil
- 1 package (13-1/4 ounces) whole wheat penne pasta
- 1 pound Italian turkey sausage links, casings removed
- 2 garlic cloves, minced
- 2 cans (14-1/2 ounces *each*) Italian stewed tomatoes
- 2 tablespoons tomato paste
- 1-1/2 cups (6 ounces) shredded part-skim mozzarella cheese, *divided*
- 1/3 cup shredded Asiago cheese, *divided*

In a large bowl, combine the squash, brussels sprouts and onion; drizzle with oil and toss to coat. Spread vegetables in a single layer in two 15-in. x 10-in. x 1-in. baking pans coated with nonstick cooking spray. Bake, uncovered, at 425° for 30-40 minutes or until tender.

Meanwhile, cook pasta according to package directions. In a large nonstick skillet, cook sausage and garlic over medium heat until meat is no longer pink; drain. Add tomatoes and tomato paste; cook and stir over medium heat until slightly thickened, about 5 minutes.

Drain pasta and return to the pan. Add sausage mixture, 1 cup mozzarella, 1/4 cup Asiago and roasted vegetables.

Transfer to a 13-in. x 9-in. x 2-in. baking dish coated with nonstick cooking spray. Cover and bake at 350° for 30-40 minutes or until heated through. Uncover; sprinkle with remaining cheeses. Bake 5 minutes longer or until cheese is melted. Yield: 8 servings.

Hearty Pasta Casserole
Loaded with colorful, flavorful roasted veggies, this recipe is very tasty. This rustic Italian-inspired casserole is also the perfect main dish to go—it transports easily and retains heat well. A great make-ahead, too!
—Taste of Home Test Kitchen

Turkey Manicotti

The addition of wholesome bulgur gives extra nutrition to this Italian entree. It's so zesty and flavorful, your family will never realize it's good for them.
—Mary Gunderson, Conrad, Iowa

Four-Cheese Chicken Fettuccine

Four-Cheese Chicken Fettuccine

As a cattle rancher, my husband's a big fan of beef. For him to comment on a poultry dish is rare. But he always tells me, "I love this casserole!" I first tasted it at a potluck; now, I fix it for my family once or twice a month, and I'm asked to take it to most every get-together.
—Rochelle Brownlee
Big Timber, Montana

PREP: 20 MIN. **BAKE:** 30 MIN.

- 8 ounces uncooked fettuccine
- 1 can (10-3/4 ounces) condensed cream of mushroom soup, undiluted
- 1 package (8 ounces) cream cheese, cubed
- 1 jar (4-1/2 ounces) sliced mushrooms, drained
- 1 cup heavy whipping cream
- 1/2 cup butter
- 1/4 teaspoon garlic powder
- 3/4 cup grated Parmesan cheese
- 1/2 cup shredded part-skim mozzarella cheese
- 1/2 cup shredded Swiss cheese
- 2-1/2 cups cubed cooked chicken

TOPPING:
- 1/3 cup seasoned bread crumbs
- 2 tablespoons butter, melted
- 1 to 2 tablespoons grated Parmesan cheese

Cook fettuccine according to package directions. Meanwhile, in a Dutch oven, combine the soup, cream cheese, mushrooms, cream, butter and garlic powder. Stir in cheeses; cook and stir until melted. Add the chicken; heat through. Drain fettuccine; add to the sauce.

Transfer to a shallow greased 2-1/2-qt. baking dish. Combine topping ingredients; sprinkle over chicken mixture. Cover and bake at 350° for 25 minutes. Uncover; bake 5-10 minutes longer or until golden brown. Yield: 6-8 servings.

Turkey Manicotti

PREP: 15 MIN. + STANDING
BAKE: 1 HOUR 20 MIN.

- 1/4 cup bulgur
- 2/3 cup boiling water
- 3/4 pound lean ground turkey
- 1-1/2 cups (12 ounces) 2% cottage cheese
- 1 teaspoon dried basil
- 1 teaspoon dried oregano
- 1/2 teaspoon salt
- 1/4 teaspoon pepper
- 14 uncooked manicotti shells
- 1 jar (28 ounces) meatless spaghetti sauce
- 1/2 cup water
- 1 cup (4 ounces) shredded part-skim mozzarella cheese

Italian Turkey and Noodles

A jar of meatless spaghetti sauce makes this easy dish a perfect supper during the week. Just add a green salad and dinner is set. Best of all, my whole family loves it.
—*Cindi Roshia, Racine, Wisconsin*

Italian Turkey And Noodles

PREP: 35 MIN. **BAKE:** 30 MIN.

- 1-1/4 pounds lean ground turkey
- 1-1/2 cups sliced fresh mushrooms
- 1/2 cup chopped onion
- 1/2 cup chopped green pepper
- 1 jar (26 ounces) meatless spaghetti sauce
- 1/2 teaspoon onion salt
- 3 cups cooked yolk-free wide noodles
- 1 cup (4 ounces) shredded part-skim mozzarella cheese

In a large nonstick skillet, cook the turkey, mushrooms, onion and green pepper over medium heat until turkey is no longer pink. Add spaghetti sauce and onion salt; bring to a boil. Reduce heat; simmer, uncovered, for 15 minutes.

Place cooked noodles in the bottom of a 2-1/2-qt. baking dish coated with nonstick cooking spray. Pour meat mixture over noodles. Sprinkle with cheese. Cover and bake at 350° for 20 minutes. Uncover; bake 10-15 minutes longer or until heated through. Yield: 6 servings.

Chicken Provencale

PREP: 15 MIN. **BAKE:** 65 MIN.

- 1 broiler/fryer chicken (3 to 4 pounds), cut up
- 1 tablespoon vegetable oil
- 1-1/2 cups chopped onions
- 3 garlic cloves, minced
- 2 cans (15-1/2 ounces each) great northern beans, rinsed and drained
- 1 can (29 ounces) diced tomatoes, undrained
- 3 medium carrots, sliced 1/4 inch thick
- 1 tablespoon chicken bouillon granules
- 1 teaspoon dried thyme
- 1/2 teaspoon dried oregano
- 1/2 teaspoon pepper

In a skillet, brown the chicken in oil; remove and set aside. Saute onion and garlic in drippings until tender. Stir in remaining ingredients.

Spoon into a 3-qt. baking dish; arrange chicken pieces on top. Cover and bake at 350° for 65-75 minutes or until meat thermometer reads 170° in breast pieces and 180° in thighs and drumsticks. Yield: 4 servings.

Chicken Provencale

When I serve this entree at a dinner party, people always comment on the tender chicken and flavorfully seasoned beans. I sometimes fix it a day ahead— it's as good as it is the first day it's made.
—*Barbara Zeilinger Columbus, Indiana*

My husband, Chad, is always ready to try a new recipe, so I surprised him with this creamy chicken casserole sprinkled with crushed tortilla chips. He loves the flavor, and I like that it's the perfect size for our small family.
—Kendra Schneider
Grifton, North Carolina

Turkey 'n' Stuffing Pie

PREP: 30 MIN. **BAKE:** 25 MIN.

- 1 egg, lightly beaten
- 1 cup chicken broth
- 1/3 cup butter, melted
- 5 cups seasoned stuffing cubes

FILLING:

- 1 can (4 ounces) mushroom stems and pieces, drained
- 1/2 cup chopped onion
- 1 tablespoon butter
- 1 tablespoon all-purpose flour
- 3 cups cubed cooked turkey
- 1 cup frozen peas
- 1 tablespoon minced fresh parsley
- 1 teaspoon Worcestershire sauce
- 1/2 teaspoon dried thyme
- 1 jar (12 ounces) turkey gravy
- 5 slices process American cheese, cut into strips

In a large bowl, combine the egg, broth and butter. Stir in stuffing. Pat onto the bottom and up the sides of a greased 9-in. pie plate; set aside.

For filling, in a large skillet, saute mushrooms and onion in butter until tender. Sprinkle with flour until well blended. Stir in the turkey, peas, parsley, Worcestershire sauce and thyme. Stir in gravy. Bring to a boil; cook and stir for 2 minutes.

Spoon into crust. Bake at 375° for 20 minutes. Arrange cheese strips in a lattice pattern over filling. Bake 5-10 minutes longer or until cheese is melted. Yield: 4-6 servings.

Chicken 'n' Chips

PREP: 10 MIN. **BAKE:** 25 MIN.

- 1 can (10-3/4 ounces) condensed cream of chicken soup, undiluted
- 1 cup (8 ounces) sour cream
- 2 tablespoons taco sauce
- 1/4 cup chopped green chilies
- 3 cups cubed cooked chicken
- 12 slices process American cheese
- 4 cups broken tortilla chips

In a bowl, combine the soup, sour cream, taco sauce and chilies. In an ungreased shallow 2-qt. baking dish, layer half of the chicken, soup mixture, cheese and tortilla chips. Repeat layers.

Bake, uncovered, at 350° for 25-30 minutes or until bubbly. Yield: 4-6 servings.

Turkey 'n' Stuffing Pie

I use stuffing as the crust for an attractive cheese-latticed turkey pie. Try it the day after Thanksgiving.
—Ruth Hastings
Louisville, Illinois

Country Cassoulet

This dish is one that I make frequently—my husband's a bean lover! We live not far from the Pennsylvania border, and there are still farms in our area of the state. Our home's on 2 acres of land, with a vegetable garden plus fruit trees and berry bushes.
—*Roberta Strohmaier*
Lebanon, New Jersey

Country Cassoulet

PREP: 65 MIN. + STANDING
BAKE: 1-1/2 HOURS

- 3/4 **pound dry navy beans**
- 3 **cups water**
- 1 **bay leaf**
- 1 **teaspoon salt**
- 1 **can (14-1/2 ounces) chicken broth**
- 1/4 **pound bacon, diced**
- 4 **chicken legs or thighs**
- 2 **carrots, quartered**
- 2 **medium onions, quartered**
- 1/4 **cup coarsely chopped celery with leaves**
- 1 **cup canned diced tomatoes**
- 2 **garlic cloves, crushed**
- 1/2 **teaspoon dried marjoram leaves**
- 1/2 **teaspoon ground sage**
- 1 **teaspoon whole cloves**
- 1/2 **pound smoked sausage, cut into 2-inch pieces**

Chopped fresh parsley

Sort beans and rinse with cold water. In a Dutch oven or soup kettle, combine the beans, water, bay leaf, salt and pepper. Bring to a boil; boil, uncovered, for 2 minutes. Remove from the heat; cover and let stand for 1 to 4 hours or until beans are softened. Do not drain.

Stir in chicken broth; bring to a boil. Reduce heat; cover and simmer for 1 hour. Meanwhile, in a small skillet, cook bacon over medium heat until crisp. Using a slotted spoon, remove to paper towels. Drain; reserve 2 tablespoons drippings. In the same skillet, brown the chicken in reserved drippings on all sides; drain and set aside.

In a 3-qt. casserole, combine the beans with cooking liquid, bacon, carrots, onions, celery, tomatoes, garlic, marjoram and sage. Place whole cloves on a double thickness of cheesecloth; bring up corners of cloth and tie with string to form a bag. Add to casserole; top with chicken.

Cover and bake at 350° for 1 hour. Uncover; add sausage. Bake 30-35 minutes longer or until beans are tender. Discard bay leaf and spice bag. Garnish with chopped parsley. Yield: 4 servings.

Turkey Potpie

The best part of a turkey dinner is the leftovers—especially when they're baked into this exceptional potpie! Relatives who visit my family on our farm always leave with this recipe.
—Debi Engelhard
Donnybrook, North Dakota

Turkey Potpie

PREP: 30 MIN. **BAKE:** 45 MIN.

- 1 cup diced carrots
- 3/4 cup chopped onion
- 1/2 cup chopped celery
- 1/4 cup chicken broth
- 3 cups cubed cooked turkey
- 1 can (10-3/4 ounces) condensed cream of chicken soup, undiluted
- 1 cup (8 ounces) sour cream
- 1 teaspoon Worcestershire sauce
- 1/2 teaspoon salt
- 1/8 teaspoon pepper

TOPPING:

- 1 cup all-purpose flour
- 2 teaspoons baking powder
- 1/2 teaspoon salt
- 1/2 cup milk
- 2 eggs
- 1 cup (4 ounces) shredded cheddar cheese, *divided*
- 3 tablespoons chopped green pepper
- 2 tablespoons chopped pimientos

In a large saucepan, bring the carrots, onion, celery and broth to a boil. Reduce heat; cover and simmer for 15 minutes or until vegetables are tender. Remove from the heat. Stir in the turkey, soup, sour cream, Worcestershire sauce, salt and pepper. Spoon into a greased 2-qt. baking dish.

In a large bowl, combine the flour, baking powder and salt. Combine milk, eggs, 3/4 cup cheese, green pepper and pimientos; stir into the flour mixture until combined. Drop by tablespoonfuls over the hot turkey mixture.

Bake, uncovered, at 350° for 40-45 minutes or until golden brown. Sprinkle with remaining cheese. Bake 3 minutes longer or until cheese is melted. Yield: 4-5 servings.

Chicken Ham Casserole

PREP: 15 MIN. **BAKE:** 25 MIN.

- 1 package (6 ounces) long grain and wild rice mix
- 2 cups cubed cooked chicken
- 1 cup cubed fully cooked ham
- 1 can (10-3/4 ounces) condensed cream of chicken soup, undiluted
- 1 can (12 ounces) evaporated milk
- 1 cup (4 ounces) shredded Colby cheese
- 1/8 teaspoon pepper
- 1/4 cup grated Parmesan cheese

Cook rice mix according to package directions. Transfer to a greased 2-qt. baking dish. Top with chicken and ham.

In a bowl, combine the soup, milk, Colby cheese and pepper; pour over chicken mixture. Sprinkle with the Parmesan. Bake, uncovered, at 350° for 25-30 minutes or until bubbly. Yield: 6 servings.

Chicken Ham Casserole

I am retired and always looking for fast-to-fix foods to serve when my children or grandchildren stop by. Leftover chicken, ham and a wild rice mix make this dish quick to assemble. If you have extra turkey, you can use it instead of the chicken.
—Lovetta Breshears
Nixa, Missouri

Chicken Spaghetti Casserole

I first made this meal-in-one when I had unexpected guests. It's popular when I'm in a hurry, because it takes minutes to assemble.
—Bernice V. Janowski, Stevens Point, Wisconsin

Leftover-Turkey Bake

PREP: 20 MIN. **BAKE:** 35 MIN.

- 1-1/2 **cups finely chopped onion**
- 1/2 **cup finely chopped celery**
- 1 **can (14-1/2 ounces) reduced-sodium chicken broth, *divided***
- 2 **eggs, lightly beaten**
- 2 **teaspoons poultry seasoning**
- 1/2 **teaspoon salt**
- 1/4 **teaspoon pepper**
- 3 **cups cubed whole grain bread**
- 3 **cups cubed white bread**
- 2 **cups cubed cooked turkey breast**
- 1/2 **cup chopped fresh *or* frozen cranberries**

In a large saucepan, bring the onion, celery and 1/2 cup broth to a boil. Reduce heat; simmer, uncovered, for 5-8 minutes or until vegetables are tender. Remove from the heat. Stir in the eggs, poultry seasoning, salt, pepper and remaining broth until blended. Add the bread cubes, turkey and cranberries; mix well.

Spoon into a 2-qt. baking dish coated with nonstick cooking spray. Cover and bake at 350° for 15 minutes. Uncover; bake 20-25 minutes longer or until lightly browned and a knife inserted near the center comes out clean. Yield: 4 servings.

Chicken Spaghetti Casserole

PREP: 20 MIN. **BAKE:** 40 MIN.

- 8 **ounces uncooked spaghetti**
- 1 **cup ricotta cheese**
- 1 **cup (4 ounces) shredded part-skim mozzarella cheese, *divided***
- 2 **tablespoons grated Parmesan cheese**
- 1/2 **teaspoon Italian seasoning**
- 1/2 **teaspoon garlic powder**
- 1 **jar (26 ounces) meatless spaghetti sauce**
- 1 **can (14-1/2 ounces) Italian diced tomatoes, undrained**
- 1 **jar (4-1/2 ounces) sliced mushrooms, drained**
- 4 **breaded fully cooked chicken patties (10 to 14 ounces)**

Cook spaghetti according to package directions. Meanwhile, in a large bowl, combine the ricotta,

Leftover-Turkey Bake

Dotted with pretty cranberries, this moist casserole is a wonderful way to use up extra turkey.
—Alice Slagter
Wyoming, Michigan

All-American Turkey Potpie

Ever since my sister-in-law shared this recipe with me, I haven't made any other kind of potpie. The crust is very easy to work with.
—Laureen Naylor
Factoryville, Pennsylvania

1/2 cup mozzarella, Parmesan, Italian seasoning and garlic powder; set aside. In another bowl, combine the spaghetti sauce, tomatoes and mushrooms.

Drain spaghetti; add 2 cups spaghetti sauce mixture and toss to coat. Transfer to a greased 13-in. x 9-in. x 2-in. baking dish; top with cheese mixture.

Place chicken patties over the top; drizzle with the remaining spaghetti sauce mixture. Sprinkle with the remaining mozzarella. Bake, uncovered, at 350° for 40-45 minutes or until bubbly. Yield: 4 servings.

All-American Turkey Potpie

PREP: 30 MIN. + CHILLING
BAKE: 35 MIN.

- 2 cups all-purpose flour
- 1/2 teaspoon salt
- 1/2 cup finely shredded cheddar cheese
- 2/3 cup shortening
- 1 tablespoon cold butter, cubed
- 3 to 4 tablespoons cold water

FILLING:
- 1 cup diced peeled potatoes
- 1/2 cup thinly sliced carrots
- 1/3 cup chopped celery
- 1/4 cup chopped onion
- 1 garlic clove, minced
- 1 tablespoon butter
- 1 cup chicken broth
- 2 tablespoons all-purpose flour
- 1/2 cup milk
- 1-1/2 cups cubed turkey
- 1/2 cup frozen peas, thawed
- 1/2 cup frozen corn, thawed
- 1/2 teaspoon salt
- 1/4 teaspoon dried tarragon
- 1/4 teaspoon pepper

In a food processor, combine flour and salt; cover and pulse to blend. Add cheese; pulse until fine crumbs form. Add shortening and butter; pulse until coarse crumbs form. While processing, gradually add water until dough forms a ball. Divide dough in half with one ball slightly larger than the other; wrap in plastic wrap. Refrigerate for 30 minutes.

For filling, in a large saucepan, saute the potatoes, carrots, celery, onion and garlic in butter for 5-6 minutes. Add broth; cover and cook for 10 minutes or until the vegetables are tender. In a small bowl, combine the flour and milk until smooth. Gradually add to the vegetable mixture. Bring to a boil; cook and stir for 2 minutes or until thickened. Add remaining ingredients; simmer 5 minutes longer.

Roll out larger pastry ball to fit a 9-in. pie plate; transfer to pie plate. Trim pastry even with edge. Pour hot turkey filling into crust. Roll out remaining pastry to fit top of pie; place over filling. Trim, seal and flute edges. Cut slits in top or make decorative cutouts in pastry.

Bake at 350° for 35-45 minutes or until the crust is light golden brown. Serve immediately. Yield: 6 servings.

Broccoli Turkey Supreme

PREP: 15 MIN. **BAKE:** 1-1/4 HOURS

- 4 cups cubed cooked turkey breast
- 1 can (10-3/4 ounces) condensed cream of chicken soup, undiluted
- 1 package (10 ounces) frozen broccoli florets, thawed and drained
- 1 package (6.9 ounces) chicken-flavored rice mix
- 1-1/3 cups milk
- 1 cup chicken broth
- 1 cup chopped celery
- 1 can (8 ounces) sliced water chestnuts, drained
- 3/4 cup mayonnaise
- 1/2 cup chopped onion

In a large bowl, combine all of the ingredients. Transfer to a greased 3-qt. baking dish. Cover and bake at 325° for 1 hour. Uncover; bake 15-20 minutes longer or until rice is tender. Yield: 8 servings.

Stuffed Pasta Shells

PREP: 15 MIN. **BAKE:** 30 MIN.

This is a different way to use up leftovers. A casserole of pasta shells filled with moist stuffing, tender chicken chunks and green peas is covered with an easy sauce.
—Judy Memo
New Castle, Pennsylvania

- 1-1/2 cups cooked stuffing
- 2 cups diced cooked chicken *or* turkey
- 1/2 cup frozen peas, thawed
- 1/2 cup mayonnaise
- 18 jumbo pasta shells, cooked and drained
- 1 can (10-3/4 ounces) condensed cream of chicken soup, undiluted
- 2/3 cup water

Paprika

Minced fresh parsley

In a large bowl, combine the stuffing, chicken, peas and mayonnaise; spoon into pasta shells. Place in a greased 13-in. x 9-in. x 2-in. baking dish. In a small bowl, combine soup and water; pour over shells. Sprinkle with paprika.

Cover and bake at 350° for 30 minutes or until heated through. Sprinkle with parsley. Yield: 6 servings.

Curried Barley Chicken

PREP: 40 MIN. **BAKE:** 1 HOUR

The sweet taste of orange marmalade tops off this nicely seasoned chicken and barley dish.
—Mary Sullivan,
Spokane, Washington

- 1/2 cup chopped onion
- 1/2 cup chopped sweet red pepper
- 1/2 cup chopped green pepper
- 1 garlic clove, minced
- 1 tablespoon olive oil
- 1 medium tart apple, chopped
- 1 to 2 tablespoons curry powder
- 2-1/2 cups chicken broth

Broccoli Turkey Supreme

I do a lot of catering, and this easy rice casserole always gets rave reviews from clients as well as friends and family. It is loaded with turkey, broccoli and water chestnuts. I'm asked for the recipe over and over.
—Marcene Christopherson
Miller, South Dakota

Pecan Chicken Casserole
This recipe came from a radio show years ago, and it's one of my favorites. The unusual crust holds a zippy egg filling flavored with chicken and a splash of hot pepper sauce.
—Jackie Heyer
Cushing, Iowa

1 cup medium pearl barley
4 boneless skinless chicken breast halves (4 ounces *each*)
1/4 teaspoon garlic salt
3 tablespoons orange marmalade

In a large skillet, saute the onion, peppers and garlic in oil until crisp-tender. Stir in apple and curry; cook 1-2 minutes. Add broth and barley; bring to a boil. Reduce heat; cover and simmer for 15 minutes.

Transfer to a greased 9-in. square baking dish. Arrange the chicken on barley mixture and sprinkle with garlic salt. Cover and bake at 375° for 45 minutes. Uncover and brush with the marmalade. Bake for 15 minutes longer or until chicken juices run clear and barley is tender. Yield: 4 servings.

Pecan Chicken Casserole

PREP: 15 MIN.
BAKE: 35 MIN. + STANDING

1 cup all-purpose flour
1 cup (4 ounces) finely shredded cheddar cheese
3/4 cup finely chopped pecans
1/2 teaspoon salt
1/4 teaspoon paprika
1/3 cup vegetable oil
FILLING:
4 eggs
1 cup (8 ounces) sour cream
1 cup chicken broth
4 cups diced cooked chicken
1/2 cup finely shredded cheddar cheese
1/4 cup finely chopped onion
1/4 cup mayonnaise
1/4 teaspoon dill seed
1/8 teaspoon hot pepper sauce

In a bowl, combine the first six ingredients. Set aside 1/2 cup of crumb mixture for topping. Press remaining crumb mixture onto the bottom of a greased 13-in. x 9-in. x 2-in. baking dish. (Crust will be crumbly.) Bake at 350° for 10 minutes or until lightly browned.

In a bowl, beat eggs. Add the remaining ingredients. Pour over baked crust. Sprinkle with reserved crumb mixture. Bake at 350° for 25-30 minutes or until a knife inserted near the center comes out clean. Let stand for 10 minutes before cutting. Yield: 12 servings.

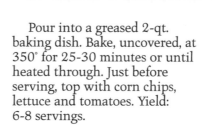

Colorful Chicken and Rice

Topped with crushed corn chips, shredded lettuce and chopped tomatoes, this marvelous meal-in-one is as pretty as it is tasty. I serve it to company along with bread and dessert, and it always gets compliments.

—Dana Wise
Quinter, Kansas

Colorful Chicken and Rice

PREP: 20 MIN. **BAKE:** 25 MIN.

- 1 can (10-3/4 ounces) condensed cream of chicken soup, undiluted
- 1 cup (8 ounces) sour cream
- 1/2 cup 4% cottage cheese
- 1 package (3 ounces) cream cheese, cubed
- 3 cups cubed cooked chicken
- 3 cups cooked rice
- 1-1/2 cups (6 ounces) shredded Monterey Jack cheese
- 1 can (4 ounces) chopped green chilies
- 1 can (2-1/4 ounces) sliced ripe olives, drained
- 1/8 teaspoon garlic salt
- 1-1/2 cups crushed corn chips
- 2 cups shredded lettuce
- 2 medium tomatoes, chopped

In a blender, combine the soup, sour cream, cottage cheese and cream cheese; cover and process until smooth. Transfer to a large bowl. Stir in the chicken, rice, Monterey Jack cheese, chilies, olives and garlic salt.

Pour into a greased 2-qt. baking dish. Bake, uncovered, at 350° for 25-30 minutes or until heated through. Just before serving, top with corn chips, lettuce and tomatoes. Yield: 6-8 servings.

Hearty Chicken Strata

PREP: 25 MIN. **BAKE:** 1-1/2 HOURS

- 10 cups bread cubes (1/2-inch cubes)
- 2 cups diced cooked chicken
- 1 cup diced potatoes
- 1 cup diced celery
- 1/2 cup diced carrots
- 1/4 cup minced fresh parsley
- 4 cups milk
- 2 cups chicken broth
- 5 eggs, beaten
- 1/4 cup butter, melted and cooled
- 1 teaspoon salt
- 1/2 teaspoon pepper
- 1 to 2 jars (12 ounces *each*) chicken gravy, warmed, optional

Arrange bread cubes in a single layer on several ungreased large baking sheets. Bake at 350° for 20-30 minutes until golden brown and crisp.

Transfer to a large bowl. Add the chicken, potatoes, celery, carrots and parsley. In another large bowl, combine the milk, broth, eggs, butter, salt and pepper. Pour over bread mixture; toss to coat.

Pour into a greased 13-in. x 9-in. x 2-in. baking dish. Bake, uncovered, at 350° for 45 minutes; stir. Bake 45 minutes longer or until a knife inserted near the center comes out clean. Serve with gravy if desired. Yield: 12-14 servings.

Hearty Chicken Strata

My great-grandparents made this traditional Amish recipe on Sundays when they had company, and it's still one of my family's favorite dishes.

—Sara Yoder
Mount Hope, Ohio

Reuben Casserole

PREP: 10 MIN. **BAKE:** 25 MIN.

- 1 jar (16 ounces) sauerkraut, rinsed and well drained
- 1-1/4 cups chopped cooked corned beef (about 1 pound)
- 1 cup (8 ounces) sour cream
- 1 small onion, chopped
- 1 garlic clove, minced
- 1 cup (4 ounces) shredded Swiss cheese
- 2 slices rye bread, cubed
- 2 tablespoons butter, melted

In a large bowl, combine the sauerkraut, corned beef, sour cream, onion and garlic.

Transfer to a greased 11-in. x 7-in. x 2-in. baking dish. Sprinkle with cheese and bread; drizzle with butter. Bake, uncovered, at 350° for 25-30 minutes or until heated through. Yield: 4 servings.

Hamburger Hot Dish

PREP: 25 MIN. **BAKE:** 25 MIN.

With a tossed green salad, this ground beef casserole makes an easy and delightful meal. You won't mind when your family asks for seconds, because the satisfying supper dish is so economical.
—Dee Eastman
Fairfield Glade, Tennessee

- 2 cups uncooked elbow macaroni
- 2 pounds ground beef
- 1 can (28 ounces) whole tomatoes, undrained and quartered
- 1 can (15 ounces) tomato sauce
- 1 jar (12 ounces) beef gravy
- 1/2 cup chopped onion
- 1 teaspoon garlic powder

Cook macaroni according to package directions. Meanwhile, in a large skillet, cook beef over medium heat until no longer pink; drain. Add the tomatoes, tomato sauce, gravy, onion and garlic powder. Drain macaroni; add to beef mixture and mix well.

Transfer to a greased shallow 3-qt. baking dish. Bake, uncovered, at 350° for 25-30 minutes or until heated through. Yield: 8 servings.

Orange-Flavored Beef and Potatoes

PREP: 15 MIN. + STANDING
BAKE: 2 HOURS

This stick-to-your-ribs dish has never failed me. While it's baking, I can prepare a simple vegetable side dish or salad to complete the meal.
—Paula Pelis Marchesi
New York, New York

- 2 green onions, sliced
- 3 tablespoons soy sauce
- 2 tablespoons water
- 2 tablespoons white wine *or* additional water
- 1 tablespoon sugar
- 4 teaspoons vegetable oil, *divided*
- 1 tablespoon orange juice
- 1 teaspoon grated orange peel
- 1 teaspoon white vinegar

Reuben Casserole

This is a great dish to serve for St. Patrick's Day—or anytime. It features corned beef, sauerkraut and other ingredients that make Reuben sandwiches so popular. It's always well received at a potluck.
—Margery Bryan
Royal City, Washington

3/4 teaspoon ground ginger
1 tablespoon quick-cooking tapioca
1-1/2 pounds beef stew meat, cut into 1-inch cubes
1 pound small red potatoes, quartered

In a large bowl, combine the green onions, soy sauce, water, wine or additional water, sugar, 3 teaspoons oil, orange juice, peel, vinegar and ginger. Stir in tapioca and let stand for 15 minutes.

Place the beef and potatoes in a greased 11-in. x 7-in. x 2-in. baking dish. Pour tapioca mixture over the top. Cover and bake at 350° for 2 hours or until meat is tender. Yield: 6 servings.

Baked Beef Stew

PREP: 25 MIN. **BAKE:** 1 1/2 HOURS

1 can (14-1/2 ounces) diced tomatoes, undrained
3/4 cup water
1/4 cup red wine *or* beef broth
3 tablespoons quick-cooking tapioca
2 teaspoons sugar
1-1/2 teaspoons seasoned salt
1 teaspoon browning sauce, optional
1/2 teaspoon dried marjoram
1/2 teaspoon pepper
2 pounds lean beef stew meat, cut into 1-inch cubes
5 small red potatoes, quartered
4 medium carrots, cut into 1-inch chunks
2 celery ribs, cut into 3/4-inch chunks
1 medium onion, cut into chunks
1/2 cup soft bread crumbs
1 cup frozen peas, thawed

In a large bowl, combine the tomatoes, water, wine or broth, tapioca, sugar, seasoned salt, browning sauce if desired, marjoram and pepper. Let stand for 15 minutes. Add the meat, potatoes, carrots, celery, onion and bread crumbs.

Pour into a greased 13-in. x 9-in. x 2-in. baking dish. Cover and bake at 375° for 1-1/4 hours. Uncover; stir in peas. Bake 15-20 minutes longer or until meat and vegetables are tender. Yield: 6-8 servings.

Baked Beef Stew
We get plenty of cold winter days here in the Midwest. Nothing warms us up like this chunky oven-baked stew.
—Joanne Wright
Niles, Michigan

Dinner in a Dish

I haven't found anyone yet who can resist this saucy casserole topped with mashed potatoes. The frozen peas and canned tomatoes add color and make a helping or two a complete meal.
—Betty Sitzman
Wray, Colorado

Dinner in a Dish

PREP: 15 MIN. **BAKE:** 35 MIN.

- **2** pounds ground beef
- **1** medium onion, chopped
- **2** cans (14-1/2 ounces *each*) diced tomatoes, undrained
- **3** cups frozen peas
- **2/3** cup ketchup
- **1/4** cup chopped fresh parsley
- **2** tablespoons all-purpose flour
- **2** teaspoons beef bouillon granules
- **2** teaspoons dried marjoram
- **1** teaspoon salt
- **1/2** teaspoon pepper
- **6** cups hot mashed potatoes (prepared with milk and butter)
- **2** eggs

In a skillet, cook beef and onion over medium heat until beef is no longer pink; drain. Stir in tomatoes, peas, ketchup, parsley, flour, bouillon and seasonings. Bring to a boil; cook and stir for 2 minutes.

Pour into an ungreased shallow 3-qt. baking dish. Combine the potatoes and eggs. Drop by 1/2 cupfuls onto beef mixture. Bake, uncovered, at 350° for 35-40 minutes or until bubbly and potatoes are lightly browned. Yield: 12 servings.

Swiss Steak Dinner

PREP: 20 MIN.
BAKE: 1 HOUR AND 50 MIN.

- **1/2** cup all-purpose flour
- **2** teaspoons salt, *divided*
- **1/2** teaspoon pepper
- **2** pounds boneless beef round steak, cut into 1/2-inch pieces
- **2** to 3 tablespoons vegetable oil
- **6** medium onions, thinly sliced
- **7** to 9 small red potatoes (about 1-1/4 pounds), halved
- **1** bay leaf
- **1** can (10-3/4 ounces) condensed tomato soup, undiluted
- **2** cups frozen cut green beans, thawed

In a large resealable plastic bag, combine flour, 1-1/2 teaspoons salt and pepper. Add beef in batches and shake to coat.

In a large skillet over medium heat, brown beef in oil on both sides. Transfer to a greased 3-qt. baking dish. Top with onions and potatoes. Sprinkle with remaining salt; gently toss to coat. Add the bay leaf. Spoon soup over top.

Cover and bake at 350° for 1-1/2 hours. Uncover; place beans around edge of dish. Bake 15-20 minutes longer or until meat and vegetables are tender. Discard bay leaf. Yield: 6 servings.

Swiss Steak Dinner

I came across this recipe in the 1950s, and it's served me well ever since. As this meaty meal bakes, the aroma gets our mouths watering!
—Gloria Cross
Cupertino, California

Crescent Beef Casserole
You'll have some tomato puree left over from this
recipe. It can be covered and refrigerated for up to one
week. Use it to make spaghetti sauce.
—Taste of Home Test Kitchen

Beef and Potato Moussaka

PREP: 25 MIN.
BAKE: 1 HOUR + STANDING

Beef and Potato Moussaka

*My son brought home this recipe
for moussaka (a classic Greek
entree) when he had a sixth-grade
assignment about Greece. It earned
high marks when we made it for
his class. Men love the hearty
meat and potatoes combination.
—Jean Puffer
Chilliwack, British Columbia*

- 1 **pound ground beef**
- 1 **medium onion, chopped**
- 1 **garlic clove, minced**
- 3/4 **cup water**
- 1 **can (6 ounces) tomato paste**
- 3 **tablespoons minced fresh parsley**
- 1 **teaspoon salt**
- 1/2 **teaspoon dried mint, optional**
- 1/4 **teaspoon ground cinnamon**
- 1/4 **teaspoon pepper**

PARMESAN SAUCE:

- 1/4 **cup butter, cubed**
- 1/4 **cup all-purpose flour**
- 2 **cups milk**
- 4 **eggs, lightly beaten**
- 1/2 **cup grated Parmesan cheese**
- 1/2 **teaspoon salt**
- 5 **medium potatoes, peeled and thinly sliced**

In a large skillet, cook the beef,
onion and garlic over medium
heat until meat is no longer pink;
drain. Stir in the water, tomato
paste, parsley, salt, mint if desired,
cinnamon and pepper. Set aside.

For sauce, melt butter in a
saucepan over medium heat. Stir
in flour until smooth; gradually
add milk. Bring to a boil; cook and
stir 2 minutes or until thickened.
Remove from the heat. Stir a small
amount of hot mixture into eggs;
return all to the pan, stirring
constantly. Add the Parmesan
cheese and salt.

Place half of the potato slices in
a greased shallow 3-qt. baking
dish. Top with half of the
Parmesan sauce and all of the
meat mixture. Arrange the
remaining potatoes over meat
mixture; top with the remaining
Parmesan sauce.

Bake, uncovered, at 350° for 1
hour or until potatoes are tender.
Let stand for 10 minutes before
serving. Yield: 8-10 servings.

Crescent Beef Casserole

PREP/TOTAL TIME: 30 MIN.

- 1 **pound lean ground beef**
- 1 **cup diced zucchini**
- 1/4 **cup chopped onion**
- 1/4 **cup chopped green pepper**
- 2 **teaspoons olive oil**

Broccoli Biscuit Squares

With a cheesy biscuit-like crust, these pretty squares disappear quickly at our house. We enjoy them for breakfast, brunch and dinner.
—Vi Janus
Pelican Lake, Wisconsin

1 cup tomato puree
1 teaspoon dried oregano
1/4 teaspoon salt
1/8 teaspoon pepper
1-1/2 cups mashed potatoes
1 cup (4 ounces) crumbled feta cheese
1 tube (8 ounces) refrigerated crescent rolls

In a large skillet, cook beef over medium heat until no longer pink; drain and set aside. In the same skillet, saute the zucchini, onion and green pepper in oil until crisp-tender. Stir in the beef, tomato puree, oregano, salt and pepper; heat through.

Spread mashed potatoes in an 11-in. x 7-in. x 2-in. baking dish coated with nonstick cooking spray. Top with beef mixture; sprinkle with feta cheese.

Unroll crescent dough. Separate into four rectangles; arrange three rectangles over the casserole. Bake, uncovered, at 375° for 12-15 minutes or until top is browned. Roll remaining dough into two crescent rolls; bake for another use. Yield: 6 servings.

Broccoli Biscuit Squares

PREP: 25 MIN. **BAKE:** 25 MIN.

1 pound ground beef
1 can (4 ounces) mushroom stems and pieces, drained
1 small onion, chopped
2 cups biscuit/baking mix
2 cups (8 ounces) shredded cheddar cheese, *divided*
1/4 cup grated Parmesan cheese
1/2 cup water
1 package (10 ounces) frozen chopped broccoli, thawed and drained
4 eggs
1/2 cup milk
1 teaspoon salt
Dash pepper

In a large skillet, cook the beef, mushrooms and onion over medium heat until meat is no longer pink; drain. In a large bowl, combine biscuit mix, 1/2 cup cheddar cheese, Parmesan cheese and water until a soft dough forms.

Press dough onto the bottom and 1/2 in. up the sides of a greased 13-in. x 9-in. x 2-in. baking dish. Stir the remaining cheddar cheese into the beef mixture; spread over dough. Sprinkle with broccoli.

In a large bowl, beat eggs, milk, salt and pepper. Pour over meat mixture. Bake, uncovered, at 400° for 25 minutes or until a knife inserted near center comes out clean. Yield: 6 servings.

Taco Casserole

This casserole, which tastes like a taco salad, is a favorite at my house. I like that it's a breeze to prepare.
—Rhonda McKee
Greensburg, Kansas

- 2 cups (16 ounces) 4% cottage cheese
- 2 eggs, lightly beaten
- 12 corn tortillas (6 inches), torn
- 3-1/2 to 4 cups shredded Monterey Jack cheese

In a large skillet, cook meat over medium heat until no longer pink; drain. Add the seasoned salt, taco seasoning mix, tomatoes, tomato sauce and chilies. Reduce heat; simmer, uncovered, for 15 to 20 minutes. In a small bowl, combine cottage cheese and eggs.

In a greased 13-in. x 9-in. x 2-in. baking dish, layer half of the meat sauce, half of the tortillas, half the cottage cheese mixture and half of the Monterey Jack cheese. Repeat layers. Bake, uncovered, at 350° for 30 minutes or until bubbly. Let stand 10 minutes before cutting. Yield: 10-12 servings.

Taco Casserole

PREP: 25 MIN. **BAKE:** 15 MIN.

- 1 pound ground beef
- 1/4 cup chopped onion
- 1/4 cup chopped green pepper
- 1 envelope taco seasoning
- 1/2 cup water
- 1 cup crushed tortilla chips
- 1 can (16 ounces) refried beans
- 1 cup (4 ounces) shredded cheddar cheese

Toppings: chopped lettuce and tomatoes, sliced ripe olives, sour cream and picante sauce

In a large skillet, cook beef, onion and green pepper over medium heat until meat is no longer pink; drain. Stir in taco seasoning and water. Cook and stir for 3 minutes or until thickened; set aside.

Place chips in a greased 8-in. square baking dish. In a small bowl, stir refried beans; spread over chips. Top with beef mixture and cheese.

Bake, uncovered, at 375° for 15-20 minutes or until heated. Top with lettuce, tomatoes and olives. Serve with sour cream and picante sauce. Yield: 4 servings.

Burrito Bake

Years ago when I was in college, my roommate would frequently make this economical casserole. It's so easy to put together, and one serving goes a long way.
—*Cindee Ness*
Horace, North Dakota

Burrito Bake

PREP: 25 MIN. **BAKE:** 30 MIN.

- 1 **pound ground beef**
- 1 **can (16 ounces) refried beans**
- 1/4 **cup chopped onion**
- 1 **envelope taco seasoning**
- 1 **tube (8 ounces) refrigerated crescent rolls**
- 2 **cups (8 ounces) shredded cheddar cheese**
- 2 **cups (8 ounces) shredded part-skim mozzarella cheese**

Toppings: chopped green pepper, shredded lettuce, chopped tomatoes and sliced ripe olives

In a large skillet, cook beef over medium heat until no longer pink; drain. Add the beans, onion and taco seasoning.

Unroll crescent roll dough. Press onto the bottom and up the sides of a greased 13-in. x 9-in. x 2-in. baking dish; seal seams and perforations.

Spread beef mixture over crust; sprinkle with cheeses. Bake, uncovered, at 350° for 30 minutes or until golden brown. Sprinkle with toppings of your choice. Yield: 6 servings.

Sweet-and-Sour Supper

PREP: 20 MIN. **BAKE:** 30 MIN.

- 1 **pound ground beef**
- 1-1/2 **teaspoons chili powder**
- 1-1/2 **teaspoons dried oregano**
- 1-1/2 **teaspoons salt**

Pepper to taste

- 3 **cups cooked long grain rice**
- 1 **can (7 ounces) mushroom stems and pieces, drained**
- 1 **medium green pepper, sliced**

SAUCE:

- 1 **cup plus 2 tablespoons sugar**
- 1/3 **cup cornstarch**
- 2-1/2 **cups cold water**
- 1/3 **cup white vinegar**
- 1/3 **cup ketchup**
- 1-1/2 **teaspoons salt**

Pepper to taste

In a large skillet, cook beef over medium heat until meat is no longer pink; drain. Stir in the chili powder, oregano, salt and pepper.

In a greased 3-qt. baking dish, layer the rice, beef mixture, mushrooms and green pepper; set aside.

In a large saucepan, combine sugar and cornstarch; stir in the remaining sauce ingredients until smooth. Bring to a boil; cook and stir for 2 minutes or until thickened.

Pour over layered ingredients. Bake, uncovered, at 350° for 30 minutes or until heated through. Yield: 4-6 servings.

Sweet-and-Sour Supper

My mother shared this recipe, which I've been making for my family for years. The homemade sweet-and-sour sauce is the key to this dish's success.
—*Dorothy Reimer*
Dewberry, Alberta

Party Beef Casserole

PREP: 30 MIN. **BAKE:** 1-3/4 HOURS

- 3 tablespoons all-purpose flour
- 1 teaspoon salt
- 1/2 teaspoon pepper
- 2 pounds boneless round steak, cut into 1/2-inch cubes
- 2 tablespoons vegetable oil
- 1 cup water
- 1/2 cup beef broth
- 1 garlic clove, minced
- 1 tablespoon dried minced onion
- 1/2 teaspoon dried thyme
- 1/4 teaspoon dried rosemary, crushed
- 2 cups sliced fresh mushrooms
- 2 cups frozen peas, thawed
- 3 cups mashed potatoes (with added milk and butter)
- 1 tablespoon butter, melted

Paprika

In a large resealable plastic bag, combine the flour, salt and pepper; add beef in batches; shake to coat. In a large skillet, cook beef over medium heat in oil until meat is no longer pink. Place beef and drippings in a greased shallow 2-1/2-qt. baking dish.

In the same skillet, add the water, broth, garlic, onion, thyme and rosemary; bring to a boil. Simmer, uncovered, for 5 minutes; stir in mushrooms. Pour over meat; stir to coat.

Cover and bake at 350° for 1-1/2 to 1-3/4 hours or until beef is tender. Uncover; sprinkle peas over meat. Spread potatoes evenly over top. Brush with butter; sprinkle with paprika. Cover and bake 15-20 minutes longer. Yield: 6-8 servings.

Chili Rellenos

PREP: 15 MIN. **BAKE:** 40 MIN.

I really don't recall where I first came across this recipe. I've had it in my files for years and fix it for my family quite often.
—Carolyn Gorrell
Portales, New Mexico

- 2 cans (4 ounces *each*) chopped green chilies
- 1 pound ground beef, cooked and drained
- 4 cups (16 ounces) shredded cheddar cheese
- 1/2 cup all-purpose flour
- 1 teaspoon salt
- 2 eggs
- 2 cups milk

Sprinkle green chilies in a greased 13-in. x 9-in. x 2-in. baking dish. Top with beef. In a large bowl, combine the cheese, flour and salt.

In a small bowl, whisk eggs and milk; stir into cheese mixture until blended. Pour over the beef. Bake, uncovered, at 350° for 40 minutes or until a knife inserted near the center comes out clean. Yield: 10-12 servings.

Editor's Note: Make a tossed salad with avocado slices and tomato wedges; drizzle with creamy ranch dressing. Serve with Chili Rellenos.

Party Beef Casserole
Round steak is economical and delicious. That's why I was thrilled to find the recipe for this comforting meal-in-one casserole. With a salad and rolls, it's an inexpensive, hearty dinner.
—Kelly Hardgrave
Hartman, Arkansas

Ole Polenta Casserole

This casserole has been a family favorite for over 25 years! Servings are great dolloped with sour cream.
—Angela Biggin
Lyons, Illinois

Oven Beef Hash

PREP/TOTAL TIME: 30 MIN.

With just the two of us, we usually have leftovers of some sort, so hash is a regular menu item at our house. It's nice to have a hash that I can pop in the oven.
—Dorothy Pritchett
Wills Point, Texas

- 3 cups diced cooked potatoes
- 1-1/2 cups cubed cooked roast beef
- 1 can (5 ounces) evaporated milk
- 1/4 cup minced fresh parsley
- 1/4 cup finely chopped onion
- 2 teaspoons Worcestershire sauce
- 1/2 teaspoon salt
- 1/8 teaspoon pepper
- 1/3 cup crushed saltines
- 1 tablespoon butter, melted

In a large bowl, combine the first eight ingredients. Spoon into a greased 1-1/2-qt. baking dish. Combine saltines and butter; sprinkle over the top. Bake, uncovered, at 350° for 30 minutes or until heated through. Yield: 4 servings.

Ole Polenta Casserole

PREP: 1 HOUR + CHILLING
BAKE: 40 MIN. + STANDING

- 1 cup yellow cornmeal
- 1 teaspoon salt
- 4 cups water, *divided*
- 1 pound ground beef
- 1 cup chopped onion
- 1/2 cup chopped green pepper
- 2 garlic cloves, minced
- 1 can (14-1/2 ounces) diced tomatoes, undrained
- 1 can (8 ounces) tomato sauce
- 1/2 pound sliced fresh mushrooms
- 1 teaspoon *each* dried basil, oregano and dill weed

Dash hot pepper sauce

- 1-1/2 cups (6 ounces) shredded part-skim mozzarella cheese
- 1/4 cup grated Parmesan cheese

For polenta, in a small bowl, whisk cornmeal, salt and 1 cup water until smooth. In a large saucepan, bring remaining water to a boil. Add cornmeal mixture, stirring constantly. Bring to a boil; cook and stir for 3 minutes or until thickened.

Reduce heat to low; cover and cook for 15 minutes. Divide the mixture between two greased 8-in. square baking dishes. Cover and refrigerate until firm, about 1-1/2 hours.

In a large skillet, cook beef, onion, green pepper and garlic over medium heat until meat is no longer pink; drain. Stir in the tomatoes, tomato sauce, mushrooms, herbs and hot pepper sauce; bring to a boil. Reduce heat; simmer, uncovered, for 20 minutes or until thickened.

Loosen one polenta from sides and bottom of dish; invert onto a waxed paper-lined baking sheet and set aside. Spoon half of the meat mixture over the remaining polenta that is still in a dish. Sprinkle with half the mozzarella and half the Parmesan cheese. Top with reserved polenta and remaining meat mixture.

Cover and bake at 350° for 40 minutes or until heated through. Uncover; sprinkle with remaining cheese. Bake 5 minutes longer or until cheese is melted. Let stand for 10 minutes before cutting. Yield: 6 servings.

Steak Potpie

This classic meat pie recipe really hits the spot on cold winter nights. With steak, vegetables and gravy, it's so satisfying.
—*Kristin Shaw, Castleton, New York*

Steak Potpie

PREP: 20 MIN. **BAKE:** 20 MIN.

1-1/4 pounds boneless beef sirloin steak, cut into 1/2-inch cubes
    2 tablespoons butter
  1/4 teaspoon pepper
    1 package (16 ounces) frozen vegetables for stew
    2 tablespoons water
  1/2 teaspoon dried thyme
    1 jar (12 ounces) mushroom *or* beef gravy
    1 tube (8 ounces) refrigerated crescent rolls

In a large ovenproof skillet, brown beef in butter. Remove beef; season with pepper and keep warm. In same skillet, combine the vegetables, water and thyme. Stir in the gravy. Bring to a boil. Reduce heat; simmer, uncovered, until the vegetables are thawed. Stir in beef; remove from the heat.

Separate crescent dough into eight triangles. Starting from the wide end of each triangle, roll up a third of the length and place over beef mixture with pointed ends toward the center. Bake, uncovered, at 375° for 16-18 minutes or until golden brown. Yield: 4-6 servings.

Broccoli Beef Supper

PREP: 15 MIN. **BAKE:** 35 MIN.

    4 cups frozen cottage fries
    1 pound ground beef
    1 package (10 ounces) frozen chopped broccoli, thawed
    1 can (2.8 ounces) french-fried onions, *divided*
    1 medium tomato, chopped
    1 can (10-3/4 ounces) condensed cream of celery soup, undiluted
    1 cup (4 ounces) shredded cheddar cheese, *divided*
  1/2 cup milk
  1/4 teaspoon garlic powder
  1/4 teaspoon pepper

Line bottom and sides of a greased 13-in. x 9-in. x 2-in. baking dish with cottage fries. Bake, uncovered, at 400° for 10 minutes.

Meanwhile, in a large skillet, cook beef over medium heat until no longer pink; drain. Layer the beef, broccoli, half of the onions and the tomato over fries. In a small bowl, combine the soup, 1/2 cup cheese, milk, garlic powder and pepper; pour over top.

Cover and bake at 400° for 20 minutes. Uncover; sprinkle with remaining cheese and onions. Bake 2 minutes longer or until cheese is melted. Yield: 8 servings.

Broccoli Beef Supper
Broccoli is one of my favorite vegetables, so I'm constantly on the lookout for new ways of preparing it. This casserole is a great entree.
—*Connie Bolton*
San Antonio, Texas

Pork & Lamb

Pork Chops with Apple Stuffing

PREP: 15 MIN. **BAKE:** 40 MIN.

A friend shared this recipe from her Slovak mother back in the 1950s, and my husband and children love it. They still do.
—Romaine Smith
Garden Grove, Iowa

- 6 bone-in pork loin chops (3/4 inch thick and 8 ounces *each*)
- 4 tablespoons butter, *divided*
- 6 cups unseasoned stuffing cubes
- 3/4 cup chopped peeled apple
- 3/4 cup finely chopped celery
- 1/2 cup raisins
- 1/2 cup hot water
- 3 teaspoons rubbed sage
- 1 teaspoon salt
- 1/4 teaspoon pepper
- 4 teaspoons Dijon mustard

In a large skillet, brown pork chops over medium heat in 2 tablespoons butter on each side; remove from pan and keep warm.

In the same pan, cook the stuffing cubes, apple, celery, raisins, water, sage, salt and pepper in remaining butter until apples and celery are crisp-tender.

Transfer to a greased 3-qt. baking dish. Top with pork chops. Spread mustard over chops. Cover and bake at 350° for 35 minutes. Uncover; bake 5-10 minutes longer or until meat juices run clear. Yield: 6 servings.

Veggie Noodle Ham Casserole

PREP: 15 MIN. **BAKE:** 50 MIN.

- 1 package (12 ounces) wide egg noodles
- 1 can (10-3/4 ounces) condensed cream of chicken soup, undiluted
- 1 can (10-3/4 ounces) condensed cream of broccoli soup, undiluted
- 1-1/2 cups milk
- 2 cups frozen corn, thawed
- 1-1/2 cups frozen California-blend vegetables, thawed
- 1-1/2 cups cubed fully cooked ham
- 2 tablespoons minced fresh parsley
- 1/2 teaspoon pepper
- 1/4 teaspoon salt
- 1 cup (4 ounces) shredded cheddar cheese, *divided*

Cook pasta according to package directions; drain. In a large bowl, combine soups and milk; stir in the noodles, corn, vegetables, ham, parsley, pepper, salt and 3/4 cup cheese.

Transfer to a greased 13-in. x 9-in. x 2-in. baking dish. Cover and bake at 350° for 45 minutes. Uncover; sprinkle with remaining cheese. Bake 5-10 minutes longer or until bubbly and cheese is melted. Yield: 8-10 servings.

Veggie Noodle Ham Casserole
This saucy main dish is really quite versatile. Without the ham, it can be a vegetarian entree or a hearty side dish.
—Judy Moody
Wheatley, Ontario

A great use for leftover ham, this dish has been served at countless church suppers. A puffy topping covers a mixture of sweet potatoes, ham and apples.
—Amanda Denton, Barre, Vermont

New England Lamb Bake

PREP: 25 MIN. **BAKE:** 1-1/2 HOURS

- 2 pounds boneless leg of lamb, cubed
- 1 large onion, chopped
- 1 tablespoon vegetable oil
- 1/4 cup all-purpose flour
- 5 cups chicken broth
- 2 large carrots, sliced
- 2 large leeks, cut into 2-inch pieces
- 2 tablespoons minced fresh parsley, *divided*
- 1 bay leaf
- 1/2 teaspoon dried rosemary
- 1/4 teaspoon dried thyme
- 1/2 teaspoon salt
- 1/4 teaspoon pepper
- 3 large potatoes, peeled and sliced
- 1/4 cup butter, cubed

In a Dutch oven, cook lamb and onion over medium heat in oil until meat is no longer pink. Stir in flour until blended. Gradually add broth. Bring to a boil; cook and stir for 1-2 minutes or until thickened, stirring to remove browned bits from pan. Add carrots, leeks, 1 tablespoon parsley and seasonings.

Spoon into a greased 3-qt. baking dish. Cover with potatoes and dot with butter. Bake at 375° for 1-1/2 to 2 hours or until the meat is tender and the potatoes are golden brown. Discard bay leaf. Sprinkle with remaining parsley. Yield: 6-8 servings.

New England Lamb Bake

This entree is hearty and perfect for warming up on a chilly winter evening. The aroma is almost as delightful as the dish itself.
—Frank Grady
Fort Kent, Maine

Apple Ham Bake

PREP: 20 MIN. **BAKE:** 35 MIN.

- 3 medium tart apples, peeled and sliced
- 2 medium sweet potatoes, peeled and thinly sliced
- 3 cups cubed fully cooked ham
- 3 tablespoons brown sugar
- 1/2 teaspoon salt
- 1/4 teaspoon pepper
- 1/4 teaspoon curry powder
- 2 tablespoons cornstarch
- 1/3 cup apple juice
- 1 cup pancake mix
- 1 cup milk
- 2 tablespoons butter, melted
- 1/2 teaspoon ground mustard

In a large skillet, combine the apples, sweet potatoes, ham, brown sugar, salt, pepper and curry. Cook over medium heat

Greek Pasta Bake

My mom taught me to cook, and I love trying and creating new recipes. I developed this one on a cold and snowy afternoon many years ago. Tangy lemon and herbs are complemented by the subtle sweetness of cinnamon.
—Carol Stevens
Basye, Virginia

until apples are crisp-tender; drain. Combine cornstarch and apple juice until smooth; stir into apple mixture. Bring to a boil; cook and stir for 1-2 minutes or until thickened.

Transfer to a greased 2-qt. baking dish. Cover and bake at 375° for 10 minutes or until sweet potatoes are tender. In a bowl, whisk together the pancake mix, milk, butter and mustard; pour over ham mixture. Bake, uncovered, for 25-30 minutes or until puffed and golden brown. Yield: 8 servings.

Greek Pasta Bake

PREP: 40 MIN. **BAKE:** 1 HOUR

- 1/2 **pound ground beef**
- 1/2 **pound ground lamb**
- 1 **large onion, chopped**
- 4 **garlic cloves, minced**
- 3 **teaspoons dried oregano**
- 1 **teaspoon dried basil**
- 1/2 **teaspoon salt**
- 1/4 **teaspoon pepper**
- 1/4 **teaspoon dried thyme**
- 1 **can (15 ounces) tomato sauce**
- 1 **can (14-1/2 ounces) diced tomatoes, undrained**
- 1 **tablespoon lemon juice**
- 1 **teaspoon sugar**
- 1/4 **teaspoon ground cinnamon**
- 2 **cups uncooked rigatoni *or* large tube pasta**
- 4 **ounces feta cheese, crumbled**

In a large skillet, cook beef and lamb over medium heat until no longer pink; drain. Stir in the onion, garlic, oregano, basil, salt, pepper and thyme; mix well. Add the tomato sauce, tomatoes and lemon juice. Bring to a boil. Reduce heat; simmer, uncovered, for 20 minutes. Stir occasionally.

Stir in the sugar and cinnamon. Simmer, uncovered, 15 minutes longer. Meanwhile, cook the pasta according to package directions; drain. Stir into meat mixture.

Transfer to a greased 2-qt. baking dish. Sprinkle with feta cheese. Cover and bake at 325° for 45 minutes. Uncover; bake 15 minutes longer or until heated through. Yield: 6 servings.

Golden Pork Chops

I've had this recipe for several years and really don't remember where I first got it. I have a large family and am always looking for easy recipes that will please all of them. This is definitely one of them.
—Betty Sparks
Windsor, Connecticut

Golden Pork Chops

PREP: 10 MIN. **BAKE:** 35 MIN.

- 1 can (14-3/4 ounces) cream-style corn
- 1/2 cup finely chopped onion
- 1/2 cup finely chopped celery
- 1/2 teaspoon paprika
- 1-1/2 cups crushed corn bread stuffing
- 4 boneless pork loin chops (3/4 inch thick and 6 ounces *each*)
- 1 tablespoon brown sugar
- 1 tablespoon spicy brown mustard

In a large bowl, combine the corn, onion, celery and paprika. Stir in stuffing. Transfer to a greased 11-in. x 7-in. x 2-in. baking dish.

Arrange pork chops over stuffing. Combine brown sugar and mustard; spread over chops. Bake, uncovered, at 400° for 35-40 minutes or until meat juices run clear. Yield: 4 servings.

Sausage Macaroni Bake

PREP: 20 MIN. **BAKE:** 20 MIN.

- 1/2 cup uncooked elbow macaroni
- 1/2 pound bulk pork sausage
- 1/4 cup chopped green pepper
- 2 tablespoons chopped onion
- 1/4 teaspoon dried oregano
- 1/8 teaspoon pepper
- 1 can (8 ounces) tomato sauce
- 1/2 cup water
- 4 tablespoons grated Parmesan cheese, *divided*

Cook macaroni according to package directions; drain and set aside. In a large skillet, cook sausage over medium heat until no longer pink; drain. Add the green pepper, onion, oregano and pepper. Stir in tomato sauce and water. Bring to a boil. Reduce heat; simmer, uncovered, for 5 minutes.

Stir in macaroni and 2 table-spoons Parmesan cheese. Transfer to an ungreased 1-qt. baking dish. Sprinkle with the remaining Parmesan. Bake, uncovered, at 350° for 20-25 minutes or until bubbly. Yield: 2 servings.

Sausage Macaroni Bake

Everyone's bound to want seconds of this satisfying Italian-style bake. Oregano seasons the pork sausage, macaroni and tomato sauce mixture that's topped with a sprinkling of Parmesan cheese.
—Kelli Bucy
Massena, Iowa

Pork and Corn Casserole

A satisfying supper includes this casserole fresh from the oven, a garden salad and buttermilk biscuits. It's a winner every time!
—Karen Sesto
South Portland, Maine

Pork and Corn Casserole

PREP: 15 MIN. **BAKE:** 30 MIN.

- 7 cups uncooked egg noodles
- 1 pound ground pork
- 1 small green pepper, chopped
- 1 can (14-3/4 ounces) cream-style corn
- 1 can (11-1/2 ounces) condensed chicken with rice soup, undiluted
- 1 jar (2 ounces) diced pimientos, drained
- 8 ounces process cheese (Velveeta), cubed
- 1/2 cup dry bread crumbs
- 2 tablespoons butter, melted

Cook noodles according to package directions; drain. Meanwhile in a large skillet, cook pork and green pepper over medium heat until meat is no longer pink; drain. In a large bowl, combine the noodles, corn, soup, pimientos, cheese and pork mixture.

Transfer to a greased shallow 2-1/2-qt. baking dish. Combine bread crumbs and butter; sprinkle over noodle mixture. Bake, uncovered, at 350° for 30-35 minutes or until bubbly and top is golden brown. Yield: 6-8 servings.

Biscuit-Topped Creamed Ham

PREP: 30 MIN. **BAKE:** 30 MIN.

- 1/4 cup chopped green pepper
- 3 tablespoons chopped onion
- 2 tablespoons butter
- 3 tablespoons all-purpose flour
- 1-3/4 cups milk
- 1 can (10-3/4 ounces) condensed cream of chicken soup, undiluted
- 2 cups cubed fully cooked ham
- 1 tablespoon lemon juice

BISCUITS:

- 1 cup all-purpose flour
- 1-1/2 teaspoons baking powder
- 1/2 teaspoon salt
- 2 tablespoons shortening
- 3/4 cup shredded cheddar cheese
- 1/3 cup milk
- 1 teaspoon diced pimientos

In a large skillet, saute green pepper and onion in butter until tender. Stir in flour until blended. Gradually add milk. Bring to a boil; cook and stir for 1-2 minutes or until thickened. Whisk in soup until blended. Stir in the ham and lemon juice; heat through.

Pour into a greased 9-in. square baking dish. Bake, uncovered, at 375° for 10 minutes. Meanwhile, in a large bowl, combine the flour, baking powder and salt; cut in shortening until mixture resembles coarse crumbs. Stir in the cheese, milk and pimientos just until moistened.

Turn onto a lightly floured surface; knead gently 4-5 times. Roll to about 1/2-in. thickness; cut out six biscuits with a 2-1/2-in. biscuit cutter. Arrange biscuits over ham mixture. Bake 18-22 minutes longer or until biscuits are golden brown. Yield: 6 servings.

Pineapple Ham Casserole

Living in Hawaii, I wanted to share this recipe which features pineapple. It's our most important fruit crop.
—Marsha Fleming, Kula, Hawaii

Pineapple Ham Casserole

PREP: 15 MIN. **BAKE:** 30 MIN.

- 2 cups uncooked wide egg noodles
- 1/2 cup chopped celery
- 2 tablespoons butter, *divided*
- 1 package (8 ounces) cream cheese, cubed
- 3/4 cup milk
- 2 cups cubed fully cooked ham
- 2 cans (8 ounces *each*) crushed pineapple, drained
- 2 teaspoons Worcestershire sauce
- 1/2 teaspoon salt

Dash pepper

- 1/4 cup dry bread crumbs

Cook noodles according to package directions; drain. In a large skillet, saute celery in 1 tablespoon butter until tender. Stir in cream cheese and milk; cook and stir until cheese is melted. Add the noodles, ham, pineapple, Worcestershire sauce, salt and pepper.

Transfer to an ungreased 1-1/2-qt. baking dish. Melt remaining butter; toss with bread crumbs. Sprinkle over the casserole. Bake, uncovered, at 350° for 30-35 minutes or until heated through. Yield: 4 servings.

Irish Pie

PREP: 15 MIN.
BAKE: 65 MIN. + STANDING

- 3 cups cubed cooked chicken
- 2 cups (8 ounces) shredded Monterey Jack cheese
- 1 teaspoon garlic salt
- 2 cups seasoned stuffing croutons
- 1 pound bulk pork sausage, cooked and drained
- 2 cups peeled cooked diced potatoes
- 2 cups (8 ounces) shredded cheddar cheese
- 3 eggs
- 1-1/2 cups milk

In a greased 3-qt. baking dish, layer the first seven ingredients in the order given. Beat the eggs and milk; pour over the cheese.

Cover and bake at 325° for 55 minutes. Uncover and bake 10 minutes longer. Let stand for 10 minutes before serving. Yield: 6-8 servings.

Irish Pie
The combination of chicken, pork sausage, potatoes and cheese makes this a hearty as well as a tasty meal.
—Roberta Ressler
Sandwich, Illinois

Cheesy Ham Macaroni

PREP: 25 MIN. **BAKE:** 25 MIN.

- 1 package (8 ounces) elbow macaroni
- 6 tablespoons butter, *divided*
- 1/4 cup all-purpose flour
- 1/2 teaspoon salt

Dash pepper

- 2 cups milk
- 2 cups (8 ounces) shredded sharp cheddar cheese
- 2 cups cubed fully cooked ham
- 1 can (4 ounces) mushroom stems and pieces, drained
- 1 jar (2 ounces) diced pimientos, drained
- 1/2 cup crushed butter-flavored crackers (about 11 crackers)

Minced fresh parsley, optional

Cook the macaroni according to package directions. Meanwhile in large saucepan, melt 4 tablespoons butter. Stir in the flour, salt and pepper until smooth; gradually whisk in milk. Bring to a boil; cook and stir for 1 minute or until thickened. Reduce heat. Add the cheese; cook and stir until melted. Stir in the ham, mushrooms and pimientos. Drain macaroni; stir into ham mixture.

Transfer to a greased shallow 2-1/2-qt. baking dish. Sprinkle with cracker crumbs; dot with remaining butter. Bake, uncovered, at 350° for 25-30 minutes or until heated through and bubbly. Sprinkle with parsley if desired. Yield: 8 servings.

Au Gratin Spinach 'n' Pork

PREP: 20 MIN. **BAKE:** 25 MIN.

This dish is nice and rich, which makes it a good choice when you crave comfort food. It's a complete family meal all by itself. With rolls and a salad, it's the perfect company casserole.
—*Sandy Szwarc*
Albuquerque, New Mexico

- 2 large onions, sliced
- 1 tablespoon vegetable oil
- 1 tablespoon butter
- 2 bacon strips, diced
- 1 pound pork chop suey meat
- 1 package (10 ounces) fresh spinach, torn
- 2 garlic cloves, minced
- 2 teaspoons grated lemon peel
- 1 teaspoon fennel seed, crushed
- 1/2 teaspoon salt
- 1/2 teaspoon pepper
- 1 cup (4 ounces) shredded Swiss cheese, *divided*
- 2 tablespoons grated Parmesan cheese

In a large skillet, saute onions in oil and butter until golden brown. Remove to paper towels to drain. In the same skillet, cook bacon over medium heat until crisp. Using a slotted spoon, remove to paper towels to drain, reserving dripping.

In the drippings, cook pork over medium heat until no longer pink. Add spinach and garlic; cook and stir for 6 minutes or until heated through. Drain thoroughly.

Cheesy Ham Macaroni

I'm often asked to bring this home-style casserole to potluck dinners, and it's a favorite of my family, too. The rich and creamy, easy-to-fix dish is a great way to use leftover baked ham.
—*Molly Seidel*
Edgewood, New Mexico

Smoked Sausage Potato Bake
My mom passed this recipe along to me. I often fix it for guests because it's pleasing to the eye as well as the appetite. I rarely have leftovers, since second helpings are a given.
—Joanne Werner
La Porte, Indiana

Stir in the lemon peel, fennel seed, salt, pepper, 1/3 cup Swiss cheese and bacon.

Place half of the onions in a greased 1-qt. baking dish; top with pork mixture and remaining onions (dish will be full). Sprinkle with Parmesan cheese and the remaining Swiss cheese. Bake, uncovered, at 350° for 25-30 minutes or until pork is tender and cheese is melted. Yield: 4-6 servings.

Pork Spanish Rice

PREP: 20 MIN. **BAKE:** 20 MIN.

My family wasn't fond of pork roast until I used it in this yummy casserole with rice.
—Betty Unrau
MacGregor, Manitoba

- 1 medium green pepper, chopped
- 1 small onion, chopped
- 2 tablespoons butter
- 1 can (14-1/2 ounces) diced tomatoes, drained
- 1 cup chicken broth
- 1/2 teaspoon salt
- 1/4 teaspoon pepper
- 1-3/4 cups cubed cooked pork
- 1 cup uncooked instant rice

In a large skillet, saute green pepper and onion in butter until tender. Stir in the tomatoes, broth, salt and pepper. Bring to a boil; stir in pork and rice.

Transfer to a greased 2-qt. baking dish. Cover and bake at 350° for 20-25 minutes or until rice is tender and liquid is absorbed. Stir before serving. Yield: 4 servings.

Smoked Sausage Potato Bake

PREP: 10 MIN. **BAKE:** 30 MIN.

- 1-3/4 cups water
- 2/3 cup milk
- 5 tablespoons butter, *divided*
- 1/2 teaspoon salt
- 2-2/3 cups mashed potato flakes
- 1 cup (8 ounces) sour cream
- 1 cup (4 ounces) shredded cheddar cheese
- 1 pound smoked sausage links, halved lengthwise and cut into 1/2-inch slices
- 1 cup (4 ounces) shredded Monterey Jack cheese
- 2 tablespoons dry bread crumbs

In a large saucepan, bring the water, milk, 4 tablespoons butter and salt to a boil. Remove from the heat; stir in potato flakes. Let stand for 30 seconds or until liquid is absorbed. Whip with a fork until fluffy. Stir in sour cream and cheddar cheese.

Spoon half into a greased 2-qt. baking dish. Top with sausage and remaining potatoes. Sprinkle with Monterey Jack cheese.

Melt remaining butter and toss with bread crumbs; sprinkle over the top. Bake, uncovered, at 350° for 30-35 minutes or until heated through and edges are golden brown. Yield: 4-6 servings.

Hash Brown Pork Bake
This filling, family-style casserole is so convenient since it uses frozen hash brown potatoes.
—Darlis Wilfer
Phelps, Wisconsin

Hash Brown Pork Bake

PREP: 15 MIN. **BAKE:** 1 HOUR

- 2 cups (16 ounces) sour cream
- 1 can (10-3/4 ounces) condensed cream of chicken soup, undiluted
- 1 package (32 ounces) frozen cubed hash brown potatoes, thawed
- 2 cups cubed cooked pork
- 1 pound process cheese (Velveeta), cubed
- 1/4 cup chopped onion
- 2 cups crushed cornflakes
- 1/2 cup butter, melted
- 1 cup (4 ounces) shredded part-skim mozzarella cheese
- 3 green pepper rings

In a large bowl, combine sour cream and soup. Stir in the hash browns, pork, process cheese and onion. Transfer to a greased 3-qt. baking dish.

Toss cornflake crumbs and butter; sprinkle over the top. Bake, uncovered, at 350° for 50 minutes. Sprinkle with mozzarella cheese. Bake 10 minutes longer or until bubbly. Garnish with green pepper rings. Yield: 8 servings.

Sausage and Broccoli Bake

PREP: 20 MIN. **BAKE:** 30 MIN.

- 1 package (10 ounces) frozen chopped broccoli
- 1 pound bulk Italian sausage
- 3 cups seasoned salad croutons
- 2 cups (8 ounces) shredded sharp cheddar cheese
- 4 eggs, lightly beaten
- 1 can (10-3/4 ounces) condensed cream of broccoli soup, undiluted
- 1-1/3 cups milk
- 1 can (2.8 ounces) french-fried onions

Cook broccoli according to package directions; drain and set aside. In a large skillet, cook sausage over medium heat until no longer pink; drain. Add the broccoli, croutons and cheese.

Transfer to a greased 2-qt. baking dish. In a bowl, combine the eggs, soup and milk. Pour over sausage mixture. Bake, uncovered, at 375° for 25 minutes. Sprinkle with french-fried onions. Bake for 3-5 minutes longer or until a knife inserted near the center comes out clean. Yield: 6-8 servings.

Sausage and Broccoli Bake
I make this easy meat and veggie bake often because it provides plenty of delicious leftovers for later. My fiance and I love broccoli, so this hearty recipe pleases us both. It would go over big as a featured entree for a brunch buffet.
—Robin Moherman
Ashland, Ohio

Sauerkraut Hot Dish

We often serve this hearty dish at family gatherings, and the men especially seem to enjoy it. My sister gave me this recipe about 15 years ago, and it has been a favorite ever since. The blend of ingredients is a pleasant surprise.
—Nedra Parker, Dunbar, Wisconsin

Greek Shepherd's Pie

PREP: 25 MIN. + STANDING
BAKE: 35 MIN. + STANDING

5-1/2	cups cubed eggplant (about 1 large)
2	teaspoons salt
4	large potatoes, peeled and cubed
1/2	cup sour cream
1/4	cup butter
2	tablespoons all-purpose flour
1/4	cup vegetable oil
1	pound ground lamb
1/2	pound ground turkey
1	jar (26 ounces) meatless spaghetti sauce
2	tablespoons dried minced onion
2	tablespoons minced fresh parsley
1	teaspoon garlic powder
1/2	teaspoon dried rosemary, crushed
1/2	teaspoon dried basil
1/2	teaspoon pepper
1	cup (4 ounces) crumbled feta cheese

Place eggplant in a colander over a plate; sprinkle with salt and toss. Let stand for 30 minutes.

Meanwhile, place potatoes in a large saucepan and cover with water. Bring to a boil. Reduce heat; cover and cook for 10-15 minutes or until tender. Drain. Mash potatoes with sour cream and butter; set aside.

Rinse eggplant and drain well. Sprinkle with flour and toss to coat. In a skillet, cook eggplant in oil over medium heat until browned and oil is absorbed. Transfer to a greased 3-qt. baking dish.

In the same skillet, cook lamb and turkey over medium heat until no longer pink; drain. Stir in the spaghetti sauce, onion, parsley and seasonings. Cook until heated through, about 5 minutes. Pour over eggplant; sprinkle with feta cheese. Spread mashed potatoes over the top.

Bake, uncovered, at 350° for 35-45 minutes or until top begins to brown. Let stand for 10-15 minutes before serving. Yield: 6 servings.

Sauerkraut Hot Dish

PREP: 15 MIN. **BAKE:** 1-1/2 HOURS

1-1/2	pounds pork stew meat
1	medium onion, chopped
2	celery ribs, chopped

Greek Shepherd's Pie

It's hard to resist a big scoop of this comforting casserole with its fluffy mashed potato topping. Eggplant, lamb and ground turkey complement each other nicely in the stick-to-your-ribs filling.
—Sharon Ann McGray
San Francisco, California

Zucchini Pork Chop Supper

My mom gave me a recipe for zucchini casserole and I added the meat because I was trying to make a one-dish supper. I look forward to fresh zucchini now.
—Linda Martin
Rhinebeck, New York

- 1 can (16 ounces) sauerkraut, undrained
- 8 ounces noodles, cooked and drained
- 1 can (10-3/4 ounces) condensed cream of mushroom soup, undiluted
- 1 can (4-1/2 ounces) whole mushrooms

Salt and pepper to taste

In a large skillet, brown pork over medium heat. Add the onions and celery; cook until vegetables are crisp-tender. Stir in sauerkraut, noodles, soup and mushrooms; sprinkle with salt and pepper.

Spoon into a greased 2-qt. baking dish. Cover and bake at 350° for 1-1/2 hours or until the meat is tender; stirring occasionally. Yield: 6-8 servings.

Zucchini Pork Chop Supper

PREP: 10 MIN. **BAKE:** 1 HOUR

- 1 package (14 ounces) seasoned cubed stuffing mix, *divided*
- 1/4 cup butter, melted
- 2 pounds zucchini, cut into 1/2-inch pieces
- 1/2 cup grated carrots
- 1 can (10-3/4 ounces) condensed cream of celery soup, undiluted
- 1/2 cup milk
- 1 cup (8 ounces) sour cream
- 1 tablespoon chopped fresh parsley *or* 1 teaspoon dried parsley flakes
- 1/2 teaspoon pepper
- 6 pork loin chops (1 inch thick and 8 ounces *each*)

Water *or* additional milk

In a large bowl, combine two-thirds of the stuffing mix with butter; place half in a greased 13-in. x 9-in. x 2-in. baking dish. In another large bowl, combine the zucchini, carrots, soup, milk, sour cream, parsley and pepper; spoon over stuffing. Sprinkle remaining buttered stuffing on top.

Crush remaining stuffing mix; place in a shallow bowl. In another shallow bowl, place the water or milk. Dip pork chops in water or milk then roll in stuffing crumbs.

Place pork on top of stuffing mixture. Bake, uncovered, at 350° for 1 hour or until pork chops are tender. Yield: 6 servings.

Linguine with Ham & Swiss Cheese

My grandmother used to make this for parties and potlucks. It was loved by all back then, and it still is today.
—Mary Savor
Woodburn, Indiana

Linguine with Ham & Swiss Cheese

PREP: 15 MIN. **BAKE:** 50 MIN.

- 8 **ounces uncooked linguine, broken in half**
- 2 **cups cubed fully cooked ham**
- 1 **can (10-3/4 ounces) condensed cream of mushroom soup, undiluted**
- 2-1/2 **cups (10 ounces) shredded Swiss cheese, *divided***
- 1 **cup (8 ounces) sour cream**
- 1 **medium onion, chopped**
- 1/2 **cup finely chopped green pepper**
- 2 **tablespoons butter, melted**

Cook linguine according to package directions; drain. In a large bowl, combine the ham, soup, 2 cups cheese, sour cream, onion, green pepper and butter. Add the pasta; toss to coat.

Transfer to a greased 13-in. x 9-in. x 2-in. baking dish. Cover and bake at 350° for 35 minutes. Uncover; sprinkle with remaining cheese. Bake 15-20 minutes longer or until cheese is melted. Yield: 8 servings.

Meaty Spinach Manicotti

PREP: 30 MIN. **BAKE:** 45 MIN.

- 2 **packages (8 ounces *each*) manicotti shells**
- 1/4 **cup butter, cubed**
- 1/4 **cup all-purpose flour**
- 2-1/2 **cups milk**
- 3/4 **cup grated Parmesan cheese**
- 1 **pound bulk Italian sausage**
- 4 **cups cubed cooked chicken *or* turkey**
- 2 **packages (10 ounces *each*) frozen chopped spinach, thawed and squeezed dry**
- 2 **eggs, beaten**
- 1 **cup (4 ounces) shredded part-skim mozzarella cheese**
- 2 **jars (26 ounces *each*) spaghetti sauce**
- 1/4 **cup minced fresh parsley**

Cook manicotti according to package directions. Meanwhile, melt butter in a saucepan. Stir in flour until smooth. Gradually add milk. Bring to a boil; cook and stir for 2 minutes or until thickened.

Add Parmesan cheese; stir until melted and set aside. Drain manicotti; set aside.

In a large skillet, cook the sausage over medium heat until no longer pink; drain. Add the chicken, spinach, eggs, mozzarella cheese and 3/4 cup white sauce. Stuff into manicotti shells.

Spread 1/2 cup spaghetti sauce in each of two ungreased 13-in. x 9-in. x 2-in. baking dishes. Top with manicotti. Pour remaining spaghetti sauce over the top.

Reheat remaining white sauce, stirring constantly. Pour over spaghetti sauce. Bake, uncovered, at 350° for 45-50 minutes. Sprinkle with parsley. Yield: 14-16 servings.

Meaty Spinach Manicotti

This hearty, stuffed pasta dish feeds a crowd. Tangy tomato sauce tops manicotti that's filled with a mouth-watering blend of Italian sausage, chicken, spinach and mozzarella cheese.
—Pat Schroeder
Elkhorn, Wisconsin

Mexican-Style Pork Chops

PREP: 15 MIN. **BAKE:** 35 MIN.

- 6 bone-in pork loin chops (1/2 inch thick and 8 ounces *each*)
- 2 tablespoons vegetable oil
- 1 medium onion, chopped
- 1 can (16 ounces) kidney beans, rinsed and drained
- 1 can (15-1/4 ounces) whole kernel corn, drained
- 1 can (10-3/4 ounces) condensed tomato soup, undiluted
- 1-1/4 cups water
- 1 cup uncooked instant rice
- 1/2 cup sliced ripe olives
- 2 to 3 teaspoons chili powder
- 1/2 teaspoon dried oregano
- 1/2 teaspoon salt
- 1/8 teaspoon pepper

In an ovenproof skillet, brown pork chops in oil on each side; remove and keep warm. In the same skillet, saute onion until tender. Stir in the remaining ingredients; bring to a boil.

Place chops over the onion mixture. Bake, uncovered, at 350° for 35-40 minutes or until meat is tender. **Yield:** 6 servings.

Mexican-Style Pork Chops

My family's fond of Mexican food, and I love to cook but not clean up. This easy, one-pot meal makes everybody happy.
—*Beverly Short*
Gold Beach, Oregon

Ham and Swiss Casserole

PREP: 15 MIN. **BAKE:** 40 MIN.

When I prepare this noodle casserole for church gatherings, it's always a hit. It can easily be doubled or tripled for a crowd.
—*Doris Barb*
El Dorado, Kansas

- 1 package (8 ounces) egg noodles, cooked and drained
- 2 cups cubed fully cooked ham
- 2 cups (8 ounces) shredded Swiss cheese
- 1 can (10-3/4 ounces) condensed cream of celery soup, undiluted
- 1 cup (8 ounces) sour cream
- 1/2 cup chopped green pepper
- 1/2 cup chopped onion

In a greased 13-in. x 9-in. x 2-in. baking dish, layer half the noodles, ham and cheese.

In a large bowl, combine the soup, sour cream, green pepper and onion; spread half over top. Repeat layers. Bake, uncovered, at 350° for 40-45 minutes or until heated through. **Yield:** 6-8 servings.

Bavarian Wiener Supper

PREP: 10 MIN. **BAKE:** 35 MIN.

This great family meal also goes over well at potluck suppers. This dish is always scraped clean and I'm asked for the recipe, which my daughter received from a friend.
—*Helen Kendig*
Lawrenceburg, Kentucky

- 1 can (10-3/4 ounces) condensed cream of mushroom soup, undiluted
- 1/2 cup mayonnaise

Best-Ever Beans and Sausage

My wife devised this dish, which is extremely popular with our friends and family. Whenever I ask, "What can I share?" the reply is always, "Bring your beans and sausage, and a couple copies of the recipe."
—*Robert Saulnier*
Clarksburg, Massachusetts

1 jar (16 ounces) sauerkraut, rinsed and well drained

1 package (1 pound) hot dogs, halved lengthwise and cut into bite-size pieces

1 teaspoon caraway seeds

4 cups cubed cooked potatoes

1/4 cup soft bread crumbs

1 tablespoon butter, melted

1/4 teaspoon paprika

In a large bowl, combine soup and mayonnaise. In another large bowl, combine the sauerkraut, hot dogs, caraway seeds and half of the soup mixture. Spread into a greased shallow 2-qt. baking dish.

In a bowl, combine potatoes and remaining soup mixture. Spoon over sauerkraut mixture.

Combine the bread crumbs, butter and paprika; sprinkle over potatoes. Bake, uncovered, at 350° for 35-40 minutes or until heated through. Yield: 8 servings.

Editor's Note: Reduced-fat or fat-free mayonnaise is not recommended for this recipe.

Best-Ever Beans And Sausage

PREP: 15 MIN.
BAKE: 1 HOUR 20 MIN.

1-1/2 pounds bulk hot pork sausage

1 medium green pepper, chopped

1 medium onion, chopped

1 can (31 ounces) pork and beans

1 can (16 ounces) kidney beans, rinsed and drained

1 can (15-1/2 ounces) great northern beans, rinsed and drained

1 can (15-1/2 ounces) black-eyed peas, rinsed and drained

1 can (15 ounces) pinto beans, rinsed and drained

1 can (15 ounces) garbanzo beans *or* chickpeas, rinsed and drained

1-1/2 cups ketchup

3/4 cup packed brown sugar

2 teaspoons ground mustard

In a large skillet, cook sausage over medium heat until no longer pink; drain. Add green pepper and onion; saute until tender. Drain. Add remaining ingredients.

Pour into a greased 13-in. x 9-in. x 2-in. baking dish. Cover and bake at 325° for 1 hour. Uncover; bake 20-30 minutes longer or until bubbly. Yield: 12-16 servings.

Seafood

Crab Thermidor

PREP: 15 MIN. **BAKE:** 20 MIN.

The taste of this dish is as impressive as its name. Imitation crabmeat keeps it affordable, but it's fabulous with the real thing, especially for special occasions.
—Mary Rose Fedorka
Jamestown, New York

- 3 tablespoons butter
- 3 tablespoons all-purpose flour
- 1/4 teaspoon salt
- 1/8 teaspoon paprika
- 1/8 teaspoon ground nutmeg
- 1-1/2 cups half-and-half cream
- 2 ounces process cheese (Velveeta), cubed
- 1 tablespoon lemon juice
- 1/2 cup shredded cheddar cheese
- 2 packages (8 ounces *each*) imitation crabmeat, flaked

Additional paprika, optional

In a large saucepan, melt butter. Stir in the flour, salt, paprika and nutmeg until smooth. Gradually add cream. Bring to a boil; cook and stir for 2 minutes or until thickened. Reduce heat. Add process cheese and lemon juice; stir until the cheese is melted. Remove from the heat and add cheddar cheese; stir until melted. Stir in crab.

Transfer to a greased 1-qt. baking dish. Sprinkle with additional paprika if desired. Bake, uncovered, at 350° for 20-25 minutes or until bubbly. Yield: 4 servings.

Pineapple Shrimp Rice Bake

PREP: 30 MIN. **BAKE:** 15 MIN.

- 2 cups chicken broth
- 1 cup uncooked long grain rice
- 1 garlic clove, minced
- 1 medium onion, chopped
- 1 medium green pepper, julienned
- 2 tablespoons vegetable oil
- 2 teaspoons soy sauce
- 1/4 teaspoon ground ginger
- 1-1/2 pounds cooked medium shrimp, peeled and deveined
- 1-1/2 cups cubed fully cooked ham
- 3/4 cup pineapple tidbits, drained

In a large saucepan, bring broth to a boil. Stir in rice. Reduce heat; cover and simmer for 25 minutes or until tender.

Meanwhile, in a large skillet, saute the garlic, onion and green pepper in oil until tender. Stir in soy sauce and ginger. Add shrimp, ham and pineapple. Stir in rice.

Transfer to a greased 2-qt. baking dish. Bake, uncovered, at 350° for 15-20 minutes or until heated through. Stir before serving. Yield: 8 servings.

Pineapple Shrimp Rice Bake
After I made this casserole for the first time, my son begged me to make it again soon. That was more than 20 years ago, and it's still a favorite among family and friends.
—Vi Manning
Spring Hill, Florida

Padre Island Shells

PREP: 20 MIN. **BAKE:** 25 MIN.

- 1/2 cup chopped green pepper
- 2 tablespoons thinly sliced green onion
- 4 tablespoons butter, *divided*
- 2 tablespoons all-purpose flour
- 1/2 teaspoon salt
- 2 cups milk
- 1 large tomato, peeled and chopped
- 2 tablespoons minced fresh parsley
- 1-1/4 cups (5 ounces) pepper Jack cheese
- 3-1/2 cups medium shell pasta, cooked and drained
- 3 cans (6 ounces *each*) crabmeat, drained, flaked and cartilage removed *or* 1 pound imitation crabmeat, flaked
- 1/2 cup dry bread crumbs

In a large saucepan, saute the green pepper and onion in 2 tablespoons butter until tender. Stir in flour and salt until blended. Gradually stir in milk. Bring to a boil; cook and stir for 2 minutes or until thickened. Stir in tomato and parsley.

Remove from the heat and add 1 cup cheese; stir until melted. Stir in pasta and crab. Transfer to a greased shallow 2-1/2-qt. baking dish. Cover and bake at 350° for 20 minutes.

Melt the remaining butter; toss with bread crumbs. Sprinkle over casserole. Top with remaining cheese. Bake, uncovered, for 5-10 minutes longer or until golden brown. Yield: 6-8 servings.

Padre Island Shells
I'm asked to fix this casserole over and over again, so there's no doubt it's worth sharing.
—Dona Grover
Rockwall, Texas

Seafood Lasagna

PREP: 15 MIN.
BAKE: 50 MIN. + STANDING

Everyone seems to enjoy this dish. I like to prepare it the day before and refrigerate it overnight. Just take it out of the fridge 30 minutes before popping it in the oven.
—Viola Walmer
Tequesta, Florida

- 3/4 cup chopped onion
- 2 tablespoons butter
- 1 package (8 ounces) cream cheese, cubed
- 1-1/2 cups (12 ounces) 4% cottage cheese
- 1 egg, lightly beaten
- 2 teaspoons dried basil
- 1 teaspoon salt
- 1/4 teaspoon pepper
- 1 can (10-3/4 ounces) condensed cream of shrimp soup, undiluted
- 1 can (10-3/4 ounces) condensed cream of mushroom soup, undiluted
- 1/2 cup white wine *or* chicken broth
- 1/2 cup milk
- 2 packages (8 ounces *each*) imitation crabmeat, flaked
- 1 can (6 ounces) small shrimp, rinsed and drained
- 9 lasagna noodles, cooked and drained
- 1/2 cup grated Parmesan cheese
- 3/4 cup shredded Monterey Jack cheese

In a large skillet, saute onion in butter until tender. Reduce heat. Add cream cheese; cook and stir

Tuna in the Straw Casserole
Shoestring potatoes give this main dish great flavor and crunch. Even my husband, who doesn't normally care for tuna, counts it among his favorites.
—Kallee McCreery
Escondido, California

until melted and smooth. Stir in the cottage cheese, egg, basil, salt and pepper. Remove from the heat and set aside. In a large bowl, combine the soups, wine or broth, milk, crab and shrimp.

Arrange three noodles in a greased 13-in. x 9-in. x 2-in. baking dish. Spread with a third of cottage cheese mixture and a third of the seafood mixture. Repeat layers twice. Sprinkle with Parmesan cheese.

Cover and bake at 350° for 40 minutes. Uncover; sprinkle with the Monterey Jack cheese. Bake 10 minutes longer or until cheese is melted and lasagna is bubbly. Let stand for 15 minutes before serving. Yield: 12 servings.

Potato Salmon Casserole

PREP: 5 MIN. **BAKE:** 35 MIN.

Experimenting in the kitchen is how I came up with this tasty recipe. It's a great way to work salmon into your menu.
—Laura Varney, Batavia, Ohio

2-1/2 cups cubed cooked potatoes
2 cups frozen peas, thawed
1 cup mayonnaise
1 can (14-3/4 ounces) salmon, drained, bones and skin removed
5 ounces process cheese (Velveeta), cubed
1 cup finely crushed cornflakes
1 tablespoon butter, melted

Place potatoes in a greased 2-qt. baking dish. Sprinkle with peas; spread with mayonnaise. Top with salmon and cheese.

Bake, uncovered, at 350° for 30 minutes. Combine cornflake crumbs and butter; sprinkle over top. Bake 5-10 minutes longer or until golden brown. Yield: 4-6 servings.

Editor's Note: Reduced-fat or fat-free mayonnaise is not recommended for this recipe.

Tuna in the Straw Casserole

PREP/TOTAL TIME: 30 MIN.

1 can (10-3/4 ounces) condensed cream of mushroom soup, undiluted
1 can (5 ounces) evaporated milk
1 can (6 ounces) tuna, drained and flaked
1 can (4 ounces) mushroom stems and pieces, drained
1 cup frozen mixed vegetables, thawed
2 cups potato sticks, *divided*

In a large bowl, combine the soup and milk until blended. Stir in the tuna, mushrooms, vegetables and 1-1/2 cups potato sticks.

Transfer to a greased 1-1/2-qt. baking dish. Bake, uncovered, at 375° for 20 minutes. Sprinkle with the remaining potatoes. Bake 5-10 minutes longer or until bubbly and potatoes are crisp. Yield: 4 servings.

Catch-of-the-Day Casserole

PREP: 15 MIN. **BAKE:** 30 MIN.

- 4 ounces uncooked small shell pasta
- 1 can (10-3/4 ounces) condensed cream of celery soup, undiluted
- 1/2 cup mayonnaise
- 1/4 cup milk
- 1/4 cup shredded cheddar cheese
- 1 package (10 ounces) frozen peas, thawed
- 1 can (7-1/2 ounces) salmon, drained, bones and skin removed
- 1 tablespoon finely chopped onion

Cook pasta according to package directions. Meanwhile, in a bowl, combine soup, mayonnaise, milk and cheese until blended. Stir in the peas, salmon and onion.

Drain pasta; add to salmon mixture. Transfer to a greased 2-qt. baking dish. Bake, uncovered, at 350° for 30-35 minutes or until bubbly. Yield: 4 servings.

Editor's Note: Reduced-fat or fat-free mayonnaise is not recommended for this recipe.

Florida Seafood Casserole

PREP: 15 MIN. **BAKE:** 25 MIN.

- 1/3 cup minced onion
- 1/4 cup butter, cubed
- 1/4 cup all-purpose flour
- 1/2 teaspoon salt
- 1/2 teaspoon pepper
- 1 cup milk
- 1 cup half-and-half cream
- 2 cups cooked rice
- 1 cup peeled cooked shrimp
- 1 cup flaked cooked crabmeat
- 1 can (8 ounces) sliced water chestnuts, drained
- 2 tablespoons lemon juice
- 1 tablespoon chopped pimiento
- 1 tablespoon snipped fresh parsley
- 1 cup (4 ounces) shredded cheddar cheese, *divided*

In a small saucepan, saute onion in butter. Stir in the flour, salt and pepper until smooth. Gradually whisk in milk and cream. Bring to a boil; cook and stir for 2 minutes or until thickened. Remove from the heat; stir in the rice, shrimp, crabmeat, water chestnuts, lemon juice, pimiento, parsley and 1/2 cup cheese.

Spoon into a greased 2-1/2-qt. baking dish. Bake, uncovered, at 350° for 25 minutes or until heated through. Sprinkle with remaining cheese just before serving. Yield: 6 servings.

Dill adds fresh flavor to this comforting combination of foods you likely keep in your freezer. When our children were growing up, they loved this meal.
—*Ruth Andrewson, Leavenworth, Washington*

Crab Supreme

PREP: 20 MIN. **BAKE:** 25 MIN.

Crab Supreme

I came across this recipe years ago in an old church cookbook. It's so good, I've even served it for Christmas Eve dinner.
—*Cheryl Ryan*
Timberville, Virginia

- 1 small onion, finely chopped
- 1/4 cup diced green pepper
- 3 tablespoons butter, *divided*
- 1 tablespoon all-purpose flour
- 3/4 cup milk
- 1/2 teaspoon chili powder
- 1/4 teaspoon salt
- 1/2 pound fresh *or* canned crabmeat, drained, flaked and cartilage removed *or* 1 cup imitation crabmeat, flaked
- 1/3 cup mayonnaise

Dash hot pepper sauce

- 2 tablespoons dry bread crumbs

Dash paprika

In a small saucepan, saute the onion and green pepper in 2 tablespoons butter. Stir in flour until blended; gradually stir in the milk. Add chili powder and salt. Bring to a boil; cook and stir for 1 minute or until thickened. Remove from the heat; stir in the crab, mayonnaise and hot pepper sauce.

Transfer to a greased shallow 1-qt. baking dish. Melt the remaining butter and toss with bread crumbs. Sprinkle over crab mixture. Bake, uncovered, at 350° for 25-30 minutes or until heated through. Sprinkle with paprika. Yield: 2-3 servings.

Editor's Note: Reduced-fat or fat-free mayonnaise is not recommended for this recipe.

Fish Stick Supper

PREP: 10 MIN. **BAKE:** 50 MIN.

- 1 package (12 ounces) frozen shredded hash brown potatoes, thawed
- 4 eggs
- 2 cups milk
- 1 tablespoon dried minced onion
- 1 tablespoon snipped fresh dill *or* 1 teaspoon dill weed
- 1-1/4 teaspoons seasoned salt
- 1/8 teaspoon pepper
- 1 cup (4 ounces) shredded cheddar cheese
- 1 package (12 ounces) frozen breaded fish sticks (about 18)

Break apart hash browns with a fork; set aside. In a large bowl, beat eggs and milk. Add minced

Seafood Rice Casserole
Cooking and creating new recipes are two of my favorite pastimes. My family loves rice and clams, so I combined them in this recipe.
—Pat Wieghorst
Phillipsburg, New Jersey

- 2 cups frozen peas
- 1 cup chopped pecans, toasted
- 1 jar (2 ounces) diced pimientos, drained
- 1/2 cup crushed potato chips

Cook pasta according to package directions. Meanwhile, in a large skillet, saute the onions and mushrooms in butter until tender. Add soup, milk, Worcestershire sauce, salt and pepper; stir until blended. Bring to a boil. Remove from the heat.

Drain pasta. Add the pasta, salmon, peas, pecans and pimientos to the skillet. Transfer to a greased shallow 3-qt. baking dish.

Cover and bake at 350° for 30-35 minutes or until heated through. Sprinkle with potato chips. Yield: 12 servings.

Creamy Shrimp Rice Bake

PREP: 30 MIN. **BAKE:** 35 MIN.

The meal-in-one convenience of this casserole is very appealing. My entire family enjoys this delicious dish.
—Marie Roberts
Lake Charles, Louisiana

- 1 large green pepper, chopped
- 1 medium onion, chopped
- 1/2 cup butter
- 1 pound uncooked medium shrimp, peeled and deveined
- 1/2 teaspoon salt
- 1/4 teaspoon cayenne pepper
- 3 cups cooked long grain rice
- 1 can (10-3/4 ounces) condensed cream of mushroom soup, undiluted
- 2 cups (8 ounces) shredded cheddar cheese, *divided*

In a large skillet, saute green pepper and onion in butter until tender. Add the shrimp, salt and cayenne; cook and stir for 2-3 minutes or until shrimp turn pink. Add the rice, soup and 1 cup cheese; stir until combined.

Pour into a greased 1-1/2-qt. baking dish. Cover and bake at 325° for 30 minutes. Sprinkle with remaining cheese. Bake, uncovered, for 5 minutes longer or until heated through and cheese is melted. Yield: 6 servings.

Seafood Rice Casserole

PREP: 10 MIN. **BAKE:** 45 MIN.

- 3 cups cooked long grain rice
- 1/3 cup chopped onion
- 2 tablespoons chopped green chilies
- 1 can (6-1/2 ounces) chopped clams, undrained
- 1 can (5 ounces) evaporated milk
- 1/4 cup seasoned bread crumbs
- 1/2 cup shredded cheddar cheese

In a 1-1/2-qt. baking dish coated with nonstick cooking spray, combine rice, onion and chilies. In a small bowl, combine clams and milk; pour over rice mixture. Sprinkle with crumbs and cheese. Bake, uncovered, at 350° for 45 minutes. Yield: 4 main-dish or 8 side-dish servings.

Flounder Florentine

I discovered this recipe several years ago when I was looking for a way to dress up fish fillets. Even though we're not big fans of fish, we enjoy this dish.
—Debbie Verbeck
Florence, New Jersey

Flounder Florentine

PREP: 20 MIN. **BAKE:** 20 MIN.

- 2 **packages (10 ounces *each*) frozen chopped spinach, thawed and drained**
- 1 **pound flounder fillets**
- 3 **tablespoons chopped onion**
- 2 **tablespoons butter**
- 3 **tablespoons all-purpose flour**
- 1/4 **teaspoon salt**
- 1/4 **teaspoon pepper**
- 1/8 **teaspoon ground nutmeg**
- 1-1/2 **cups fat-free milk**
- 1 **tablespoon grated Parmesan cheese**
- 1/4 **teaspoon paprika**

Sprinkle spinach in a 13-in. x 9-in. x 2-in. baking dish coated with nonstick cooking spray. Top with fillets.

In a large saucepan, saute onion in butter until tender. Stir in the flour, salt, pepper and nutmeg until smooth. Gradually add milk. Bring to a boil; cook and stir for 2 minutes or until thickened.

Pour over fillets; sprinkle with Parmesan cheese and paprika. Bake, uncovered, at 350° for 20 minutes or until fish flakes easily with a fork. Yield: 4 servings.

Pasta Crab Casserole

PREP: 25 MIN. **BAKE:** 25 MIN.

- 8 **ounces uncooked spiral pasta**
- 2 **large onions, chopped**
- 1/2 **pound fresh mushrooms, sliced**
- 1/2 **cup chopped green pepper**
- 2 **garlic cloves, minced**
- 1/2 **cup butter**
- 2 **packages (8 ounces *each*) imitation crabmeat, chopped**
- 1/2 **cup sour cream**
- 2 **teaspoons salt**
- 1-1/2 **teaspoons dried basil**
- 1-1/2 **cups (6 ounces) shredded cheddar cheese**

Cook pasta according to package directions. Meanwhile, in a skillet, saute the onions, mushrooms, green pepper and garlic in butter until crisp-tender. Remove from the heat. Drain pasta; add to the vegetable mixture. Stir in the crab, sour cream, salt and basil.

Transfer to two greased 8-in. square baking dishes. Sprinkle with cheese. Cover and freeze one casserole for up to 1 month. Cover and bake the second casserole at 350° for 20 minutes. Uncover; bake 5 minutes longer or until heated through.

To use frozen casserole: Thaw in the refrigerator for 24 hours. Remove from refrigerator 30 minutes before baking. Cover and bake at 350° for 55-60 minutes or until heated through. Yield: 2 casseroles (4-6 servings each).

Pasta Crab Casserole

This is an easy dish to freeze ahead for company. A yummy combination of spiral pasta, crab and sauteed veggies is coated with a buttery sauce, then covered with cheddar cheese. All that's needed to complete the meal is warm garlic bread and a tossed green salad.
—Georgia Mountain
Tampa, Florida

Meatless

Corn Bread Veggie Bake

PREP: 10 MIN. **BAKE:** 25 MIN.

Pantry items in this simple side dish mean that it just takes minutes to prepare.
—Sharon Van Ornum
Hilton, New York

- 1 can (10-3/4 ounces) condensed cream of mushroom soup, undiluted
- 1 cup milk, *divided*
- 1-1/2 cups frozen mixed vegetables, thawed
- 1 package (8-1/2 ounces) corn bread/muffin mix
- 1 egg, lightly beaten
- 2/3 cup french-fried onions

In a large bowl, combine the soup, 2/3 cup milk and vegetables. Transfer to a greased 11-in. x 7-in. x 2-in. baking dish. In a large bowl, combine the corn bread mix, egg and remaining milk just until blended. Carefully spread over vegetable mixture.

Sprinkle with onions (pan will be full). Bake at 350° for 25-30 minutes or until lightly browned and a toothpick inserted near the center comes out clean. Yield: 6 servings.

Southwest Vegetarian Bake

PREP: 40 MIN.
BAKE: 35 MIN. + STANDING

- 3/4 cup uncooked brown rice
- 1-1/2 cups water
- 1 can (15 ounces) black beans, rinsed and drained
- 1 can (11 ounces) Mexicorn, drained
- 1 can (10 ounces) diced tomatoes and green chilies
- 1 cup salsa
- 1 cup (8 ounces) reduced-fat sour cream
- 1 cup (4 ounces) shredded reduced-fat cheddar cheese
- 1/4 teaspoon pepper
- 1/2 cup chopped red onion
- 1 can (2-1/4 ounces) sliced ripe olives, drained
- 1 cup (4 ounces) shredded reduced-fat Mexican cheese blend

In a large saucepan, bring rice and water to a boil. Reduce heat; cover and simmer for 35-40 minutes or until tender.

In a large bowl, combine the beans, Mexicorn, tomatoes, salsa, sour cream, cheddar cheese, pepper and rice. Transfer to a shallow 2-1/2-qt. baking dish coated with nonstick cooking spray. Sprinkle with onion and olives.

Bake, uncovered, at 350° for 30 minutes. Sprinkle with Mexican cheese. Bake 5-10 minutes longer or until heated through and cheese is melted. Let stand for 10 minutes before serving. Yield: 8 servings.

Southwest Vegetarian Bake
Creamy and comforting, this spicy, meatless casserole hits the spot on chilly nights. But it's great any time I have a taste for Mexican food with all the fixings.
—Patricia Gale
Monticello, Illinois

Chickpea-Stuffed Shells

PREP: 15 MIN. **BAKE:** 30 MIN.

- 18 uncooked jumbo pasta shells
- 1 can (15 ounces) garbanzo beans *or* chickpeas, rinsed and drained
- 2 egg whites
- 1 carton (15 ounces) reduced-fat ricotta cheese
- 1/2 cup minced fresh parsley
- 1/3 cup grated Parmesan cheese
- 1 small onion, quartered
- 1 garlic clove, minced
- 1 jar (28 ounces) meatless spaghetti sauce, *divided*
- 1-1/2 cups (6 ounces) shredded part-skim mozzarella cheese

Cook pasta shells according to package directions. Meanwhile, place the chickpeas and egg whites in a food processor; cover and process until smooth. Add the ricotta, parsley, Parmesan, onion and garlic; cover and process until well blended. Pour 1-1/4 cups of spaghetti sauce into an ungreased 13-in. x 9-in. x 2-in. baking dish; set aside.

Drain pasta shells; stuff with chickpea mixture. Place over sauce. Drizzle with remaining sauce. Bake, uncovered, at 350° for 30 minutes. Sprinkle with mozzarella cheese. Bake 5-10 minutes longer or until cheese is melted and sauce is bubbly. Yield: 6 servings.

Swiss Macaroni

PREP: 20 MIN. **BAKE:** 30 MIN.

My friends are always happy when I bring this comforting casserole to a gathering.
—Carolyn Steele
Marathon Shores, Florida

- 1 package (7 ounces) elbow macaroni
- 1 jar (2 ounces) diced pimientos, drained
- 2 eggs, lightly beaten
- 1 cup half-and-half cream
- 1 small onion, chopped
- 2 tablespoons minced fresh parsley
- 1-1/2 teaspoons salt
- 1/8 teaspoon pepper
- 1 cup soft bread crumbs
- 1 cup (4 ounces) shredded Swiss cheese
- 1/4 cup butter, melted

Cook macaroni according to package directions; drain. Transfer to a greased 11-in. x 7-in. x 2-in. baking dish. Stir in the pimientos. In a large bowl, combine the eggs, cream, onion, parsley, salt and pepper.

Pour over macaroni mixture. Sprinkle with bread crumbs and cheese; drizzle with butter. Bake, uncovered, at 350° for 30 minutes or until golden brown. Yield: 6-8 servings.

Chickpea-Stuffed Shells

I never guessed my picky eaters would agree to try chickpeas, but they gobble them up when I disguise them this way. This pasta dish receives raves from my husband, young son and daughter and dinner guests, too. No one can guess my secret ingredient is nutritious legumes!
—Susan Brown
Saugerties, New York

Black Bean Lasagna

I'm a schoolteacher who loves exchanging recipes with my colleagues. This is a great recipe for a crowd. It's tasty, nutritious and feeds plenty.
—Deborah Kolek
Winchester Center, Connecticut

the spaghetti sauce, green pepper and tomatoes.

In a blender, cover and process the ricotta cheese until pureed. Add to the spaghetti sauce mixture. Stir in the mushrooms, onion, garlic, basil, oregano and 1-1/2 cups mozzarella cheese. Add the spaghetti; toss to coat.

Transfer to a 13-in. x 9-in. x 2-in. baking dish coated with nonstick cooking spray. Sprinkle with remaining mozzarella. Cover; bake at 350° for 40-45 minutes or until heated through. Yield: 9 servings.

Black Bean Lasagna

PREP: 30 MIN.
BAKE: 30 MIN. + STANDING

- 1 large onion, chopped
- 1 medium green pepper, chopped
- 4 to 6 garlic cloves, minced

- 2 tablespoons vegetable oil
- 1 can (28 ounces) crushed tomatoes
- 1-1/2 teaspoons salt
- 1-1/2 teaspoons chili powder
- 1 teaspoon ground cumin
- 1/8 teaspoon cayenne pepper
- 1 can (15 ounces) black beans, rinsed and drained
- 1 cup canned pinto beans, rinsed and drained
- 1 carton (15 ounces) ricotta cheese
- 1 egg white, beaten
- 2 tablespoons minced fresh parsley
- 1 tablespoon chopped seeded jalapeno pepper
- 2 cups (8 ounces) shredded cheddar cheese
- 4 flour tortillas (7 inches), halved

In a large saucepan, saute the onion, green pepper and garlic in oil until tender. Stir in tomatoes, salt, chili powder, cumin and

cayenne. Bring to a boil. Reduce heat; simmer, uncovered, for 10 minutes. Stir in the black beans and pinto beans. Heat through.

In a large bowl, combine the ricotta cheese, egg white, parsley and jalapeno. Spread a third of the bean mixture into a greased 13-in. x 9-in. x 2-in. baking dish. Top with half of the cheddar cheese, tortillas and ricotta mixture. Repeat layers. Spread remaining bean mixture over top.

Cover and bake at 350° for 30-35 minutes or until bubbly. Let stand 15 minutes before cutting. Yield: 12 servings.

Editor's Note: When cutting or seeding hot peppers, use rubber or plastic gloves to protect your hands. Avoid touching your face.

Puffy Chile Rellenos Casserole

Here's a wonderfully zesty casserole that's much lower in fat and easier to assemble than traditional chile rellenos. I don't remember where I got the recipe, but I've enjoyed this layered entree for years.
—Marilyn Morey, Mallard, Iowa

Puffy Chile Rellenos Casserole

PREP: 20 MIN.
BAKE: 40 MIN. + STANDING

- 6 cans (4 ounces *each*) whole green chilies, drained
- 8 flour tortillas (6 inches), cut into 1-inch strips
- 2 cups (8 ounces) shredded part-skim mozzarella cheese
- 2 cups (8 ounces) shredded reduced-fat cheddar cheese
- 3 cups egg substitute
- 3/4 cup fat-free milk
- 1/2 teaspoon garlic powder
- 1/2 teaspoon ground cumin
- 1/2 teaspoon pepper
- 1/4 teaspoon salt
- 1 teaspoon paprika
- 1 cup salsa

Cut along one side of each chili and open to lie flat. Coat a 13-in. x 9-in. x 2-in. baking dish with nonstick cooking spray. Layer half of the chilies, tortilla strips, mozzarella and cheddar cheeses in prepared dish. Repeat layers.

In a small bowl, beat the egg substitute, milk, garlic powder, cumin, pepper and salt. Pour over cheese. Sprinkle with paprika.

Bake, uncovered, at 350° for 40-45 minutes or until puffy and a knife inserted 2 in. from the edge of the pan comes out clean.

Let stand for 10 minutes before cutting. Serve with salsa. Yield: 12 servings.

Editor's Note: When cutting or seeding hot peppers, use rubber or plastic gloves to protect your hands. Avoid touching your face.

Pinto Beans And Rice

PREP: 15 MIN. **BAKE:** 30 MIN.

- 1 large onion, chopped
- 2 tablespoons vegetable oil
- 3/4 cup ketchup
- 2 to 4 tablespoons brown sugar
- 1 teaspoon prepared mustard
- 1 teaspoon Liquid Smoke, optional
- 1 teaspoon salt
- 1/4 teaspoon pepper
- 3 cups cooked long grain rice
- 2 cans (15 ounces *each*) pinto beans, rinsed and drained

In a large skillet, saute onion in oil until tender. Remove from the heat; stir in ketchup, brown sugar, mustard, Liquid Smoke if desired, salt and pepper. Stir in rice and beans.

Transfer to a greased 1-1/2-qt. baking dish. Bake, uncovered, at 350° for 30-35 minutes or until heated through. Yield: 6 servings.

Pinto Beans and Rice
I love to try different foods, and I especially like to see the reaction of my family when I put new dishes on the dinner table. This was a success. I've since served it at many potlucks and have been asked for the recipe every time.
—Linda Romano
Mt. Airy, North Carolina

Breakfast &Brunch

Overnight Sausage and Grits

PREP: 10 MIN. + CHILLING
BAKE: 1 HOUR

This recipe is so appealing because it can be prepared the night before and then popped into the oven an hour before you want to eat. This satisfying dish works well as a side with pancakes or waffles or as your main course.
—Susan Ham, Cleveland, Tennessee

3	cups hot cooked grits
1	pound bulk pork sausage, cooked and crumbled
2-1/2	cups (10 ounces) shredded cheddar cheese
3	eggs
1-1/2	cups milk
3	tablespoons butter, melted
1/4	teaspoon garlic powder

In a large bowl, combine the grits, sausage and cheese. Beat the eggs and milk; stir into grits. Add butter and garlic powder. Transfer to a greased 13-in. x 9-in. x 2-in. baking dish. Cover and refrigerate 8 hours or overnight.

Remove from refrigerator 30 minutes before baking. Bake, uncovered, at 350° for 1 hour or until a knife inserted near the center comes out clean. Let stand for 5 minutes before cutting. Yield: 10-12 servings.

Brunch Strata

PREP: 45 MIN.
BAKE: 35 MIN. + STANDING

3	cups sliced fresh mushrooms
3	cups chopped zucchini
2	cups cubed fully cooked ham
1-1/2	cups chopped onions
1-1/2	cups chopped green peppers
2	garlic cloves, minced
1/3	cup vegetable oil
2	packages (8 ounces *each*) cream cheese, softened
1/2	cup half-and-half cream
12	eggs
4	cups cubed day-old bread
3	cups (12 ounces) shredded cheddar cheese
1	teaspoon salt
1/2	teaspoon pepper

In a skillet, saute the mushrooms, zucchini, ham, onions, green peppers and garlic in oil until vegetables are tender. Drain and pat dry; set aside.

In a large mixing bowl, beat the cream cheese and cream until smooth. Beat in eggs. Stir in the bread, cheese, salt, pepper and vegetable mixture.

Pour into two greased 11-in. x 7-in. x 2-in. baking dishes. Bake, uncovered, at 350° for 35-40 minutes or until a knife inserted near the center comes out clean. Let stand for 10 minutes before serving. Yield: 2 casseroles (8 servings each).

Brunch Strata
Ham, zucchini, mushrooms and cheese flavor this rich egg dish. It adds appeal to a breakfast or lunch buffet and cuts easily, too. Make sure you bring the recipe—everyone will want it!
—Arlene Butler
Ogden, Utah

Cheesy O'Brien Egg Scramble

It's so easy to prepare this breakfast bake, and it's perfect for a brunch buffet. Full of bacon, cheese, hash browns and eggs, the all-in-one dish is a real crowd-pleaser.
—Margaret Edmondson, Red Oak, Iowa

Brunch Lasagna

This sensational dish takes a while to bake, but it is well worth the wait. Pop it into the oven before guests arrive—add fresh fruit and muffins—and you have an instant brunch. You can serve it as a delicious supper, too, drizzled with a little salsa.
—Judy Munger
Warren, Minnesota

Brunch Lasagna

PREP: 25 MIN.
BAKE: 45 MIN. + STANDING

- 8 uncooked lasagna noodles
- 8 eggs
- 1/2 cup milk
- **Butter-flavored nonstick cooking spray**
- 2 jars (16 ounces each) Alfredo sauce
- 3 cups diced fully cooked ham
- 1/2 cup chopped green pepper
- 1/4 cup chopped green onions
- 1 cup (4 ounces) shredded cheddar cheese
- 1/4 cup grated Parmesan cheese

Cook noodles according to package directions. Meanwhile, in a large bowl, beat eggs and milk. In a large nonstick skillet coated with butter-flavored cooking spray, cook eggs over medium-low heat until set but moist. Remove from the heat. Drain noodles.

Spread 1/2 cup Alfredo sauce in a greased 10-in. square or 13-in. x 9-in. x 2-in. baking dish.

Layer with four lasagna noodles (trim noodles if necessary to fit dish), ham, green pepper and onions.

Top with half of the remaining Alfredo sauce and the remaining noodles. Layer with scrambled eggs, cheddar cheese and remaining Alfredo sauce. Sprinkle with Parmesan cheese.

Bake, uncovered, at 375° for 45-50 minutes or until heated through and bubbly. Let stand for 10 minutes before cutting. Yield: 10-12 servings.

Cheesy O'Brien Egg Scramble

PREP: 20 MIN. **BAKE:** 20 MIN.

- 1 package (28 ounces) frozen O'Brien hash brown potatoes
- 1/2 teaspoon garlic salt
- 1/4 teaspoon pepper
- 1 can (10-3/4 ounces) condensed cheddar cheese soup, undiluted
- 1 pound sliced bacon, cooked and crumbled

Blueberry Brunch Bake

Taste and convenience is what this recipe provides, which makes it especially nice for overnight company. It's simple to make the day before and then bake it in the morning. Just sit back and enjoy your guests and a great breakfast.
—Carol Forcum
Marion, Illinois

12 eggs, lightly beaten
2 tablespoons butter
2 cups (8 ounces) shredded cheddar cheese

In a large skillet, prepare hash browns according to package directions. Sprinkle with garlic salt and pepper. Transfer to a greased 2-1/2-qt. baking dish. Top with soup. Set aside 1/2 cup of bacon; sprinkle remaining bacon over soup.

In a bowl, whisk the eggs. In another large skillet, heat butter until hot. Add eggs; cook and stir over medium heat until eggs are nearly set. Spoon over bacon. Sprinkle with cheese and reserved bacon. Bake, uncovered, at 350° for 20-25 minutes or until cheese is melted. Yield: 12 servings.

Blueberry Brunch Bake

PREP: 15 MIN. + CHILLING
BAKE: 50 MIN.

1 loaf (1 pound) day-old French bread, cut into 1/2-inch cubes
1-1/2 cups fresh *or* frozen unsweetened blueberries
12 ounces cream cheese, softened
8 eggs
1/2 cup plain yogurt
1/3 cup sour cream
1 teaspoon vanilla extract
1/2 teaspoon ground cinnamon
1/2 cup milk
1/3 cup maple syrup
Additional blueberries, optional
Additional maple syrup

Place half of the bread cubes in a greased shallow 3-qt. baking dish. Sprinkle with blueberries.

In a large mixing bowl, beat cream cheese until smooth. Beat in the eggs, yogurt, sour cream, vanilla and cinnamon. Gradually add milk and 1/3 cup syrup until blended. Pour half over the bread. Top with the remaining bread and cream cheese mixture. Cover and refrigerate overnight.

Remove from the refrigerator 30 minutes before baking. Cover and bake at 350° for 30 minutes. Uncover; bake 20-25 minutes longer or until a knife inserted near the center comes out clean. Sprinkle with additional blueberries if desired. Let stand for 5 minutes. Serve with additional syrup. Yield: 6-8 servings.

Editor's Note: If using frozen blueberries, do not thaw before adding to batter.

Overnight Stuffed French Toast

This brunch dish is so rich that no one will suspect it's low in fat. You can use any fresh berry that your family likes.
—Bren Childress
Broken Arrow, Oklahoma

Overnight Stuffed French Toast

PREP: 20 MIN. + CHILLING
BAKE: 45 MIN.

- 20 **slices French bread (1 inch thick)**
- 1 **package (8 ounces) fat-free cream cheese**
- 3 **cups egg substitute**
- 2 **cups fat-free milk**
- 1/3 **cup plus 1-3/4 cups sugar-free maple-flavored syrup,** *divided*
- 1 **teaspoon vanilla extract**
- 1/4 **teaspoon ground cinnamon**
- 2-1/2 **cups sliced fresh strawberries**

Arrange 10 slices bread in a 13-in. x 9-in. x 2-in. baking dish coated with nonstick cooking spray. Spread each slice with cream cheese. Top with remaining bread. In a large bowl, whisk the egg substitute, milk, 1/3 cup syrup, vanilla and cinnamon; pour over bread. Cover and refrigerate overnight.

Remove from the refrigerator 30 minutes before baking. Bake, uncovered, at 350° for 45-50 minutes or until top is lightly browned and a thermometer reads at least 160°. Serve with strawberries and remaining syrup. Yield: 10 servings.

Eggsquisite Breakfast Casserole

PREP: 20 MIN. **BAKE:** 45 MIN.

- 1 **pound sliced bacon, diced**
- 2 **packages (4-1/2 ounces each) sliced dried beef, cut into thin strips**
- 1 **can (4-1/2 ounces) sliced mushrooms**
- 1/2 **cup all-purpose flour**
- 1/8 **teaspoon pepper**
- 4 **cups milk**
- 16 **eggs**
- 1 **cup evaporated milk**
- 1/4 **teaspoon salt**
- 1/4 **cup butter, cubed**

Chopped fresh parsley, optional

In a large skillet, cook bacon over medium heat until crisp. Using a slotted spoon, remove bacon to paper towels; drain, reserving 1/4 cup drippings. In the same skillet, combine the beef, mushrooms, flour, pepper and reserved drippings until thoroughly combined. Gradually add milk. Bring to a boil; cook and stir for 2 minutes or until thickened. Stir in bacon; set aside.

In a large bowl, whisk eggs, evaporated milk and salt. In another large skillet, heat butter until hot. Add egg mixture; cook and stir over medium heat until eggs are completely set.

Place half of the eggs in a greased 13-in. x 9-in. x 2-in. baking dish; pour half the sauce over the eggs. Repeat layers. Cover and bake at 300° for 45-50 minutes or until heated through. Let stand for 5 minutes before serving. Yield: 12-16 servings.

Eggsquisite Breakfast Casserole

I developed this recipe over 20 years ago. The creamy, warm sauce tastes especially good on cold winter mornings. I hope your family enjoys it as much as mine!
—Bee Fischer
Jefferson, Wisconsin

Spring-Ahead Brunch Bake

The great taste of this enchilada-style dish makes it popular with my family. If your family likes things spicy, add more hot pepper sauce.
—Lois Jacobsen
Dallas, Wisconsin

Remove from the refrigerator 30 minutes before baking. Bake, uncovered, at 325° for 32-36 minutes or until heated through. Yield: 12 servings.

Spring-Ahead Brunch Bake

PREP: 20 MIN. + CHILLING
BAKE: 35 MIN.

- 2 cups sliced fresh mushrooms
- 1/2 cup sliced green onions
- 1/2 cup chopped green pepper
- 2 tablespoons butter
- 8 slices deli ham
- 8 flour tortillas (7 inches), warmed
- 1-1/2 cups (6 ounces) shredded Swiss cheese
- 1/2 cup shredded cheddar cheese
- 1 tablespoon all-purpose flour
- 4 eggs
- 2 cups milk
- 1/4 teaspoon garlic powder
- 1/4 teaspoon salt
- 1/8 teaspoon hot pepper sauce

In a large skillet, saute mushrooms, onions and green pepper in butter until tender; set aside. Place one slice of ham on each tortilla. Top each with about 1/4 cup mushroom mixture. Combine cheeses; set aside 1/4 cup. Sprinkle remaining cheese over tortillas.

Roll up tortillas. Place seam side down in a greased 11-in. x 7-in. x 2-in. baking dish. In a large bowl, beat the flour, eggs, milk, garlic powder, salt and hot pepper sauce until blended.

Pour over tortillas. Sprinkle with reserved cheese. Cover and refrigerate for at least 30 minutes. Bake, uncovered, at 350° for 35-45 minutes or set. Yield: 8 servings.

Southwestern Egg Bake

PREP: 20 MIN.
BAKE: 35 MIN. + STANDING

I got this recipe after I tried it at my niece's graduation party. Good

thing there was plenty—it went fast!
—Terry Bray, Haines City, Florida

- 5 green onions, thinly sliced
- 1 tablespoon butter
- 8 eggs
- 1 cup milk
- 1 can (4 ounces) chopped green chilies
- 1/4 teaspoon salt
- 1/4 teaspoon pepper
- 1/4 teaspoon ground cumin
- 2-1/2 cups (10 ounces) shredded Monterey Jack cheese
- 6 bacon strips, cooked and crumbled

In a small skillet, saute onions in butter until tender; set aside. In a large bowl, combine the eggs, milk, chilies, salt, pepper and cumin. Stir in the cheese, bacon and reserved onions.

Transfer to a greased 2-qt. baking dish. Bake, uncovered, at 350° for 35-40 minutes or until a knife inserted near the center comes out clean. Let stand for 10 minutes before serving. Yield: 6-8 servings.

Ham 'n' Cheese Strata

Our daughter wouldn't mind if I made this every weekend! I do prepare it for each holiday, serving it alongside fresh cinnamon buns and a fruit salad.

—Marilyn Kroeker, Steinbach, Manitoba

Ham 'n' Cheese Strata

PREP: 15 MIN. + CHILLING
BAKE: 50 MIN. + STANDING

- 12 slices white bread, crusts removed
- 1 pound fully cooked ham, diced
- 2 cups (8 ounces) shredded cheddar cheese
- 6 eggs
- 3 cups milk
- 2 teaspoons Worcestershire sauce
- 1 teaspoon ground mustard
- 1/2 teaspoon salt
- 1/4 teaspoon pepper

Dash cayenne pepper

- 1/4 cup finely chopped onion
- 1/4 cup finely chopped green pepper
- 1/4 cup butter, melted
- 1 cup crushed cornflakes

Arrange six slices of bread in the bottom of a greased 13-in. x 9-in. x 2-in. baking dish. Top with ham and cheese. Cover with remaining bread.

In a bowl, beat the eggs, milk, Worcestershire sauce, mustard, salt, pepper and cayenne. Stir in onion and green pepper; pour over all. Cover and refrigerate overnight.

Remove from the refrigerator 30 minutes before baking. Pour butter over bread; sprinkle with cornflakes. Bake, uncovered, at 350° for 50-60 minutes or until a knife inserted near the center comes out clean. Let stand for 10 minutes before serving. Yield: 8-10 servings.

Apple Pan Goody

PREP: 20 MIN. **BAKE:** 20 MIN.

- 4 to 5 medium tart apples, peeled and sliced
- 3/4 cup dried cranberries
- 6 tablespoons brown sugar
- 1 teaspoon ground cinnamon, *divided*
- 3 tablespoons butter
- 6 eggs
- 1-1/2 cups orange juice
- 1-1/2 cups all-purpose flour
- 3/4 teaspoon salt
- 2 tablespoons sugar

Maple syrup, optional

In a large skillet, saute the apples, cranberries, brown sugar and 3/4 teaspoon cinnamon in butter until apples begin to soften, about 6 minutes. Transfer to a greased 13-in. x 9-in. x 2-in. baking dish.

In a blender, combine the eggs, orange juice, flour and salt; cover and process until smooth. Pour over apple mixture. Sprinkle with sugar and remaining cinnamon.

Bake, uncovered, at 425° for 20-25 minutes or until a knife inserted near the center comes out clean. Serve with syrup if desired. Yield: 8 servings.

Apple Pan Goody

I found the recipe for this unique casserole years ago and adapted it to my family's taste. Dotted with dried cranberries, the tender apple bake is sweetened with brown sugar and a little cinnamon. We enjoy it on breakfast buffets, but it also makes a tasty side dish, particularly with a pork entree.

—Jeanne Bredemeyer
Orient, New York

Potato Egg Supper

PREP: 20 MIN. **BAKE:** 30 MIN.

4 cups diced cooked peeled potatoes
8 bacon strips, cooked and crumbled
4 hard-cooked eggs, sliced
1 can (10-3/4 ounces) condensed cream of mushroom soup, undiluted
1/2 cup milk
1 small onion, chopped
1 tablespoon chopped green pepper
1 tablespoon chopped sweet red pepper
1 cup (4 ounces) shredded cheddar cheese

Place half of the potatoes in a greased 2-qt. baking dish. Top with bacon, eggs and remaining potatoes. In a saucepan, combine the soup, milk, onion and peppers. Cook over medium heat until heated through. Pour over the potatoes.

Cover and bake at 350° for 20 minutes. Uncover; sprinkle with cheese. Bake 10-15 minutes longer or until heated through. Yield: 4 servings.

Six-Veggie Bake

PREP: 15 MIN. + CHILLING
BAKE: 30 MIN.

The original recipe for this strata-like dish called for sausage. I replaced the sausage with fresh vegetables. Just add a salad and you'll have a great dinner.
—Kate Hilts, Fairbanks, Alaska

1 loaf (1 pound) Italian bread, cut into 1/2-inch cubes
1 can (14-1/2 ounces) diced tomatoes, undrained
1 package (10 ounces) frozen chopped spinach, thawed and squeezed dry
1 cup chopped fresh mushrooms
1 cup (4 ounces) shredded part-skim mozzarella cheese
1/2 cup chopped green pepper
1/2 cup chopped zucchini
2 green onions, chopped
1 teaspoon dried basil
1/2 teaspoon dried oregano
1 cup fat-free milk
1 cup egg substitute
1 teaspoon salt-free seasoning blend
1/4 teaspoon pepper

In a large bowl, combine the first 10 ingredients. Transfer to a 13-in. x 9-in. x 2-in. baking dish coated with nonstick cooking spray.

In a small bowl, combine the milk, egg substitute, seasoning blend and pepper; pour over the vegetable mixture. Cover and refrigerate for 2 hours or overnight.

Remove from the refrigerator 30 minutes before baking. Cover and bake at 425° for 15 minutes. Uncover; bake 15 minutes longer or until a knife inserted near the center comes out clean. Yield: 16 servings.

Potato Egg Supper

I serve this convenient, all-in-one casserole with a green salad or pickled beets. I've taken it to church suppers many times. It's always a hit.
—Rosemary Flexman
Waukesha, Wisconsin

Toffee Apple French Toast
I love quick breakfast recipes that can be assembled the night before, saving time on busy mornings. I created this dish by incorporating my family's favorite apple dip with French toast.
—Renee Endress
Galva, Illinois

Toffee Apple French Toast

PREP: 25 MIN. + CHILLING
BAKE: 35 MIN.

- 8 cups cubed French bread (1-inch cubes)
- 2 medium tart apples, peeled and chopped
- 1 package (8 ounces) cream cheese, softened
- 3/4 cup packed brown sugar
- 1/4 cup sugar
- 1-3/4 cups milk, *divided*
- 2 teaspoons vanilla extract, *divided*
- 1/2 cup English toffee bits *or* almond brickle chips
- 5 eggs

Place half of the bread cubes in a greased 13-in. x 9-in. x 2-in. baking dish; top with apples. In a large mixing bowl, beat the cream cheese, sugars, 1/4 cup milk and 1 teaspoon vanilla until smooth; stir in toffee bits. Spread over apples. Top with remaining bread cubes.

In another mixing bowl, beat the eggs and remaining milk and vanilla until blended; pour over bread. Cover and refrigerate overnight.

Remove from the refrigerator 30 minutes before baking. Bake, uncovered, at 350° for 35-45 minutes or until a knife inserted near the center comes out clean. Yield: 8 servings.

Amish Breakfast Casserole

PREP: 15 MIN.
BAKE: 35 MIN. + STANDING

We enjoyed a hearty breakfast bake during a visit to an Amish inn. When I asked for the recipe, one of the ladies told me the ingredients right off the top of her head. Try breakfast sausage in place of bacon.
—Beth Notaro, Kokomo, Indiana

- 1 pound sliced bacon, diced
- 1 medium sweet onion, chopped
- 6 eggs, lightly beaten
- 4 cups frozen shredded hash brown potatoes, thawed
- 2 cups (8 ounces) shredded cheddar cheese
- 1-1/2 cups (12 ounces) 4% cottage cheese
- 1-1/4 cups shredded Swiss cheese

In a large skillet, cook bacon and onion over medium heat until bacon is crisp. Using a slotted spoon, remove to paper towels to drain. In a bowl, combine the remaining ingredients; stir in bacon mixture. Transfer to a greased 13-in. x 9-in. x 2-in. baking dish.

Bake, uncovered, at 350° for 35-40 minutes or until set and bubbly. Let stand for 10 minutes before cutting. Yield: 12 servings.

Side Dishes

Autumn Squash

PREP: 15 MIN. **BAKE:** 20 MIN.

I make this pretty dish with squash from my garden. It has a delicious, crunchy topping.
—Joanne Linde
Williams Lake, British Columbia

- 1 **cup mashed cooked acorn *or* butternut squash**
- 1/2 **cup crushed butter-flavored crackers, *divided***
- 4 **tablespoons butter, melted, *divided***
- 1 **egg, lightly beaten**
- 1 **tablespoons brown sugar**
- 1 **to 2 teaspoons prepared mustard**
- 1/8 **teaspoon salt**
- 1/8 **teaspoon pepper**

In a large bowl, combine the squash, 1/4 cup cracker crumbs, 2 tablespoons butter, egg, brown sugar, mustard, salt and pepper.

Pour into a greased 2-1/2-cup baking dish. Combine remaining crumbs and butter; sprinkle over top. Bake, uncovered, at 350° for 20 minutes or until a knife inserted near the center comes out clean. Yield: 2 servings.

Brown Rice Vegetable Casserole

PREP: 20 MIN.
BAKE: 1 HOUR 20 MIN.

- 3 **cups chicken broth**
- 1-1/2 **cups uncooked brown rice**
- 2 **cups chopped onions, *divided***
- 3 **tablespoons soy sauce**
- 2 **tablespoons butter, melted**
- 1/2 **teaspoon dried thyme**
- 4 **cups fresh cauliflowerets**
- 4 **cups fresh broccoli florets**
- 2 **medium sweet red peppers, julienned**
- 2 **garlic cloves, minced**
- 3 **tablespoons olive oil**
- 1 **cup salted cashew halves**
- 2 **cups (8 ounces) shredded cheddar cheese, optional**

In a greased 3-qt. baking dish, combine the broth, rice, 1 cup onions, soy sauce, butter and thyme. Cover and bake at 350° for 65-70 minutes or until rice is tender.

Meanwhile, in a large skillet, saute the cauliflower, broccoli, peppers, garlic and remaining onions in oil until crisp-tender; spoon over rice mixture.

Cover and bake for 10 minutes. Uncover; sprinkle with cashews and cheese if desired. Bake 5-7 minutes longer or until cheese is melted. Yield: 8-10 servings.

Brown Rice Vegetable Casserole
One taste of this crowd-pleasing casserole brings compliments and requests for my recipe. It's been in my file for as long as I can remember.
—Gloria De Beradinis
Greentown, Pennsylvania

Mushroom Wild Rice Bake

*The wild rice adds a wonderful flavor to this casserole.
I like to serve it on special occasions.*
—Jann Marie Foster
Minneapolis, Minnesota

Hungarian Noodle Side Dish

I first served this creamy, rich noodle dish at our ladies meeting at church. Everyone liked it and many of the ladies wanted the recipe. The original recipe was from a friend, but I changed it a bit to suit our tastes.
—Betty Sugg
Akron, New York

Hungarian Noodle Side Dish

PREP: 15 MIN. **BAKE:** 45 MIN.

- 3 chicken bouillon cubes
- 1/4 cup boiling water
- 1 can (10-3/4 ounces) condensed cream of mushroom soup, undiluted
- 1/2 cup chopped onion
- 2 tablespoons Worcestershire sauce
- 2 tablespoons poppy seeds
- 1/8 to 1/4 teaspoon garlic powder
- 1/8 to 1/4 teaspoon hot pepper sauce
- 2 cups (16 ounces) 4% cottage cheese
- 2 cups (16 ounces) sour cream
- 1 package (16 ounces) medium noodles, cooked and drained
- 1/4 cup shredded Parmesan cheese

Paprika

In a large bowl, dissolve bouillon in water. Add the soup, onion Worcestershire sauce, poppy seeds, garlic powder and hot pepper sauce; mix well. Stir in the cottage cheese, sour cream and noodles; mix well.

Pour into a greased 2-1/2-qt. baking dish. Sprinkle with the Parmesan cheese and paprika. Cover and bake at 350° for 45-50 minutes or until heated through. Yield: 8-10 servings.

Mushroom Wild Rice Bake

PREP: 15 MIN. + SOAKING
BAKE: 1 HOUR 25 MIN.

- 1 cup uncooked wild rice
- 2 cups boiling water
- 1 pound sliced fresh mushrooms
- 1 medium onion, chopped
- 2 tablespoons butter
- 3/4 cup uncooked long grain rice
- 1/2 cup sliced almonds
- 3 cups chicken broth
- 1-1/2 cups heavy whipping cream
- 1 teaspoon salt
- 1/8 teaspoon pepper
- 3 tablespoons grated Parmesan cheese

Beefy Eggplant Parmigiana

I developed this recipe one summer when my husband planted eggplant and tomatoes. I was thrilled when this special casserole won high honors at a national beef contest.
—Celeste Copper
Baton Rouge, Louisiana

Place wild rice in a bowl and cover with boiling water; soak for 1 hour. Drain and set aside.

In a large skillet, saute mushrooms and onion in butter until tender. In a large bowl, combine the mushroom mixture, wild rice, long grain rice, almonds, broth, cream, salt and pepper.

Transfer to a greased 2-1/2-qt. baking dish. Cover and bake at 350° for 1-1/4 hours. Uncover; sprinkle with Parmesan cheese. Bake 10 minutes longer or until rice is tender. Yield: 8-10 servings.

Beefy Eggplant Parmigiana

PREP: 1 HOUR 10 MIN.
BAKE: 35 MIN. + STANDING

- 1/3   cup chopped onion
- 1/4   cup finely chopped celery
- 1   teaspoon dried parsley flakes
- 1/8   teaspoon garlic powder
- 2   tablespoons vegetable oil
- 1   can (14-1/2 ounces) Italian stewed tomatoes
- 1/4   cup tomato paste
- 1/2   teaspoon dried oregano
- 1-1/4 teaspoons salt, *divided*
- 1/2   teaspoon pepper, *divided*
- 1   bay leaf
- 3/4   cup all-purpose flour
- 1   cup buttermilk
- 1   medium eggplant, peeled and cut into 3/8-inch slices

Additional vegetable oil

- 1/2   cup grated Parmesan cheese
- 1   pound ground beef, cooked and drained
- 2   cups (8 ounces) shredded part-skim mozzarella cheese, *divided*
- 1-1/2 teaspoons minced fresh parsley

In a large saucepan, saute the onion, celery, parsley and garlic powder in oil until tender. Stir in the tomatoes, tomato paste, oregano, 1/2 teaspoon salt, 1/4 teaspoon pepper and bay leaf. Bring to a boil. Reduce heat; cover and simmer for 1 hour. Discard bay leaf.

In a shallow dish, combine flour and remaining salt and pepper. Place buttermilk in another shallow dish. Dip eggplant in buttermilk, then in flour mixture.

In a large skillet, cook eggplant in batches in 1 in. of hot oil until golden brown on each side; drain.

Place half of eggplant in a greased 13-in. x 9-in. x 2-in. baking dish. Top with half of Parmesan cheese, beef, tomato mixture and mozzarella cheese. Top with remaining eggplant, Parmesan cheese, beef and tomato mixture.

Bake, uncovered, at 350° for 30 minutes or until heated through. Sprinkle with the remaining mozzarella cheese. Bake 5-10 minutes longer or until cheese is melted. Let stand for 10 minutes before serving. Sprinkle with parsley. Yield: 8 servings.

Asparagus Mushroom Casserole

This colorful casserole is a palate-pleaser. Asparagus, mushrooms, onions and pimientos make a mouth-watering medley. Lemon and nutmeg give this dish a slightly tangy taste.
—*M. Kay Lacey, Apache Junction, Arizona*

Asparagus Mushroom Casserole

PREP: 10 MIN. **BAKE:** 35 MIN.

- 4 cups sliced fresh mushrooms
- 1 cup chopped onion
- 4 tablespoons butter, *divided*
- 2 tablespoons all-purpose flour
- 1 teaspoon chicken bouillon granules
- 1/2 teaspoon salt
- 1/8 teaspoon ground nutmeg
- 1/8 teaspoon pepper
- 1 cup 2% milk
- 1 package (12 ounces) frozen cut asparagus, thawed and drained
- 1/4 cup diced pimientos
- 1-1/2 teaspoons lemon juice
- 3/4 cup soft bread crumbs

In a nonstick skillet, cook mushrooms and onion in 3 tablespoons butter until tender. Remove vegetables with a slotted spoon and set aside. Stir the flour, bouillon, salt, nutmeg and pepper into drippings until smooth. Gradually add milk. Bring to a boil; cook and stir for 2 minutes or until thickened. Stir in asparagus, pimientos, lemon juice and the mushroom mixture.

Pour into a 1-1/2-qt. baking dish coated with nonstick cooking spray. Melt remaining butter; toss with bread crumbs. Sprinkle over top. Bake, uncovered, at 350° for 35-40 minutes or until heated through. Yield: 6 servings.

Scalloped Potatoes

PREP: 15 MIN. **BAKE:** 1-1/4 HOURS

- 3 tablespoons butter, *divided*
- 1 tablespoon all-purpose flour
- 1 teaspoon salt
- 1/4 teaspoon pepper
- 1-1/2 cups milk
- 4 cups thinly sliced peeled potatoes (about 2 pounds)
- 1 medium onion, finely chopped
- 1 small green pepper, finely chopped
- 1/2 cup dry bread crumbs
- 3/4 cup shredded cheddar cheese

In a small saucepan, melt 2 tablespoons butter; stir in flour, salt and pepper. Gradually add milk. Bring to a boil; cook and stir for 2 minutes or until thickened.

In a greased 1-1/2-qt. baking dish, arrange half the potatoes, onion and green pepper in layers; cover with half of the sauce. Repeat layers. Cover and bake at 350° for 35 minutes. Melt remaining butter; combine with bread crumbs and sprinkle over potatoes. Bake, uncovered, about 40 minutes longer or until potatoes are tender. Sprinkle with cheddar cheese. Let stand for 5 minutes before serving. Yield: 4 servings.

Scalloped Potatoes
As a child, I thought the crisp cheese-and-crumb topping on these potatoes made them a special treat. I remember how my aunt always saw to it everyone got some of that topping with their individual serving.
—*Eleanore Hill*
Fresno, California

Scalloped Carrots

PREP: 25 MIN. BAKE: 35 MIN.

- 6 cups water
- 12 medium carrots, sliced 1/4 inch thick (about 4 cups)
- 1 medium onion, finely chopped
- 1/2 cup butter, *divided*
- 1/4 cup all-purpose flour
- 1 teaspoon salt
- 1/4 teaspoon celery salt
- 1/4 teaspoon ground mustard

Dash pepper

- 2 cups milk
- 2 cups (8 ounces) shredded cheddar cheese
- 3 slices whole wheat bread, cut into small cubes

Place 1 in. of water in a large saucepan; add carrots. Bring to a boil. Reduce heat; cover and simmer for 7-9 minutes or until crisp-tender. Drain.

In another saucepan, saute onion in 1/4 cup butter. Stir in the flour, salt, celery salt, mustard and pepper until blended. Gradually add milk. Bring to a boil; cook and stir for 2 minutes or until thickened.

In a greased 11-in. x 7-in. x 2-in. baking dish, layer half of the carrots, cheese and white sauce. Repeat layers. Melt remaining butter; toss with bread cubes. Sprinkle over top. Bake, uncovered, at 350° for 35-40 minutes or until hot and bubbly. Yield: 4-6 servings.

Scalloped Carrots

A cookbook my husband gave me as a wedding gift included this recipe, which he remembers having the dish as a child at church dinners. Now I make it whenever I need a special vegetable side. It's rich even after reheating.
—Joyce Tornholm
New Market, Iowa

Colorful Vegetable Casserole

PREP: 25 MIN. BAKE: 25 MIN.

With its eye-opening zippy flavor, horseradish really livens up this blend of cauliflower, broccoli and carrots. It's a great way to eat your vegetables!
—Precious Owens
Elizabethtown, Kentucky

- 3 cups fresh cauliflowerets
- 3 cups sliced carrots
- 3 cups fresh broccoli florets
- 1 cup mayonnaise
- 1/4 cup finely chopped onion
- 3 tablespoons prepared horseradish
- 1/4 teaspoon salt
- 1/8 teaspoon pepper
- 1/3 cup dry bread crumbs
- 2 tablespoons butter, melted
- 1/8 teaspoon paprika

In a large saucepan; add 1-in. of water. Add cauliflower and carrots. Bring to a boil. Reduce heat; cover and simmer for 4-8 minutes. Add broccoli; cook 4-6 minutes longer or until all the vegetables are crisp-tender. Drain.

In a small bowl, combine the mayonnaise, onion, horseradish, salt and pepper. Add vegetables; toss to coat.

Pour into a greased 2-qt. baking dish. In a small bowl, combine the bread crumbs, butter and paprika until crumbly; sprinkle over vegetables. Bake, uncovered, at 350° for 25-30 minutes or until heated through. Yield: 12-14 servings.

Garden Casserole

This delicious, cheesy casserole uses lots of veggies and herbs from my garden. The dish includes a sunny medley of eggplant, zucchini and tomatoes.
—Phyllis Hickey
Bedford, New Hampshire

Garden Casserole

PREP: 25 MIN. + STANDING
BAKE: 20 MIN.

- 2 **pounds eggplant, peeled**
- 5 **teaspoons salt,** *divided*
- 1/4 **cup olive oil**
- 2 **medium onions, finely chopped**
- 2 **garlic cloves, minced**
- 2 **medium zucchini, sliced 1/2 inch thick**
- 5 **medium tomatoes, peeled and chopped**
- 2 **celery ribs, sliced**
- 1/4 **cup minced fresh parsley**
- 1/4 **cup minced fresh basil** *or* **1 tablespoon dried basil**
- 1/2 **teaspoon pepper**
- 1/2 **cup grated Romano cheese**
- 1 **cup seasoned bread crumbs**
- 2 **tablespoons butter, melted**
- 1 **cup (4 ounces) shredded part-skim mozzarella cheese**

Cut eggplant into 1/2-in.-thick slices; sprinkle both sides with 3 teaspoons salt. Place in a deep dish; cover and let stand for 30 minutes. Rinse with cold water; drain and dry on paper towels.

Cut eggplant into 1/2-in. cubes. Transfer to a large skillet; saute in oil until lightly browned. Add the onions, garlic and zucchini; cook 3 minutes. Add the tomatoes, celery, parsley, basil, pepper and remaining salt. Cover and simmer for 10 minutes. Remove from the heat; stir in Romano cheese.

Pour into a greased 13-in. x 9-in. x 2-in. baking dish. Combine crumbs and butter; sprinkle on top. Bake, uncovered, at 375° for 15 minutes. Sprinkle with mozzarella cheese. Bake 5 minutes longer or until cheese is melted. Yield: 12 servings.

Broccoli Casserole

PREP: 20 MIN. **BAKE:** 35 MIN.

Everybody who has tried this side dish absolutely raves about it. People who don't even like broccoli beg me to make it.
—Elaine Hubbard
Poconto Lake, Pennsylvania

- 2 **packages (16 ounces** *each***) frozen broccoli florets**
- 1 **can (10-3/4 ounces) condensed cream of mushroom soup, undiluted**
- 1 **cup (8 ounces) sour cream**
- 1-1/2 **cups (6 ounces) shredded sharp cheddar cheese,** *divided*
- 1 **can (6 ounces) french-fried onions,** *divided*

Cook broccoli according to package directions; drain well. In a large saucepan, combine the soup, sour cream, 1 cup cheese and 1-1/4 cups onions. Cook over medium heat for 4-5 minutes or until heated through. Stir in the broccoli.

Pour into a greased 2-qt. baking dish. Bake, uncovered, at 325° for 25-30 minutes or until bubbly. Sprinkle with the remaining cheese and onions. Bake 10-15 minutes longer or until cheese is melted. Yield: 6-8 servings.

Garlic Potato Bake
I created this recipe for an end-of-summer harvest picnic. Everyone loved it, so now I serve it at all my special dinners.
—Shelly Lehman
Powell, Wyoming

Garlic Potato Bake

PREP: 30 MIN. **BAKE:** 30 MIN.

- 18 medium potatoes, peeled and diced
- 3 whole garlic bulbs, separated into cloves and peeled
- 3 cups (12 ounces) shredded cheddar cheese
- 1 package (8 ounces) cream cheese, cubed
- 6 eggs, lightly beaten
- 1 tablespoon minced chives
- 1-1/2 to 2 teaspoons salt
- 1/4 teaspoon white pepper

Diced sweet red, yellow and orange peppers, fresh rosemary sprigs and minced chives, optional

Place potatoes and garlic in a large kettle and cover with water. Bring to a boil. Reduce heat; cover and simmer for 15-20 minutes or until potatoes and garlic are tender. Drain.

In a large mixing bowl, beat the potatoes and garlic, cheddar cheese, cream cheese, eggs, chives, salt and pepper until blended.

Spoon into two greased shallow 3-qt. baking dishes. Bake, uncovered, at 350° for 30-35 minutes or until a thermometer reads 160°. Garnish with peppers, rosemary and chives if desired. Yield: 25 servings.

Cheesy Noodle Casserole

PREP: 25 MIN. **BAKE:** 25 MIN.

- 2 packages (1 pound *each*) wide egg noodles
- 1/2 cup butter, cubed
- 1/4 cup all-purpose flour
- 1 teaspoon garlic salt
- 1 teaspoon onion salt
- 5 to 6 cups milk
- 2 pounds process cheese (Velveeta), cubed

TOPPING:
- 1/2 cup dry bread crumbs
- 2 tablespoons butter, melted

Cook noodles according to package directions; drain. Meanwhile, in a Dutch oven, melt butter. Stir in the flour, garlic salt and onion salt until smooth; gradually stir in milk. Bring to a boil; cook and stir for 2 minutes or until thickened. Add the cheese; stir until melted. Stir in the noodles.

Transfer to two greased shallow 2-qt. baking dishes. Combine bread crumbs and butter until crumbly; sprinkle over casseroles. Bake, uncovered, at 350° for 25-30 minutes or until golden brown. Yield: 2 casseroles (12 servings each).

Cheesy Noodle Casserole
This creamy side dish is such an excellent meal extender that I always keep it in mind whenever I feel my menu needs a boost. It's a quick and easy casserole to fix, and is always devoured in a hurry!
—Shirley McKee
Varna, Illinois

Summer Squash Bake

PREP: 15 MIN. **BAKE:** 30 MIN.

- 3 cups sliced yellow summer squash
- 2 tablespoons water
- 1/2 cup finely chopped green pepper
- 1/2 cup finely chopped onion
- 1/2 cup chopped pecans
- 1/2 cup mayonnaise
- 2/3 cup shredded cheddar cheese, *divided*
- 1/2 teaspoon sugar
- 1/2 teaspoon salt
- 1/4 teaspoon pepper

Place squash and water in a 1-1/2-qt. microwave-safe bowl. Cover and microwave on high for 2-3 minutes or until crisp-tender; drain well. Stir in the green pepper, onion, pecans, mayonnaise, 1/3 cup cheese, sugar, salt and pepper.

Transfer to a lightly greased shallow 1-1/2-qt. baking dish. Cover and bake at 350° for 25 minutes. Uncover; sprinkle with remaining cheese. Bake 5 minutes longer or until cheese is melted. Yield: 6 servings.

Editor's Note: Reduced-fat or fat-free mayonnaise is not recommended for this recipe. This recipe was tested in a 1,100-watt microwave.

Summer Squash Bake

This colorful side makes the most of fresh summer squash. A handful of chopped pecans adds a nutty crunch to the creamy side dish.
—Gail Smrtic
Broken Arrow, Oklahoma

Creamy Baked Spinach

PREP: 15 MIN. **BAKE:** 20 MIN.

Cream cheese turns ordinary spinach into a side dish that's pretty enough to serve company. This casserole is a snap to stir up because it relies on convenient frozen chopped spinach.
—Beverly Albrecht
Beatrice, Nebraska

- 2 packages (10 ounces *each*) frozen chopped spinach
- 2 packages (3 ounces *each*) cream cheese, softened
- 4 tablespoons butter, *divided*
- 1/4 teaspoon salt
- 1/2 cup seasoned bread crumbs

Cook spinach according to package directions; drain well. Stir in cream cheese, 2 tablespoons butter and salt.

Transfer to a greased 1-qt. baking dish. Melt remaining butter; toss with bread crumbs. Sprinkle over spinach mixture. Bake, uncovered, at 350° for 20 minutes or until lightly browned. Yield: 4-6 servings.

Saucy Green Bean Bake

Here's a different way to serve green beans. It's a nice change of pace from plain vegetables yet doesn't require much work on your part. Keep it in mind the next time your schedule is full and you have to set dinner on the table.
—June Formanek
Belle Plaine, Iowa

Saucy Green Bean Bake

PREP/TOTAL TIME: 30 MIN.

- 1   can (8 ounces) tomato sauce
- 2   tablespoons diced pimientos
- 1   tablespoon prepared mustard
- 1/4   teaspoon salt
- 1/8   teaspoon pepper
- 1   pound fresh *or* frozen cut green beans, cooked
- 1/2   cup chopped onion
- 1/3   cup chopped green pepper
- 1   garlic clove, minced
- 2   tablespoons butter
- 3/4   cup shredded process cheese (Velveeta)

In a large bowl, combine the first five ingredients. Add the green beans; toss to coat. Transfer to an ungreased 1-qt. baking dish. Cover and bake at 350° for 20 minutes.

Meanwhile, in a large skillet, saute the onion, green pepper and garlic in butter until tender. Sprinkle over beans. Top with cheese. Bake, uncovered, for 3-5 minutes or until cheese is melted. Yield: 4-6 servings.

Festive Cauliflower Casserole

PREP: 20 MIN. **BAKE:** 30 MIN.

My family asks for this dish every Christmas. It complements turkey or ham and can be put together the day before the meal.
—Nancy McDonald
Burns, Wyoming

- 1   large head cauliflower (about 2 pounds), cut into florets
- 1/4   cup diced green pepper
- 1   jar (4-1/2 ounces) sliced mushrooms, drained
- 1/4   cup butter, cubed
- 1/3   cup all-purpose flour
- 3/4   teaspoon salt
- 2   cups milk
- 1   jar (2 ounces) diced pimientos, drained
- 1   cup (4 ounces) shredded Swiss cheese, *divided*

In a large saucepan, bring 1 in. of water and the cauliflower to a boil. Reduce heat; cover and simmer for 5-10 minutes or until crisp-tender; drain. Place in a greased 8-in. square baking dish.

In a large saucepan, saute green pepper and mushrooms in butter until tender. Add flour and salt; stir until blended. Gradually add milk. Bring to a boil; cook and stir for 2 minutes or until thickened. Remove from the heat; add pimientos. Add 3/4 cup cheese, stirring until melted; pour over cauliflower.

Cover and bake at 350° for 20 minutes. Uncover; sprinkle with remaining cheese. Bake 10-15 minutes longer or until cheese is melted. Yield: 6-8 servings.

Hearty Baked Beans

This saucy dish is flavorful and filling, chock-full of ground beef, bacon and four varieties of beans. I've had the recipe for over 10 years and make it often for big appetites at home and potlucks at work and church.
—Cathy Swancutt, Junction City, Oregon

Hearty Baked Beans

PREP: 15 MIN. **BAKE:** 1 HOUR

- 1 pound ground beef
- 2 large onions, chopped
- 3/4 pound sliced bacon, cooked and crumbled
- 4 cans (15 ounces *each*) pork and beans
- 1 bottle (18 ounces) honey barbecue sauce
- 1 can (16 ounces) kidney beans, rinsed and drained
- 1 can (15-1/4 ounces) lima beans, rinsed and drained
- 1 can (15 ounces) black beans, rinsed and drained
- 1/2 cup packed brown sugar
- 3 tablespoons cider vinegar
- 1 tablespoon Liquid Smoke, optional
- 1 teaspoon salt
- 1/2 teaspoon pepper

In a large skillet, cook beef and onions over medium heat until meat is no longer pink; drain. Transfer to a 5-qt. Dutch oven. Stir in the remaining ingredients. Cover and bake at 350° for 1 hour or until heated through. Yield: 18 servings.

Biscuit-Topped Tomato Casserole

PREP: 30 MIN. **BAKE:** 20 MIN.

- 2 tablespoons cornstarch
- 1 tablespoon sugar
- 2 tablespoons cold water
- 8 medium tomatoes, seeded and chopped
- 1 medium green pepper, chopped
- 1 teaspoon salt
- 1/8 teaspoon pepper

TOPPING:

- 1 cup all-purpose flour
- 2 teaspoons baking powder
- 1 teaspoon garlic powder
- 1/4 teaspoon baking soda
- 1/4 teaspoon chicken bouillon granules
- 1/4 cup cold butter, cubed
- 1/2 cup shredded cheddar cheese
- 1/2 cup plus 1 tablespoon buttermilk

In a large saucepan, combine cornstarch and sugar. Stir in water until smooth. Stir in tomatoes. Bring to a boil; cook and stir for 2 minutes or until thickened. Remove from the heat. Stir in the green pepper, salt and pepper; keep warm.

In a large bowl, combine the first five topping ingredients. Cut in butter until mixture resembles coarse crumbs. Stir in cheese and buttermilk just until moistened.

Transfer tomato mixture to a greased 11-in. x 7-in. x 2-in. baking dish. Drop topping into eight mounds onto hot tomato mixture. Bake, uncovered, at 400° for 20-25 minutes or until a toothpick inserted in biscuits comes out clean. Yield: 6 servings.

Biscuit-Topped Tomato Casserole

I use fresh tomatoes from our garden to prepare this delightful, old-fashioned dish. Since it's just my husband and me, I sometimes halve the tomato mixture, then make the rest of the topping into garlic-cheese drop biscuits to eat with other meals.
—Jayme Buzard
Wichita, Kansas

Sweet Onion Corn Bake

This tasty corn casserole gets plenty of flavor from sweet onions, cream-style corn and cheddar cheese plus a little zip from hot pepper sauce. It's a popular addition to our church potlucks.
—Jeannette Travis, Forth Worth, Texas

End of Summer Vegetable Bake

End of Summer Vegetable Bake
When my husband worked as a deputy ag commissioner, he'd bring me bushels of vegetables from area farms. This pretty side dish is the result—it's easy to fix but impressive enough for company. We're busy retirees with five grown kids and a menagerie ranging from show dogs to miniature donkeys.
—Judy Williams
Hayden, Idaho

PREP: 40 MIN.
BAKE: 25 MIN. + STANDING

- 1 small head cauliflower, broken into small florets (about 5 cups)
- 1 medium bunch broccoli, cut into small florets (about 4 cups)
- 1 medium onion, chopped
- 2 garlic cloves, minced
- 1 tablespoon butter
- 2 medium tomatoes, chopped
- 3/4 teaspoon dried basil
- 3/4 teaspoon dried oregano
- 3/4 teaspoon salt
- 1/4 teaspoon pepper
- 1/4 teaspoon hot pepper sauce
- 4 eggs
- 1/3 cup half-and-half cream
- 1-1/2 cups (6 ounces) shredded Swiss cheese, *divided*
- 1/4 cup shredded Parmesan cheese

Place the cauliflower and broccoli in a saucepan with a small amount of water. Bring to a boil. Reduce heat; cover and simmer for 5-10 minutes or until crisp-tender. Drain and set aside.

In a large skillet, saute onion and garlic in butter until tender. Stir in the tomatoes, seasonings, cauliflower and broccoli. Cook, uncovered, until heated through, about 4 minutes, stirring occasionally. Remove from the heat and set aside.

In a large bowl, beat eggs and cream; stir in 1 cup Swiss cheese, Parmesan cheese and the vegetable mixture. Transfer to a greased shallow 2-qt. baking dish. Sprinkle with remaining Swiss cheese.

Bake, uncovered, at 375° for 25-30 minutes or until a knife inserted near the center comes out clean. Let stand for 10 minutes before serving. Yield: 12 servings.

Sweet Onion Corn Bake

PREP: 15 MIN.
BAKE: 45 MIN. + STANDING

- 2 large sweet onions, thinly sliced
- 1/2 cup butter, cubed
- 1 cup (8 ounces) sour cream
- 1/2 cup milk

Asparagus Pea Medley

A rich and creamy sauce beautifully coats asparagus and peas. This makes a great side for any special occasion meal.
—M. Joalyce Graham
Starke, Florida

1/2 teaspoon dill weed

1/4 teaspoon salt

2 cups (8 ounces) shredded cheddar cheese, *divided*

1 egg, lightly beaten

1 can (14-3/4 ounces) cream-style corn

1 package (8-1/2 ounces) corn bread/muffin mix

4 drops hot pepper sauce

In a large skillet, saute onions in butter until tender. In a small bowl, combine the sour cream, milk, dill and salt until blended; stir in 1 cup of cheese. Stir into the onion mixture; remove from the heat and set aside.

In a large bowl, combine the egg, corn, corn bread mix and hot pepper sauce. Pour into a greased 13-in. x 9-in. x 2-in. baking dish. Spoon onion mixture over top. Sprinkle with remaining cheese.

Bake, uncovered, at 350° for 45-50 minutes or until the top is set and lightly browned. Let stand for 10 minutes before cutting. Yield: 12-15 servings.

Asparagus Pea Medley

PREP: 20 MIN. **BAKE:** 35 MIN.

2 packages (10-1/2 ounces *each*) frozen cut asparagus

1 package (10 ounces) frozen peas, thawed

1 jar (8 ounces) sliced mushrooms, drained

1 jar (2 ounces) diced pimientos, drained

5 tablespoons butter, *divided*

3 tablespoons all-purpose flour

3/4 cup milk

1 jar (5 ounces) sharp American cheese spread

1/4 teaspoon salt

1/4 teaspoon pepper

1/3 cup dry bread crumbs

Cook asparagus according to package directions, omitting the salt. Drain, reserving 3/4 cup cooking liquid. Place asparagus in a greased 11-in. x 7-in. x 2-in. baking dish. Top with peas, mushrooms and pimientos; set aside.

In a small saucepan, melt 3 tablespoons butter. Stir in flour until smooth; gradually add milk and reserved cooking liquid. Bring to a boil; cook and stir for 2 minutes or until thickened. Reduce heat; add the cheese spread, salt and pepper. Stir until blended. Pour over vegetables. Melt remaining butter; toss with bread crumbs. Sprinkle over cheese sauce.

Cover and refrigerate for 8 hours or overnight. Or bake, uncovered, at 350° for 35-40 min. or until bubbly. If refrigerated before baking, remove from the refrigerator 30 minutes before baking. Yield: 8-10 servings.

Pecan Sweet Potato Bake

The recipe for this luscious souffle was handed down through my husband's family, and it's become a tradition for me to serve it during the holidays. Everyone loves it!
—Nanci Keatley
Salem, Oregon

Pecan Sweet Potato Bake

PREP: 20 MIN. **BAKE:** 30 MIN.

- **3 cups mashed sweet potatoes**
- **2 eggs**
- **1/2 cup sugar**
- **1/4 cup half-and-half cream**
- **1/4 cup butter, softened**
- **2 teaspoons vanilla extract**
- **1/8 teaspoon salt**

TOPPING:
- **1/2 cup packed brown sugar**
- **2 tablespoons all-purpose flour**
- **1/4 cup cold butter, cubed**
- **1/2 cup chopped pecans**

In a large mixing bowl, combine the first seven ingredients; beat until light and fluffy. Transfer to a greased 11-in. x 7-in. x 2-in. baking dish.

For topping, combine the brown sugar and flour in a bowl; cut in butter until crumbly. Fold in pecans. Sprinkle over sweet potato mixture.

Bake, uncovered, at 350° for 30-35 minutes or until a knife inserted near the center comes out clean. Yield: 6-8 servings.

Calico Squash Casserole

PREP: 20 MIN. **BAKE:** 30 MIN.

- **2 cups sliced yellow summer squash (1/4 inch thick)**
- **1 cup sliced zucchini (1/4 inch thick)**
- **1 medium onion, chopped**
- **1/4 cup sliced green onions**
- **1 cup water**
- **1 teaspoon salt, *divided***
- **2 cups crushed butter-flavored crackers**
- **1/2 cup butter, melted**
- **1 can (10-3/4 ounces) condensed cream of chicken soup, undiluted**
- **1 can (8 ounces) sliced water chestnuts, drained**
- **1 large carrot, shredded**
- **1/2 cup mayonnaise**
- **1 jar (2 ounces) diced pimientos, drained**
- **1 teaspoon rubbed sage**
- **1/2 teaspoon white pepper**
- **1 cup (4 ounces) shredded sharp cheddar cheese**

In a large saucepan, combine the first five ingredients; add 1/2 teaspoon salt. Cover and cook until squash is tender, about 6 minutes. Drain well; set aside.

Combine crumbs and butter; spoon half into a greased shallow 1-1/2-qt. baking dish. In a large bowl, combine the soup, water chestnuts, carrot, mayonnaise, pimientos, sage, pepper and remaining salt; fold into squash mixture. Spoon over crumbs.

Sprinkle with cheese and the remaining crumb mixture. Bake, uncovered, at 350° for 30 minutes or until lightly browned. Yield: 8 servings.

Calico Squash Casserole

I have a thriving country garden and try a lot of recipes using my squash. It's a pleasure to present this beautiful casserole at dinnertime.
—Lucille Terry
Frankfort, Kentucky

Italian Zucchini Casserole

Compliments crop up as fast as zucchini vines when folks sample this casserole. Even those who generally don't like zucchini find they enjoy it in this savory side dish.
—Kimberly Speta
Kennedy, New York

  3 cups sliced peeled cooked sweet potatoes
  3 cups sliced peeled tart apples (about 2 large)
3/4 cup packed brown sugar
3/4 teaspoon ground nutmeg
1/4 teaspoon ground allspice
1/4 teaspoon salt
Dash pepper
  1 tablespoon butter

In a greased 1-1/2-qt. baking dish, layer half of the sweet potatoes and apples. In a small bowl, combine the brown sugar, nutmeg, allspice, salt and pepper; sprinkle half over apples. Dot with half of the butter. Repeat layers.

Cover and bake at 350° for 15 minutes. Uncover; baste with pan juices. Bake 15 minutes longer or until apples are tender. Yield: 8 servings.

Italian Zucchini Casserole

PREP: 35 MIN. **BAKE:** 30 MIN.

  3 medium zucchini, sliced (about 6-1/2 cups)
  3 tablespoons olive oil, *divided*
  1 medium onion, sliced
  1 garlic clove, minced
  1 can (28 ounces) diced tomatoes, undrained
  1 tablespoon minced fresh basil *or* 1 teaspoon dried basil
1-1/2 teaspoons minced fresh oregano *or* 1/2 teaspoon dried oregano
1/2 teaspoon garlic salt
1/4 teaspoon pepper
1-1/2 cups stuffing mix
1/2 cup grated Parmesan cheese
3/4 cup shredded part-skim mozzarella cheese

In a large skillet, cook zucchini in 1 tablespoon oil 5-6 minutes or until tender; drain and set aside. In the same skillet, saute the onion and garlic in remaining oil for 1 minute. Add the tomatoes, basil, oregano, garlic salt and pepper. Bring to a boil. Reduce heat; simmer, uncovered, for 10 minutes. Remove from the heat; gently stir in zucchini.

Transfer to a greased 13-in. x 9-in. x 2-in. baking dish. Top with stuffing mix; sprinkle with Parmesan cheese. Cover and bake at 350° for 20 minutes. Uncover; sprinkle with mozzarella cheese. Bake 10 minutes longer or until cheese is melted. Yield: 6-8 servings.

Broccoli Rice Casserole

This hearty side is my favorite dish to make for a potluck. With the green of the broccoli and the rich cheese sauce, it's pretty to serve, and it makes a tasty partner with almost any kind of meat.
—*Margaret Mayes, La Mesa, California*

Broccoli Rice Casserole

PREP: 10 MIN. **BAKE:** 25 MIN.

- 1 small onion, chopped
- 1/2 cup chopped celery
- 1 package (10 ounces) frozen chopped broccoli, thawed
- 1 tablespoon butter
- 1 jar (8 ounces) process cheese sauce
- 1 can (10-3/4 ounces) condensed cream of mushroom soup, undiluted
- 1 can (5 ounces) evaporated milk
- 3 cups cooked rice

In a large skillet, saute the onion, celery and broccoli in butter for 3-5 minutes or until crisp-tender. Stir in the cheese sauce, soup and milk until smooth.

Place rice in a greased 8-in. square baking dish. Pour cheese mixture over; do not stir. Bake, uncovered, at 325° for 25-30 minutes or until bubbly. Yield: 8-10 servings.

Acorn Squash Feta Casserole

PREP: 25 MIN.
BAKE: 1 HOUR 35 MIN.

- 2 large acorn squash (about 1-1/2 pounds *each*)
- 1 medium onion, chopped
- 2 garlic cloves, minced
- 3 tablespoons butter
- 1/2 cup chopped green pepper
- 1/2 cup chopped sweet red pepper
- 2 eggs
- 1 cup (8 ounces) plain yogurt
- 1 cup (4 ounces) crumbled feta cheese
- 1-1/4 teaspoons salt
- 1/2 teaspoon pepper

Dash cayenne pepper, optional

- 1/4 cup sunflower kernels

Cut squash in half; discard seeds. Place squash cut side down in a greased 15-in. x 10-in. x 1-in. baking pan; add 1/2 in. of hot water. Bake, uncovered, at 350° for 35-40 minutes. Drain water from pan; turn squash cut side up. Bake 10 minutes longer or until squash is tender; cool slightly. Carefully scoop out squash; place in a large bowl and mash. Set aside.

In a large skillet, saute onion and garlic in butter until tender. Add peppers; saute until crisp-tender. In a large bowl, whisk

eggs and yogurt until blended. Stir in the squash, onion mixture, feta cheese, salt, pepper and cayenne if desired.

Transfer to a greased 11-in. x 7-in. x 2-in. baking dish. Sprinkle with sunflower kernels. Cover and bake at 375° for 25 minutes. Uncover; bake 25-30 minutes longer or until a knife inserted near the center comes out clean. Yield: 6-8 servings.

Acorn Squash Feta Casserole
I get loads of compliments on this out-of-the-ordinary recipe whenever I serve it. The dish marries squash and feta cheese with onion, garlic, bell peppers and a sprinkling of sunflower kernels. Leftovers are delicious hot or cold!
—*Maisy Vliet Holland, Michigan*

Festive Green Bean Casserole

This recipe came from a cookbook my son gave to me over 20 years ago. It's a delicious dish that I make often for get-togethers and potluck suppers.
—June Mullins, Livonia, Missouri

Special Scalloped Corn

PREP: 10 MIN. **BAKE:** 30 MIN.

- 1 can (14-3/4 ounces) cream-style corn
- 2 eggs
- 1/2 cup crushed saltines (about 15 crackers)
- 1/4 cup butter, melted
- 1/4 cup evaporated milk
- 1/4 cup shredded carrot
- 1/4 cup chopped green pepper
- 1 tablespoon chopped celery
- 1 teaspoon chopped onion
- 1/2 teaspoon sugar
- 1/2 teaspoon salt
- 1/2 cup shredded cheddar cheese

In a large bowl, combine the first 11 ingredients. Transfer to a greased 1-qt. baking dish. Sprinkle with cheese. Bake, uncovered, at 350° for 30-35 minutes or until a knife inserted near the center comes out clean. Yield: 4 servings.

Festive Green Bean Casserole

PREP/TOTAL TIME: 30 MIN.

- 1 cup chopped sweet red pepper
- 1 small onion, finely chopped
- 1 tablespoon butter
- 1 can (10-3/4 ounces) condensed cream of celery soup, undiluted
- 1/2 cup milk
- 1 teaspoon Worcestershire sauce
- 1/8 teaspoon hot pepper sauce
- 2 packages (16 ounces *each*) frozen French-style green beans, thawed and drained
- 1 can (8 ounces) sliced water chestnuts, drained
- 1 cup (4 ounces) shredded cheddar cheese

In a skillet, saute red pepper and onion in butter until tender. Add the soup, milk, Worcestershire sauce and hot pepper sauce; stir until smooth. Stir in beans and water chestnuts.

Transfer to an ungreased 1-1/2-qt. baking dish. Sprinkle with cheese. Bake, uncovered, at 350° for 15 minutes or until heated through. Yield: 6-8 servings.

Special Scalloped Corn

Carrots and green pepper make this a colorful dish, which also grabs attention at a potluck. For those occasions, I double the recipe.
—Mrs. J. Brown
Fort Dodge, Iowa

Slow Cooker

Appetizers & Beverages 126

Soups & Sandwiches 144

Poultry & Seafood 168

Beef & Ground Beef 186

Pork & Lamb 210

Side Dishes 228

Desserts 242

Indexes 371

Appetizers &Beverages

Warm Spiced Cider Punch

PREP: 5 MIN. **COOK:** 4 HOURS

This is a nice warm-up punch—I like to serve it when there is a nip in the air. The aroma of the apple cider, orange juice and spices is wonderful as the punch simmers in the slow cooker.
—Susan Smith, Forest, Virginia

- 4 **cups apple cider** *or* **unsweetened apple juice**
- 2-1/4 **cups water**
- 3/4 **cup orange juice concentrate**
- 3/4 **teaspoon ground nutmeg**
- 3/4 **teaspoon ground ginger**
- 3 **whole cloves**
- 2 **cinnamon sticks**
- 4 **orange slices, halved**

In a 3-qt. slow cooker, combine the apple cider, water, orange juice concentrate, nutmeg and ginger. Place cloves and cinnamon sticks on a double thickness of cheesecloth; bring up corners of cloth and tie with string to form a bag. Place bag in slow cooker. Cover and cook on low for 4-5 hours or until heated through. Remove and discard spice bag. Garnish with orange slices. Yield: 8 servings.

Hot Chili Cheese Dip

PREP: 20 MIN. **COOK:** 4 HOURS

- 1 **medium onion, finely chopped**
- 2 **garlic cloves, minced**
- 2 **teaspoons vegetable oil**
- 2 **cans (15 ounces** *each***) chili without beans**
- 2 **cups salsa**
- 2 **packages (3 ounces** *each***) cream cheese, cubed**
- 2 **cans (2-1/4 ounces** *each***) sliced ripe olives, drained**

Tortilla chips

In a skillet, saute onion and garlic in oil until tender. Transfer to a 3-qt. slow cooker. Stir in the chili, salsa, cream cheese and olives. Cover and cook on low for 4 hours or until heated through, stirring occasionally. Stir before serving with tortilla chips. Yield: 6 cups.

Hot Chili Cheese Dip
I simplify party preparation by using my slow cooker to create this thick, cheesy dip. Your guests won't believe how good it is.
—Jeanie Carrigan Madera, California

Spiced Coffee

Even those who usually don't drink coffee will find this special blend with a hint of chocolate appealing. I keep a big batch simmering at parties.
—Joanne Holt, Bowling Green, Ohio

Buffet Meatballs

PREP: 10 MIN. **COOK:** 4 HOURS

- 1 cup grape juice
- 1 cup apple jelly
- 1 cup ketchup
- 1 can (8 ounces) tomato sauce
- 4 pounds frozen Italian-style meatballs

In a small saucepan, combine the juice, jelly, ketchup and tomato sauce. Cook and stir over medium heat until jelly is melted; remove from the heat. Place meatballs in a 5-qt. slow cooker. Pour sauce over the top and gently stir to coat. Cover and cook on low for 4 hours or until heated through. Yield: about 11 dozen.

Buffet Meatballs

Only five ingredients are needed to fix these easy appetizers. Grape juice and apple jelly are the secrets behind the sweet yet tangy sauce that complements convenient packaged meatballs.
—Janet Anderson
Carson City, Nevada

In a 3-qt. slow cooker, combine the coffee, sugar, chocolate syrup and anise extract. Place cinnamon sticks and cloves in a double thickness of cheesecloth; bring up corners of cloth and tie with string to form a bag. Add to slow cooker. Cover and cook on low for 2-3 hours.

Discard spice bag. Ladle coffee into mugs; garnish each with a cinnamon stick if desired. Yield: 8 cups.

Slow-Cooked Salsa

PREP: 15 MIN.
COOK: 2-1/2 HOURS + COOLING

I love the fresh taste of homemade salsa, but as a working mother, I don't have much time to make it. So I created this delicious slow-cooked version that is so easy it practically makes itself!
—Toni Menard, Lompoc, California

- 10 plum tomatoes, cored
- 2 garlic cloves
- 1 small onion, cut into wedges

Spiced Coffee

PREP: 10 MIN. **COOK:** 2 HOURS

- 8 cups brewed coffee
- 1/3 cup sugar
- 1/4 cup chocolate syrup
- 1/2 teaspoon anise extract
- 4 cinnamon sticks (3 inches)
- 1-1/2 teaspoons whole cloves

Additional cinnamon sticks, optional

Mulled Pomegranate Sipper

PREP: 10 MIN. **COOK:** 1 HOUR

- 1 bottle (64 ounces) cranberry-apple juice
- 2 cups unsweetened apple juice
- 1 cup pomegranate juice
- 2/3 cup honey
- 1/2 cup orange juice
- 3 cinnamon sticks (3 inches)
- 10 whole cloves
- 2 tablespoons grated orange peel

In a 5-qt. slow cooker, combine the first five ingredients. Place the cinnamon sticks and cloves on a double thickness of cheesecloth; bring up corners of cloth and tie with string to form a bag. Add to slow cooker. Cover and cook on low for 1-2 hours. Discard spice bag. Yield: 16 servings (about 3 quarts).

Cranberry Meatballs

PREP: 20 MIN. **COOK:** 6 HOURS

Whether you serve them as appetizers or the main course, these tasty meatballs are sure to be a hit. Cranberry and chili sauces give them extra sweetness. For a main dish, I suggest serving them over egg noodles.
—*Nina Hall, Spokane, Wisconsin*

- 2 eggs, beaten
- 1 cup dry bread crumbs
- 1/3 cup minced fresh parsley
- 2 tablespoons finely chopped onion
- 1-1/2 pounds lean ground beef
- 1 can (16 ounces) jellied cranberry sauce
- 1 bottle (12 ounces) chili sauce
- 1/3 cup ketchup
- 2 tablespoons brown sugar
- 1 tablespoon lemon juice

In a large bowl, combine the eggs, bread crumbs, parsley and onion. Crumble beef over mixture and mix well. Shape into 1-1/2-in. balls. Place in a 3-qt. slow cooker.

In a small bowl, combine the cranberry sauce, chili sauce, ketchup, brown sugar and lemon juice. Pour over meatballs. Cover and cook on low for 6 hours or until meat is no longer pink. Yield: 6 servings.

Slow-Cooker Cheese Dip

PREP: 15 MIN. **COOK:** 4 HOURS

I brought this slightly spicy cheese dip to a gathering with friends, where it was a huge hit.
—*Marion Bartone*
Conneaut, Ohio

- 1 pound ground beef
- 1/2 pound bulk spicy pork sausage
- 2 pounds process American cheese, cubed
- 2 cans (10 ounces *each*) diced tomatoes and green chilies

Tortilla chips

In a large skillet, cook beef and sausage over medium heat until

Mulled Pomegranate Sipper
This warm, comforting cider fills the entire house with a wonderful aroma.
—*Lisa Renshaw*
Kansas City, Missouri

Barbecue Sausage Bites

A popular appetizer, this dish pairs pineapple chunks with barbecue sauce and three kinds of sausage. It requires just a few minutes of prep, which makes it a super recipe for entertaining.
—Rebekah Randolph
Greer, South Carolina

no longer pink; drain. Transfer to a 5-qt. slow cooker. Add cheese and tomatoes; mix well. Cover and cook on low for 4 hours or until the cheese is melted, stirring occasionally. Serve with tortilla chips. Yield: 3 quarts.

Old-Fashioned Peach Butter

PREP: 10 MIN.
COOK: 9 HOURS + COOLING

Cinnamon and ground cloves add down-home flavor to this spread for toast or biscuits. Using the slow cooker eliminates much of the stirring required when simmering fruit butter on the stovetop.
—Marilou Robinson
Portland, Oregon

14	cups coarsely chopped peeled fresh *or* frozen peaches (about 5-1/2 pounds)
2-1/2	cups sugar
4-1/2	teaspoons lemon juice
1-1/2	teaspoons ground cinnamon
3/4	teaspoon ground cloves
1/2	cup quick-cooking tapioca

In a large bowl, combine the peaches, sugar, lemon juice, cinnamon and cloves. Transfer to a 5-qt. slow cooker. Cover and cook on low for 8-10 hours or until peaches are very soft, stirring occasionally.

Stir in the tapioca. Cook, uncovered, on high for 1 hour or until thickened. Pour into jars or freezer containers; cool to room temperature, about 1 hour. Refrigerate or freeze. Yield: 9 cups.

Barbecue Sausage Bites

PREP: 10 MIN. **COOK:** 2-1/2 HOURS

1	package (1 pound) miniature smoked sausages
3/4	pound fully cooked bratwurst
3/4	pound smoked kielbasa *or* Polish sausage
1	bottle (18 ounces) barbecue sauce
2/3	cup orange marmalade
1/2	teaspoon ground mustard
1/8	teaspoon ground allspice
1	can (20 ounces) pineapple chunks, drained

In a 3-qt. slow cooker, combine the sausages. In a bowl, whisk barbecue sauce, marmalade, mustard and allspice. Pour over sausage mixture; stir to coat.

Cover and cook on high for 2-1/2 to 3 hours or until heated through. Stir in pineapple. Serve with toothpicks. Yield: 12-14 servings.

Party Sausages

Don't want any leftovers on January 2? Serve these sausages January 1. I've never had even one end up uneaten.
—Jo Ann Renner
Xenia, Ohio

Party Sausages

PREP: 15 MIN. **COOK:** 1 HOUR

- 2 pounds fully cooked smoked sausage links
- 1 bottle (8 ounces) Catalina salad dressing
- 1 bottle (8 ounces) Russian salad dressing
- 1/2 cup packed brown sugar
- 1/2 cup pineapple juice

Cut sausages diagonally into 1/2-in. slices; cook in a skillet over medium heat until lightly browned. Transfer sausages to a 3-qt. slow cooker; discard drippings. Add dressings, sugar and juice to skillet; cook and stir over medium-low heat until sugar is dissolved. Pour over sausages. Heat on low for 1-2 hours or until heated through. Serve hot. Yield: 16 servings.

Hearty Broccoli Dip

PREP: 10 MIN. **COOK:** 2 HOURS

You'll need just five ingredients to stir up this no-fuss appetizer. People often ask me to bring this creamy dip to potlucks and parties.
—Sue Call, Beech Grove, Indiana

- 1 pound ground beef
- 1 pound process American cheese, cubed
- 1 can (10-3/4 ounces) condensed cream of mushroom soup, undiluted
- 1 package (10 ounces) frozen chopped broccoli, thawed
- 2 tablespoons salsa

Tortilla chips

In a large skillet, cook beef over medium heat until no longer pink; drain. Transfer to a 3-qt. slow cooker. Add the cheese, soup, broccoli and salsa; mix well. Cover and cook on low for 2-3 hours or until heated through, stirring after 1 hour. Serve with tortilla chips. Yield: 5-1/2 cups.

Parmesan Fondue

PREP/TOTAL TIME: 15 MIN.

- 1-1/2 to 2 cups milk
- 2 packages (8 ounces *each*) cream cheese, cubed
- 1-1/2 cups grated Parmesan cheese
- 1/2 teaspoon garlic salt
- 1 loaf (1 pound) French bread, cubed

In a large saucepan, cook and stir the milk and cream cheese over low heat until cheese is melted. Stir in Parmesan cheese and garlic salt; cook and stir until heated through. Transfer to a 1-1/2-qt. slow cooker or fondue pot; keep warm. Serve with bread cubes. Yield: about 3-1/2 cups.

Parmesan Fondue

This recipe was given to me many years ago at a New Year's potluck. Since then, it has been a tradition to serve it at our holiday open house. The creamy mixture is always a hit.
—Gwynne Fleener
Coeur d'Alene, Idaho

Marinated Chicken Wings

PREP: 5 MIN. + MARINATING
COOK: 3-1/2 HOURS

- 20 whole chicken wings (about 4 pounds)
- 2 cups soy sauce
- 1/2 cup white wine *or* chicken broth
- 1/2 cup vegetable oil
- 2 to 3 garlic cloves, minced
- 2 tablespoons sugar
- 2 teaspoons ground ginger

Cut chicken wings into three sections; discard wing tips. In a large bowl, combine remaining ingredients. Pour half the sauce into a large resealable plastic bag; add wings. Seal bag and toss to coat; refrigerate overnight. Cover and refrigerate remaining marinade.

Drain and discard the marinade from wings. Place wings in a 5-qt. slow cooker; top with reserved sauce. Cover and cook on low for 3-1/2 to 4 hours or until chicken juices run clear. Transfer wings to a serving dish; discard cooking juices. Yield: 18-20 servings.

Editor's Note: This recipe was prepared with the first and second sections of the wings.

Marinated Chicken Wings

I've made these nicely flavored chicken wings many times for get-togethers. They're so moist and tender—I always get lots of compliments and many requests for the recipe.
—*Janie Botting*
Sultan, Washington

Nacho Rice Dip

PREP: 20 MIN. **COOK:** 15 MIN.

Spanish rice mix adds a tasty twist to this effortless appetizer. Every time I serve this dip at parties my guests gobble it up.
—*Audra Hungate, Holt, Missouri*

- 1 package (6.8 ounces) Spanish rice and vermicelli mix
- 2 tablespoons butter
- 2 cups water
- 1 can (14-1/2 ounces) diced tomatoes, undrained
- 1 pound ground beef
- 1 pound (16 ounces) process cheese (Velveeta), cubed
- 1 can (14-1/2 ounces) stewed tomatoes
- 1 jar (8 ounces) process cheese sauce

Tortilla chips

In a large saucepan, cook rice mix in butter until golden. Stir in water and diced tomatoes; bring to a boil. Reduce heat; cover and simmer for 15-20 minutes or until rice is tender.

Meanwhile, in a skillet, cook beef over medium heat until no longer pink. Drain and add to the rice. Stir in the cheese, stewed tomatoes and cheese sauce; cook and stir until cheese is melted. Transfer to a 3-qt. slow cooker; cover and keep warm on low. Serve with tortilla chips. Yield: about 8 cups.

Moist 'n' Tender Wings

PREP: 15 MIN. **COOK:** 8 HOURS

- 25 whole chicken wings (about 5 pounds)
- 1 bottle (12 ounces) chili sauce
- 1/4 cup lemon juice
- 1/4 cup molasses
- 2 tablespoons Worcestershire sauce
- 6 garlic cloves, minced
- 1 tablespoon chili powder
- 1 tablespoon salsa
- 1 teaspoon garlic salt
- 3 drops hot pepper sauce

Cut chicken wings into three sections; discard wing tips. Place the wings in a 5-qt. slow cooker. In a bowl, combine the remaining ingredients; pour over chicken. Stir to coat. Cover and cook on low for 8 hours or until chicken is tender. Yield: about 4 dozen.

Editor's Note: This recipe was prepared with the first and second sections of the wings.

Moist 'n' Tender Wings

These no-fuss wings are fall-off-the-bone tender. Chili sauce offers a bit of spice while molasses lends a hint sweetness. For a main course, serve with a side dish of rice.
—*Sharon Morcilio*
Joshua Tree, California

Sweet 'n' Spicy Meatballs

PREP: 25 MIN. **BAKE:** 15 MIN.

You'll usually find a batch of these meatballs in my freezer. The slightly sweet sauce nicely complements the spicy pork sausage.
—*Genie Brown, Roanoke, Virginia*

- 2 pounds bulk hot pork sausage
- 1 egg, lightly beaten
- 1 cup packed brown sugar
- 1 cup red wine vinegar
- 1 cup ketchup
- 1 tablespoon soy sauce
- 1 teaspoon ground ginger

In a large bowl, combine the sausage and egg. Shape into 1-in. balls. Place on a greased rack in a shallow baking pan. Bake at 400° for 15-20 minutes or until meat is no longer pink; drain.

Meanwhile, in a saucepan, combine the brown sugar, vinegar, ketchup, soy sauce and ginger. Bring to a boil. Reduce heat; simmer, uncovered, until sugar is dissolved.

Transfer meatballs to a 3-qt. slow cooker. Add the sauce and stir gently to coat. Cover and keep warm on low until serving. Yield: about 4 dozen.

Reuben Spread

PREP: 5 MIN. **COOK:** 3 HOURS

This hearty dip tastes like a Reuben sandwich. It's requested at all the gatherings we attend.
—*Pam Rohr, Troy, Ohio*

- 2-1/2 cups cubed cooked corned beef
- 1 jar (16 ounces) sauerkraut, rinsed and well drained
- 2 cups (8 ounces) shredded Swiss cheese
- 2 cups (8 ounces) shredded cheddar cheese
- 1 cup mayonnaise

Snack rye bread

In a 3-qt. slow cooker, combine the first five ingredients. Cover and cook on low for 3 hours, stirring occasionally. Serve warm with rye bread. Yield: about 5 cups.

Simmered Smoked Links

A tasty sweet-sour sauce glazes bite-size sausages in this recipe. Serve these effortless appetizers with toothpicks at parties or holiday get-togethers.
—Maxine Cenker
Weirton, West Virginia

Cheesy Pizza Fondue

PREP: 10 MIN. **COOK:** 4 HOURS

I keep these dip ingredients on hand for spur-of-the-moment gatherings. Folks can't resist chewy bread cubes coated with this savory sauce.
—Nel Carver, Moscow, Idaho

- 1 jar (29 ounces) meatless spaghetti sauce
- 2 cups (8 ounces) shredded part-skim mozzarella cheese
- 1/4 cup shredded Parmesan cheese
- 2 teaspoons dried oregano
- 1 teaspoon dried minced onion
- 1/4 teaspoon garlic powder
- 1 loaf (1 pound) unsliced Italian bread, cut into cubes

In a 1-1/2-qt. slow cooker, combine the spaghetti sauce, cheeses, oregano, onion and garlic powder. Cook for 4-6 hours or until cheese is melted and sauce is hot. Serve with bread cubes. Yield: 12 servings (4 cups).

Mulled Dr. Pepper

PREP: 10 MIN. **COOK:** 2 HOURS

When neighbors or friends visit us on a chilly evening, I'll serve this warm beverage.
—Bernice Morris
Marshfield, Missouri

- 8 cups Dr. Pepper
- 1/4 cup packed brown sugar
- 1/4 cup lemon juice
- 1/2 teaspoon ground allspice
- 1/4 teaspoon salt
- 1/4 teaspoon ground nutmeg
- 1/2 teaspoon whole cloves
- 3 cinnamon sticks (3 inches)

In a 3-qt. slow cooker, combine the first six ingredients. Place cinnamon sticks and cloves on a double thickness of cheesecloth; bring up corners of the cloth and tie with kitchen string to form bag. Place in slow cooker. Cover and cook on low for 2 hours or until desired temperature is reached. Discard spice bag. Yield: 8-10 servings.

Simmered Smoked Links

PREP: 5 MIN. **COOK:** 4 HOURS

- 2 packages (16 ounces *each*) miniature smoked sausage links
- 1 cup packed brown sugar
- 1/2 cup ketchup
- 1/4 cup prepared horseradish

Place sausages in a 3-qt. slow cooker. Combine the brown sugar, ketchup and horseradish; pour over sausages. Cover and cook on low for 4 hours. Yield: 16-20 servings.

Tropical Tea

I recommend brewing a batch of this fragrant, flavorful tea in a slow cooker for your next family gathering.
—*Irene Helen Zundel*
Carmichaels, Pennsylvania

Tropical Tea

PREP: 15 MIN. **COOK:** 2 HOURS

- **6 cups boiling water**
- **6 individual tea bags**
- **1-1/2 cups orange juice**
- **1-1/2 cups unsweetened pineapple juice**
- **1/3 cup sugar**
- **1 medium navel orange, sliced and halved**
- **2 tablespoons honey**

In a 5-qt. slow cooker, combine boiling water and tea bags. Cover and let stand for 5 minutes. Discard the tea bags. Stir in the remaining ingredients. Cover and cook on low for 2-4 hours or until heated through. Serve warm. Yield: about 2-1/2 quarts.

Sweet-and-Sour Smokies

PREP: 5 MIN. **COOK:** 4 HOURS

This warm appetizer is so simple to make but so tasty. It uses cherry pie filling, chunks of pineapple and a little brown sugar to create a fruity sauce that's just perfect for mini sausage links.
—*Debi Hetland, Rochelle, Illinois*

- **2 packages (16 ounces *each*) miniature smoked sausages**
- **2 cans (21 ounces *each*) cherry pie filling**
- **1 can (20 ounces) pineapple chunks, drained**
- **3 tablespoons brown sugar**

Place sausages in a 5-qt. slow cooker. In a bowl, combine the pie filling, pineapple and brown sugar; pour over sausages. Cover and cook on low for 4 hours. Yield: 16-20 servings.

Raspberry Fondue Dip

PREP/TOTAL TIME: 25 MIN.

- **1 package (10 ounces) frozen sweetened raspberries**
- **1 cup apple butter**
- **1 tablespoon red-hot candies**
- **2 teaspoons cornstarch**

Assorted fresh fruit

Place raspberries in a bowl; set aside to thaw. Strain raspberries, reserving 1 tablespoon juice; discard seeds.

In a small saucepan, combine strained berries, apple butter and red-hots; cook over medium heat until the candies are dissolved, stirring occasionally. In a small bowl, combine cornstarch and reserved juice until smooth; stir into berry mixture. Bring to a boil; cook and stir over medium heat for 1-2 minutes or until thickened.

Serve warm or cold with fruit. To serve warm, transfer to a serving dish, 1-1/2-qt. slow cooker or fondue pot. Yield: 1 cup.

Raspberry Fondue Dip

My guests are delighted when I serve this fun, nontraditional fondue. Creamy apple butter and cinnamon red hots add tangy flair!
—*Edna Hoffman*
Hebron, Indiana

Shredded Steak Sandwiches

PREP: 15 MIN. **COOK:** 6 HOURS

3 pounds boneless beef round steak, cut into large pieces
2 large onions, chopped
3/4 cup thinly sliced celery
1-1/2 cups ketchup
1/2 to 3/4 cup water
1/3 cup lemon juice
1/3 cup Worcestershire sauce
3 tablespoons brown sugar
3 tablespoons cider vinegar
2 to 3 teaspoons salt
2 teaspoons prepared mustard
1-1/2 teaspoons paprika
1 teaspoon chili powder
1/2 teaspoon pepper
1/8 to 1/4 teaspoon hot pepper sauce
12 to 14 sandwich rolls, split

Place meat in a 5-qt. slow cooker. Add onions and celery. In a bowl, combine ketchup, water, lemon juice, Worcestershire sauce, brown sugar, vinegar, salt, mustard, paprika, chili powder, pepper and hot pepper sauce. Pour over meat.

Cover and cook on high for 6-8 hours. Remove meat; cool slightly. Shred with a fork. Return to the sauce and heat through. Serve on rolls. Yield: 12-14 servings.

Chili Sandwiches

PREP: 30 MIN. + STANDING **COOK:** 3 HOURS

No one will be able to resist these special sandwiches stuffed with spicy chili. Of course, the chili also makes a wonderfully filling meal by itself.
—*Kerry Haglund*
Wyoming, Minnesota

1 pound dried navy beans
2 pounds beef stew meat
2 cups water
1 pound sliced bacon, diced
1 cup chopped onion
1 cup shredded carrots
1 cup chopped celery
1/3 cup *each* chopped green and sweet red pepper
4 garlic cloves, minced
3 cans (14-1/2 ounces *each*) diced tomatoes, undrained
1 cup barbecue sauce
1 cup chili sauce
1/2 cup honey
1/4 cup hot pepper sauce
1 tablespoon chili powder
1 tablespoon baking cocoa
1 tablespoon Dijon mustard
1 tablespoon Worcestershire sauce
1 bay leaf
4 teaspoons beef bouillon granules
30 hamburger buns, split

Place beans in a large saucepan; add water to cover by 2 in. Bring to a boil; boil for 2 minutes. Remove from the heat; cover and let stand for 1 to 4 hours or until beans are softened. Drain and rinse beans, discarding liquid.

In a large kettle or Dutch oven, simmer beans and beef in water for 2 hours or until very tender; drain. Shred beef and place beef and beans in a 5-qt. slow cooker.

In a skillet, cook bacon over

Shredded Steak Sandwiches
When I was a newlywed over 30 years ago, I received this recipe and it's been a favorite since then. The saucy steak barbecue makes a quick meal served on sliced buns or over rice, potatoes or buttered noodles.
—*Lee Deneau*
Lansing, Michigan

Chicken Soup with Beans

I put lime-flavored tortilla chips at the bottom of individual bowls before ladling in this Southwestern soup. Loaded with chicken, beans, corn, tomatoes and green chilies, it's satisfying and fuss-free.
—Penny Peronia
West Memphis, Arkansas

medium heat until crisp. Transfer bacon to slow cooker. Discard all but 3 tablespoons drippings. Saute the onion, carrots, celery, peppers and garlic in drippings until tender. Transfer to the slow cooker. Add all the remaining ingredients except buns. Cover and cook on high for 3-4 hours, stirring often. Discard bay leaf. Spoon 1/2 cup onto each bun. Yield: 30 servings.

Navy Bean Vegetable Soup

PREP: 15 MIN. **COOK:** 9 HOURS

My family likes bean soup, so I came up with this hearty version. Leftovers freeze well for first-rate future meals.
—Eleanor Mielke
Mitchell, South Dakota

- 4 medium carrots, thinly sliced
- 2 celery ribs, chopped
- 1 medium onion, chopped
- 2 cups cubed fully cooked ham

- 1-1/2 cups dried navy beans
- 1 package (1.70 ounces) vegetable soup mix
- 1 envelope onion soup mix
- 1 bay leaf
- 1/2 teaspoon pepper
- 8 cups water

In a 5-qt. slow cooker, combine the first nine ingredients. Stir in water. Cover and cook on low for 9-10 hours or until beans are tender. Discard bay leaf. Yield: 12 servings (3 quarts).

Chicken Soup With Beans

PREP: 10 MIN. **COOK:** 6 HOURS

- 1 large onion, chopped
- 2 garlic cloves, minced
- 1 tablespoon vegetable oil
- 1-1/4 pounds boneless skinless chicken breasts, cooked and cubed
- 2 cans (15-1/2 ounces *each*) great northern beans, rinsed and drained
- 2 cans (11 ounces *each*) white *or* shoepeg corn, drained

- 1 can (10 ounces) diced tomatoes and green chilies, undrained
- 3 cups water
- 1 can (4 ounces) chopped green chilies
- 2 tablespoons lime juice
- 1 teaspoon lemon-pepper seasoning
- 1 teaspoon ground cumin
- 1/4 teaspoon salt
- 1/4 teaspoon pepper

In a small skillet, saute onion and garlic in oil until tender. Transfer to a 5-qt. slow cooker. Stir in the chicken, beans, corn, tomatoes, water, chopped green chilies, lime juice and seasoning. Cover and cook on low for 6-7 hours or until heated through. Yield: 12 servings (3 quarts).

Slow-Cooker Barbecue Beef

PREP: 15 MIN. **COOK:** 8 HOURS

- 1 boneless beef sirloin tip roast (about 3 pounds), cut into large chunks
- 3 celery ribs, chopped
- 1 large onion, chopped
- 1 medium green pepper, chopped
- 1 cup ketchup
- 1 can (6 ounces) tomato paste
- 1/2 cup packed brown sugar
- 1/4 cup cider vinegar
- 3 tablespoons chili powder
- 2 tablespoons lemon juice
- 2 tablespoons molasses
- 2 teaspoons salt
- 2 teaspoons Worcestershire sauce
- 1 teaspoon ground mustard
- 8 to 10 sandwich rolls, split

Place beef in a 5-qt. slow cooker. Add the celery, onion and green pepper. In a bowl, combine the ketchup, tomato paste, brown sugar, vinegar, chili powder, lemon juice, molasses, salt, Worcestershire sauce and mustard. Pour over beef mixture. Cover and cook on low for 8-9 hours or until meat is tender.

Skim fat from cooking juices if necessary. Shred beef. Toast rolls if desired. Use a slotted spoon to serve beef on rolls. Yield: 8-10 servings.

Spicy Beefy Chili

PREP: 15 MIN. **COOK:** 4 HOURS

- 2 pounds ground beef
- 2 to 3 hot chili peppers of your choice
- 3 cans (16 ounces *each*) kidney beans, rinsed and drained
- 1 can (6 ounces) tomato paste
- 1 medium onion, chopped
- 1 medium green pepper, seeded and chopped
- 2 teaspoons chili powder
- 2 teaspoons cider vinegar
- 1 teaspoon garlic powder
- 1 teaspoon dried oregano
- 1/4 to 1/2 teaspoon ground cinnamon
- 1/4 teaspoon pepper
- 2 to 4 cups tomato juice

In a large skillet, cook beef over medium heat until no longer pink; drain. Transfer to a 5-qt. slow cooker. Remove seeds from the chili peppers if desired; chop peppers. Add to the slow cooker. Stir in the beans, tomato paste, onion, green pepper, seasonings and 2 cups tomato juice.

Cover and cook on low for 4-6 hours or until heated through, adding more tomato juice if needed to achieve desired thickness. Yield: 8 servings.

Editor's Note: When cutting or seeding hot peppers, use rubber or plastic gloves to protect your hands. Avoid touching your face.

Barbecued Turkey Chili

PREP: 5 MIN. **COOK:** 4 HOURS

- 1   can (16 ounces) kidney beans, rinsed and drained
- 1   can (15-1/2 ounces) hot chili beans
- 1   can (15 ounces) turkey chili with beans
- 1   can (14-1/2 ounces) diced tomatoes, undrained
- 1/3   cup barbecue sauce

In a 3-qt. slow cooker, combine all of the ingredients. Cover and cook on high for 4 hours or until heated through and flavors are blended. Yield: 4-6 servings.

Italian Sausage Hoagies

PREP: 15 MIN. **COOK:** 4 HOURS

In southeastern Wisconsin, our cuisine is influenced by both Germans and Italians who immigrated to this area. When preparing this recipe, we usually substitute German bratwurst for the Italian sausage, so we blend the two influences with delicious results.
—*Craig Wachs, Racine, Wisconsin*

- 10   uncooked Italian sausage links
- 2   tablespoons olive oil
- 1   jar (26 ounces) meatless spaghetti sauce
- 1/2   medium green pepper, julienned
- 1/2   medium sweet red pepper, julienned
- 1/2   cup water
- 1/4   cup grated Romano cheese
- 2   tablespoons dried oregano
- 2   tablespoons dried basil
- 2   loaves French bread (20 inches)

In a large skillet, brown sausage in oil over medium-high heat; drain. Transfer to a 5-qt. slow cooker. Add the spaghetti sauce, peppers, water, cheese, oregano and basil. Cover and cook on low for 4 hours or until sausage is no longer pink.

Slice each French bread lengthwise but not all of the way through; cut each loaf widthwise into five pieces. Fill each with sausage, peppers and sauce. Yield: 10 servings.

Split Pea 'n' Ham Soup

PREP: 5 MIN. **COOK:** 4 HOURS

Easy prep and fantastic flavor make this one of my favorite meals to make. When I get home, I just add the milk, and supper is served!
—*Deanna Waggy*
South Bend, Indiana

- 1   package (16 ounces) dried split peas
- 2   cups diced fully cooked lean ham
- 1   cup diced carrots
- 1   medium onion, chopped
- 2   garlic cloves, minced
- 2   bay leaves
- 1/2   teaspoon salt
- 1/2   teaspoon pepper
- 5   cups boiling water
- 1   cup hot milk

Barbecued Turkey Chili

The first time I made this, it won first prize at a chili cook-off. It takes just minutes to mix together, and the slow cooker does the rest. It's often requested by friends and family when we all get together.
—*Melissa Webb*
Ellsworth Air Force Base
South Dakota

Shrimp Chowder

Because the chowder is ready in less than 4 hours, it can be prepared in the afternoon and served to dinner guests that night.
—Will Zunio
Gretna, Louisiana

2 cans (12 ounces *each*) evaporated milk

2 cans (10-3/4 ounces *each*) condensed cream of potato soup, undiluted

2 cans (10-3/4 ounces *each*) condensed cream of chicken soup, undiluted

1 can (11 ounces) white *or* shoepeg corn, drained

1 teaspoon Creole seasoning

1/2 teaspoon garlic powder

2 pounds cooked small shrimp, peeled and deveined

1 package (3 ounces) cream cheese, cubed

Turkey Chili

PREP: 20 MIN. **COOK:** 6-1/2 HOURS

I've taken my mother's milder recipe for chili and made it thicker and more robust. It's a favorite, especially in fall and winter.
—Celesta Zanger
Bloomfield Hills, Michigan

1 pound lean ground turkey

3/4 cup chopped onion

3/4 cup chopped celery

3/4 cup chopped green pepper

1 can (28 ounces) diced tomatoes, undrained

1 jar (26 ounces) meatless spaghetti sauce

1 can (15-1/2 ounces) hot chili beans

1-1/2 cups water

1/2 cup frozen corn

2 tablespoons chili powder

1 teaspoon ground cumin

1/4 teaspoon pepper

1/8 to 1/4 teaspoon cayenne pepper

1 can (16 ounces) kidney beans, rinsed and drained

1 can (15 ounces) pinto beans, rinsed and drained

In a large nonstick skillet cook the turkey, onion, celery and green pepper over medium heat until meat is no longer pink and vegetables are tender. Drain; transfer to a 5-qt. slow cooker. Add the tomatoes, spaghetti sauce, chili beans, water, corn and seasonings. Cover and cook on high for 1 hour.

Reduce heat to low; cook for 5-6 hours. Add kidney and pinto beans; cook 30 minutes longer. Yield: 13 servings.

Shrimp Chowder

PREP: 15 MIN. **BAKE:** 3-1/2 HOURS

1/2 cup chopped onion

2 teaspoons butter

In a small skillet, saute onion in butter until tender. In a 5-qt. slow cooker, combine the onion mixture, milk, soups, corn, Creole seasoning and garlic powder.

Cover and cook on low for 3 hours. Stir in shrimp and cream cheese. Cook 30 minutes longer or until shrimp are heated through and cheese is melted. Stir to blend. Yield: 12 servings (3 quarts).

Editor's Note: The following spices may be substituted for the Creole seasoning: 1/2 teaspoon *each* paprika and garlic powder, and a pinch each cayenne pepper, dried thyme and ground cumin.

Colony Mountain Chili

My husband created this chili for a local cooking contest, and it won the People's Choice Award. It's loaded with beef, Italian sausage, tomatoes and beans and seasoned with chili powder, cumin and red pepper flakes for zip.
—Marjorie O'Dell
Bow, Washington

Colony Mountain Chili

PREP: 25 MIN. **COOK:** 6 HOURS

- 1 **pound boneless beef sirloin steak, cut into 3/4-inch cubes**
- 4 **Italian sausage links, casings removed and cut into 3/4-inch slices**
- 2 **tablespoons olive oil, *divided***
- 1 **medium onion, chopped**
- 3 **garlic cloves, minced**
- 2 **green onions, thinly sliced**
- 2 **teaspoons beef bouillon granules**
- 1 **cup boiling water**
- 1 **can (6 ounces) tomato paste**
- 3 **tablespoons chili powder**
- 2 **tablespoons brown sugar**
- 2 **tablespoons Worcestershire sauce**
- 2 **teaspoons ground cumin**
- 1 **to 2 teaspoons crushed red pepper flakes**
- 1 **teaspoon salt**
- 1/2 **teaspoon pepper**

- 3 **cans (14-1/2 ounces *each*) stewed tomatoes, cut up**
- 2 **cans (15 ounces *each*) pinto beans, rinsed and drained**

Shredded cheddar cheese

In a large skillet, brown the beef and sausage in 1 tablespoon oil; drain. Transfer meat to a 5-qt. slow cooker. In the same skillet, saute the onion, garlic and green onions in remaining oil until tender. Transfer to slow cooker.

In a small bowl, dissolve bouillon in water. Stir in the tomato paste, chili powder, brown sugar, Worcestershire sauce and seasonings until blended; add to slow cooker. Stir in tomatoes and beans. Cover and cook on high for 6-8 hours or until the meat is tender. Serve with cheese if desired. Yield: 10 servings.

Slow-Cooked Pork Barbecue

PREP: 15 MIN. **COOK:** 5 HOURS

- 1 **boneless pork loin roast (3 to 4 pounds), cut in half**
- 1-1/2 **teaspoons seasoned salt**

- 1 **teaspoon garlic powder**
- 1 **cup barbecue sauce**
- 1 **cup cola**
- 8 **to 10 sandwich rolls, split**

Place roast in a 5-qt. slow cooker. Sprinkle with seasoned salt and garlic powder. Cover and cook on low for 4 hours or until meat is tender.

Remove meat; skim fat from cooking juices. Shred meat with a fork and return to the slow cooker. Combine barbecue sauce and cola; pour over meat. Cover and cook on high for 1-2 hours or until sauce is thickened. Serve on rolls. Yield: 8-10 servings.

Slow-Cooked Pork Barbecue

I need only five ingredients to fix this sweet and tender pork for sandwiches. I think it's perfect just the way it is, but feel free to adjust the sauce ingredients to suit your family's tastes.
—Connie Johnson
Springfield, Missouri

This classic, homemade soup with a hint of cayenne is chock-full of vegetables, chicken and noodles. I revised this recipe from my father-in-law. It's great with a salad and crusty bread.
—Norma Reynolds
Overland Park, Kansas

Chunky Potato Soup

PREP: 30 MIN. **COOK:** 5 HOURS

5-1/2	cups cubed peeled potatoes, *divided*
2-3/4	cups water
1/3	cup butter, cubed
1-1/3	cups cubed fully cooked ham
2	celery ribs, chopped
2/3	cup chopped onion
3/4	teaspoon garlic powder
3/4	teaspoon paprika
1/8	teaspoon pepper
1/2	pound process cheese (Velveeta), cubed
2/3	cup sour cream

Milk, optional

Place 4-1/2 cups of the potatoes in a saucepan; add water. Bring to a boil. Reduce heat; cover and cook for 15-20 minutes or until tender. Remove from the heat (do not drain). Mash potatoes; stir in butter.

In a 3-qt. slow cooker, combine the ham, celery, onion, garlic powder, paprika, pepper and remaining cubed potatoes. Stir in the mashed potatoes; top with cheese. Cover and cook on low for 5-6 hours or until potatoes and other vegetables are tender. Stir in the sour cream until blended. Thin soup with milk if desired. Yield: 6 servings.

Chunky Potato Soup

I make this thick soup for our annual St. Patrick's Day party, and there is never any left over.
—Mary Jo O'Brien
Hastings, Minnesota

Hearty Chicken Noodle Soup

PREP: 20 MIN.
COOK: 5-1/2 HOURS

12	fresh baby carrots, cut into 1/2-inch pieces
4	celery ribs, cut into 1/2-inch pieces
3/4	cup finely chopped onion
1	tablespoon minced fresh parsley
1/2	teaspoon pepper
1/4	teaspoon cayenne pepper
1-1/2	teaspoons mustard seed
2	garlic cloves, peeled and halved
1-1/4	pounds boneless skinless chicken breast halves
1-1/4	pounds boneless skinless chicken thighs
4	cans (14-1/2 ounces *each*) chicken broth
1	package (9 ounces) refrigerated linguine

Chicken Chili

Assemble this midday and your dinner will be ready and waiting for you. It's a fantastic chili that's nicely seasoned, but not too spicy.
—Taste of Home Test Kitchen

Veggie Meatball Soup

PREP: 10 MIN. **COOK:** 4 HOURS

It's a snap to put together this hearty soup before I leave for work. I just add cooked pasta when I get home, and I have a few minutes to relax before supper is ready.
—Charla Tinney
Tyrone, Oklahoma

> 3 cups beef broth
> 2 cups frozen mixed vegetables, thawed
> 1 can (14-1/2 ounces) stewed tomatoes
> 15 frozen fully cooked meatballs, thawed
> 3 bay leaves
> 1/4 teaspoon pepper
> 1 cup spiral pasta, cooked and drained

In a 3-qt. slow cooker, combine the first six ingredients. Cover and cook on low for 4-5 hours. Just before serving, stir in pasta; heat through. Discard bay leaves. Yield: 6 servings.

In a 5-qt. slow cooker, combine the first six ingredients. Place mustard seed and garlic on a double thickness of cheesecloth; bring up corners of cloth and tie with kitchen string to form a bag. Place in slow cooker. Add chicken and broth. Cover and cook on low for 5-6 hours or until chicken juices run clear.

Discard spice bag. Remove chicken; cool slightly. Stir linguine into soup; cover and cook for 30 minutes or until tender. Cut chicken into pieces and return to soup; heat through. Yield: 12 servings (3 quarts).

Chicken Chili

PREP: 10 MIN. **COOK:** 5 HOURS

> 1-1/2 pounds boneless skinless chicken breasts, cut into 1/2-inch cubes
> 1 cup chopped onion
> 3 tablespoons vegetable oil
> 1 can (15 ounces) cannellini *or* white kidney beans, rinsed and drained
> 1 can (14-1/2 ounces) diced tomatoes, undrained
> 1 can (14-1/2 ounces) diced tomatoes with mild green chilies, undrained
> 1 cup frozen corn
> 1 teaspoon salt
> 1 teaspoon ground cumin
> 1 teaspoon minced garlic
> 1/2 teaspoon celery salt
> 1/2 teaspoon ground coriander
> 1/2 teaspoon pepper
> Sour cream and shredded cheddar cheese, optional

In a large skillet, saute chicken and onion in oil for 5 minutes or until chicken is browned. Transfer to a 5-qt. slow cooker. Stir in the beans, tomatoes, corn and seasonings. Cover and cook on low for 5 hours or until chicken is no longer pink. Garnish with sour cream and cheese if desired. Yield: 6 servings.

Turkey Sloppy Joes

This tangy sandwich filling is so easy to prepare in the slow cooker, and it goes over well at gatherings large and small. I often take it to potlucks, and I'm always asked for my secret ingredient.
—Marylou LaRue
Freeland, Michigan

PREP: 15 MIN. **COOK:** 4 HOURS

- 1 **pound ground turkey breast**
- 1 **small onion, chopped**
- 1/2 **cup chopped celery**
- 1/4 **cup chopped green pepper**
- 1 **can (10-3/4 ounces) reduced-fat reduced-sodium condensed tomato soup, undiluted**
- 1/2 **cup ketchup**
- 1 **tablespoon brown sugar**
- 2 **tablespoons prepared mustard**
- 1/4 **teaspoon pepper**
- 8 **hamburger buns, split**

In a large saucepan coated with nonstick cooking spray, cook the turkey, onion, celery and green pepper over medium heat until meat is no longer pink; drain if necessary. Stir in the soup, ketchup, brown sugar, mustard and pepper.

Transfer to a 3-qt. slow cooker. Cover and cook on low for 4 hours. Serve on buns. Yield: 8 servings.

Tangy Bean Soup

PREP: 15 MIN. **COOK:** 4-1/2 HOURS

- 2 **cans (14-1/2 ounces *each*) chicken broth**
- 1 **package (16 ounces) frozen mixed vegetables**
- 1 **can (15 ounces) black beans, rinsed and drained**
- 1 **can (15 ounces) pinto beans, rinsed and drained**
- 1 **can (14-1/2 ounces) diced tomatoes, undrained**
- 1 **medium onion, chopped**
- 1 **tablespoon chili powder**
- 1 **tablespoon minced fresh cilantro**
- 4 **garlic cloves, minced**
- 1/4 **teaspoon pepper**

CORNMEAL DUMPLINGS:
- 1/2 **cup all-purpose flour**
- 1/2 **cup shredded cheddar cheese**
- 1/3 **cup cornmeal**
- 1 **tablespoon sugar**
- 1 **teaspoon baking powder**
- 1 **egg**
- 2 **tablespoons milk**
- 2 **teaspoons vegetable oil**

In a 5-qt. slow cooker, combine the first 10 ingredients. Cover and cook on high for 4-5 hours.

For dumplings, combine the flour, cheese, cornmeal, sugar and baking powder in a large bowl. In another bowl, combine the egg, milk and oil; add to dry ingredients just until moistened (batter will be stiff).

Drop by heaping tablespoons onto soup. Cover and cook on high 30 minutes longer (without lifting cover) or until a toothpick inserted in a dumpling comes out clean. Yield: 6 servings.

Tangy Bean Soup
The great Southwestern flavor makes this soup a real winner with my family. The cornmeal dumplings add a comforting twist to the soup.
—Joan Hallford
North Richland Hills, Texas

Slow-Cooked Chili

PREP: 15 MIN. **COOK:** 4 HOURS

- 2 pounds ground beef
- 2 cans (16 ounces *each*) kidney beans, rinsed and drained
- 2 cans (14-1/2 ounces *each*) diced tomatoes, undrained
- 1 can (8 ounces) tomato sauce
- 2 medium onions, chopped
- 1 green pepper, chopped
- 2 garlic cloves, minced
- 2 tablespoons chili powder
- 2 teaspoons salt, optional
- 1 teaspoon pepper

Shredded cheddar cheese, optional

In a large skillet, cook beef over medium heat until no longer pink; drain. Transfer to a 5-qt. slow cooker. Add the beans, tomatoes, tomato sauce, onions, green pepper, garlic and seasonings. Cover and cook on low for 8-10 hours or on high for 4 hours. Garnish individual servings with cheese if desired. Yield: 10 servings.

Slow-Cooked Chili

This chunky chili can cook for up to 10 hours on low in the slow cooker. It's so good to come home to the wonderful aroma.
—Sue Call
Beech Grove, Indiana

Two-Bean Vegetable Soup

PREP: 20 MIN. **COOK:** 9 HOURS

You have to try this hearty soup to appreciate its unique flavors and beautiful appearance. With all the rich foods served during the holidays, it's nice to offer this soup loaded with fiber and vitamins.
—Christina Till
South Haven, Michigan

- 3/4 cup chopped onion
- 1/2 cup chopped celery
- 1/2 cup chopped green pepper
- 2 tablespoons olive oil
- 1 large potato, peeled and diced
- 1 medium sweet potato, peeled and diced
- 1 to 2 garlic cloves, minced
- 3 cups chicken *or* vegetable broth
- 2 medium fresh tomatoes, chopped
- 1 can (16 ounces) kidney beans, rinsed and drained
- 1 can (15 ounces) garbanzo beans *or* chickpeas, rinsed and drained
- 2 teaspoons soy sauce
- 1 teaspoon paprika
- 1/2 teaspoon dried basil
- 1/4 teaspoon salt
- 1/4 teaspoon ground turmeric
- 1 bay leaf

Dash cayenne pepper

In a large skillet, saute the onion, celery and green pepper in oil until crisp-tender. Add the potato, sweet potato and garlic; saute 3-5 minutes longer. Transfer to a 5-qt. slow cooker. Stir in the remaining ingredients. Cover and cook on low for 9-10 hours or until vegetables are tender. Discard bay leaf. Yield: 12 servings (about 3 quarts).

Hearty Black Bean Soup

PREP: 10 MIN. **COOK:** 9 HOURS

Cumin and chili powder spice up this thick soup. If you have leftover

Italian Beef Sandwiches

I'm a paramedic/firefighter, and slow-cooked recipes like this one suit my unpredictable schedule. My husband, children and the hungry bunch at the firehouse love these robust sandwiches which have a little zip.
—Kristen Swihart
Perrysburg, Ohio

meat—smoked sausage, browned ground beef or roast—toss it in for the last 30 minutes of cooking.
—Amy Chop
Oak Grove, Louisiana

- 3 medium carrots, halved and thinly sliced
- 2 celery ribs, thinly sliced
- 1 medium onion, chopped
- 4 garlic cloves, minced
- 1 can (30 ounces) black beans, rinsed and drained
- 2 cans (14-1/2 ounces *each*) chicken broth
- 1 can (15 ounces) crushed tomatoes
- 1-1/2 teaspoons dried basil
- 1/2 teaspoon dried oregano
- 1/2 teaspoon ground cumin
- 1/2 teaspoon chili powder
- 1/2 teaspoon hot pepper sauce
Hot cooked rice

In a 3-qt. slow cooker, combine the first 12 ingredients. Cover and cook on low for 9-10 hours or until vegetables are tender. Serve over rice. Yield: 8 servings (about 2 quarts).

Italian Beef Sandwiches

PREP: 10 MIN. **COOK:** 8 HOURS

- 1 jar (11-1/2 ounces) pepperoncinis
- 1 boneless beef chuck roast (3-1/2 to 4 pounds)
- 1/4 cup water
- 1-3/4 teaspoons dried basil
- 1-1/2 teaspoons garlic powder
- 1-1/2 teaspoons dried oregano
- 1-1/4 teaspoons salt
- 1/4 teaspoon pepper
- 1 large onion, sliced and quartered
- 10 to 12 hard rolls, split

Drain pepperoncinis, reserving liquid. Remove and discard stems of peppers; set peppers aside. Cut roast into large chunks; place a third of the meat in a 5-qt. slow cooker. Add water.

In a small bowl, combine the seasonings; sprinkle half over beef. Layer with half of the remaining meat, then onion, reserved peppers and liquid. Top with remaining meat and herb mixture.

Cover and cook on low for 8-9 hours or until meat is tender. Shred beef with two forks. Using a slotted spoon, serve beef and peppers on rolls. Yield: 10-12 servings.

Editor's Note: Look for pepperoncinis (pickled peppers) in the pickle and olive section of your grocery store.

Poultry &Seafood

Spicy Seafood Stew

PREP: 30 MIN. **COOK:** 4-3/4 HOURS

This zippy stew is very easy and quick to prepare. The hardest part is peeling and dicing the potatoes, and even that can be done the night before. Just place the potatoes in water and store them in the refrigerator overnight to speed up assembly the next day.
—*Bonnie Marlow, Ottoville, Ohio*

- 2 pounds potatoes, peeled and diced
- 1 pound carrots, sliced
- 1 jar (26 ounces) spaghetti sauce
- 2 jars (6 ounces *each*) sliced mushrooms, drained
- 1-1/2 teaspoons ground turmeric
- 1-1/2 teaspoons minced garlic
- 1 teaspoon cayenne pepper
- 3/4 teaspoon salt
- 1-1/2 cups water
- 1 pound sea scallops
- 1 pound uncooked medium shrimp, peeled and deveined

In a 5-qt. slow cooker, combine the first eight ingredients. Cover and cook on low for 4-1/2 to 5 hours or until potatoes are tender.

Stir in the water, scallops and shrimp. Cover and cook for 15-20 minutes or until scallops are opaque and shrimp turn pink. Yield: 9 servings.

Chicken Saltimbocca

PREP: 25 MIN. + CHILLING
COOK: 4 HOURS

- 6 boneless skinless chicken breast halves
- 6 thin slices deli ham
- 6 slices Swiss cheese
- 1/4 cup all-purpose flour
- 1/4 cup grated Parmesan cheese
- 1/2 teaspoon salt
- 1/4 teaspoon pepper
- 2 tablespoons vegetable oil
- 1 can (10-3/4 ounces) condensed cream of chicken soup, undiluted
- 1/2 cup dry white wine *or* chicken broth

Hot cooked rice

Flatten chicken to 1/4-in. thickness. Top each piece with a slice of ham and cheese. Roll up tightly; secure with toothpicks. In a shallow bowl, combine the flour, Parmesan cheese, salt and pepper. Roll chicken in flour mixture; refrigerate for 1 hour.

In a skillet, brown roll-ups in oil on all sides; transfer to a 3-qt. slow cooker. Combine the soup and wine or broth; pour over chicken. Cover and cook on low for 4-5 hours or until a meat thermometer reads 170°. Remove roll-ups and stir sauce. Serve with rice. Yield: 6 servings.

Chicken Saltimbocca
White wine dresses up cream of chicken soup to make a lovely sauce for chicken, ham and Swiss cheese roll-ups. This tried-and-true recipe comes from my mother.
—*Carol McCollough
Missoula, Montana*

Sweet-and-Sour Chicken

Who would believe that this "stir-fry" supper was cooked in a slow cooker! Adding the onions, pineapple and snow peas later in the process keeps them from becoming overcooked.
—Dorothy Hess, Hartwell, Georgia

Italian Shrimp 'n' Pasta

PREP: 10 MIN.
COOK: 7 HOURS 20 MIN.

- 1 pound boneless skinless chicken thighs, cut into 2-inch x 1-inch strips
- 2 tablespoons vegetable oil
- 1 can (28 ounces) crushed tomatoes
- 2 celery ribs, chopped
- 1 medium green pepper, cut into 1-inch pieces
- 1 medium onion, coarsely chopped
- 2 garlic cloves, minced
- 1 tablespoon sugar
- 1/2 teaspoon salt
- 1/2 teaspoon Italian seasoning
- 1/8 to 1/4 teaspoon cayenne pepper
- 1 bay leaf
- 1/2 cup uncooked orzo pasta *or* other small pasta
- 1 pound cooked medium shrimp, peeled and deveined

In a large skillet, brown chicken in oil; transfer to a 3-qt. slow cooker. Add the tomatoes, celery, green pepper, onion, garlic, sugar and seasonings; mix well. Cover and cook on low for 7-8 hours or until chicken juices run clear. Discard bay leaf.

Stir in the pasta; cover and cook on high for 15 minutes or until pasta is tender. Stir in shrimp; cover and cook for 5 minutes or until the shrimp are heated through. Yield: 6-8 servings.

Sweet-and-Sour Chicken

PREP: 15 MIN.
COOK: 3 HOURS 20 MIN.

- 1-1/4 pounds boneless skinless chicken breasts, cut into 1-inch strips
- 1 tablespoon vegetable oil
- Salt and pepper to taste
- 1 can (8 ounces) pineapple chunks
- 1 can (8 ounces) sliced water chestnuts, drained
- 2 medium carrots, sliced
- 2 tablespoons soy sauce
- 4 teaspoons cornstarch
- 1 cup sweet-and-sour sauce
- 1/4 cup water
- 1-1/2 teaspoons ground ginger

Italian Shrimp 'n' Pasta

This dish is always a hit! The shrimp, orzo, tomatoes and cayenne pepper remind me of a Creole favorite, but the Italian seasoning adds a different twist. The strips of chicken thighs stay nice and moist during the slow cooking.
—Karen Scaglione
Nanuet, New York

Spiced Lemon Chicken

I took a favorite recipe and modified it to work in our slow cooker. We enjoy this seasoned, lemony chicken with buttered noodles or rice.
—Nancy Rambo
Riverside, California

3 green onions, cut into
   1-inch pieces
1-1/2 cups fresh *or* frozen snow
   peas
Hot cooked rice

In a large skillet, saute chicken in oil for 4-5 minutes; drain. Sprinkle with salt and pepper. Drain pineapple, reserving juice; set pineapple aside. In a 5-qt. slow cooker, combine the chicken, water chestnuts, carrots, soy sauce and pineapple juice. Cover and cook on low for 3 hours or until chicken juices run clear.

In a small bowl, combine the cornstarch, sweet-and-sour sauce, water and ginger until smooth. Stir into the slow cooker. Add onions and reserved pineapple; cover and cook on high for 15 minutes or until thickened. Add peas; cook 5 minutes longer. Serve with rice. Yield: 5 servings.

Spiced Lemon Chicken

PREP: 20 MIN. **COOK:** 4 HOURS

1 medium onion, chopped
1/3 cup water
1/4 cup lemon juice
1 tablespoon vegetable oil
1/2 to 1 teaspoon salt
1/2 teaspoon *each* garlic
   powder, chili powder and
   paprika
1/2 teaspoon ground ginger
1/4 teaspoon pepper
4 boneless skinless chicken
   breast halves (4 ounces
   each)
4-1/2 teaspoons cornstarch
4-1/2 teaspoons cold water
Hot cooked noodles
Chopped fresh parsley, optional

In a greased 3-qt. slow cooker, combine the onion, water, lemon juice, oil and seasonings. Add chicken; turn to coat. Cover and cook on low for 4-5 hours or until a meat thermometer reads 170°. Remove chicken and keep warm.

In a saucepan, combine the cornstarch and cold water until smooth. Gradually add the cooking juices. Bring to a boil; cook and stir for 2 minutes or until thickened. Serve with chicken over noodles. Sprinkle with parsley if desired. Yield: 4 servings.

Turkey Thigh Supper
*This family-pleasing meal-in-one
has it meaty turkey thighs, tasty
vegetables and a homemade sauce.
You can substitute chicken breasts
for the turkey or honey-flavored
barbecue sauce for
the soup mixture.*
—Betty Gingrich
Oxford, Arkansas

Turkey Thigh Supper

PREP: 10 MIN. **COOK:** 7 HOURS

- 3 **medium red potatoes, cut into chunks**
- 1/2 **pound fresh baby carrots**
- 2 **medium onions, cut into chunks**
- 4 **turkey thighs, skin removed**
- 1 **can (10-3/4 ounces) condensed tomato soup, undiluted**
- 1/3 **cup water**
- 1 **teaspoon minced garlic**
- 1 **teaspoon Italian seasoning**
- 1/2 **to 1 teaspoon salt**

In a 5-qt. slow cooker, layer the potatoes, carrots and onions. Top with turkey. Combine the soup, water, garlic, Italian seasoning and salt; pour over turkey. Cover and cook on high for 7-8 hours or until a meat thermometer reads 180° and vegetables are tender. Yield: 4 servings.

Herbed Chicken And Shrimp

PREP: 15 MIN.
COOK: 4 HOURS 20 MIN.

- 1 **teaspoon salt**
- 1 **teaspoon pepper**
- 1 **broiler/fryer chicken (3 to 4 pounds), cut up and skin removed**
- 1/4 **cup butter**
- 1 **large onion, chopped**
- 1 **can (8 ounces) tomato sauce**
- 1/2 **cup white wine *or* chicken broth**
- 1 **garlic clove, minced**
- 1 **teaspoon dried basil**
- 1 **pound uncooked medium shrimp, peeled and deveined**

Combine salt and pepper; rub over the chicken pieces. In a skillet, brown chicken on all sides in butter. Transfer to an ungreased 5-qt. slow cooker. In a bowl, combine the onion, tomato sauce, wine or broth, garlic and basil; pour over chicken.

Cover and cook on low for 4-5 hours or until a meat thermometer reads 170° in the breast meat and 180° in the thighs and drumsticks. Stir in the shrimp. Cover and cook on high for 20-30 minutes or until shrimp turn pink. Yield: 4 servings.

Herbed Chicken and Shrimp
*Chicken and shrimp are perfect
partners in this delicious entree
that's easy to prepare, yet elegant
enough to serve for company. While
I clean the house, it practically
cooks itself. I serve it with pasta or
rice and a green salad.*
—Diana Knight
Reno, Nevada

Nostalgic Chicken And Dumplings

PREP: 20 MIN.
COOK: 4 HOURS 50 MIN.

- 6 bone-in chicken breast halves (10 ounces *each*), skin removed
- 2 whole cloves
- 12 pearl onions
- 1 bay leaf
- 1 garlic clove, minced
- 1/2 teaspoon salt
- 1/2 teaspoon dried thyme
- 1/2 teaspoon dried marjoram
- 1/4 teaspoon pepper
- 1/2 cup reduced-sodium chicken broth
- 1/2 cup white wine *or* additional chicken broth
- 3 tablespoons cornstarch
- 1/4 cup cold water
- 1/2 teaspoon browning sauce, optional
- 1 cup reduced-fat biscuit/baking mix
- 6 tablespoons fat-free milk
- 1 tablespoon minced fresh parsley

Place the chicken in a 5-qt. slow cooker. Insert cloves into one onion; add to slow cooker. Add bay leaf and remaining onions. Sprinkle chicken with the garlic, salt, thyme, marjoram and pepper. Pour broth and wine or additional broth over chicken mixture. Cover and cook on low for 4-1/2 to 5 hours or until chicken juices run clear and a meat thermometer reads 170°.

Remove chicken to a serving platter and keep warm. Discard cloves and bay leaf. Increase the temperature to high. In a small bowl, combine cornstarch, water and browning sauce if desired until smooth. Stir into slow cooker.

In another small bowl, combine biscuit mix, milk and parsley. Drop by tablespoonfuls onto simmering liquid. Cover and cook on low for 20-25 minutes or until a toothpick inserted into dumplings comes out clean (do not lift cover while simmering). Serve dumplings and gravy with chicken. Yield: 6 servings.

Nostalgic Chicken and Dumplings

Enjoy old-fashioned goodness without all the fuss when you fix this supper in your slow cooker. You'll soon crave the wonderfully light dumplings and a full-flavored sauce.
—Brenda Edwards
Hereford, Arizona

Apple Chicken Stew

PREP: 20 MIN. **COOK:** 4 HOURS

My husband and I like to visit the apple orchards in nearby Nebraska City. When we do, we always buy cider to use in this sensational stew.
—Carol Mathias, Lincoln, Nebraska

- 4 medium potatoes, cubed
- 4 medium carrots, cut into 1/4-inch slices
- 1 medium red onion, halved and sliced
- 1 celery rib, thinly sliced
- 1-1/2 teaspoons salt
- 3/4 teaspoon dried thyme
- 1/2 teaspoon pepper
- 1/4 to 1/2 teaspoon caraway seeds
- 2 pounds boneless skinless chicken breasts, cubed
- 2 tablespoons olive oil
- 1 large tart apple, peeled and cubed
- 1-1/4 cups apple cider *or* juice

Sweet Pepper Chicken
Sweet red and green pepper strips add attractive color to this delicious chicken. I usually cut up the veggies while the meat is browning.
—Ann Johnson
Dunn, North Carolina

1 tablespoon cider vinegar
1 bay leaf
Minced fresh parsley

In a 5-qt. slow cooker, layer the potatoes, carrots, onion and celery. Combine the salt, thyme, pepper and caraway seeds; sprinkle half over vegetables.

In a skillet, saute chicken in oil until browned; transfer to slow cooker. Top with apple. Combine apple cider and vinegar; pour over chicken and apple. Sprinkle with remaining salt mixture. Top with bay leaf.

Cover and cook on high for 4-5 hours or until vegetables are tender and chicken juices run clear. Discard bay leaf. Stir before serving. Sprinkle with parsley. Yield: 6-8 servings.

Sweet Pepper Chicken

PREP: 20 MIN. **COOK:** 4 HOURS

6 **bone-in chicken breast halves (10 ounces *each*), skin removed**
1 **tablespoon vegetable oil**
2 **cups sliced fresh mushrooms**
1 **medium onion, halved and sliced**
1 **medium green pepper, julienned**
1 **medium sweet red pepper, julienned**
1 **can (10-3/4 ounces) condensed cream of chicken soup, undiluted**
1 **can (10-3/4 ounces) condensed cream of mushroom soup, undiluted**
Hot cooked rice

In a large skillet, brown chicken in oil on both sides. Transfer to a 5-qt. slow cooker. Top with mushrooms, onion and peppers. Combine the soups; pour over vegetables. Cover and cook on low for 4-5 hours or until a meat thermometer reads 170°. Serve with rice. Yield: 6 servings.

Sunday Chicken Supper

This hearty supper makes a special dish any day of the week. It serves two, which is just perfect for us.
—Ruthann Martin
Louisville, Ohio

Sunday Chicken Supper

PREP: 15 MIN. **COOK:** 6 HOURS

- 2 **small carrots, cut into 2-inch pieces**
- 1/2 **medium onion, chopped**
- 1/2 **celery rib, cut into 2-inch pieces**
- 1 **cup cut fresh green beans (2-inch pieces)**
- 2 **small red potatoes, halved**
- 2 **bone-in chicken breast halves (7 ounces *each*), skin removed**
- 2 **bacon strips, cooked and crumbled**
- 3/4 **cup hot water**
- 1 **teaspoon chicken bouillon granules**
- 1/4 **teaspoon salt**
- 1/4 **teaspoon dried thyme**
- 1/4 **teaspoon dried basil**

Pinch pepper

In a 3-qt. slow cooker, layer the first seven ingredients in the order listed. Combine the water, bouillon, salt, thyme, basil and pepper; pour over the top. Do not stir. Cover and cook on low for 6-8 hours or until vegetables are tender and meat thermometer reads 170°. Remove chicken and vegetables. Thicken cooking juices for gravy if desired. Yield: 2 servings.

Citrus Turkey Roast

PREP: 15 MIN. **COOK:** 5-1/4 HOURS

- 1 **tablespoon garlic powder**
- 1 **tablespoon paprika**
- 1 **tablespoon olive oil**
- 2 **teaspoons Worcestershire sauce**
- 1/2 **teaspoon salt**
- 1/2 **teaspoon pepper**
- 1 **frozen boneless turkey roast, thawed (3 pounds), cut in half**
- 8 **garlic cloves, peeled**
- 1 **cup chicken broth, *divided***
- 1/4 **cup water**
- 1/4 **cup white wine *or* additional chicken broth**
- 1/4 **cup orange juice**
- 1 **tablespoon lemon juice**
- 2 **tablespoons cornstarch**

Combine the garlic powder, paprika, oil, Worcestershire sauce, salt and pepper; rub over turkey.

Place in a 5-qt. slow cooker. Add the garlic, 1/2 cup broth, water, wine or additional broth, orange juice and lemon juice. Cover and cook on low for 5-6 hours or until a meat thermometer reads 170°.

Remove turkey and keep warm. Discard garlic cloves. For gravy, combine the cornstarch and remaining broth until smooth; stir into cooking juices. Cover and cook on high for 15 minutes or until thickened. Slice turkey; serve with gravy. Yield: 12 servings.

Citrus Turkey Roast

I was skeptical at first about fixing turkey in a slow cooker. But once I tasted this dish, I was hooked. With a little cornstarch to thicken the juices, the gravy is easily made.
—Kathy Kittell
Lenexa, Kansas

Rosemary Cashew Chicken

PREP: 10 MIN. **COOK:** 4 HOURS

- 1 broiler/fryer chicken (3 to 4 pounds), cut up and skin removed
- 1 medium onion, thinly sliced
- 1/3 cup orange juice concentrate
- 1 teaspoon dried rosemary, crushed
- 1 teaspoon salt
- 1/4 teaspoon cayenne pepper
- 2 tablespoons all-purpose flour
- 3 tablespoons water
- 1/4 to 1/2 cup chopped cashews

Hot cooked pasta

Place chicken in a 3-qt. slow cooker. Combine the onion, orange juice concentrate, rosemary, salt and cayenne; pour over chicken. Cover and cook on low for 4-5 hours or until a meat thermometer reads 170° in the breast meat and 180° in the thighs and drumsticks. Remove the chicken and keep warm.

In a saucepan, combine flour and water until smooth. Stir in cooking juices. Bring to a boil; cook and stir for 2 minutes or until thickened. Stir in cashews. Pour over chicken. Serve with pasta. Yield: 4-6 servings.

Rosemary Cashew Chicken

This elegant entree with fresh herbs and crunchy cashews is mouth-watering.
—*Ruth Andrewson*
Leavenworth, Washington

Southwest Turkey Stew

PREP: 15 MIN. **COOK:** 5 HOURS

I prefer main dishes that help me to stay on my diet but still allow me to eat with the rest of the family. This stew is a hit with my husband and our young children.
—*Stephanie Wilson, Helix, Oregon*

- 1-1/2 pounds turkey tenderloins, cubed
- 2 teaspoons canola oil
- 1 can (15 ounces) turkey chili with beans, undrained
- 1 can (14-1/2 ounces) diced tomatoes
- 1 medium sweet red pepper, cut into 3/4-inch pieces
- 1 medium green pepper, cut into 3/4-inch pieces
- 3/4 cup chopped onion
- 3/4 cup salsa
- 3 garlic cloves, minced
- 1-1/2 teaspoons chili powder
- 1/2 teaspoon salt
- 1/2 teaspoon ground cumin
- 1 tablespoon minced fresh cilantro, optional

In a nonstick skillet, brown turkey in oil; transfer to a 3-qt. slow cooker. Stir in the chili, tomatoes, peppers, onion, salsa, garlic, chili powder, salt and cumin. Cover and cook on low for 5-6 hours or until turkey juices run clear. Garnish with cilantro if desired. Yield: 6 servings.

Turkey in Cream Sauce

PREP: 20 MIN. **COOK:** 7 HOURS

I've been relying on this recipe for tender turkey since I first moved out on my own years ago. I serve it whenever I invite new guests to the house, and I'm constantly writing

Hearty Chicken Enchiladas

My husband, Nathan, and I really like Mexican food, and this is our favorite dish. You can adjust it to suit your taste, adding corn, rice or refried beans.
—*Jenny Miller*
Raleigh, North Carolina

out the recipe for them.
—*Kathy-Jo Winterbottom*
Pottstown, Pennsylvania

1-1/4 **cups white wine** *or* **chicken broth**
1 **medium onion, chopped**
2 **garlic cloves, minced**
2 **bay leaves**
2 **teaspoons dried rosemary, crushed**
1/2 **teaspoon pepper**
3 **turkey breast tenderloins (3/4 pound** *each***)**
3 **tablespoons cornstarch**
1/2 **cup half-and-half cream** *or* **milk**
1/2 **teaspoon salt**

In a 3-qt. slow cooker, combine the wine or broth, onion, garlic and bay leaves. Combine rosemary and pepper; rub over turkey. Place in slow cooker. Cover and cook on low for 7-8 hours or until a meat thermometer reads 170°.

Remove turkey and keep warm. Strain cooking juices; pour into a saucepan. Combine cornstarch,

cream and salt until smooth; gradually add to juices. Bring to a boil; cook and stir for 2 minutes or until thickened. Slice turkey; serve with cream sauce. Yield: 9 servings.

Hearty Chicken Enchiladas

PREP: 15 MIN.
COOK: 8 HOURS 25 MIN.

1 **pound boneless skinless chicken breasts**
2 **cans (15 ounces** *each***) enchilada sauce**
1 **can (4 ounces) chopped green chilies**
1 **can (15 ounces) black beans, rinsed and drained**
8 **flour tortillas (6 inches)**
1 **cup (4 ounces) shredded Mexican cheese blend**
Sour cream, optional

In a 3-qt. slow cooker, combine the chicken, enchilada sauce

and chilies. Cover and cook on low for 8 hours or until a meat thermometer reads 170°.

Remove chicken and shred with two forks. Reserve 1-2/3 cups cooking juices. Pour the remaining cooking juices into a large bowl; add the beans and shredded chicken. Coat two freezer-safe 8-in. square baking dishes with nonstick cooking spray; add 1/2 cup reserved juices to each.

Place about 1/3 cup chicken mixture down the center of each tortilla. Roll up and place seam side down in prepared dishes. Pour remaining reserved juices over top; sprinkle with cheese.

Cover and freeze one dish for up to 3 months. Cover and bake the second dish at 350° for 20 minutes. Uncover; bake 5 minutes longer or until cheese is lightly browned. Serve with sour cream if desired.

To use frozen enchiladas: Thaw in the refrigerator overnight. Remove from the refrigerator 30 minutes before baking. Bake as directed. Yield: 2 casseroles (4 servings each).

Sweet 'n' Tangy Chicken

My slow cooker comes in handy during the haying and harvest seasons. We're so busy that if supper isn't prepared before I serve lunch, it doesn't seem to get done on time. This recipe is hearty, delicious and fuss-free.
—Joan Airey, Rivers, Manitoba

Sweet 'n' Tangy Chicken

PREP: 15 MIN. **COOK:** 4-1/2 HOURS

- 1 medium onion, chopped
- 1-1/2 teaspoons minced garlic
- 1 broiler/fryer chicken (3 pounds), cut up and skin removed
- 2/3 cup ketchup
- 1/3 cup packed brown sugar
- 1 tablespoon chili powder
- 1 tablespoon lemon juice
- 1 teaspoon dried basil
- 1/2 teaspoon salt
- 1/4 teaspoon pepper
- 1/8 teaspoon hot pepper sauce
- 2 tablespoons cornstarch
- 3 tablespoons cold water

In a 3-qt. slow cooker, combine onion and garlic; top with chicken. In a small bowl, combine the ketchup, brown sugar, chili powder, lemon juice, basil, salt, pepper and pepper sauce; pour over chicken.

Cover and cook on low for 4-1/2 to 5 hours or until chicken juices run clear. Remove chicken and keep warm.

Transfer cooking juices to a saucepan. Combine cornstarch and water until smooth; stir into juices. Bring to a boil; cook and stir for 2 minutes or until thickened. Serve over chicken. Yield: 4 servings.

Lemonade Chicken

PREP: 10 MIN. **COOK:** 3 HOURS

- 6 boneless skinless chicken breast halves (4 ounces each)
- 3/4 cup lemonade concentrate
- 3 tablespoons ketchup
- 2 tablespoons brown sugar
- 1 tablespoon cider vinegar
- 2 tablespoons cornstarch
- 2 tablespoons cold water

Place chicken in a 5-qt. slow cooker. Combine the lemonade, ketchup, brown sugar and vinegar; pour over chicken. Cover and cook on low for 2-1/2 hours or until a meat thermometer reads 170°.

Remove chicken and keep warm. For gravy, combine cornstarch and water until smooth; stir into cooking juices. Cover and cook on high for 30 minutes or until thickened. Return chicken to the slow cooker; heat through. Yield: 6 servings.

Lemonade Chicken

I don't know where this recipe originally came from, but my mother used to make it for our family when I was little. Now I love to make it, too.
—Jenny Cook
Eau Claire, Wisconsin

Wild Rice Turkey Dinner

PREP: 10 MIN. **COOK:** 7 HOURS

- 3/4 cup uncooked wild rice
- 1 medium butternut squash, peeled, seeded and cut into 1-inch pieces
- 1 medium onion, cut into 1-inch pieces
- 2 turkey breast tenderloins (8 ounces *each*)
- 3 cups chicken broth
- 1/2 teaspoon salt
- 1/2 teaspoon pepper
- 1/2 teaspoon dried thyme
- 1/2 cup dried cranberries

In a 5-qt. slow cooker, layer the rice, squash, onion and turkey. Add broth; sprinkle with salt, pepper and thyme. Cover and cook on low for 7-8 hours or until a meat thermometer reads 170°.

Remove turkey; cut into slices. Stir cranberries into rice mixture; serve with a slotted spoon. Serve with turkey. Yield: 4 servings.

Mushroom Chicken Cacciatore

PREP: 20 MIN. **COOK:** 4 HOURS

An Italian treatment is given to chicken by cooking it in a zesty tomato sauce and serving it over spaghetti.
—*Jane Bone, Cape Coral, Florida*

- 4 boneless skinless chicken breast halves (about 1-1/2 pounds)
- 2 tablespoons vegetable oil
- 1 can (15 ounces) tomato sauce
- 2 cans (4 ounces *each*) sliced mushrooms, drained
- 1 medium onion, chopped
- 1/4 cup red wine *or* chicken broth
- 2 garlic cloves, minced
- 1-1/4 teaspoons dried oregano
- 1/2 teaspoon dried thyme
- 1/8 to 1/4 teaspoon salt
- 1/8 teaspoon pepper

Hot cooked spaghetti

In a large skillet, brown chicken in oil on both sides. Transfer to a 3-qt. slow cooker. In a bowl, combine the tomato sauce, mushrooms, onion, wine or broth, garlic, oregano, thyme, salt and pepper; pour over chicken. Cover and cook on low for 4-5 hours or until a meat thermometer reads 170°. Serve over spaghetti. Yield: 4 servings.

Lemony Turkey Breast

PREP: 10 MIN. **COOK:** 5 HOURS

Lemon and a hint of garlic add a lovely touch to these moist slices of turkey breast. I usually serve the gravy over a combination of white and brown rice, along with broccoli for a healthy meal.
—*Lynn Laux, Ballwin, Missouri*

- 1 bone-in turkey breast (5 pounds), cut in half
- 1 medium lemon, halved
- 1 teaspoon salt-free lemon-pepper seasoning

Wild Rice Turkey Dinner
We live in the northwoods of Wisconsin, and the wild rice, squash and cranberries I use for this dish are locally grown. I combine these ingredients with turkey tenderloins for a complete and satisfying supper.
—*Tabitha Dodge*
Conover, Wisconsin

Beef & Ground Beef

Garlic Beef Stroganoff

PREP: 20 MIN. **COOK:** 7 HOURS

I'm a mom and work full-time, so I try to use my slow cooker whenever possible. This Stroganoff is perfect because I can get it ready in the morning before the kids get up.
—*Erika Anderson*
Wausau, Wisconsin

- 2 teaspoons beef bouillon granules
- 1 cup boiling water
- 1 can (10-3/4 ounces) condensed cream of mushroom soup, undiluted
- 2 jars (4-1/2 ounces *each*) sliced mushrooms, drained
- 1 large onion, chopped
- 3 garlic cloves, minced
- 1 tablespoon Worcestershire sauce
- 1-1/2 to 2 pounds boneless round steak, trimmed and cut into thin strips
- 2 tablespoons vegetable oil
- 1 package (8 ounces) cream cheese, cubed
  Hot cooked noodles

In a 3-qt. slow cooker, dissolve bouillon in water. Add the soup, mushrooms, onion, garlic and Worcestershire sauce. In a skillet, brown beef in oil.

Transfer to the slow cooker. Cover and cook on low for 7-8 hours or until the meat is tender. Stir in cream cheese until smooth. Serve over noodles. Yield: 6-8 servings.

Slow-Cooked Stew

PREP: 20 MIN. **COOK:** 9 HOURS

- 4 cups reduced-sodium V8 juice
- 3 tablespoons quick-cooking tapioca
- 1 tablespoon sugar
- 1/4 teaspoon pepper
- 2 cups frozen cut green beans
- 2 cups fresh baby carrots, halved lengthwise
- 2 celery ribs, thinly sliced
- 1 small onion, chopped
- 1-1/2 pounds beef stew meat, cut into 1-inch cubes
  Hot cooked noodles

Combine the V8, tapioca, sugar and pepper; let stand for 15 minutes. In a 5-qt. slow cooker, combine the beans, carrots, celery and onion. Top with beef. Add V8 mixture. Cover and cook on low for 9-10 hours or until beef is tender. Serve over noodles. Yield: 10 servings.

Slow-Cooked Stew

You can't beat this combination of tender beef and colorful vegetables in a savory sauce over noodles. It's great to come home to an easy meal that looks and tastes like you fussed all day.
—*Diane Delaney*
Harrisburg, Pennsylvania

Hamburger Supper

My mother-in-law shared this recipe with me when my husband and I were first married. Over the past 50 years, I've relied on this meal-in-one more times than I can count.
—Dolores Hickenbottom, Greensburg, Pennsylvania

Old-World Sauerbraten

Old-World Sauerbraten

I serve this popular German entree with potato pancakes and vegetables. Crushed gingersnaps, lemon and vinegar give the marinated beef and gravy their appetizing sweet-sour flavor.
—Susan Garoutte
Georgetown, Texas

PREP: 10 MIN. + MARINATING
COOK: 6 HOURS 10 MIN.

- 1-1/2 **cups water,** *divided*
- 1-1/4 **cups cider vinegar,** *divided*
- 2 **large onions, sliced,** *divided*
- 1 **medium lemon, sliced**
- 15 **whole cloves,** *divided*
- 6 **bay leaves,** *divided*
- 6 **whole peppercorns**
- 2 **tablespoons sugar**
- 2 **teaspoons salt**
- 1 **boneless beef sirloin tip roast (3 pounds), cut in half**
- 1/4 **teaspoon pepper**
- 12 **gingersnap cookies, crumbled**

In a resealable plastic bag, combine 1 cup water, 1 cup vinegar, half of onions, lemon, 10 cloves, four bay leaves, peppercorns, sugar and salt. Add roast. Seal bag and turn to coat; refrigerate overnight, turning occasionally.

Drain and discard marinade. Place roast in a 5-qt. slow cooker; add pepper and remaining water, vinegar, onions, cloves and bay leaves. Cover and cook on low for 6-8 hours or until meat is tender.

Remove roast and keep warm. Discard bay leaves and cloves. Stir in gingersnaps. Cover and cook on high for 10-15 minutes or until gravy is thickened. Slice roast; serve with gravy. **Yield:** 12 servings.

Hamburger Supper

PREP: 20 MIN. **COOK:** 4 HOURS

- 1 **pound ground beef**
- 1/4 **cup hot water**
- 3 **small potatoes, peeled and diced**
- 1 **medium onion, chopped**
- 1 **can (15 ounces) peas and carrots, drained**
- 1 **can (14-1/2 ounces) diced tomatoes, undrained**
- 1 **tablespoon sugar**
- 1/2 **teaspoon salt**
- 1/4 **teaspoon pepper**

Shape beef into four patties. In a skillet, cook patties over medium heat until no longer pink. Place in

Tender Beef 'n' Bean Stew

When I am juggling a lot of the kids' sports schedules, this is the recipe I turn to for an easy and satisfying dinner. Add a green salad and some corn bread or homemade rolls for a perfect meal.
—Juline Goelzer
Arroyo Grande, California

Enchilada Casserole

PREP: 20 MIN. **COOK:** 6 HOURS

Tortilla chips and a side salad turn this casserole into a complete, mouth-watering meal.
—Denise Waller
Omaha, Nebraska

a 5-qt. slow cooker. Add water to skillet and stir to loosen browned bits from pan. Pour into slow cooker. Add remaining ingredients. Cover and cook on low for 4-6 hours or until potatoes are tender. Yield: 4 servings.

Tender Beef 'n' Bean Stew

PREP: 15 MIN. **COOK:** 8-1/2 HOURS

- 1 pound lean beef stew meat, cut into 1-inch cubes
- 2 cans (16 ounces *each*) kidney beans, rinsed and drained
- 1 can (14-1/2 ounces) diced tomatoes, undrained
- 1-1/2 cups frozen corn
- 1 cup hot water
- 1 cup chopped onion
- 2 celery ribs, chopped

- 1 can (4 ounces) chopped green chilies
- 1 can (2-1/4 ounces) sliced ripe olives, drained
- 2 tablespoons uncooked long grain rice
- 1 to 2 tablespoons chili powder
- 2 teaspoons beef bouillon granules
- 1/4 teaspoon salt
- 1 can (8 ounces) tomato sauce
Shredded cheddar cheese and sour cream, optional

In a 5-qt. slow cooker, combine the first 13 ingredients. Cover and cook on low for 8-9 hours or until the beef is tender. Stir in the tomato sauce; cover and cook for 30 minutes or until heated through. Garnish with the cheese and sour cream if desired. Yield: 10 servings.

- 1 pound ground beef
- 2 cans (10 ounces *each*) enchilada sauce
- 1 can (10-3/4 ounces) condensed cream of onion soup, undiluted
- 1/4 teaspoon salt
- 1 package (8-1/2 ounces) flour tortillas, torn
- 3 cups (12 ounces) shredded cheddar cheese

In a skillet, cook beef over medium heat until no longer pink; drain. Stir in enchilada sauce, soup and salt.

In a 3-qt. slow cooker, layer a third of the beef mixture, tortillas and cheese. Repeat the layers twice. Cover and cook on low for 6-8 hours or until heated through. Yield: 4 servings.

Sweet 'n' Tangy Pot Roast

The first time I cooked for my husband-to-be more than 20 years ago, I made him this roast. For dessert, I served chocolate pudding spooned over marshmallows. He thought he'd died and gone to heaven!
—Carol Mulligan
Honeoye Falls, New York

Sweet 'n' Tangy Pot Roast

PREP: 10 MIN. **COOK:** 9-1/2 HOURS

- 1 boneless beef chuck roast (3 pounds), cut in half
- 1/2 teaspoon salt
- 1/2 teaspoon pepper
- 1 cup water
- 1 cup ketchup
- 1/4 cup red wine *or* beef broth
- 1 envelope brown gravy mix
- 2 teaspoons Dijon mustard
- 1 teaspoon Worcestershire sauce
- 1/8 teaspoon garlic powder
- 3 tablespoons cornstarch
- 1/4 cup cold water

Place roast in a 5-qt. slow cooked. Sprinkle with salt and pepper. In a bowl, combine the water, ketchup, wine or broth, gravy mix, mustard, Worcestershire sauce and garlic powder; pour over meat. Cover and cook on low for 9-10 hours or until meat is tender.

Combine cornstarch and cold water until smooth. Stir into slow cooker. Cover and cook on high for 30 minutes or until gravy is thickened. Remove meat from slow cooker. Slice and serve with gravy. Yield: 8 servings.

Slow-Cooked Cabbage Rolls

PREP: 20 MIN. **COOK:** 6 HOURS

- 1 large head cabbage
- 1 egg, beaten
- 1 can (8 ounces) tomato sauce
- 3/4 cup quick-cooking rice
- 1/2 cup chopped green pepper
- 1/2 cup crushed saltines (about 15 crackers)
- 1 envelope onion soup mix
- 1-1/2 pounds lean ground beef
- 1 can (46 ounces) V8 juice

Salt to taste

Grated Parmesan cheese, optional

Cook cabbage in boiling water just until leaves fall off head. Set aside 12 large leaves for rolls; drain well. (Refrigerate remaining cabbage for another use.) Cut out the thick vein from the bottom of each reserved leaf, making a V-shaped cut; set aside.

In a bowl, combine the egg, tomato sauce, rice, green pepper, cracker crumbs and soup mix. Crumble beef over mixture and mix well. Place about 1/3 cup meat mixture on each cabbage leaf; overlap cut ends of leaf. Fold in sides, beginning from the cut end. Roll up completely to enclose filling. Secure with toothpicks if desired.

Place cabbage rolls in a 3-qt. slow cooker. Pour V8 juice over rolls. Cover and cook on low for 6-7 hours or until filling reaches 160°. Just before serving, sprinkle with salt and cheese if desired. Yield: 6 servings.

Slow-Cooked Cabbage Rolls

I've worked full-time for more than 30 years, and this super slow-cooker recipe has been a lifesaver. It's great to have dinner ready when you walk in the door.
—Rosemary Jarvis
Sparta, Tennessee

Corned Beef 'n' Cabbage

PREP: 5 MIN. **COOK:** 8 HOURS

- 1 large onion, cut into wedges
- 1 cup apple juice
- 1 bay leaf
- 1 corned beef brisket with spice packet (2-1/2 to 3 pounds), cut in half
- 1 small head cabbage, cut into wedges

Place the onion in a 5-qt. slow cooker. Combine the apple juice, bay leaf and contents of spice packet; pour over onion. Place in brisket slow cooker. Top with cabbage. Cover and cook on low for 8-10 hours or until meat and vegetables are tender. Discard bay leaf before serving. Yield: 6 servings.

Hearty Hash Brown Dinner

PREP: 15 MIN. **COOK:** 4-1/2 HOURS

This meal-in-one with vegetables and ground beef is frequent fare at my house. It's great for potlucks, too. French-fried onions sprinkled on after cooking create a crispy, delicious topping.
—Marge Berg, Gibbon, Minnesota

- 3 cups frozen shredded hash brown potatoes, thawed
- 1/2 teaspoon salt
- 1/4 teaspoon pepper
- 1 pound ground beef
- 1/2 cup chopped onion

Corned Beef 'n' Cabbage

The apple juice gives this recipe a tasty twist and a mild flavor. The long slow-cooking assures that the meat will be tender.
—Jo Ann Honey
Longmont, Colorado

- 1 package (16 ounces) frozen California-blend vegetables
- 1 can (10-3/4 ounces) condensed cream of chicken soup, undiluted
- 1 cup milk
- 12 ounces process cheese (Velveeta), cubed
- 1 can (2.8 ounces) french-fried onions

Place potatoes in a lightly greased 5-qt. slow cooker; sprinkle with salt and pepper. In a large skillet, cook beef and onion over medium heat until meat is no longer pink; drain. Spoon over potatoes. Top with vegetables. Combine soup and milk; pour over vegetables. Cover and cook on low for 4 to 4-1/2 hours.

Top with cheese; cover and cook 30 minutes longer or until cheese is melted. Just before serving, sprinkle with french-fried onions. Yield: 4 servings.

Beef and Barley

PREP: 15 MIN. **COOK:** 4 HOURS

I like to serve this to company. I'm not sure where the recipe originated for this country-style dish, but I've had it for years and rely on it when I'm hosting a meal for several people.
—Linda Ronk, Melbourne, Florida

- 2 pounds ground beef
- 1 can (15 ounces) diced carrots, undrained
- 1 can (14-1/2 ounces) diced tomatoes, undrained
- 1 can (10-3/4 ounces) condensed tomato soup, undiluted

Green Chili Beef Burritos

Recipes that are leaner in fat and calories—like the one for these delicious burritos—helped me lose 30 pounds.
—Shirley Davidson
Thornton, Colorado

sauce into an ungreased 5-qt. slow cooker. Layer with a third of the noodles, a third of the beef, a third of the remaining sauce and a third of the cheeses. Repeat layers twice.

Cover and cook on low for 4 hours or until cheese is melted and lasagna is heated through. Yield: 12-16 servings.

Green Chili Beef Burritos

PREP: 20 MIN.
COOK: 8 HOURS + COOLING

- 2 boneless beef top sirloin roasts (3 pounds *each*)
- 4 cans (4 ounces *each*) chopped green chilies
- 1 medium onion, chopped
- 3 medium jalapeno peppers, seeded and chopped
- 3 garlic cloves, sliced
- 3 teaspoons chili powder
- 1-1/2 teaspoons ground cumin
- 1 teaspoon salt-free seasoning blend, optional
- 1 cup reduced-sodium beef broth
- 24 fat-free flour tortillas (8 inches), warmed

Chopped tomatoes, shredded lettuce and reduced-fat cheddar cheese, optional

Trim fat from roasts; cut meat into large chunks. Place in a 5-qt. slow cooker. Top with the chilies, onion, jalapenos, garlic, chili powder, cumin and seasoning blend if desired. Pour broth over all. Cover and cook on low for 8-9 hours.

Remove beef; cool slightly. Shred with two forks. Cool cooking liquid slightly; skim fat. In a blender, cover and process cooking liquid in small batches until smooth. Return liquid and beef to slow cooker; heat through. Place 1/3 cup beef mixture on each tortilla. Top with tomatoes, lettuce and cheese if desired. Fold in ends and sides. Yield: 2 dozen.

Editor's Note: When cutting or seeding hot peppers, use rubber or plastic gloves to protect your hands. Avoid touching your face.

Cabbage Patch Stew

I like to serve steaming helpings of this hearty stew in old-fashioned soup plates with thick, crusty slices of homemade bread. For a quicker prep, substitute coleslaw mix for the chopped cabbage.
—*Karen Ann Bland*
Gove, Kansas

Cabbage Patch Stew

PREP: 20 MIN. **COOK:** 6 HOURS

- 1   **pound ground beef**
- 1   **cup chopped onion**
- 2   **celery ribs, chopped**
- 11   **cups coarsely chopped cabbage (about 2 pounds)**
- 2   **cans (14-1/2 ounces *each*) stewed tomatoes**
- 1   **can (15 ounces) pinto beans, rinsed and drained**
- 1   **can (10 ounces) diced tomatoes with green chilies**
- 1/2   **cup ketchup**
- 1   **to 1-1/2 teaspoons chili powder**
- 1/2   **teaspoon dried oregano**
- 1/2   **teaspoon pepper**
- 1/4   **teaspoon salt**

Shredded cheddar cheese and sour cream, optional

In a large skillet, cook the beef, onion and celery over medium heat until meat is no longer pink and vegetables are tender; drain.

Transfer to a 5-qt. slow cooker. Stir in the cabbage, stewed tomatoes, beans, diced tomatoes, ketchup, chili powder, oregano, pepper and salt. Cover and cook on low for 6-8 hours or until cabbage is tender. Serve with cheese and sour cream if desired. Yield: 8 servings.

Flank Steak Fajitas

PREP: 10 MIN. **COOK:** 8 HOURS

- 1-1/2   **to 2 pounds beef flank steak, cut into thin strips**
- 1   **can (10 ounces) diced tomatoes and green chilies, undrained**
- 2   **garlic cloves, minced**
- 1   **jalapeno pepper, seeded and chopped**
- 1   **tablespoon minced fresh cilantro *or* parsley**
- 1   **teaspoon chili powder**
- 1/2   **teaspoon ground cumin**
- 1/4   **teaspoon salt**
- 1   **medium sweet red pepper, julienned**
- 1   **medium green pepper, julienned**
- 8   **to 10 flour tortillas (7 to 8 inches)**

Sour cream, salsa and shredded cheddar cheese, optional

Place beef in a 3-qt. slow cooker. In a bowl, combine the tomatoes, garlic, jalapeno, cilantro, chili powder, cumin and salt; pour over beef. Cover and cook on low for 7-8 hours. Stir in red and green peppers. Cook 1 hour longer or until meat and peppers are tender. Thicken juices if desired.

Using a slotted spoon, place about 1/2 cup beef mixture down the center of each tortilla; fold sides over filling. Serve with sour cream, salsa and cheese if desired. Yield: 8-10 servings.

Editor's Note: When cutting or seeding hot peppers, use rubber or plastic gloves to protect your hands. Avoid touching your face.

Flank Steak Fajitas

My family loves Mexican food, and this is one of our favorites. The slow cooker tenderizes the flank steak for these filling fajitas, which have just the right amount of spice.
—*Twila Burkholder*
Middleburg, Pennsylvania

Coffee Beef Pot Roast

PREP: 15 MIN. **COOK:** 8 HOURS

- 1 boneless beef sirloin tip roast (2-1/2 pounds), cut in half
- 2 teaspoons canola oil
- 1-1/2 cups sliced fresh mushrooms
- 1/3 cup sliced green onions
- 2 garlic cloves, minced
- 1-1/2 cups brewed coffee
- 1 teaspoon Liquid Smoke, optional
- 1/2 teaspoon salt
- 1/2 teaspoon chili powder
- 1/4 teaspoon pepper
- 1/4 cup cornstarch
- 1/3 cup cold water

In a large nonstick skillet, brown roast on all sides in oil over medium-high heat. Place in a 5-qt. slow cooker. In the same skillet, saute mushrooms, onions and garlic until tender; stir in the coffee, Liquid Smoke if desired, salt, chili powder and pepper. Pour over roast. Cover and cook on low for 8-10 hours or until meat is tender.

Remove roast and keep warm. Pour cooking juices into a 2-cup measuring cup; skim fat. In a saucepan, combine cornstarch and water until smooth. Gradually stir in 2 cups cooking juices. Bring to a boil; cook and stir for 2 minutes or until thickened. Serve with sliced beef. Yield: 6 servings.

Stuffed Flank Steak

PREP: 20 MIN.
COOK: 8 HOURS + 10 MIN.

This recipe came with my first slow cooker. Now I'm on my fourth slow cooker and still use the recipe.
—*Kathy Clark, Byron, Minnesota*

- 1 beef flank steak (2 pounds)
- 1 medium onion, chopped
- 1 garlic clove, minced
- 1 tablespoon butter
- 1-1/2 cups soft bread crumbs (about 3 slices)
- 1/2 cup chopped fresh mushrooms
- 1/4 cup minced fresh parsley
- 1/4 cup egg substitute
- 3/4 teaspoon poultry seasoning
- 1/2 teaspoon salt
- 1/8 teaspoon pepper
- 1/2 cup beef broth
- 2 teaspoons cornstarch
- 4 teaspoons water

Flatten steak to 1/2-in. thickness; set aside. In a nonstick skillet, saute onion and garlic in butter until tender. Add the bread crumbs, mushrooms, parsley, egg substitute, poultry seasoning, salt and pepper; mix well. Spread over steak to within 1 in. of edge. Roll up jelly-roll style, starting with a long side; tie with kitchen string. Place in a 5-qt. slow cooker; add broth. Cover and cook on low for 8-10 hours.

Remove meat to a serving platter and keep warm. Skim fat from cooking juices; pour into a

Coffee Beef Pot Roast

Day-old coffee is the key to this flavorful beef roast that simmers in the slow cooker until it's fall-apart tender. Try it once and I'm sure you'll cook it again.
—*Charles Trahan*
San Dimas, California

small saucepan. Combine cornstarch and water until smooth; stir into juices. Bring to a boil; cook and stir for 1-2 minutes or until thickened. Remove string before slicing steak; serve with gravy. Yield: 8 servings.

Pizza Casserole

PREP: 25 MIN. **COOK:** 1 HOUR

A friend from church gave me the recipe for this family-pleasing casserole. It's always one of the first dishes emptied at potlucks, and it can easily be adapted to personal tastes.
—*Julie Sterchi, Harrisburg, Illinois*

- 3 **pounds ground beef**
- 1/2 **cup chopped onion**
- 1 **jar (28 ounces) spaghetti sauce**
- 2 **jars (4-1/2 ounces *each*) sliced mushrooms, drained**
- 1 **teaspoon salt**
- 1/2 **teaspoon garlic powder**
- 1/2 **teaspoon dried oregano**

Dash pepper

- 1 **package (16 ounces) wide egg noodles, cooked and drained**
- 2 **packages (3-1/2 ounces *each*) sliced pepperoni**
- 2 **cups (8 ounces) shredded cheddar cheese**
- 2 **cups (8 ounces) shredded part-skim mozzarella cheese**

In a Dutch oven, brown beef and onion over medium heat until meat is no longer pink; drain. Add the spaghetti sauce, mushrooms, salt, garlic powder, oregano and pepper; heat through.

Spoon 4 cups into a 6-qt. slow cooker. Top with half of the noodles, pepperoni and cheeses. Repeat layers. Cover and cook on high for 1 hour or until cheese is melted. Yield: 12 servings.

Editor's Note: To use a 3-qt. slow cooker, cut the recipe in half.

Artichoke Beef Stew

PREP: 25 MIN. **COOK:** 7-1/2 HOURS

- 1/3 **cup all-purpose flour**
- 1 **teaspoon salt**

Artichoke Beef Stew

The recipe for this special stew was given to me by a dear friend before she moved to another state. She served it with dumplings, but my husband prefers noodles.
—*Janell Schmidt*
Athelstane, Wisconsin

- 1/2 **teaspoon pepper**
- 2-1/2 **pounds lean beef stew meat, cut into 1-inch cubes**
- 3 **tablespoons vegetable oil**
- 1 **can (10-1/2 ounces) condensed beef consomme, undiluted**
- 2 **medium onions, halved and sliced**
- 1 **cup red wine *or* beef broth**
- 1 **garlic clove, minced**
- 1/2 **teaspoon dill weed**
- 2 **jars (6-1/2 ounces *each*) marinated artichoke hearts, drained and chopped**
- 20 **small fresh mushrooms, halved**

Hot cooked noodles

In a shallow bowl or large resealable plastic bag, combine the flour, salt and pepper. Add beef and toss to coat. In a skillet, brown beef in oil.

Transfer to a 3-qt. slow cooker with a slotted spoon. Gradually add consomme to the skillet. Bring to a boil; stir to loosen browned bits from pan. Stir in onions, wine or broth, garlic and dill. Pour over beef. Cover and cook for low for 7-8 hours or until the meat is nearly tender. Stir in the artichokes and mushrooms; cook 30 minutes longer or until heated through. Serve over noodles. Yield: 6-8 servings.

Moroccan Braised Beef

Curry powder is a blend of up to 20 spices, herbs and seeds. Add a pinch of curry to your favorite soups, stews, salads and even rice for an exotic flavor. In this Moroccan stew, begin by mixing 2 teaspoons curry, then adjust to your taste.
—Taste of Home Test Kitchen

Moroccan Braised Beef

PREP: 20 MIN. **COOK:** 7 HOURS

- 1/3 cup all-purpose flour
- 2 pounds boneless beef chuck roast, cut into 1-inch cubes
- 3 tablespoons olive oil
- 2 cans (14-1/2 ounces *each*) beef broth
- 2 cups chopped onions
- 1 can (14-1/2 ounces) diced tomatoes, undrained
- 1 cup dry red wine
- 2 to 3 teaspoons curry powder
- 1 tablespoon paprika
- 1 teaspoon salt
- 1 teaspoon ground cumin
- 1 teaspoon ground coriander
- 1/2 teaspoon cayenne pepper
- 1-1/2 cups golden raisins

Hot cooked couscous, optional

Place flour in a large resealable plastic bag; add beef and toss to coat. In a large skillet, brown beef in oil. Transfer to a 5-qt. slow cooker. Stir in the broth, onions, tomatoes, wine and seasonings. Cover and cook on low for 7-8 hours or until the meat is tender.

During the last 30 minutes of cooking, stir in the raisins. Serve with couscous if desired. Yield: 6 servings.

Barbecued Beef Brisket

PREP: 10 MIN. **COOK:** 4 HOURS

- 1 teaspoon salt
- 1 teaspoon chili powder
- 1/2 teaspoon garlic powder
- 1/4 teaspoon onion powder
- 1/4 teaspoon celery seed
- 1/4 teaspoon pepper
- 1 fresh beef brisket (2-1/2 pounds), trimmed

SAUCE:

- 1/2 cup ketchup
- 1/2 cup chili sauce
- 1/4 cup packed brown sugar
- 2 tablespoons cider vinegar
- 2 tablespoons Worcestershire sauce
- 1 to 1-1/2 teaspoons Liquid Smoke, optional
- 1/2 teaspoon ground mustard

In a small bowl, combine the first six ingredients; rub over brisket. Place in a 3-qt. slow cooker. In a large bowl, combine the sauce ingredients. Pour half over the brisket; set the remaining sauce aside.

Cover and cook on high for 4-5 hours or until meat is tender. Serve with the reserved sauce. Yield: 8 servings.

Editor's Note: This is a fresh beef brisket, not corned beef. The meat comes from the first cut of the brisket.

Barbecued Beef Brisket
I enjoy fixing a sit-down meal for my husband and myself every evening, so this is often on the menu. It's fairly inexpensive, takes little effort to prepare and tastes wonderful.
—Anita Keppinger
Philomath, Oregon

Slow-Cooked Swiss Steak

PREP: 10 MIN. **COOK:** 6 HOURS

- 2 tablespoons all-purpose flour
- 1/2 teaspoon salt
- 1/4 teaspoon pepper
- 1-1/2 pounds boneless beef round steak, cut into six pieces
- 1 medium onion, cut into 1/4-inch slices
- 1 celery rib, cut into 1/2-inch slices
- 2 cans (8 ounces *each*) tomato sauce

In a large resealable plastic bag, combine the flour, salt and pepper. Add the steak; seal bag and toss to coat.

Place the onion in a greased 3-qt. slow cooker. Top with the steak, celery and tomato sauce. Cover and cook on low for 6-8 hours or until meat is tender. Yield: 6 servings.

Corned Beef Dinner

PREP: 10 MIN. **COOK:** 9 HOURS

This flavorful meal is a must for St. Patrick's Day but great anytime of the year. While I usually cook it on the stovetop, a slow cooker makes it even easier. It serves four nicely with enough leftover meat for Reuben sandwiches or other dishes.
—Michelle Rhodes
Cleveland, Ohio

- 4 to 5 medium red potatoes, quartered
- 2 cups fresh baby carrots, halved lengthwise
- 3 cups chopped cabbage
- 1 corned beef brisket (3-1/2 pounds) with spice packet, cut in half
- 3 cups water
- 1 tablespoon caraway seeds

Place the potatoes, carrots and cabbage in a 5-qt. slow cooker. Place brisket over vegetables. Add the water, caraway seeds and contents of spice packet. Cover and cook on low for 9-10 hours or until the meat and vegetables are tender. Yield: 8 servings.

Mushroom Round Steak

PREP: 25 MIN. **COOK:** 8 HOURS

I think our family would starve it I didn't have a slow cooker—I use it twice a week. This saucy beef entree is perfect with mashed potatoes.
—Linda Krivanek
Oak Creek, Wisconsin

- 1/2 cup all-purpose flour
- 1 teaspoon salt
- 1/4 teaspoon pepper
- 2 to 2-1/2 pounds boneless beef round steak (1/2 inch thick), cut into serving-size pieces
- 2 tablespoons vegetable oil
- 1 can (10-1/2 ounces) condensed French onion soup, undiluted
- 1 can (8 ounces) mushroom stems and pieces, drained

Slow-Cooked Swiss Steak

This is a favorite for me to make, because I can flour and season the steaks and refrigerate them overnight. The next morning, I just put all the ingredients in the slow cooker, and I have a delicious dinner at the end of the day with hardly any effort.
—Sarah Burks
Wathena, Kansas

3/4 cup water
1/4 cup ketchup
1 tablespoon Worcestershire sauce
2 tablespoons cornstarch
1/4 cup cold water
1 cup (8 ounces) sour cream

In a large resealable plastic bag, combine the flour, salt and pepper. Add beef, a few pieces at a time, and shake to coat. In a large skillet, brown the beef in batches in oil. Transfer meat to a 3-qt. slow cooker with a slotted spoon.

In a bowl, combine the soup, mushrooms, water, ketchup and Worcestershire sauce. Pour over meat. Cover and cook on low for 8 hours or until meat is tender.

Remove beef with a slotted spoon; keep warm. Transfer cooking liquid to a saucepan. Combine cornstarch and cold water until smooth; gradually stir into cooking liquid. Bring to a boil; cook and stir for 1-2 minutes or until thickened. Stir a small amount of hot liquid into sour cream. Return all to the pan; cook on low until heated through. Serve over meat. Yield: 6 servings.

Beef 'n' Bean Torta

PREP: 30 MIN. **COOK:** 4 HOURS

1 pound ground beef
1 small onion, chopped
1 can (15 ounces) pinto *or* black beans, rinsed and drained
1 can (10 ounces) diced tomatoes and green chilies, undrained
1 can (2-1/4 ounces) sliced ripe olives, drained
1-1/2 teaspoons chili powder
1/2 teaspoon salt
1/8 teaspoon pepper

Beef 'n' Bean Torta

The zesty Southwestern flavor makes this dish a hit with my family. And it's easy to prepare. I serve it on nights when we have only a few minutes to eat before running off to meetings or sports events.
—Joan Hallford
North Richland Hills, Texas

3 drops hot pepper sauce
4 flour tortillas (8 inches)
1 cup (4 ounces) shredded cheddar cheese
Minced fresh cilantro, optional
Salsa, sour cream, shredded lettuce and chopped tomatoes, optional

Cut four 20-in. x 3-in. strips of heavy-duty foil; crisscross so they resemble spokes of a wheel. Place strips on the bottom and up the sides of a 5-qt. slow cooker. Coat strips with nonstick cooking spray.

In a large skillet, cook beef and onion over medium heat until meat is no longer pink; drain. Stir in the beans, tomatoes, olives, chili powder, salt, pepper and hot pepper sauce. Spoon about 1-2/3 cups into prepared slow cooker; top with one tortilla and 1/4 cup cheese. Repeat layers three times.

Cover and cook on low for 4-5 hours or until heated through. Using foil strips as handles, remove the tortilla stack to a platter. Sprinkle with cilantro if desired. Serve with salsa, sour cream, lettuce and tomatoes if desired. Yield: 4 servings.

Hearty Beef Vegetable Stew

A co-worker gave me this wonderful recipe. It's awesome! Everyone loves it, including our two young children.
—Angela Nelson
Ruther Glen, Virginia

Hearty Beef Vegetable Stew

PREP: 10 MIN. + STANDING
COOK: 5 HOURS

1	can (28 ounces) crushed tomatoes, undrained
3	tablespoons quick-cooking tapioca
2	tablespoons dried basil
1	tablespoon sugar
1/2	teaspoon salt
1/8	teaspoon pepper
1-1/2	pounds red potatoes, cut into 1-inch cubes
3	medium carrots, cut into 1-inch slices
1	medium onion, chopped
1/2	cup chopped celery
1-1/2	pounds lean chuck roast, cut into 1-inch cubes
2	teaspoons canola oil

In a bowl, combine the tomatoes, tapioca, basil, sugar, salt and pepper; let stand for 15 minutes. Place the potatoes, carrots, onion and celery in a 5-qt. slow cooker.

In a large nonstick skillet, brown meat in oil over medium heat. Drain and transfer meat to slow cooker. Pour tomato mixture over the top. Cover and cook on high for 5-6 hours or until meat and vegetables are tender. Yield: 6 servings.

Bavarian Pot Roast

PREP: 10 MIN. **COOK:** 5 HOURS

1	boneless beef top round roast (about 4 pounds), cut in half
1-1/2	cups apple juice
1	can (8 ounces) tomato sauce
1	small onion, chopped
2	tablespoons white vinegar
1	tablespoon salt
2	to 3 teaspoons ground cinnamon
1	tablespoon minced fresh gingerroot
1/4	cup cornstarch
1/2	cup water

In a Dutch oven coated with nonstick cooking spray, brown roast on all sides over medium-high heat; drain. Transfer to a 5-qt. slow cooker. In a bowl, combine the juice, tomato sauce, onion, vinegar, salt, cinnamon and ginger; pour over roast. Cover and cook on high for 5-7 hours.

In a small bowl, combine cornstarch and water until smooth; stir into cooking juices until well combined. Cover and cook 1 hour longer or until the meat is tender and gravy begins to thicken. Yield: 12 servings.

Bavarian Pot Roast

I grew up eating pot roast but disliked it until I got this recipe at a church social, and changed a few ingredients. My 7-year-old especially enjoys the seasoned apple gravy.
—Patricia Gasmund
Rockford, Illinois

Seasoned Short Ribs

PREP: 15 MIN. **COOK:** 6 HOURS

- 1-1/2 cups tomato juice
- 1/2 cup maple syrup
- 1/4 cup chopped onion
- 3 tablespoons cider vinegar
- 1 tablespoon Worcestershire sauce
- 1 tablespoon Dijon mustard
- 2 teaspoons minced garlic
- 1/4 teaspoon ground cinnamon
- 1/4 teaspoon ground cloves
- 4 pounds bone-in beef short ribs
- 1 teaspoon pepper
- 1 tablespoon cornstarch
- 2 tablespoons cold water

In a small bowl, combine the first nine ingredients; set aside. Cut ribs into serving-size pieces; place on a broiler pan. Sprinkle with pepper. Broil 4-6 in. from the heat for 3-5 minutes on each side or until browned; drain on paper towels.

Place ribs in a 5-qt. slow cooker; top with tomato juice mixture. Cover and cook on low for 6-7 hours or until meat is tender.

In a small bowl, combine cornstarch and cold water until smooth. Pour 1 cup cooking liquid into a small saucepan; skim off fat. Bring to a boil; stir in cornstarch mixture. Return to a boil; cook and stir for 2 minutes or until thickened. Serve over ribs. Yield: 4 servings.

Seasoned Short Ribs

These juicy, barbecue-style short ribs are sure to be a hit with your family. Line your broiler pan with foil for easy cleanup.
—*Taste of Home Test Kitchen*

Meal-in-One Casserole

PREP: 15 MIN. **COOK:** 4 HOURS

Salsa gives zip to this hearty meal. Because this recipe makes more than my husband and I can eat, I freeze half of it. We think it tastes even better the second time.
—*Dorothy Pritchett*
Wills Point, Texas

- 1 pound ground beef
- 1 medium onion, chopped
- 1 medium green pepper, chopped
- 1 can (15-1/4 ounces) whole kernel corn, drained
- 1 can (4 ounces) mushroom stems and pieces, drained
- 1 teaspoon salt
- 1/4 teaspoon pepper
- 1 jar (11 ounces) salsa
- 5 cups cooked medium egg noodles
- 1 can (28 ounces) diced tomatoes, undrained
- 1 cup water
- 1 cup (4 ounces) shredded cheddar cheese *or* blend of cheddar, Monterey Jack and American cheese

In a skillet, cook beef and onion over medium heat until meat is no longer pink; drain.

Transfer to a 5-qt. slow cooker. Top with the green pepper, corn and mushrooms. Sprinkle with salt and pepper. Pour salsa over mushrooms. Top with noodles. Pour tomatoes and water over all. Sprinkle with cheese. Cover and cook on low for 4 hours or until heated through. Yield: 4-6 servings.

Meatball Stew

I came up with this delicious meal-in-one as another way to use frozen meatballs. It's quick to put together in the morning and ready when my husband gets home in the evening.
—Iris Schultz
Miamisburg, Ohio

Creamy Beef and Pasta

PREP: 15 MIN. **COOK:** 6 HOURS

A friend shared the recipe for this fix-it-and-forget-it meal. I often make it for our children when my husband and I go out. Even the baby-sitters have commented how much they like it.
—Carol Losier
Baldwinsville, New York

- 2 cans (10-3/4 ounces) condensed cream of mushroom soup, undiluted
- 2 cups (8 ounces) shredded cheddar cheese *or* part-skim mozzarella cheese
- 1 pound ground beef, cooked and drained
- 2 cups uncooked small pasta
- 2 cups milk
- 1/2 to 1 teaspoon onion powder
- 1/2 to 1 teaspoon salt
- 1/4 to 1/2 teaspoon pepper

In a 3-qt. slow cooker, combine all ingredients. Cover and cook on low for 6 hours or until pasta is tender. Yield: 4-6 servings.

Meatball Stew

PREP: 15 MIN. **COOK:** 9 HOURS

- 3 medium potatoes, peeled and cut into 1/2-inch cubes
- 1 package (16 ounces) fresh baby carrots, quartered
- 1 large onion, chopped
- 3 celery ribs, sliced
- 1 package (12 ounces) frozen fully cooked meatballs
- 1 can (10-3/4 ounces) condensed tomato soup, undiluted
- 1 can (10-1/2 ounces) beef gravy
- 1 cup water
- 1 envelope onion soup mix
- 2 teaspoons beef bouillon granules

Place the potatoes, carrots, onion, celery and meatballs in a 5-qt. slow cooker. In a bowl, combine the remaining ingredients. Pour over meatball mixture. Cover and cook on low for 9-10 hours or until the vegetables are crisp-tender. Yield: 6 servings.

Pork & Lamb

Creamy Ham And Potatoes

PREP: 20 MIN. **COOK:** 8 HOURS

Serve this satisfying dish with a green salad and dessert for a complete meal. The tasty mixture of hearty ham and tender potatoes is brimming with homemade flavor.
—Peggy Key, Grant, Alabama

- 4 medium red potatoes, thinly sliced
- 2 medium onions, finely chopped
- 1-1/2 cups cubed fully cooked ham
- 2 tablespoons butter
- 2 tablespoons all-purpose flour
- 1 teaspoon ground mustard
- 1/2 teaspoon salt
- 1/2 teaspoon pepper
- 1 can (10-3/4 ounces) condensed cream of celery soup, undiluted
- 1-1/3 cups water
- 1 cup (4 ounces) shredded cheddar cheese, optional

In a 3-qt. slow cooker, layer the potatoes, onions and ham.

In a large saucepan, melt butter. Stir in the flour, mustard, salt and pepper until smooth. Combine soup and water; gradually stir into flour mixture. Bring to a boil; cook and stir for 2 minutes or until thickened.

Pour over ham. Cover and cook on low for 8-9 hours or until potatoes are tender. If desired, sprinkle with cheese before serving. Yield: 4 servings.

Sweet 'n' Sour Ribs

PREP: 10 MIN. **COOK:** 8 HOURS

- 3 to 4 pounds boneless country-style pork ribs
- 1 can (20 ounces) pineapple tidbits, undrained
- 2 cans (8 ounces *each*) tomato sauce
- 1/2 cup thinly sliced onion
- 1/2 cup thinly sliced green pepper
- 1/2 cup packed brown sugar
- 1/4 cup cider vinegar
- 1/4 cup tomato paste
- 2 tablespoons Worcestershire sauce
- 1 garlic clove, minced

Salt and pepper to taste

Place ribs in an ungreased 5-qt. slow cooker. In a large bowl, combine the remaining ingredients; pour over the ribs.

Cover and cook on low for 8-10 hours or until meat is tender. Thicken the sauce if desired. Yield: 8 servings.

Sweet 'n' Sour Ribs

If you're looking for a change from typical barbecue ribs, you'll enjoy this recipe my mom always prepared on birthdays and special occasions. The succulent ribs have a tangy taste that my family loves. I usually serve them with garlic mashed potatoes and a salad or coleslaw.
—Dorothy Voelz
Champaign, Illinois

Slow-Cooked Lamb Chops

PREP: 10 MIN. **COOK:** 5-1/2 HOURS

- 4 bacon strips
- 4 lamb shoulder blade chops, trimmed
- 2-1/4 cups thinly sliced peeled potatoes
- 1 cup thinly sliced carrots
- 1/2 teaspoon dried rosemary, crushed
- 1/4 teaspoon garlic powder
- 1/4 teaspoon salt
- 1/4 teaspoon pepper
- 1/4 cup chopped onion
- 2 garlic cloves, minced
- 1 can (10-3/4 ounces) condensed cream of mushroom soup, undiluted
- 1/3 cup milk
- 1 jar (4-1/2 ounces) sliced mushrooms, drained

Wrap bacon around lamb chops; secure with toothpicks. Place in a 3-qt. slow cooker. Cover and cook on high for 1-1/2 hours.

Remove chops; discard toothpicks and bacon. Drain liquid from slow cooker. Add potatoes and carrots; top with lamb chops. Sprinkle with the rosemary, garlic powder, salt, pepper, onion and garlic.

In a bowl, combine soup and milk. Add mushrooms. Pour over the chops. Cover and cook on low for 4-6 hours or until meat and vegetables are tender. Yield: 4 servings.

Meaty Cassoulet

PREP: 15 MIN. + STANDING
COOK: 5 HOURS

Fresh dinner rolls and a salad go great with this hearty bean stew.
—*Suzanne McKinley, Lyons, Georgia*

- 1 pound (2 cups) dried great northern beans
- 2 fresh garlic sausage links
- 3 bacon strips, diced
- 1-1/2 pounds boneless pork, cut into 1-inch cubes
- 1 pound boneless lamb, cut into 1-inch cubes
- 1-1/2 cups chopped onions
- 3 garlic cloves, minced
- 2 teaspoons salt
- 1 teaspoon dried thyme
- 4 whole cloves
- 2 bay leaves
- 2-1/2 cups chicken broth
- 1 can (8 ounces) tomato sauce

Sort beans and rinse with cold water. Place beans in a Dutch oven; add water to cover by 2 in. Bring to a boil; boil for 2 minutes. Remove from the heat; cover and let stand for 1 to 4 hours or until beans are softened. Drain and rinse beans, discarding liquid.

In a large skillet over medium-high heat, brown sausage; remove with a slotted spoon to a 5-qt. slow cooker. Add bacon to skillet; cook until crisp. Remove with a slotted spoon to slow cooker.

In bacon drippings, cook pork and lamb until browned on all sides. Remove pork and lamb with a slotted spoon to slow cooker. Stir in beans and remaining ingredients.

Slow-Cooked Lamb Chops

This is my best recipe for lamb chops. It's great for people who are trying lamb for the first time, since the meat turns out extra tender. I decided to wrap the chops in bacon because that's how I've always done venison. I think it really enhances the taste.
—*Sandra McKenzie*
Braham, Minnesota

Slow-Cooked Ham

PREP: 5 MIN. **COOK:** 8 HOURS

- 1/2 cup packed brown sugar
- 1 teaspoon ground mustard
- 1 teaspoon prepared horseradish
- 4 tablespoons regular cola, *divided*
- 1 boneless smoked ham (5 to 6 pounds), cut in half

In a bowl, combine the brown sugar, mustard, horseradish and 2 tablespoons cola; mix well. Rub over ham. Place in a 5-qt. slow cooker; pour remaining cola over ham. Cover and cook on low for 8-10 hours or until a meat thermometer reads 140°. Yield: 15-20 servings.

Pizza Rigatoni

PREP: 15 MIN. **COOK:** 4 HOURS

This zesty, layered casserole turns a slow cooker into a pizzeria. The dish is loaded with cheese, Italian sausage, pepperoni and pasta.
—*Marilyn Cowan*
North Manchester, Indiana

- 1-1/2 pounds bulk Italian sausage
- 3 cups uncooked rigatoni *or* large tube pasta
- 4 cups (16 ounces) shredded part-skim mozzarella cheese
- 1 can (10-3/4 ounces) condensed cream of mushroom soup, undiluted
- 1 small onion, chopped
- 2 cans (one 15 ounces, one 8 ounces) pizza sauce

- 1 package (3-1/2 ounces) sliced pepperoni
- 1 can (6 ounces) pitted ripe olives, drained and halved

In a skillet, cook sausage over medium heat until no longer pink; drain. Cook pasta according to package directions; drain.

In a 5-qt. slow cooker, layer half of the sausage, pasta, cheese, soup, onion, pizza sauce, pepperoni and olives. Repeat the layers. Cover and cook on low for 4 hours. Yield: 6-8 servings.

Pennsylvania Pot Roast

PREP: 10 MIN.
COOK: 8 HOURS 10 MIN.

I adapted this one-dish meal from a Pennsylvania Dutch recipe. I start the pot roast cooking before I leave for church, add vegetables when I get home, and then just sit back and relax until it's done.
—*Donna Wilkinson*
Clarksburg, Maryland

- 1 boneless pork shoulder roast (2-1/2 to 3 pounds), cut in half
- 1-1/2 cups beef broth
- 1/2 cup sliced green onions
- 1 teaspoon dried basil
- 1 teaspoon dried marjoram
- 1/2 teaspoon salt
- 1/2 teaspoon pepper
- 1 bay leaf
- 6 medium red potatoes, cut into 2-inch chunks
- 4 medium carrots, cut into 2-inch chunks

Slow-Cooked Ham

Entertaining doesn't get much easier than when you serve this five-ingredient entree. I first prepared it for Christmas with great results. Leftovers are delicious in casseroles.
—*Heather Spring*
Sheppard Air Force Base, Texas

Cider Pork Roast

PREP: 20 MIN.
COOK: 5 HOURS 10 MIN.

- 1 boneless pork loin roast (2 pounds)
- 3/4 teaspoon salt
- 1/4 teaspoon pepper
- 2 cups apple cider *or* unsweetened apple juice, *divided*
- 3 spring fresh rosemary
- 1/2 cup dried cherries
- 5 teaspoons cornstarch

Sprinkle pork with salt and pepper. In a nonstick skillet coated with nonstick cooking spray, brown pork for about 4 minutes on each side. Pour 1 cup apple cider in a 3-qt. slow cooker. Place two sprigs rosemary in slow cooker; top with meat and remaining rosemary. Place cherries around roast. Cover and cook on low for 5-6 hours or until a meat thermometer reads 160°.

Remove meat; keep warm. Strain cooking liquid; reserve liquid and transfer to a small saucepan. Stir in 3/4 cup cider; bring to a boil. Combine the cornstarch and remaining cider until smooth. Gradually whisk into cider mixture. Bring to a boil; cook and stir for 1-2 minutes or until thickened. Serve with meat. Yield: 6 servings.

Italian Pork Chop Dinner

PREP: 30 MIN. **COOK:** 4 HOURS

I serve these appetizing pork chops with spaghetti, a tossed salad and garlic bread alongside.
—Martina Williams
Grovetown, Georgia

- 6 bacon strips, diced
- 1/2 pound fresh mushrooms, sliced
- 1 medium onion, finely chopped
- 1 garlic clove, minced
- 3/4 cup all-purpose flour
- 4 teaspoons Italian seasoning, *divided*
- 1/4 teaspoon salt
- 1/4 teaspoon garlic powder
- 1/8 teaspoon pepper
- Dash cayenne pepper
- 6 bone-in pork loin chops (1 inch thick)
- 1 can (14-1/2 ounces) diced tomatoes, undrained
- 1 can (14-1/2 ounces) chicken broth
- 1 can (6 ounces) tomato paste
- 1 package (10 ounces) frozen peas, thawed
- Hot cooked pasta

In a large skillet, cook the bacon over medium heat until crisp. Using a slotted spoon, remove to paper towels. In the drippings, saute mushrooms, onion and garlic until tender. Transfer to a 5-qt. slow cooker with a slotted spoon. In a shallow bowl, combine flour, 3 teaspoons Italian seasoning, salt, garlic powder, pepper and cayenne; coat pork chops with flour mixture.

In the same skillet, brown the pork chops; transfer to the slow cooker. Top with tomatoes and bacon. Combine the broth, tomato paste and remaining Italian seasoning; add to slow cooker.

Cover and cook on low for 4-6

Cider Pork Roast

Apple cider, dried cherries and fresh rosemary put the pizzazz in this pleasing pork roast. It's even more flavorful when drizzled with the sweet pan juices.
—Terry Danner
Rochelle, Illinois

Pork Chops with Sauerkraut
Tender pork chops are paired with tangy sauerkraut in this filling main dish. It's a snap to put together.
—Stephanie Miller
Omaha, Nebraska

hours or until pork is tender; add peas during the last 30 minutes. Serve with pasta. Yield: 6 servings.

Pork Chops With Sauerkraut

PREP: 15 MIN. **COOK:** 3 HOURS

- 4 bone-in center-cut pork loin chops (8 ounces *each* and 1/2 inch thick)
- 2 tablespoons vegetable oil
- 1 jar (32 ounces) sauerkraut, undrained
- 3/4 cup packed brown sugar
- 1 medium green pepper, sliced
- 1 medium onion, sliced

In a large skillet over medium heat, brown pork chops in oil for 3-4 minutes on each side; drain.

In a 5-qt. slow cooker, combine the sauerkraut and brown sugar. Top with the pork chops, green pepper and onion. Cover and cook on low for 3 to 3-1/2 hours or until a meat thermometer reads 160°. Serve with a slotted spoon. Yield: 4 servings.

Busy-Day Barbecued Ribs

PREP: 5 MIN. **COOK:** 5 HOURS

I don't have a lot of time on weekends to spend in the kitchen. That's when this recipe comes in handy. I put all the ingredients in the slow cooker, and before I know it, dinner is ready!
—Sherry Smalley
South Milwaukee, Wisconsin

- 3-1/2 to 4 pounds country-style pork ribs
- 1 can (10-3/4 ounces) condensed tomato soup, undiluted
- 1/2 cup packed brown sugar
- 1/3 cup cider vinegar
- 1 tablespoon soy sauce
- 1 teaspoon celery seed
- 1 teaspoon chili powder

Place ribs in a 5-qt. slow cooker. Combine remaining ingredients; pour over ribs. Cover and cook on high for 1 hour. Reduce heat to low and cook 4-5 hours longer. Thicken sauce for gravy if desired. Yield: 6-8 servings.

Burgundy Lamb Shanks

For those who love fall-from-the-bone lamb, this recipe fits the bill. Burgundy wine adds a special touch to the sauce that's served alongside the entree.
—Mrs. F. W. Creutz
Southold, New York

Burgundy Lamb Shanks

PREP: 10 MIN. **COOK:** 8-1/4 HOURS

 4 **lamb shanks (about 20 ounces *each*)**
Salt and pepper to taste
 2 **tablespoons dried parsley flakes**
 2 **teaspoons minced garlic**
 1/2 **teaspoon dried oregano**
 1/2 **teaspoon grated lemon peel**
 1/2 **cup chopped onion**
 1 **medium carrot, chopped**
 1 **teaspoon olive oil**
 1 **cup burgundy wine *or* beef broth**
 1 **teaspoon beef bouillon granules**

Sprinkle lamb with salt and pepper. Place in a 5-qt. slow cooker. Sprinkle with the parsley, garlic, oregano and lemon peel.

In a small saucepan, saute onion and carrot in oil for 3-4 minutes or until tender. Stir in wine or broth and bouillon. Bring to a boil, stirring occasionally. Pour over lamb. Cover and cook on low for 8 hours or until meat is tender.

Remove lamb and keep warm. Strain cooking juices and skim fat. In a small saucepan, bring juices to a boil; cook until liquid is reduced by half. Serve with lamb. Yield: 4 servings.

Polish Kraut And Apples

PREP: 10 MIN. **COOK:** 4 HOURS

 1 **can (14 ounces) sauerkraut, rinsed and well drained**
 1 **package (16 ounces) smoked Polish sausage *or* kielbasa**
 3 **medium tart apples, peeled and cut into eighths**
 1/2 **cup packed brown sugar**
 1/2 **teaspoon caraway seeds, optional**
 1/8 **teaspoon pepper**
 3/4 **cup apple juice**

Place half of sauerkraut in a 3-qt. slow cooker. Top with the sausage, apples, brown sugar, caraway seeds if desired and pepper. Top with remaining sauerkraut. Pour apple juice over all. Cover and cook on low for 4-5 hours or until apples are tender. Yield: 4 servings.

Polish Kraut and Apples

My family loves this hearty meal on cold winter nights. The apples, brown sugar and smoked sausage give this dish a fantastic flavor. I like making it because the prep time is very short.
—Caren Markee
Cary, Illinois

Kapuzta

PREP: 20 MIN. **COOK:** 6 HOURS

- 1-1/2 **pounds pork stew meat**
- 1 **medium onion, chopped**
- 1-1/2 **pounds smoked Polish sausage, cut in 1/2-inch slices**
- 1 **quart sauerkraut, rinsed and well drained**
- 2 **cups coarsely chopped cabbage**
- 1 **tablespoon caraway seeds**
- 1 **can (10-3/4 ounces) condensed cream of mushroom soup, undiluted**

Pepper to taste

In a large skillet, cook pork and onion until pork is no longer pink. Transfer to a 5-qt. slow cooker. Stir in the remaining ingredients. Cover and cook on low for 6-8 hours or until pork is tender. Yield: 6-8 servings.

Barbecued Ribs

PREP: 15 MIN. **COOK:** 4 HOURS

These simple-to-prepare ribs call for everyday ingredients. So I never complain when my family asks me to make them. Everyone enjoys their down-home goodness.
—Alpha Wilson
Roswell, New Mexico

- 3 **pounds pork spareribs**
- 1/2 **teaspoon salt**
- 1/4 **teaspoon pepper**
- 1-3/4 **cups sliced onions**
- 1 **bottle (18 ounces) barbecue sauce**

Place ribs meat side up on a broiling pan. Sprinkle with salt and pepper. Broil 4-6 in. from the heat for 15-20 minutes or until browned. Cool; cut into serving-size pieces.

Place onions in a 5-qt. slow cooker; top with ribs. Pour barbecue sauce over all. Cover and cook on high for 1 hour; reduce heat to low and cook 3-4 hours or until ribs are tender. Yield: 4 servings.

Southwestern Stew

PREP: 10 MIN. **COOK:** 6 HOURS

The flavors of this recipe blend beautifully in this stew. It's so good, it's become our traditional Super Bowl Sunday meal.
—Virginia Price
Cheyenne, Wyoming

- 1-1/2 **pounds boneless pork, trimmed and cut into 1/2-inch cubes**
- 2 **tablespoons vegetable oil**
- 1 **medium onion, chopped**
- 1 **can (15-1/2 ounces) yellow hominy, drained**
- 1 **can (14-1/2 ounces) diced tomatoes, undrained**
- 1 **can (4 ounces) chopped green chilies**
- 1/2 **cup water**
- 1/2 **teaspoon chili powder**
- 1/4 **teaspoon garlic powder**
- 1/4 **teaspoon ground cumin**
- 1/4 **teaspoon salt**
- 1/4 **teaspoon pepper**

In a large skillet, brown pork in oil over medium-high heat. Add onion and cook for 2 minutes or until tender.

Transfer to a 3-qt. slow cooker;

Kapuzta

This is a truly authentic Old-World recipe—friends of our family who moved here from Poland gave it to my mother years ago. It's been a favorite Sunday dinner with all of us ever since then. I've found that it's always a hit at potluck dinners, too.
—Liz Krocak
Montogomery, Minnesota

Pork and Pinto Beans

I first tasted this dish at an office potluck, and now I serve it often when company comes. I set out an array of toppings and let everyone fix their own taco salad.
—Darlene Brenden
Salem, Oregon

add remaining ingredients. Cover and cook on high for 2 hours. Reduce heat to low and cook 4 hours longer. Yield: 4-6 servings.

Mushroom Pork Tenderloins

PREP: 5 MIN. **COOK:** 4 HOURS

Pork tenderloin is cooked in a savory gravy to perfection—it's the best you'll ever taste. Prepared with canned soups, it couldn't be easier to assemble.
—Donna Hughes
Rochester, New Hampshire

- 2 pork tenderloins (1 pound *each*)
- 1 can (10-3/4 ounces) condensed cream of mushroom soup, undiluted
- 1 can (10-3/4 ounces) condensed golden mushroom soup, undiluted
- 1 can (10-1/2 ounces) condensed French onion soup, undiluted

Hot mashed potatoes, optional

Place pork in a 3-qt. slow cooker. In a bowl, combine the soups; stir until smooth. Pour over pork. Cover and cook on low for 4-5 hours or until the meat is tender, and a meat thermometer reads 160° Serve with mashed potatoes if desired. Yield: 6 servings.

Pork and Pinto Beans

PREP: 25 MIN. + STANDING
COOK: 8 HOURS

- 1 pound dried pinto beans
- 1 boneless pork loin roast (3 to 4 pounds), cut in half
- 1 can (14-1/2 ounces) stewed tomatoes
- 5 medium carrots, chopped
- 4 celery ribs, chopped
- 1-1/2 cups water
- 2 cans (4 ounces *each*) chopped green chilies
- 2 tablespoons chili powder
- 4 garlic cloves, minced
- 2 teaspoons ground cumin
- 1 teaspoon dried oregano

Dash pepper
- 2 packages (10-1/2 ounces *each*) corn tortilla chips *or* 30 flour tortillas (10 inches)

Chopped green onions, sliced ripe olives, chopped tomatoes, shredded cheddar cheese, sour cream *and/or* shredded lettuce

Sort beans and rinse with cold water. Place beans in a Dutch oven; add water to cover by 2 in. Bring to a boil; boil for 2 minutes. Remove from the heat; cover and let stand for 1 to 4 hours or until beans are softened.

Drain and rinse beans, discarding liquid. Place roast in a 5-qt. slow cooker. In a bowl, combine the beans, tomatoes, carrots, celery, water, chilies, chili powder, garlic, cumin, oregano and pepper. Pour over roast. Cover and cook on high for 3 hours. Reduce heat to low; cook 5 hours longer or until beans are tender.

Remove meat, shred with two forks and return to slow cooker. With a slotted spoon, serve meat mixture over corn chips or in tortillas; serve with toppings of your choice. Yield: 10 servings.

Garlic-Apple Pork Roast

I've become famous among my friends for this tasty meal. The garlic and apple flavors really complement the pork. It's great with steamed fresh asparagus and roasted red potatoes.
—Jennifer Loos
Washington Boro, Pennsylvania

Garlic-Apple Pork Roast

PREP: 10 MIN. **COOK:** 8 HOURS

- 1 boneless whole pork loin roast (3-1/2 to 4 pounds), cut in half
- 1 jar (12 ounces) apple jelly
- 1/2 cup water
- 2-1/2 teaspoons minced garlic
- 1 tablespoon dried parsley flakes
- 1 to 1-1/2 teaspoons seasoned salt
- 1 to 1-1/2 teaspoons pepper

Place roast in a 5-qt. slow cooker. In a bowl, combine the jelly, water and garlic; pour over roast. Sprinkle with parsley, salt and pepper.

Cover and cook on low for 8 to 8-1/2 hours or until a meat thermometer reads 160° and meat is tender. Let stand for 5 minutes before slicing. Serve with cooking juices if desired. Yield: 12 servings.

Creamy Ham 'n' Broccoli

PREP: 10 MIN.
COOK: 2 HOURS + STANDING

- 3 cups cubed fully cooked ham
- 1 package (10 ounces) frozen chopped broccoli, thawed
- 1 can (10-3/4 ounces) condensed cream of mushroom soup, undiluted
- 1 jar (8 ounces) process cheese sauce
- 1 can (8 ounces) sliced water chestnuts, drained
- 1-1/4 cups uncooked instant rice
- 1 cup milk
- 1 celery rib, chopped
- 1 medium onion, chopped
- 1/8 to 1/4 teaspoon pepper
- 1/2 teaspoon paprika

In a 3-qt. slow cooker, combine the first 10 ingredients. Cover and cook on high for 2-3 hours or until the rice is tender. Let stand for 10 minutes before serving. Sprinkle with paprika. Yield: 6-8 servings.

Creamy Ham 'n' Broccoli

This sensational dish is so wonderful to come home to, especially on a cool fall or winter day. It's a delicious way to use up leftover holiday ham, too.
—Jill Pennington
Jacksonville, Florida

Side Dishes

Pineapple Baked Beans

PREP: 10 MIN. **COOK:** 4 HOURS

Tangy pineapple dresses up these hearty baked beans. Brown the beef while you open cans and chop the vegetables, and it won't take long to get this side dish ready for the slow cooker.
—*Gladys De Boer*
Castleford, Idaho

- 1 **pound ground beef**
- 1 **can (28 ounces) baked beans**
- 1 **can (8 ounces) pineapple tidbits, drained**
- 1 **jar (4-1/2 ounces) sliced mushrooms, drained**
- 1 **large onion, chopped**
- 1 **large green pepper, chopped**
- 1/2 **cup barbecue sauce**
- 2 **tablespoons soy sauce**
- 1 **garlic clove, minced**
- 1/2 **teaspoon salt**
- 1/4 **teaspoon pepper**

In a skillet, cook beef over medium heat until no longer pink; drain. Transfer to a 5-qt. slow cooker. Add remaining ingredients and mix well. Cover and cook on low for 4-8 hours or until bubbly. Serve in bowls. Yield: 12-16 side-dish or 6-8 main-dish servings.

Slow-Cooked Vegetables

PREP: 10 MIN. **COOK:** 7 HOURS

- 4 **celery ribs, cut into 1-inch pieces**
- 4 **small carrots, cut into 1-inch pieces**
- 2 **medium tomatoes, cut into chunks**
- 2 **medium onions, thinly sliced**
- 2 **cups cut fresh green beans (1-inch pieces)**
- 1 **medium green pepper, cut into 1-inch pieces**
- 1/4 **cup butter, melted**
- 3 **tablespoons quick-cooking tapioca**
- 1 **tablespoon sugar**
- 2 **teaspoons salt, optional**
- 1/8 **teaspoon pepper**

Place the vegetables in a 3-qt. slow cooker. In a small bowl, combine the butter, tapioca, sugar, salt if desired and pepper; pour over vegetables and stir well.

Cover and cook on low for 7-8 hours or until vegetables are tender. Serve with a slotted spoon. Yield: 8 servings.

Slow-Cooked Vegetables
An assortment of garden-fresh vegetables is simmered into this satisfying side dish. My sister-in-law shared this recipe with me. It's a favorite at holiday gatherings and potlucks.
—*Kathy Westendorf*
Westgate, Iowa

Scalloped Taters

PREP: 10 MIN. **COOK:** 4-1/2 HOURS

- 1 package (2 pounds) frozen cubed hash brown potatoes
- 1 can (10-3/4 ounces) condensed cream of chicken soup, undiluted
- 1-1/2 cups milk
- 1 cup (4 ounces) shredded cheddar cheese
- 1/2 cup plus 1 tablespoon butter, melted, *divided*
- 1/4 cup dried minced onions
- 1/2 teaspoon salt
- 1/8 teaspoon pepper
- 3/4 cup crushed cornflakes

In a large bowl, combine the hash browns, soup, milk, cheese, 1/2 cup butter, onion, salt and pepper. Pour into a greased 5-qt. slow cooker. Cover and cook on low for 4-1/2 to 5 hours or until potatoes are tender.

Just before serving, combine the cornflake crumbs and remaining butter in a pie plate. Bake at 350° for 4-6 minutes or until golden brown. Stir the potatoes; sprinkle with crumb topping. Yield: 12 servings.

Corn Spoon Bread

PREP: 15 MIN. **COOK:** 3 HOURS

The holidays would not be complete if I didn't serve this old-fashioned side dish. It's moister than corn pudding made in the oven, plus the cream cheese is a nice addition.
—Tamara Ellefson
Frederic, Wisconsin

- 1 package (8 ounces) cream cheese, softened
- 1/3 cup sugar
- 1 cup milk
- 1/2 cup egg substitute
- 2 tablespoons butter, melted
- 1 teaspoon salt
- 1/4 teaspoon ground nutmeg
- Dash pepper
- 2-1/3 cups frozen corn, thawed
- 1 can (14-3/4 ounces) cream-style corn
- 1 package (8-1/2 ounces) corn bread/muffin mix

In a large mixing bowl, beat cream cheese and sugar until smooth. Gradually beat in milk. Beat in the egg substitute, butter, salt, nutmeg and pepper until blended. Stir in corn and cream-style corn. Stir in corn bread mix just until moistened.

Pour into a greased 3-qt. slow cooker. Cover and cook on high for 3-4 hours or until center is almost set. Yield: 8 servings.

Slow-Cooked Sage Dressing

PREP: 15 MIN. **COOK:** 4 HOURS

This recipe is such a help when I fix a large meal. It leaves room in the oven for other dishes since it's made in a slow cooker.
—Ellen Benninger
Stoneboro, Pennsylvania

- 14 to 15 cups day-old bread cubes
- 3 cups chopped celery
- 1-1/2 cups chopped onion
- 1-1/2 teaspoons rubbed sage

Scalloped Taters
Convenient frozen hash browns make this creamy side dish a snap to assemble. And, it's great with almost any entree. This is a good way to make potatoes when your oven is busy with other dishes.
—Lucinda Wolker
Somerset, Pennsylvania

Zippy Bean Stew

This bean stew is a staple for my co-workers and me once the weather turns cool. Although this is a low-fat dish, it definitely doesn't taste like it!
—Debbie Matthews
Bluefield, West Virginia

Zippy Bean Stew

PREP: 10 MIN. **COOK:** 4 HOURS

- 1 can (14-1/2 ounces) vegetable broth *or* reduced-sodium chicken broth
- 1 can (16 ounces) kidney beans, rinsed and drained
- 1 can (15 ounces) pinto beans, rinsed and drained
- 1 can (14-1/2 ounces) diced tomatoes and green chilies
- 1 can (4 ounces) chopped green chilies, undrained
- 2 cups frozen corn, thawed
- 3 cups water
- 1 large onion, chopped
- 2 medium carrots, sliced
- 2 garlic cloves, minced
- 2 teaspoons chili powder

Combine all ingredients in a 3-qt. slow cooker. Cover and cook on high for 4-5 hours or until heated through and flavors are blended. Yield: 6 servings.

- 1 teaspoon salt
- 1/2 teaspoon pepper
- 1-1/4 cups butter, melted

Combine the bread, celery, onion, sage, salt and pepper. Add butter and toss. Spoon into a 5-qt. slow cooker. Cover and cook on low for 4-5 hours, stirring once. Yield: about 12 servings.

Squash Stuffing Casserole

PREP: 15 MIN. **COOK:** 4 HOURS

My friends just rave about this rich side dish. It's so easy to jazz up summer squash, zucchini and carrots with canned soup and stuffing mix.
—Pamela Thorson
Hot Springs, Arkansas

- 1/4 cup all-purpose flour
- 1 can (10-3/4 ounces) condensed cream of chicken soup, undiluted
- 1 cup (8 ounces) sour cream
- 2 medium yellow summer squash, cut into 1/2-inch slices
- 1 small onion, chopped
- 1 cup shredded carrots
- 1 package (8 ounces) stuffing mix
- 1/2 cup butter, melted

In a bowl, combine the flour, soup and sour cream until blended. Add the vegetables and gently stir to coat. Combine the stuffing mix and butter; sprinkle half into a 5-qt. slow cooker. Top with vegetable mixture and remaining stuffing mixture. Cover and cook on low for 4-5 hours or until vegetables are tender. Yield: 8 servings.

Side Dishes *231*

Marmalade-Glazed Carrots

This side dish is ideal when you'd like to serve your vegetables in a different way for a special dinner. Cinnamon and nutmeg season baby carrots that are simmered with orange marmalade and brown sugar.
—Barb Rudyk
Vermilion, Alberta

Marmalade Carrots

PREP: 10 MIN. **COOK:** 5-1/2 HOURS

- 1 package (2 pounds) fresh baby carrots
- 1/2 cup orange marmalade
- 3 tablespoons cold water, *divided*
- 2 tablespoons brown sugar
- 1 tablespoon butter, melted
- 1/2 teaspoon ground cinnamon
- 1/4 teaspoon salt
- 1/4 teaspoon ground nutmeg
- 1/8 teaspoon pepper
- 1 tablespoon cornstarch

In a 3-qt. slow cooker, combine the carrots, marmalade, 1 tablespoon water, brown sugar, butter and seasonings. Cover and cook on low for 5-6 hours or until carrots are tender.

Combine cornstarch and remaining water until smooth; stir into carrot mixture. Cover and cook on high for 30 minutes or until thickened. Serve with a slotted spoon. Yield: 6 servings.

Cheesy Potatoes

PREP: 10 MIN. **COOK:** 8 HOURS

- 6 medium potatoes, peeled and cut into 1/4-inch strips
- 2 cups (8 ounces) shredded cheddar cheese
- 1 can (10-3/4 ounces) condensed cream of chicken soup, undiluted
- 1 small onion, chopped *or* 1 tablespoon dried minced onion
- 7 tablespoons butter, melted, *divided*
- 1 teaspoon salt
- 1 teaspoon pepper
- 1 cup (8 ounces) sour cream
- 2 cups seasoned stuffing cubes

Toss the potatoes and cheese; place in a 5-qt. slow cooker. Combine the soup, onion, 4 tablespoons butter, salt and pepper; pour over potato mixture.

Cover and cook on low for 8-10 hours or until potatoes are tender. Stir in sour cream. Toss stuffing cubes and remaining butter; sprinkle over potatoes. Yield: 10-12 servings.

Cheesy Potatoes

For a satisfying side dish that feeds a crowd, try these saucy potatoes. A simple topping of buttered croutons accents the creamy combination.
—Melissa Marzolf
Marysville, Michigan

Cheddar Spirals

PREP: 20 MIN. **COOK:** 2-1/2 HOURS

- 1 package (16 ounces) spiral pasta
- 2 cups half-and-half cream
- 1 can (10-3/4 ounces) condensed cheddar cheese soup
- 1/2 cup butter, melted
- 4 cups (16 ounces) shredded cheddar cheese

Cook pasta according to package directions; drain. In a 5-qt. slow cooker, combine the cream, soup and butter until smooth; stir in the cheese and pasta. Cover and cook on low for 2-1/2 hours or until cheese is melted. Yield: 12-15 servings.

Cheddar Spirals

Our kids just love this and will sample a spoonful right from the slow cooker when they walk by. Sometimes I add cocktail sausages, sliced Polish sausage or cubed ham to the cheesy pasta for a hearty, all-in-one dinner.
—*Heidi Ferkovich*
Park Falls, Wisconsin

Pineapple Sweet Potatoes

PREP: 10 MIN. **COOK:** 4 HOURS

Pineapple and pecans make a pretty topping for this no-fuss, fall side dish. Making it in the slow cooker leaves extra space in the oven when preparing a holiday turkey and other dishes.
—*Bette Fulcher, Lexington, Texas*

- 4 eggs
- 1 cup milk
- 1/2 cup butter, softened
- 6 to 6-1/2 cups mashed sweet potatoes (without added milk *or* butter)
- 1 teaspoon vanilla extract
- 1 teaspoon salt
- 1 teaspoon ground cinnamon
- 1/2 teaspoon ground nutmeg
- 1/2 teaspoon lemon extract
- 1 can (8 ounces) sliced pineapple, drained
- 1/4 cup chopped pecans

In a large mixing bowl, combine the first nine ingredients. Transfer to a 3-qt. slow cooker. Top with pineapple slices and pecans. Cover and cook on low for 4-5 hours or until a thermometer reads 160°. Yield: 12-14 servings.

Roasted Red Pepper Sauce

PREP: 15 MIN. **COOK:** 4 HOURS

I often use Greek olives with the artichoke hearts to add zing to this pasta sauce. Roast the peppers yourself if you have the time.
—*Mrs. Timothy Tosh*
Lumberton, New Jersey

- 4 pounds plum tomatoes (about 17), coarsely chopped
- 1 large sweet onion, chopped
- 1 can (29 ounces) tomato puree
- 3 jars (7 ounces *each*) roasted sweet red peppers, drained and chopped
- 2 jars (6-1/2 ounces *each*) marinated artichoke hearts, drained and chopped
- 1/2 pound fresh mushrooms, quartered
- 2 cans (2-1/4 ounces *each*) sliced ripe olives, drained
- 1/4 cup sugar
- 1/4 cup balsamic vinegar
- 1/4 cup olive oil

Vegetable Medley
This is a wonderful side dish to make when garden vegetables are plentiful. The colorful combination is a great complement to any entree.
—*Terry Maly*
Olathe, Kansas

3 garlic cloves, minced
1 tablespoon dried basil
1 tablespoon dried oregano
1 teaspoon salt
Hot cooked pasta

In a 5-qt. slow cooker, combine the first 14 ingredients. Cover and cook on high for 4 hours or until flavors are blended. Serve over pasta. Yield: about 15 cups.

Hearty Pork 'n' Beans

PREP: 15 MIN. **COOK:** 4 HOURS

Serve these sweet chunky beans at a barbecue or potluck. They're also a good main dish with French bread or corn bread.
—*Janice Toms, Saline, Louisiana*

1 pound ground beef
1 medium green pepper, chopped

1 small onion, chopped
1 package (16 ounces) smoked sausage, halved lengthwise and thinly sliced
1 can (16 ounces) pork and beans, undrained
1 can (15-1/4 ounces) lima beans, rinsed and drained
1 can (15 ounces) pinto beans, rinsed and drained
1 cup ketchup
1/2 cup packed brown sugar
1 teaspoon salt
1/2 teaspoon garlic powder
1/4 teaspoon pepper

In a skillet, cook beef, green pepper and onion over medium heat until meat is no longer pink; drain.

In a 5-qt. slow cooker, combine the remaining ingredients. Stir in beef mixture. Cover and cook on high for 4-5 hours or until heated through. Yield: 12 side-dish or 8 main-dish servings.

Vegetable Medley

PREP: 5 MIN. **COOK:** 5 HOURS

4 cups diced peeled potatoes
1-1/2 cups frozen whole kernel corn *or* 1 can (15-1/4 ounces) whole kernel corn, drained
4 medium tomatoes, seeded and diced
1 cup sliced carrots
1/2 cup chopped onion
3/4 teaspoon salt
1/2 teaspoon sugar
1/2 teaspoon dill weed
1/8 teaspoon pepper

In a 3-qt. slow cooker, combine all ingredients. Cover and cook on low for 5-6 hours or until vegetables are tender. Yield: 8 servings.

Creamy Red Potatoes

This side dish features cubed red potatoes that are cooked in a creamy coating until tender. Be sure to stir the mixture before serving to help the sauce thicken.

—Elaine Ryan
Holley, New York

Creamy Red Potatoes

PREP: 5 MIN. **COOK:** 5 HOURS

- 7 cups cubed uncooked red potatoes
- 1 cup (8 ounces) 4% cottage cheese
- 1/2 cup sour cream
- 1/2 cup cubed process cheese (Velveeta)
- 1 tablespoon dried minced onion
- 2 garlic cloves, minced
- 1/2 teaspoon salt

Paprika and minced chives, optional

Place the potatoes in a 3-qt. slow cooker. In a blender or food processor, puree cottage cheese and sour cream until smooth. Transfer to a bowl; stir in the process cheese, onion, garlic and salt. Pour over potatoes and mix well.

Cover and cook on low for 5-6 hours or until potatoes are tender. Stir well before serving. Garnish with paprika and chives if desired. Yield: 8 servings.

Spiced Acorn Squash

PREP: 10 MIN. **COOK:** 4 HOURS

- 3/4 cup packed brown sugar
- 1 teaspoon ground cinnamon
- 1 teaspoon ground nutmeg
- 2 small acorn squash, halved and seeded
- 3/4 cup raisins
- 4 tablespoons butter
- 1/2 cup water

In a small bowl, combine the brown sugar, cinnamon and nutmeg; spoon into squash halves. Sprinkle with raisins. Top each with 1 tablespoon of butter. Wrap each squash half individually in heavy-duty foil; seal tightly.

Pour water into a 5-qt. slow cooker. Place the squash cut side up in slow cooker (packets may be stacked). Cover and cook on high for 4 hours or until the squash is tender. Open foil packets carefully to allow steam to escape. Yield: 4 servings.

Spiced Acorn Squash

Working full-time, I found I didn't always have time to cook the meals my family loved. So I re-created many of our favorites in the slow cooker. This cinnamony treatment for squash is one of them.

—Carol Greco
Centereach, New York

Sausage Dressing

PREP: 20 MIN. **COOK:** 4 HOURS

- 1 pound bulk pork sausage
- 1 large onion, chopped
- 2 celery ribs, chopped
- 1 package (14 ounces) seasoned stuffing croutons
- 1 can (14-1/2 ounces) chicken broth
- 1 large tart apple, chopped
- 1 cup chopped walnuts *or* pecans
- 1/2 cup egg substitute
- 1/4 cup butter, melted
- 1-1/2 teaspoons rubbed sage
- 1/2 teaspoon pepper

In a large skillet, cook the sausage, onion and celery over medium heat until meat is no longer pink; drain. Transfer to a greased 5-qt. slow cooker. Stir in the remaining ingredients. Cover and cook on low for 4-5 hours or until heated through and a thermometer reads 160°. Yield: 12 servings.

Hearty Wild Rice

PREP: 15 MIN. **COOK:** 5 HOURS

My father-in-law used to make this casserole in the oven. I switched it to the slow cooker so I wouldn't need to keep an eye on it. This tasty rice dish complements many meals.
—Mrs. Garnet Pettigrew
Columbia City, Indiana

- 1 pound ground beef
- 1/2 pound bulk pork sausage
- 6 celery ribs, diced
- 2 cans (10-1/2 ounces *each*) condensed beef broth, undiluted
- 1-1/4 cups water
- 1 medium onion, chopped
- 1 cup uncooked wild rice
- 1 can (4 ounces) mushroom stems and pieces, drained
- 1/4 cup soy sauce

In a large skillet, cook beef and sausage over medium heat until no longer pink; drain. Transfer to a 5-qt. slow cooker. Add the celery, broth, water, onion, rice, mushrooms and soy sauce; mix well. Cover and cook on high for 1 hour. Reduce heat to low; cover and cook for 4 hours or until the rice is tender. Yield: 10-12 servings.

Mushroom Potatoes

PREP: 25 MIN. **COOK:** 6 HOURS

Sliced potatoes are jazzed up with mushrooms, onions, canned soup and cheese to create this versatile recipe. With its comforting flavor, it's a nice accompaniment to most meats.
—Linda Bernard
Golden Meadow, Louisiana

- 7 medium potatoes, peeled and thinly sliced
- 1 medium onion, sliced
- 4 garlic cloves, minced
- 2 green onions, chopped
- 1 can (8 ounces) mushroom stems and pieces, drained
- 1/4 cup all-purpose flour
- 2 teaspoons salt

Sausage Dressing

I rely on this slow-cooker recipe at Thanksgiving when there's no room in the oven to bake stuffing. The results are fantastic—very moist and appetizing. Even family members who don't usually eat stuffing had some.
—Mary Kendall
Appleton, Wisconsin

Sausage Spanish Rice
Both my husband and I work the midnight shift, so I'm always on the lookout for slow-cooker recipes. It's good as a side dish, but we often enjoy it as the main course because it's so hearty.
—Michelle McKay
Garden City, Michigan

Sausage Spanish Rice

PREP: 5 MIN. **COOK:** 5 HOURS

- 1 pound fully cooked kielbasa or Polish sausage, cut into 1/4-inch slices
- 2 cans (14-1/2 ounces *each*) diced tomatoes, undrained
- 2 cups water
- 1-1/2 cups uncooked converted rice
- 1 cup salsa
- 1 medium onion
- 1/2 cup chopped green pepper
- 1/2 cup chopped sweet red pepper
- 1 can (4 ounces) chopped green chilies
- 1 envelope taco seasoning

In a 3-qt. slow cooker, combine all the ingredients; stir to combine. Cover and cook on low for 5-6 hours or until rice is tender. Yield: 9 servings.

- 1/2 teaspoon pepper
- 1/4 cup butter, cubed
- 1 can (10-3/4 ounces) condensed cream of mushroom soup, undiluted
- 1 cup (4 ounces) shredded Colby-Monterey Jack cheese

In a 3-qt. slow cooker, layer half of the potatoes, onion, garlic, green onions, mushrooms, flour, salt, pepper and butter. Repeat layers. Pour soup over the top.

Cover and cook on low for 6-8 hours or until potatoes are tender; sprinkle with cheese during the last 30 minutes of cooking time. Yield: 8-10 servings.

Rich Spinach Casserole

PREP: 10 MIN. **COOK:** 2-1/2 HOURS

I found this recipe in an old slow-cooker cookbook. When I took the side dish to our church sewing circle, it was a big hit.
— Vioda Geyer, Uhrichsville, Ohio

- 2 packages (10 ounces *each*) frozen chopped spinach, thawed and well drained
- 2 cups (16 ounces) 4% cottage cheese
- 1 cup cubed process cheese (Velveeta)
- 3/4 cup egg substitute
- 2 tablespoons butter, cubed
- 1/4 cup all-purpose flour
- 1/2 teaspoon salt

In a 3-qt. slow cooker, combine all ingredients; mix well. Cover and cook on low for 2-1/2 hours or until the cheese is melted. Yield: 8 servings.

Creamy Corn

A handful of ingredients are all you'll need for this comforting side. I first tasted it at a potluck with our camping club. It's easy to assemble and frees up time to prepare the main course.
—Judy McCarthy
Derby, Kansas

Creamy Corn

PREP: 5 MIN. **COOK:** 4 HOURS

- 2 packages (16 ounces *each*) frozen corn
- 1 package (8 ounces) cream cheese, cubed
- 1/3 cup butter, cubed
- 1/2 teaspoon garlic powder
- 1/2 teaspoon salt
- 1/4 teaspoon pepper

In a 3-qt. slow cooker, combine all ingredients. Cover and cook on low for 4 hours or until heated through and cheese is melted. Stir well before serving. Yield: 6 servings.

Michigan Bean Bake

PREP: 10 MIN. **BAKE:** 8 HOURS

Just let this go all day for a great-tasting baked bean side dish.
—Sondra Bergy, Lowell, Michigan

- 1 jar (48 ounces) great northern beans, rinsed and drained
- 1-1/2 pounds lean pork, cut into 1-inch cubes

- 1/2 teaspoon salt
- 1 bottle (14 ounces) ketchup
- 3 tablespoons prepared mustard
- 1-1/2 cups packed brown sugar
- 1/4 large sweet onion, chopped

Combine all ingredients; mix gently but well. Place in a 3-qt. slow cooker. Cover and cook on low for 8-10 hours. Or, place in beanpot or baking dish. Bake at 325°, uncovered, for 5 to 6 hours; cover last hour. Yield: 10-12 servings.

Au Gratin Garlic Potatoes

PREP: 10 MIN. **COOK:** 6 HOURS

- 1/2 cup milk
- 1 can (10-3/4 ounces) condensed cheddar cheese soup, undiluted
- 1 package (8 ounces) cream cheese, cubed
- 1 garlic clove, minced
- 1/4 teaspoon ground nutmeg
- 1/8 teaspoon pepper

- 2 pounds potatoes, peeled and sliced
- 1 small onion, chopped
Paprika, optional

In a saucepan, heat milk over medium heat until bubbles form around side of saucepan. Remove from the heat. Add the soup, cream cheese, garlic, nutmeg and pepper; stir until smooth.

Place the potatoes and onion in a 3-qt. slow cooker. Pour the milk mixture over the potato mixture; mix well. Cover and cook on low for 6-7 hours or until potatoes are tender. Sprinkle with paprika if desired. Yield: 6-8 servings.

Au Gratin Garlic Potatoes

Cream cheese and a can of cheese soup turn ordinary sliced potatoes into a rich side dish that's the perfect extra with any meal.
—Tonya Vowels
Vine Grove, Kentucky

Desserts

Black and Blue Cobbler

PREP: 15 MIN.
COOK: 2 HOURS + STANDING

It never occurred to me that I could bake a cobbler in my slow cooker, until I saw some recipes and decided to try my favorite fruity dessert recipe. It took a bit of experimenting, but the tasty results are "berry" well worth it.
—Martha Creveling
Orlando, Florida

1	cup all-purpose flour
1-1/2	cups sugar, *divided*
1	teaspoon baking powder
1/4	teaspoon salt
1/4	teaspoon ground cinnamon
1/4	teaspoon ground nutmeg
2	eggs, beaten
2	tablespoons milk
2	tablespoons vegetable oil
2	cups fresh *or* frozen blackberries
2	cups fresh *or* frozen blueberries
3/4	cup water
1	teaspoon grated orange peel

Whipped cream *or* vanilla ice cream, optional

In a bowl, combine flour, 3/4 cup sugar, baking powder, salt, cinnamon and nutmeg. Combine eggs, milk and oil; stir into dry ingredients just until moistened. Spread the batter evenly onto the bottom of a greased 5-qt. slow cooker.

In a saucepan, combine berries, water, orange peel and remaining sugar; bring to a boil. Remove from the heat; immediately pour over batter. Cover and cook on high for 2 to 2-1/2 hours or until a toothpick inserted into the batter comes out clean. Turn cooker off. Uncover and let stand for 30 minutes before serving. Serve with whipped cream or ice cream if desired. Yield: 6 servings.

Granola Apple Crisp

PREP: 20 MIN. **COOK:** 5 HOURS

8	medium tart apples, peeled and sliced
1/4	cup lemon juice
1-1/2	teaspoons grated lemon peel
2-1/2	cups granola with fruit and nuts
1	cup sugar
1	teaspoon ground cinnamon
1/2	cup butter, melted

In a large bowl, toss the apples, lemon juice and peel. Transfer to a greased 3-qt. slow cooker. Combine the cereal, sugar and cinnamon; sprinkle over apples. Drizzle with butter. Cover and cook on low for 5-6 hours or until the apples are tender. Serve warm. Yield: 6-8 servings.

Granola Apple Crisp
Tender apple slices are tucked beneath a sweet, crunchy topping in this comforting crisp. For variety, replace the apples with your favorite fruit.
—Barbara Schindler
Napoleon, Ohio

These warm, spiced pears look elegant, yet they're incredibly easy to make. Your friends won't believe this fancy-looking dessert actually took just a few minutes of your time.
—*Elizabeth Hanes, Peralta, New Mexico*

Slow-Cooker Berry Cobbler

Slow-Cooker Berry Cobbler

I adapted my mom's yummy cobbler recipe for slow cooking. With the hot summers here in Arizona, we can still enjoy this delectable dessert, and I don't have to turn on the oven.
—*Karen Jarocki*
Yuma, Arizona

PREP: 15 MIN. **COOK:** 2 HOURS

1-1/4	cups all-purpose flour, *divided*
2	tablespoons plus 1 cup sugar, *divided*
1	teaspoon baking powder
1/4	teaspoon ground cinnamon
1	egg, lightly beaten
1/4	cup fat-free milk
2	tablespoons canola oil
1/8	teaspoon salt
2	cups unsweetened raspberries
2	cups unsweetened blueberries
2	cups reduced-fat frozen vanilla yogurt, optional

In a bowl, combine 1 cup flour, 2 tablespoons sugar, baking powder and cinnamon. In another bowl, combine the egg, milk and oil; stir into dry ingredients just until moistened (batter will be thick). Spread batter evenly onto the bottom of a 5-qt. slow cooker coated with nonstick cooking spray.

In a bowl, combine salt and remaining flour and sugar; add berries and toss to coat. Spread over batter. Cover and cook on high for 2 to 2-1/2 hours or until a toothpick inserted into cobbler comes out without crumbs. Top each serving with 1/4 cup frozen yogurt if desired. **Yield:** 8 servings.

Burgundy Pears

PREP: 10 MIN. **COOK:** 3 HOURS

6	medium ripe pears
1/3	cup sugar
1/3	cup Burgundy wine *or* grape juice
3	tablespoons orange marmalade
1	tablespoon lemon juice
1/4	teaspoon ground cinnamon
1/4	teaspoon ground nutmeg

Dash salt

Whipped cream cheese

Peel pears, leaving stems intact. Core from the bottom. Stand pears upright in a 5-qt. slow cooker. In a small bowl, combine the sugar, wine or grape juice, marmalade, lemon juice, cinnamon, nutmeg and salt.

Soups

Chicken & Turkey 248

Beef & Ground Beef 268

Pork, Ham & Sausage 286

Meatless 302

Cream Soups & Chowders 318

Beans & Lentils 338

Chili 354

Indexes 371

Chicken & Turkey

Chicken Noodle Soup

PREP: 35 MIN.
COOK: 2 HOURS + COOLING

- 1 stewing chicken (2 to 3 pounds)
- 2-1/2 quarts water
- 3 teaspoons salt
- 2 teaspoons chicken bouillon granules
- 1/2 medium onion, chopped
- 1/8 teaspoon pepper
- 1/4 teaspoon dried marjoram
- 1/4 teaspoon dried thyme
- 1 bay leaf
- 1 cup diced carrots
- 1 cup diced celery
- 1-1/2 cups uncooked fine noodles

In a large soup kettle, place first 11 ingredients. Cover and slowly bring to a boil; skim foam. Reduce heat; cover and simmer 1-1/2 hours or until chicken is tender.

Remove chicken from broth; let stand until cool enough to handle. Remove chicken from bones; discard bones and skin. Cut chicken into chunks. Skim fat from broth; bring to a boil. Add noodles; cook until noodles are done. Return chicken to kettle; adjust seasonings to taste. Discard bay leaf. Yield: 8-10 servings.

After-Thanksgiving Turkey Soup

PREP: 15 MIN.
COOK: 2-1/2 HOURS + COOLING

As much as my family loves Thanksgiving, they look forward to this cream soup using leftover turkey even more. It makes a big batch that we can enjoy for days.
—*Valorie Walker*
Bradley, South Carolina

- 1 leftover turkey carcass (from a 12- to 14-pound turkey)
- 3 medium onions, chopped
- 2 large carrots, diced
- 2 celery ribs, diced
- 1 cup butter, cubed
- 1 cup all-purpose flour
- 2 cups half-and-half cream
- 1 cup uncooked long grain rice
- 2 teaspoons salt
- 1 teaspoon chicken bouillon granules
- 3/4 teaspoon pepper

Place turkey carcass in a soup kettle or Dutch oven and cover with water. Slowly bring to a boil. Reduce heat; cover and simmer for 1 hour. Remove carcass; set aside until cool enough to handle. Set aside 3 qt. broth. Remove turkey from bones and discard bones. Cut turkey into bite-size pieces; set aside.

In a soup kettle or Dutch oven, saute the onions, carrots and celery in butter until tender. Reduce heat; stir in flour until blended. Gradually add 1 qt. of reserved broth. Bring to a boil; cook and stir for 2 minutes or until thickened.

Add the cream, rice, salt, bouillon, pepper, remaining broth and reserved turkey. Reduce heat; cover and simmer for 30-35 minutes or until rice is tender. Yield: 16 servings (about 4 quarts).

Chicken Noodle Soup

I often add potatoes and corn to this soup. When I'm ambitious, I'll even make my own homemade noodles.
—*Diane Edgecomb*
Humboldt, South Dakota

Curried Chicken Rice Soup

This is a terrific way to use up leftover chicken and cooked rice. With its mild curry flavor and colorful chunks of carrots and celery, the thick mixture draws rave reviews every time I fix it.
—Judie Anglen, Riverton, Wyoming

Flower Garden Soup

Fresh vegetables and dried herbs flavor traditional chicken soup in this bountiful blend.
—Taste of Home Test Kitchen

Flower Garden Soup

PREP: 15 MIN. **COOK:** 30 MIN.

6	medium carrots
1	medium zucchini
4	celery ribs, chopped
1	medium onion, chopped
8	cans (14-1/2 ounces *each*) chicken broth
1	teaspoon dried basil
1	teaspoon dried oregano
4	cups cubed cooked chicken

Using a zest stripper or paring knife, cut a lengthwise strip on each carrot, forming a notch. Repeat at equal intervals around carrot. Repeat with zucchini. Cut carrots and zucchini into 1/4-in. slices; set zucchini aside.

In a Dutch oven or soup kettle, combine the carrots, celery, onion, broth, basil and oregano. Bring to a boil. Reduce heat; cover and simmer for 20-30 minutes or until vegetables are crisp-tender.

Add chicken and reserved zucchini; simmer, uncovered, for 10 minutes or until zucchini is tender. Yield: 8 servings (2 quarts).

Curried Chicken Rice Soup

PREP/TOTAL TIME: 30 MIN.

2	large carrots, diced
2	celery ribs, diced
1	small onion, chopped
3/4	cup butter
3/4	cup all-purpose flour
1	teaspoon seasoned salt
1/2	to 1 teaspoon curry powder
3	cans (12 ounces *each*) evaporated milk
4	cups chicken broth
2	to 3 cups cubed cooked chicken
2	cups cooked long grain rice

In a large saucepan, saute carrots, celery and onion in butter for 2 minutes. Stir in flour, seasoned salt and curry until smooth. Gradually add milk. Bring to a boil; cook and stir for 2 minutes or until thickened.

Gradually add broth. Stir in chicken and rice. Return to a boil. Reduce heat; simmer, uncovered, for 10 minutes or until vegetables are tender. Yield: 10-12 servings (about 3 quarts).

Southwestern Turkey Dumpling Soup

Here's a Western twist on traditional turkey dumpling soup. I especially like this recipe because it's fast and easy.
—Lisa Williams
Steamboat Springs, Colorado

Santa Fe Cheese Soup

PREP/TOTAL TIME: 25 MIN.

You'll likely have the majority of ingredients for this colorful soup in your pantry. To save time, I start warming the canned ingredients on the stove while I cube the cheese.
—Modie Phillips, Lubbock, Texas

- 1   can (15-1/4 ounces) whole kernel corn, drained
- 1   can (15 ounces) pinto beans, rinsed and drained
- 1   can (14-1/2 ounces) chicken broth
- 1   can (10 ounces) diced tomatoes and green chilies, undrained
- 1   can (10 ounces) premium chunk white chicken, drained
- 1   can (4 ounces) chopped green chilies
- 1   pound process American cheese, cubed

Crushed tortilla chips, optional

In a 3-qt. saucepan, combine the first seven ingredients. Cook and stir until the cheese is melted. Garnish with tortilla chips if desired. Yield: 6-8 servings (2 quarts).

Southwestern Turkey Dumpling Soup

PREP: 15 MIN. **COOK:** 30 MIN.

- 1   can (15 ounces) tomato sauce
- 1   can (14-1/2 ounces) diced tomatoes, undrained
- 1-3/4   cups water
- 1   envelope chili seasoning
- 3   cups diced cooked turkey *or* chicken
- 1   can (16 ounces) kidney beans, rinsed and drained
- 1   can (15 ounces) black beans, rinsed and drained
- 1   can (15-1/4 ounces) whole kernel corn, drained

- 1-1/2   cups biscuit/baking mix
- 1/2   cup cornmeal
- 3/4   cup shredded cheddar cheese, *divided*
- 2/3   cup milk

In a Dutch oven, combine the first five ingredients; bring to a boil. Reduce heat; cover and simmer for 10 minutes, stirring occasionally. Add beans and corn.

In a large bowl, combine biscuit mix, cornmeal and 1/2 cup cheese; stir in milk. Drop by heaping tablespoonfuls onto the simmering soup. Cover and cook for 12-15 minutes or until dumplings are firm. Sprinkle with remaining cheese; cover and simmer 1 minute longer or until the cheese is melted. Yield: 6-8 servings (2-1/2 quarts).

Chicken Vegetable Soup

I love eating a big bowl of this colorful, fresh-tasting soup on a winter's day. What a great way to warm up!
—Ruth Wimmer, Bland, Virginia

Meatball Alphabet Soup

PREP: 20 MIN. **COOK:** 35 MIN.

- 1 egg, lightly beaten
- 2 tablespoons quick-cooking oats
- 2 tablespoons grated Parmesan cheese
- 1/4 teaspoon garlic powder
- 1/4 teaspoon Italian seasoning
- 1/2 pound lean ground turkey
- 1 cup chopped onion
- 1 cup chopped celery
- 1 cup chopped carrots
- 1 cup diced peeled potatoes
- 1 tablespoon olive oil
- 2 garlic cloves, minced
- 4 cans (14-1/2 ounces *each*) reduced-sodium chicken broth
- 1 can (28 ounces) diced tomatoes, undrained
- 1 can (6 ounces) tomato paste
- 1/4 cup minced fresh parsley
- 1 teaspoon dried basil
- 1 teaspoon dried thyme
- 3/4 cup uncooked alphabet pasta

In a bowl, combine the first five ingredients. Crumble turkey over mixture and mix well. Shape into 1/2-in. balls. In a nonstick skillet, brown meatballs in small batches over medium heat until no longer pink. Remove from heat; set aside.

In a large saucepan or Dutch oven, saute the onion, celery, carrots and potatoes in oil for 5 minutes or until crisp-tender. Add garlic; saute for 1 minute longer. Add the broth, tomatoes, tomato paste, parsley, basil and thyme; bring to a boil. Add pasta; cook for 5-6 minutes. Reduce heat; add meatballs. Simmer, uncovered, for 15-20 minutes or until vegetables are tender. Yield: 9 servings (about 2 quarts).

Chicken Vegetable Soup

PREP: 10 MIN. **COOK:** 35 MIN.

- 2 cups chicken broth
- 1 cup fresh *or* frozen corn
- 1 small celery rib, chopped
- 1 small carrot, chopped
- 1 small onion, chopped
- 1 cup cubed cooked chicken
- 1/2 cup canned diced tomatoes

Salt and pepper to taste

Meatball Alphabet Soup

Bite-size meatballs made from ground turkey perk up this fun alphabet soup. A variety of vegetables accents the rich tomato broth that is nicely seasoned with herbs.
—Taste of Home Test Kitchen

Zesty Chicken Soup

This spicy soup, loaded with chicken and vegetables, freezes well.
—Gwen Nelson
Castro Valley, California

In a saucepan, combine the first five ingredients. Bring to a boil. Reduce heat; cover and simmer for 25-30 minutes or until vegetables are tender. Stir in the chicken, tomatoes, salt and pepper; heat through. Yield: 2 servings.

Zesty Chicken Soup

PREP: 25 MIN. **COOK:** 40 MIN.

- 1-1/4 **pounds boneless skinless chicken breasts**
- 4 **cups water**
- 1 **medium onion, chopped**
- 2 **celery ribs, chopped**
- 4 **garlic cloves, minced**
- 1 **tablespoon canola oil**
- 1 **can (14-1/2 ounces) Mexican diced tomatoes**
- 1 **can (14-1/2 ounces) diced tomatoes**
- 1 **can (8 ounces) tomato sauce**
- 1 **cup medium salsa**
- 3 **medium zucchini, halved and sliced**
- 2 **medium carrots, sliced**
- 1 **cup frozen white corn**
- 1 **can (4 ounces) chopped green chilies**
- 3 **teaspoons ground cumin**
- 2 **teaspoons chili powder**
- 1 **teaspoon dried basil**
- **Shredded cheddar cheese and tortilla chips, optional**

Place chicken in a Dutch oven or soup kettle; add water. Bring to a boil; reduce heat. Cover and simmer for 10-15 minutes or until chicken juices run clear. Remove chicken; cut into 1/2-in. cubes. Return to cooking liquid.

In a large skillet, saute the onion, celery and garlic in oil until tender; add to the Dutch oven. Stir in the tomatoes, tomato sauce, salsa, zucchini, carrots, corn, chilies, cumin, chili powder and basil. Bring to a boil. Reduce heat; cover and simmer for 20-25 minutes or until vegetables are tender.

Garnish with cheese and tortilla chips if desired. Soup may be frozen for up to 3 months. Yield: 10 servings (3-3/4 quarts).

Turkey Tomato Soup

Turkey and tomatoes are high on my list of favorite foods. My husband grows the best tomatoes ever, and I made up this recipe to complement both ingredients. It's wonderful anytime of year, but I prefer to make it when the tomatoes, green peppers, basil and garlic are all fresh from our garden.
—Carol Brunelle, Ascutney, Vermont

Turkey Tomato Soup

PREP: 10 MIN. **COOK:** 2-1/2 HOURS

- 4 pounds tomatoes, seeded and chopped (about 8 large tomatoes)
- 3 medium green peppers, chopped
- 2 cans (14-1/2 ounces *each*) reduced-sodium chicken broth
- 1 can (14-1/2 ounces) vegetable broth
- 1-1/2 cups water
- 1-1/2 teaspoons beef bouillon granules
- 2 garlic cloves, minced
- 1 teaspoon dried oregano
- 1 teaspoon dried basil
- 1/2 teaspoon pepper
- 3 cups cubed cooked turkey breast
- 3 cups cooked elbow macaroni

Minced fresh basil, optional

In a large saucepan or Dutch oven, combine the first 10 ingredients. Bring to a boil. Reduce heat; cover and simmer for 2 hours. Stir in turkey and macaroni; heat through. Garnish with fresh basil if desired. Yield: 12 servings (3 quarts).

Italian Chicken Soup

PREP: 10 MIN. **COOK:** 45 MIN.

- 1 fennel bulb, chopped
- 1/2 cup chopped onion
- 2 teaspoons olive oil
- 4 cups reduced-sodium chicken broth
- 2 cups water
- 1-1/2 cups chopped carrots
- 1 teaspoon salt
- 1/4 teaspoon dried thyme
- 1/4 teaspoon dried basil
- 1/4 teaspoon pepper
- 2 cups cubed cooked chicken breast
- 1/2 cup uncooked orzo pasta
- 2 tablespoons finely chopped fennel fronds

In a Dutch oven or soup kettle, saute fennel bulb and onion in oil until fennel is softened. Add the broth, water, carrots and seasonings. Bring to a boil. Reduce heat; cover and simmer for 15 minutes.

Stir in chicken and orzo. Cover and cook for 20 minutes or until orzo is tender. Stir in fennel fronds. Yield: 4 servings.

Italian Chicken Soup
This satisfying soup gets its Italian flair from fennel, thyme, basil and orzo pasta. If you don't start with a reduced-sodium or sodium-free stock, you might want to decrease the amount of salt called for in the recipe.
—Taste of Home Test Kitchen

Turkey Soup With Slickers

PREP: 20 MIN.
COOK: 2-1/2 HOURS + COOLING

- 1 leftover turkey carcass (from a 14-pound turkey)
- 5 quarts water
- 1/2 cup chopped onion
- 1/2 cup chopped carrot
- 1/2 cup chopped celery
- 3 tablespoons dried parsley flakes
- 2 teaspoons salt
- 1/2 teaspoon pepper
- 2 bay leaves
- 1 egg
- 2-1/2 to 3 cups all-purpose flour
- 1/2 teaspoon dill weed
- 1/2 teaspoon poultry seasoning
- 1 cup frozen peas

In a Dutch oven or soup kettle, add the first nine ingredients. Slowly bring to a boil; skim foam. Reduce heat; cover and simmer for 2 hours. Discard bay leaves. Remove carcass; set aside until cool enough to handle. Remove turkey from bones; discard bones. Cut turkey into bite-size pieces; set aside.

In a large bowl, beat 1 cup of the broth and egg. Stir in enough flour to form a stiff dough. Turn onto a floured surface; knead 8-10 times or until smooth. Divide dough in half; roll out each piece to 1/8-in. thickness. Cut into 2-in. x 1/4-in. strips.

Add dill and poultry seasoning to remaining broth; bring to a gentle boil. Drop slickers into broth; cover and cook for 30-35 minutes or until tender. Add peas and reserved turkey; heat through. Yield: 8-10 servings (2-1/2 quarts).

Turkey Soup with Slickers

Our grandson calls this "bone soup" because I make it with Thanksgiving turkey bones! The recipe for slickers—half dumplings, half egg noodles—comes from my grandmother.
—Christine Fleeman
Salem, Oregon

Chinese Chicken Soup

PREP/TOTAL TIME: 25 MIN.

This attractive, simple soup begins with frozen stir-fry vegetables. Minced gingerroot adds to the Oriental flavor.
—Taste of Home Test Kitchen

- 3 cans (14-1/2 ounces *each*) chicken broth
- 1 package (16 ounces) frozen stir-fry vegetable blend
- 2 cups cubed cooked chicken
- 1 teaspoon minced fresh gingerroot
- 1 teaspoon soy sauce
- 1/4 teaspoon sesame oil

In a large saucepan, combine all the ingredients. Bring to a boil. Reduce heat; cover and simmer for 15 minutes or until heated through. Yield: 6 servings.

Chicken Gumbo

PREP: 40 MIN. **COOK:** 35 MIN.

Chicken, ham, shrimp, rice and a host of good-for-you vegetables make this gumbo a surefire people-pleaser.
—Willa Govoro, St. Clair, Missouri

- 6 celery ribs, chopped
- 3 medium green peppers, chopped
- 3 medium onions, chopped
- 3/4 cup butter, cubed

10 quarts chicken broth

7 cans (14-1/2 ounces *each*) diced tomatoes, undrained

3 bay leaves

2 tablespoons minced fresh parsley

1 tablespoon pepper

2 to 3 tablespoons garlic powder

2 teaspoons salt

2 cups uncooked long grain rice

10 cups cubed cooked chicken

6 cups cubed fully cooked ham

1 package (16 ounces) frozen chopped okra

2 pounds cooked small shrimp, peeled and deveined, optional

In a large soup kettle or kettles, saute the celery, green peppers and onions in butter until tender. Add the next seven ingredients; bring to a boil. Stir in rice. Reduce heat; cover and simmer for 15-20 minutes or until rice is tender.

Stir in the chicken, ham, okra and shrimp. Simmer for 8-10 minutes or until shrimp turn pink and okra is tender. Discard bay leaves. Yield: 48 servings (6 quarts).

Southern Chicken Rice Soup

PREP: 25 MIN.
COOK: 2-1/2 HOURS + COOLING

1 broiler/fryer chicken (about 3 pounds)

10 cups water

2 teaspoons salt

1/2 cup uncooked long grain rice

1/2 cup chopped onion

1/2 cup chopped celery

1/2 cup thinly sliced carrots

1/2 cup sliced fresh *or* frozen okra

1 can (14-1/2 ounces) stewed tomatoes, diced

Southern Chicken Rice Soup

A favorite for soup night at our church, this recipe's one my husband concocted after he retired. I frequently find it on the table when I get home from work.
—*Rosalie Biar*
Thorndale, Texas

1 tablespoon chopped green chilies

1 garlic clove, minced

1-1/2 teaspoons chili powder

1 teaspoon seasoned salt

1/2 teaspoon lemon-pepper seasoning

1/2 teaspoon Creole seasoning

Place chicken, water and salt in a soup kettle or Dutch oven. Slowly bring to a boil; skim foam. Reduce heat; cover and simmer for 45-60 minutes or until the chicken is tender.

Remove chicken and set side until cool enough to handle. Remove meat from bones and discard bones and skin. Cut chicken into bite-size pieces. Skim fat from broth. Add the rice, vegetables and seasonings. Cook, uncovered, over medium heat for 30 minutes.

Add the chicken. Simmer for 30 minutes or until vegetables are tender. Yield: 10 servings (about 2-1/2 quarts).

Editor's Note: The following spices may be substituted for the Creole seasoning: 1/2 teaspoon each paprika and garlic powder, and a pinch each cayenne pepper, dried thyme and ground cumin.

Turkey Noodle Soup

My husband must eat a very low-fat diet, so I'm always experimenting to find foods that will agree with his stomach, too. This easy, economical recipe makes two generous servings. Sometimes I substitute chicken, or a different pasta or vegetable.
—Doris Nehoda, Coos Bay, Oregon

Harvest Turkey Soup

PREP: 35 MIN.
COOK: 2-1/2 HOURS + COOLING

Harvest Turkey Soup

The recipe for this super soup has evolved over the years. The herbs and spices make it taste terrific!
—Linda Sand
Winsted, Connecticut

1	leftover turkey carcass (from a 12-pound turkey)
5	quarts water
2	large carrots, shredded
1	cup chopped celery
1	large onion, chopped
4	chicken bouillon cubes
1	can (28 ounces) stewed tomatoes
3/4	cup fresh *or* frozen peas
3/4	cup uncooked long grain rice
1	package (10 ounces) frozen chopped spinach
1	tablespoon salt, optional
3/4	teaspoon pepper
1/2	teaspoon dried marjoram
1/2	teaspoon dried thyme

Place the turkey carcass and water in a Dutch oven or large soup kettle; slowly bring to a boil. Reduce heat; cover and simmer for 1-1/2 hours. Remove carcass and set aside until cool enough to handle. Remove meat from bones and discard bones. Cut turkey into bite-size pieces; set aside.

Strain broth. Add the carrots, celery, onion and bouillon; bring to a boil. Reduce heat; cover and simmer for 30 minutes. Add the tomatoes, peas, rice, spinach, seasonings and reserved turkey. Return to a boil; cook, uncovered, for 20 minutes or until rice is tender. Yield: 22 servings (5-1/2 quarts).

Turkey Noodle Soup

PREP: 15 MIN. **COOK:** 35 MIN.

2	cups water
3/4	cup cubed cooked turkey breast
1	celery rib with leaves, sliced
1/4	cup chopped onion
2	garlic cloves, minced
1/2	teaspoon salt
1/8	teaspoon dried marjoram
1/8	teaspoon pepper
1	bay leaf
1/2	cup cubed peeled potatoes
1/4	cup frozen peas
1/4	cup uncooked yolk-free wide noodles

Dash browning sauce, optional

Chicken Soup with Stuffed Noodles

Before retiring, I worked as a cook for 15 years. Now I spend lots of time in my kitchen preparing new, interesting foods for the family. You'll love this rich, homey soup.
—Jennifer Bucholtz
Kitchener, Ontario

In a large saucepan, combine the first nine ingredients; bring to a boil. Reduce heat; cover and simmer for 10 minutes or until celery is tender.

Add the potatoes, peas and noodles; cover and simmer 15 minutes longer or until potatoes are tender. Discard bay leaf. Stir in browning sauce if desired. Yield: 2 servings.

Chicken Soup With Stuffed Noodles

PREP: 20 MIN.
COOK: 1-3/4 HOURS + COOLING

- 1 broiler/fryer chicken (3 to 3-1/2 pounds), cut up
- 2-1/2 quarts water
- 2 teaspoons salt
- 1/4 teaspoon pepper
- 4 medium carrots, sliced
- 2 celery ribs, sliced
- 1 medium onion, diced

NOODLES:

- 1-1/4 cups all-purpose flour
- 1 teaspoon salt
- 1 egg
- 5 tablespoons water
- 1 teaspoon vegetable oil

FILLING:

- 2 eggs
- 1-1/4 cups seasoned bread crumbs
- 3 tablespoons butter, melted

Place chicken, water, salt and pepper in a large soup kettle. Cover and slowly bring to a boil; skim foam. Reduce heat; cover and simmer 45-60 minutes or until chicken is tender. Remove chicken and set aside until cool enough to handle. Add vegetables to broth; cook until tender, about 5-10 minutes. Remove chicken from

bones; discard bones and skin. Cut chicken into chunks; return to broth.

Meanwhile, for noodles, mix flour and salt in a medium bowl. Make a well in the center. Beat together the egg, water and oil; pour into well. Stir together, forming a dough.

Turn dough onto a floured surface; knead 8-10 times. Roll into a 16-in. x 12-in. rectangle. Combine filling ingredients; mix well. Sprinkle over dough to within 1/2 in. of edge; pat down. Moisten edges with water. Roll up jelly-roll style from long end; cut into 1/2-in. slices. Add noodles to gently boiling soup and cook for 6-8 minutes or until tender. Yield: 10 servings (2-1/2 quarts).

Lemony Turkey Rice Soup

*While growing up in Texas,
I spent a lot of time helping my
grandma cook. Lemon and cilantro
add a deliciously different twist
to this favorite turkey soup.*
—Margarita Cuellar
East Chicago, Indiana

Lemony Turkey Rice Soup

PREP/TOTAL TIME: 20 MIN.

- 6 cups chicken broth, *divided*
- 1 can (10-3/4 ounces) condensed cream of chicken soup, undiluted
- 2 cups cooked rice
- 2 cups diced cooked turkey
- 1/4 teaspoon pepper
- 2 tablespoons cornstarch
- 1/4 to 1/3 cup lemon juice
- 1/4 to 1/2 cup minced fresh cilantro

In a large saucepan, combine 5-1/2 cups broth, soup, rice, turkey and pepper. Bring to a boil; boil for 3 minutes. In a small bowl, combine cornstarch and remaining broth until smooth. Gradually stir into hot soup. Cook and stir for 1-2 minutes or until thickened and heated through. Remove from the heat; stir in lemon juice and cilantro. Yield: 8 servings (about 2 quarts).

Vegetable Chicken Noodle Soup

PREP: 10 MIN. **COOK:** 30 MIN.

- 1 cup chopped onions
- 1 cup chopped carrots
- 1 cup chopped celery
- 1 garlic clove, minced
- 2 teaspoons olive oil
- 1/4 cup all-purpose flour
- 1/2 teaspoon dried oregano
- 1/4 teaspoon dried thyme
- 1/4 teaspoon poultry seasoning
- 6 cups reduced-sodium chicken broth
- 4 cups cubed peeled potatoes
- 1 teaspoon salt
- 2 cups cubed cooked chicken breast
- 2 cups uncooked yolk-free wide noodles
- 1 cup fat-free evaporated milk

In a Dutch oven or soup kettle, saute onion, carrots, celery and garlic in oil for 5 minutes or until tender. Stir in the flour, oregano, thyme and poultry seasoning until blended; saute 1 minute longer. Gradually add broth, potatoes and salt; bring to a boil. Reduce heat; cover and simmer 15-20 minutes or until potatoes are tender.

Stir in the chicken and noodles; simmer for 10 minutes or until noodles are tender. Reduce heat. Stir in the milk; heat through (do not boil). Yield: 8 servings (about 2 quarts).

Vegetable Chicken Noodle Soup

*When the weather turns chilly, I like
to make this warmer-upper. There's
old-fashioned goodness in every
spoonful of this thick, hearty soup!*
—Julee Wallberg
Reno, Nevada

Chunky Chicken Soup

Here's a satisfying soup that you'll find yourself serving year-round. Every spoonful is loaded with the fantastic flavor of chicken, celery, carrots and peas.
—*Kathy Both*
Rocky Mountain House, Alberta

Brown Rice Turkey Soup

I don't recall where I got this recipe, but it's my all-time, favorite turkey soup. Everyone who has tried it agrees. The sweet red pepper is what gives the soup its distinctive tang.
—*Bobby Langley*
Rocky Mount, North Carolina

Brown Rice Turkey Soup

PREP/TOTAL TIME: 30 MIN.

1	cup diced sweet red pepper
1/2	cup chopped onion
1/2	cup sliced celery
2	garlic cloves, minced
2	tablespoons butter
3	cans (14-1/2 ounces *each*) reduced-sodium chicken broth
3/4	cup white wine *or* additional reduced-sodium chicken broth
1	teaspoon dried thyme
1/4	teaspoon pepper
2	cups cubed cooked turkey breast
1	cup instant brown rice
1/4	cup sliced green onions

In a Dutch oven, saute the red pepper, onion, celery and garlic in butter for 5-7 minutes or until vegetables are tender. Add the broth, wine or additional broth, thyme and pepper. Bring to a boil.

Reduce heat; cover and simmer for 5 minutes. Stir in turkey and rice. Bring to a boil; simmer, uncovered, for 5 minutes or until rice is tender. Garnish with green onions. Yield: 5 servings.

Chunky Chicken Soup

PREP: 15 MIN. **COOK:** 70 MIN.

3	boneless skinless chicken thighs, cut into 1-inch pieces
1	cup sliced celery
1/2	cup chopped onion
2	tablespoons vegetable oil
6	cups chicken broth
1-1/2	cups sliced carrots
1	teaspoon dried thyme
1/2	teaspoon salt, optional
1/4	teaspoon pepper
1/2	cup uncooked macaroni
1-1/2	cups frozen peas

In a 3-qt. saucepan, cook the chicken, celery and onion in oil until chicken juices run clear. Add the broth, carrots, thyme, salt if desired and pepper; bring to a boil. Reduce heat; cover and simmer for 45 minutes or until the vegetables are tender.

Stir in macaroni and peas. Cover and simmer for 15 minutes or until the macaroni is tender. Yield: 8 servings (2 quarts).

Homemade Chicken Broth

PREP: 10 MIN.
COOK: 2-1/2 HOURS + CHILLING

Rich with chicken taste, this traditional broth is lightly seasoned with herbs. Besides making wonderful chicken soups, it can be used in casseroles, rice dishes and other recipes that call for chicken broth.
—*Taste of Home Test Kitchen*

- 2-1/2 **pounds bony chicken pieces**
- 2 **celery ribs with leaves, cut into chunks**
- 2 **medium carrots, cut into chunks**
- 2 **medium onions, quartered**
- 2 **bay leaves**
- 1/2 **teaspoon dried rosemary, crushed**
- 1/2 **teaspoon dried thyme**
- 8 **to 10 whole peppercorns**
- 2 **quarts cold water**

Place all ingredients in a soup kettle or Dutch oven. Slowly bring to a boil; reduce heat. Skim foam. Cover and simmer for 2 hours.

Set chicken aside until cool enough to handle. Remove meat from bones. Discard bones; save meat for another use. Strain broth, discarding vegetables and seasonings. Refrigerate for 8 hours or overnight. Skim fat from surface. Yield: about 6 servings.

Southwestern Chicken Soup
The spices really liven up this filling soup. This recipe is easily doubled and freezes well.
—Anne Smithson
Cary, North Carolina

Southwestern Chicken Soup

PREP: 10 MIN. **COOK:** 1-1/4 HOURS

- 6 **cups reduced-sodium chicken broth**
- 1 **can (14-1/2 ounces) crushed tomatoes, undrained**
- 1 **can (14-1/2 ounces) diced tomatoes, undrained**
- 1 **pound boneless skinless chicken breast, cut into 1/2-inch cubes**
- 1 **large onion, chopped**
- 1/3 **cup minced fresh cilantro**
- 1 **can (4 ounces) chopped green chilies**
- 1 **garlic clove, minced**
- 1 **teaspoon chili powder**
- 1 **teaspoon ground cumin**
- 1/2 **teaspoon dried oregano**
- 1/4 **teaspoon cayenne pepper**
- 3 **cups frozen corn, thawed**

Tortilla chips
- 1 **cup (4 ounces) shredded reduced-fat cheddar *or* Mexican cheese blend**

In a large saucepan, combine the first 12 ingredients. Bring to a boil. Reduce heat; cover and simmer for 1 hour. Add corn; cook 10 minutes longer. Top each serving with tortilla chips; sprinkle with cheese. Yield: 8 servings.

Grandma's Chicken 'n' Dumpling Soup

PREP: 20 MIN. + COOLING
COOK: 2-3/4 HOURS

- 1   broiler/fryer chicken (3-1/2 to 4 pounds), cut up
- 2-1/4 quarts cold water
- 5   chicken bouillon cubes
- 6   whole peppercorns
- 3   whole cloves
- 1   can (10-3/4 ounces) condensed cream of chicken soup, undiluted
- 1   can (10-3/4 ounces) condensed cream of mushroom soup, undiluted
- 1-1/2 cups chopped carrots
- 1   cup fresh *or* frozen peas
- 1   cup chopped celery
- 1   cup chopped peeled potatoes
- 1/4 cup chopped onion
- 1-1/2 teaspoons seasoned salt
- 1/4 teaspoon pepper
- 1   bay leaf

DUMPLINGS:

- 2   cups all-purpose flour
- 4   teaspoons baking powder
- 1   teaspoon salt
- 1/4 teaspoon pepper
- 1   egg, beaten
- 2   tablespoons butter, melted
- 3/4 to 1 cup milk

Snipped fresh parsley, optional

Place chicken, water, bouillon, peppercorns and cloves in an 8-qt. Dutch oven or soup kettle. Cover and slowly bring to a boil; skim foam. Reduce heat; cover and simmer 45-60 minutes or until chicken is tender. Strain broth; return to kettle.

Remove chicken and set aside until cool enough to handle. Remove meat from bones; discard bones and skin and cut chicken into chunks. Cool broth and skim off fat.

Return chicken to Dutch oven with soups, vegetables and seasonings; bring to a boil. Reduce heat; cover and simmer for 1 hour. Uncover; increase heat to a gently boil. Discard bay leaf.

For dumplings, combine dry ingredients in a medium bowl. Stir in egg, butter and enough milk to make a moist stiff batter. Drop by teaspoonfuls into soup. Cover and cook without lifting the lid for 18-20 minutes. Sprinkle with parsley if desired. Yield: 12 servings (3 quarts).

Chicken Soup With Spaetzle

PREP: 20 MIN. + COOLING
COOK: 2-1/2 HOURS + COOLING

Here's a new and interesting twist to traditional chicken soup. Everyone who samples it can't resist the delicious soup paired with homemade spaetzle.
—Elaine Lange
Grand Rapids, Michigan

- 1   broiler/fryer chicken (2 to 3 pounds), cut into pieces
- 2   tablespoons vegetable oil
- 8   cups chicken broth
- 2   bay leaves
- 1/2 teaspoon dried thyme
- 1/4 teaspoon pepper

Grandma's Chicken 'n' Dumpling Soup

I've enjoyed making this savory soup for some 30 years. Every time I serve it, I remember Grandma, who was very special to me and was known as a great cook.
—Paulette Balda
Prophetstown, Illinois

Turkey Barley Soup

This satisfying soup has an appealing blend of flavors, and it's good for you, too. It's a great way to use up leftover holiday turkey.
—Betty Kleberger
Florissant, Missouri

Turkey Barley Soup

PREP: 15 MIN. **COOK:** 55 MIN.

- 2 cans (one 49-1/2 ounces, one 14-1/2 ounces) chicken broth
- 4 cups cubed cooked turkey
- 2 medium carrots, halved and thinly sliced
- 1 large potato, peeled and cubed
- 2 cups frozen cut green beans
- 1 medium green pepper, chopped
- 1 celery rib, chopped
- 3 garlic cloves, minced
- 1/2 cup uncooked medium pearl barley
- 2 bay leaves
- 1 teaspoon dried thyme
- 1 teaspoon rubbed sage
- 1/2 teaspoon salt

In a Dutch oven or soup kettle, combine all of the ingredients. Bring to a boil. Reduce heat; simmer, uncovered, for 45-55 minutes or until barley and vegetables are tender. Discard bay leaves. May be frozen for up to 3 months. Yield: 10 servings (3 quarts).

- 1 cup sliced carrots
- 1 cup sliced celery
- 3/4 cup chopped onion
- 1 garlic clove, minced
- 1/3 cup medium pearl barley
- 2 cups sliced fresh mushrooms

SPAETZLE:

- 1-1/4 cups all-purpose flour
- 1/8 teaspoon baking powder
- 1/8 teaspoon salt
- 1 egg, lightly beaten
- 1/4 cup water
- 1/4 cup milk

In a large kettle or Dutch oven, brown chicken pieces in oil. Add the broth, bay leaves, thyme and pepper. Slowly bring to a boil; skim foam. Reduce heat; cover and simmer for 45-60 minutes or until chicken is tender. Remove chicken and set aside until cool enough to handle. Remove meat from bones; discard bones and skin and cut chicken into bite-size pieces. Cool broth and skim off fat.

Return chicken to broth along with the carrots, celery, onion, garlic and barley. Bring to a boil. Reduce heat; cover and simmer for 35 minutes. Add mushrooms and simmer 8-10 minutes longer. Discard bay leaves.

In a small bowl, combine first three spaetzle ingredients. Stir in egg, water and milk; blend well. Drop batter by 1/2 teaspoonfuls into simmering soup. Cook for 10 minutes. Yield: 8-10 servings (2-1/2 quarts).

Turkey Meatball Soup

You don't need to cook the tender, homemade meatballs or boil the egg noodles separately, so you can easily stir up this savory soup in no time. I usually double the recipe for our family of seven.
—Carol Losier, Baldwinsville, New York

Turkey Meatball Soup

PREP: 25 MIN. **COOK:** 30 MIN.

 2 cans (14-1/2 ounces *each*) chicken broth
 1 celery rib with leaves, thinly sliced
 1 medium carrot, thinly sliced
 1/4 cup chopped onion
 1 tablespoon butter
 1 egg, beaten
 1/2 cup dry bread crumbs
 2 tablespoons dried parsley flakes
 1 tablespoon Worcestershire sauce
 1/4 teaspoon pepper
 1/2 pound lean ground turkey
 1 cup uncooked egg noodles

In a large saucepan, bring the broth, celery and carrot to a boil. Reduce heat; cover and simmer for 10 minutes.

Meanwhile, in a small skillet, saute onion in butter until tender. Transfer to a large bowl. Add the egg, bread crumbs, parsley, Worcestershire sauce and pepper. Crumble turkey over mixture and mix well. Shape into 1-in. balls.

Add meatballs to simmering broth. Bring to a boil. Reduce heat; cover and simmer for 15 minutes. Add noodles. Cover and simmer for 5 minutes or until noodles are tender. Yield: 5 servings.

Tex-Mex Chicken Soup

PREP: 10 MIN. **COOK:** 45 MIN.

 1/2 cup chopped onion
 2 garlic cloves, minced
 1 tablespoon vegetable oil
 4 cups chicken broth
 3 cups cubed cooked chicken
 3 medium zucchini, sliced
 1 can (14-1/2 ounces) diced tomatoes, undrained
 1 can (11 ounces) whole kernel corn, drained
 1 can (8 ounces) tomato sauce
 1/2 cup salsa
 2 teaspoons ground cumin
 1 teaspoon salt, optional
 3/4 teaspoon pepper
 1/2 teaspoon dried oregano
 Shredded cheddar cheese, optional
 Tortilla chips, optional

In a 4-qt. soup kettle, saute onion and garlic in oil until tender. Add broth, chicken, vegetables, tomato sauce, salsa and seasonings; bring to a boil. Reduce heat; cover and simmer for 30 minutes. Serve with cheese and tortilla chips if desired. Yield: 12 servings (3 quarts).

Tex-Mex Chicken Soup

We keep busy here on our ranch, so I'm always looking for dishes that can be prepared in a hurry but are still filling and tasty. This soup is a real winner!
—MayDell Spiess
Industry, Texas

Beef & Ground Beef

Tortellini Vegetable Soup

PREP: 15 MIN. **COOK:** 65 MIN.

Because of its rich spicy flavor, this soup has been a favorite in our home for years. I think you'll agree the tortellini adds an interesting twist.
—Tammy Nadeau
Presque Isle, Maine

- 1   pound ground beef
- 7   cups beef broth
- 2   cans (14-1/2 ounces *each*) stewed tomatoes
- 3/4 cup ketchup
- 3/4 cup thinly sliced carrots
- 3/4 cup thinly sliced celery
- 3/4 cup finely chopped onion
- 1   tablespoon dried basil
- 1-1/2 teaspoons seasoned salt
- 1   teaspoon sugar
- 1/4 teaspoon pepper
- 4   bay leaves
- 1-1/2 cups frozen cheese tortellini

Grated Parmesan cheese, optional

In a Dutch oven or soup kettle, cook beef over medium heat until no longer pink; drain. Add the next 11 ingredients; bring to a boil. Reduce heat; cover and simmer for 30 minutes.

Add tortellini; cook for 20-30 minutes or until tender. Discard bay leaves. Garnish individual servings with Parmesan cheese if desired. Yield: 10-12 servings (3-1/4 quarts).

Ground Beef Vegetable Soup

PREP: 10 MIN. **COOK:** 45 MIN.

- 3/4 pound ground beef
- 2   cans (14-1/2 ounces *each*) beef broth
- 2   cups water
- 1   can (28 ounces) diced tomatoes, undrained
- 3   celery ribs, chopped
- 2   large carrots, sliced
- 2   medium onions, sliced
- 1   medium potato, peeled and cubed
- 1-1/2 cups fresh cauliflowerets
- 2   tablespoons minced fresh tarragon *or* 2 teaspoons dried tarragon
- 1   tablespoon garlic powder
- 1   tablespoon minced fresh parsley
- 1/2 teaspoon salt
- 1/8 teaspoon pepper
- 3/4 cup uncooked macaroni

In a Dutch oven, cook beef over medium heat until no longer pink; drain. Add the broth, water, tomatoes, celery, carrots, onions, potato, cauliflower, tarragon, garlic powder, parsley, salt and pepper. Bring to a boil. Reduce heat; cover and simmer for 30 minutes or until vegetables are tender, stirring occasionally.

Cook macaroni according to package directions; drain. Stir into soup; heat through. Yield: 8 servings (3-3/4 quarts).

Ground Beef Vegetable Soup
This soup is sure to chase the chill away after a day of raking leaves or running errands. A variety of veggies along with ground beef and macaroni make this a hearty main dish.
—Raymonde Bourgeois
Swastika, Ontario

Easy Vegetable Soup

Canned tomatoes, beans and frozen vegetables give you a head start when preparing this crowd-pleaser. Set a bowl of tortilla chips next to the soup for a crunchy alternative to crackers.
—*Jan Sharp, Blue Springs, Missouri*

Scotch Broth Soup

PREP: 3 HOURS 20 MIN. + CHILLING
COOK: 1 HOUR

> 2   **pounds meaty beef soup bones (beef shanks *or* short ribs)**
> 8   **cups water**
> 6   **whole peppercorns**
> 1-1/2 **teaspoons salt**
> 1   **cup chopped carrots**
> 1   **cup chopped turnips**
> 1   **cup chopped celery**
> 1/2 **cup chopped onion**
> 1/4 **cup medium pearl barley**

In a large soup kettle, combine soup bones, water, peppercorns and salt. Slowly bring to a boil, about 30 minutes. Reduce heat; cover and simmer for 2-1/2 hours or until the meat comes easily off the bones.

Set beef bones aside until cool enough to handle. Strain broth; cool and chill. Skim off fat. Remove meat from bones; discard bones and cut meat into bite-size pieces. Return meat to broth along with remaining ingredients. Bring to a boil. Reduce heat; cover and simmer about 1 hour or until vegetables and barley are tender. Yield: 6-8 servings (2 quarts).

Scotch Broth Soup

Early in winter, I make up big pots of this chunky soup to freeze in plastic containers. Then I can bring out one or two containers at a time. I heat the frozen soup in a saucepan on low all morning, for a piping hot lunch.
—*Ann Main*
Moorefield, Ontario

Easy Vegetable Soup

PREP: 5 MIN. **COOK:** 30 MIN.

> 1   **pound ground beef**
> 1   **medium onion, chopped**
> 1   **can (28 ounces) diced tomatoes, undrained**
> 1   **package (16 ounces) frozen vegetable blend of your choice**
> 1   **can (16 ounces) kidney beans, undrained**
> 1   **can (14-1/2 ounces) beef broth**
> 1   **envelope taco seasoning**
> 1   **garlic clove, minced**
> **Shredded cheddar cheese, optional**

In a large saucepan, cook beef and onion over medium heat until meat is no longer pink; drain. Add the tomatoes, vegetables, beans, broth, taco seasoning and garlic; bring to a boil. Reduce heat; simmer, uncovered, for 10 minutes. Garnish with cheese if desired. Yield: 10-12 servings (2-3/4 quarts).

Four-Onion Soup

This mellow, rich-tasting onion soup is such a mainstay for our family that I felt compelled to share the recipe. Topped with toasted French bread and melted cheese, it's special enough to serve to guests.
—Margaret Adams
Pacific Grove, California

Wild Rice Soup

PREP/TOTAL TIME: 20 MIN.

I tasted this thick and hearty soup at a food fair I helped judge. It didn't earn a ribbon, but I thought it was a real winner. It originally called for uncooked wild rice, but I use a quick-cooking rice blend.
—Kathy Herink, Gladbrook, Iowa

- 1 pound ground beef
- 2 cups chopped celery
- 2 cups chopped onions
- 3 cups water
- 1 can (14-1/2 ounces) chicken broth
- 1 can (10-3/4 ounces) condensed cream of mushroom soup, undiluted
- 1 package (6.75 ounces) quick-cooking long grain and wild rice mix
- 5 bacon strips, cooked and crumbled

In a 3-qt. saucepan, cook the beef, celery and onions until beef is no longer pink; drain. Add the water, broth, soup and rice with contents of the seasoning packet. Bring to a boil. Reduce heat; cover and simmer for 5 minutes. Garnish with bacon. Yield: 8 servings (about 2 quarts).

Four-Onion Soup

PREP: 35 MIN. **COOK:** 50 MIN.

- 1 medium yellow onion
- 1 medium red onion
- 5 green onions with tops
- 1 medium leek (white portion only)
- 1 garlic clove, minced
- 2 tablespoons butter
- 2 cans (14-1/2 ounces *each*) beef broth
- 1 can (10-1/2 ounces) condensed beef consomme, undiluted
- 1 teaspoon Worcestershire sauce
- 1/2 teaspoon ground nutmeg
- 1 cup (4 ounces) shredded Swiss cheese
- 6 slices French bread (3/4 inch thick), toasted
- 6 tablespoons grated Parmesan cheese, optional

Slice all onions and leek 1/4 in. thick. In a large saucepan, cook onions, leek and garlic in butter over medium-low heat for 15 minutes or until tender and golden, stirring occasionally. Add the broth, consomme, Worcestershire sauce and nutmeg; bring to a boil. Reduce heat; cover and simmer for 30 minutes.

Sprinkle 1 tablespoon of Swiss cheese in the bottom of six oven-proof 8-oz. bowls. Ladle hot soup into bowls. Top each with a slice of bread. Sprinkle with remaining Swiss cheese and Parmesan cheese if desired. Broil 6-8 in. from the heat or until cheese melts. Serve immediately. Yield: 6 servings.

Spice It Up Soup

*Turkey Italian sausage and jalapeno peppers add kick to this chunky soup.
The original recipe called for a lot of butter and three cooking pots. I
eliminated the butter and tossed the ingredients together in just one pot.
My husband really enjoys this meaty soup, so I make plenty and freeze
what's left over in individual servings for his lunches.*
—Guyla Cooper, Enville, Tennessee

Meatball Vegetable Soup

*Frozen meatballs make this
satisfying soup easy to put
together. I often double the recipe
and simmer it in the slow cooker for
an even easier preparation.*
—Marcia Piaskowski
Plantsville, Connecticut

Meatball Vegetable Soup

PREP/TOTAL TIME: 25 MIN.

- 2/3 cup uncooked medium pasta shells
- 4 cups chicken broth
- 1 can (14-1/2 ounces) diced tomatoes, undrained
- 1 can (10-1/2 ounces) condensed French onion soup, undiluted
- 12 frozen cooked Italian meatballs, thawed and quartered
- 1-1/2 cups chopped fresh spinach
- 1 cup frozen sliced carrots, thawed
- 3/4 cup canned kidney beans, rinsed and drained
- 3/4 cup garbonzo beans or chickpeas, rinsed and drained

Cook pasta according to package directions. Meanwhile, combine the remaining ingredients in a Dutch oven or soup kettle. Bring to a boil. Reduce heat; cover and simmer for 15 minutes or until vegetables are tender. Drain pasta and stir into soup. Yield: 6-8 servings (about 2-1/2 quarts).

Spice It Up Soup

PREP: 10 MIN. **COOK:** 40 MIN.

- 1 pound uncooked hot turkey Italian sausage links, sliced
- 1/2 pound lean ground beef
- 1 large onion, chopped
- 1 medium green pepper, chopped
- 3 garlic cloves, minced
- 2 cans (14-1/2 ounces *each*) beef broth
- 2 cups water
- 2 cups fresh *or* frozen corn
- 1 can (14-1/2 ounces) diced tomatoes with green chilies, undrained
- 1 cup diced carrots
- 1/3 cup minced fresh cilantro
- 2 jalapeno peppers, seeded and chopped
- 1/2 teaspoon salt
- 1/2 teaspoon ground cumin

In a large saucepan, cook the sausage, beef, onion, green pepper and garlic over medium heat until meat is no longer pink; drain. Stir in the remaining ingredients. Bring to a boil. Reduce heat; cover and simmer for 30-40 minutes or until heated through. Yield: 8 servings.

Three's-a-Charm
Shamrock Soup

*There's no better way to use up
leftover St. Patrick's Day corned
beef, cabbage and potatoes than
to make a hearty soup. This
second-time-around soup
is one of my best.*
—Deborah McMirtrey
Estes Park, Colorado

In a large saucepan or Dutch oven, brown meat in oil. Add the onions, celery and garlic. Cook until beef is no longer pink. Add water and broth; bring to a boil. Add carrots and barley. Reduce heat; cover and simmer for 45-60 minutes or until barley is tender.

Add the beans, zucchini, tomatoes, cabbage, parsley and seasonings; simmer 15-20 minutes longer or until vegetables are tender. Top individual bowls with Parmesan cheese if desired. Yield: 16-20 servings (about 4 quarts).

Goulash Soup

PREP: 10 MIN. **COOK:** 3-1/2 HOURS

I found this recipe in a church cookbook and modified it slightly so it tastes just like the goulash soup we had while visiting Germany a few years ago. It's now become a family favorite at our house.
—Lois Teske, Buckley, Illinois

- 1-1/2 **pounds lean beef stew meat, cut into 1-inch cubes**
- 2 **pounds beef soup bones**
- 1 **quart fresh tomatoes, peeled and chopped**
- 1 **medium onion, chopped**
- 4 **large potatoes, peeled and diced**
- 6 **carrots, sliced**
- 3 **celery ribs, sliced**
- 3 **cups chopped cabbage**
- 3 **tablespoons Worcestershire sauce**
- 2 **to 4 teaspoons salt**
- 1/2 **teaspoon pepper**
- 3 **tablespoons minced fresh parsley**

In a large kettle or Dutch oven, cover stew meat and soup bones with water. Slowly bring to a simmer over low heat. Simmer, covered, about 2 hours or until meat is tender.

Set beef bones aside until cool enough to handle. Remove meat from bones; discard bones and cut meat into bite-size pieces.

Return broth and meat to pan. Add the next nine ingredients. Bring to a boil. Reduce heat; simmer, covered, about 1 hour or until vegetables are tender.

Sprinkle with parsley. Yield: about 16 servings (4 quarts).

Three's-a-Charm Shamrock Soup

PREP: 10 MIN. **COOK:** 40 MIN.

- 6 **celery ribs, chopped**
- 4 **medium carrots, sliced**
- 2 **cups cubed peeled potatoes**
- 5 **cups water**
- 3 **cups diced cooked corned beef**
- 2 **cups chopped cooked cabbage**
- 1 **teaspoon dill weed**
- 1 **teaspoon salt**
- 1 **teaspoon seasoned salt**
- 1/2 **teaspoon white pepper**

In a large soup kettle, bring the celery, carrots, potatoes and water to a boil. Reduce heat; cover and simmer until vegetables are tender, about 20 minutes.

Stir in remaining ingredients. Cover and simmer for 15-20 minutes or until heated through. Yield: 10 servings (2-1/2 quarts).

Italian Wedding Soup

PREP: 20 MIN. **COOK:** 15 MIN.

- 1 egg
- 3/4 cup grated Parmesan cheese
- 1/2 cup dry bread crumbs
- 1 small onion, chopped
- 3/4 teaspoon salt, *divided*
- 1-1/4 teaspoons pepper, *divided*
- 1-1/4 teaspoons garlic powder, *divided*
- 2 pounds ground beef
- 2 quarts chicken broth
- 1/3 cup chopped fresh spinach
- 1 teaspoon onion powder
- 1 teaspoon dried parsley flakes
- 1-1/4 cups cooked medium pasta shells

In a large bowl, combine the egg, cheese, bread crumbs, onion, 1/4 teaspoon salt, 1/4 teaspoon pepper and 1/4 teaspoon garlic powder. Crumble beef over mixture and mix well. Shape into 1-in. balls.

In a Dutch oven, brown meatballs in small batches; drain. Add the broth, spinach, onion powder, parsley and remaining salt, pepper and garlic powder; bring to a boil. Reduce heat; simmer, uncovered, for 5 minutes. Stir in pasta; heat through. **Yield:** 12 servings (3 quarts).

Italian Wedding Soup
This soup is always a delight! I add cooked pasta at the end of the cooking time to keep it from getting mushy.
—Nancy Ducharme
Deltona, Florida

Beef Barley Soup

PREP: 30 MIN. + COOLING
COOK: 1 HOUR 55 MIN.

When most folks think of barley, they picture it served up in a delicious soup. I'm no exception! This filling soup is a meal in itself.
—Jan Spencer
McLean, Saskatchewan

- 2 pounds bone-in beef short ribs
- 5 cups water
- 1 can (14-1/2 ounces) diced tomatoes, undrained
- 1 medium onion, chopped
- 1 to 1-1/2 teaspoons salt, optional
- 1/8 teaspoon pepper
- 2 cups sliced carrots
- 1 cup sliced celery
- 1 cup chopped cabbage
- 2/3 cup quick-cooking barley
- 1/4 cup minced fresh parsley

In a soup kettle, combine the ribs, water, tomatoes, onion, salt if desired and pepper; bring to a boil over medium heat. Reduce heat; cover and simmer for 1-1/2 to 2 hours or until meat is tender. Remove ribs; cool. Skim fat.

Remove meat from bones and cut into bite-size pieces; return to broth. Add the carrots, celery and cabbage; bring to a boil. Reduce heat; cover and simmer 15 minutes. Add barley; return to a boil. Reduce heat; cover and cook 10-15 minutes or until barley and vegetables are tender. Add parsley. **Yield:** 8 servings (2 quarts).

Hamburger Garden Soup

On our 4 acres in the country, we have a large vegetable and herb garden and raise our own steer. The only think I need to buy for this soup is the garlic!
—Alma Grady
Falls Creek, Pennsylvania

Hamburger Garden Soup

PREP: 10 MIN. **COOK:** 50 MIN.

> 1 **pound ground beef**
> 1 **cup chopped onion**
> 1 **garlic clove, minced**
> 1 **can (28 ounces) diced tomatoes, undrained**
> 2 **cups fresh *or* frozen corn**
> 2 **cups water**
> 3 **tablespoons minced fresh parsley**
> 2 **tablespoons minced fresh basil *or* 2 teaspoons dried basil**
> 2 **tablespoons minced fresh thyme *or* 2 teaspoons dried thyme**
> 1-1/2 **teaspoons minced fresh rosemary *or* 1/2 teaspoon dried rosemary, crushed**
> 1 **teaspoon salt**
> 1/2 **teaspoon pepper**

In a large saucepan, cook the beef, onion and garlic over medium heat until meat is no longer pink; drain. Add remaining ingredients; bring to a boil. Reduce heat; simmer, uncovered, for 30 minutes or until heated through. Yield: 5 servings.

Stroganoff Soup

PREP: 15 MIN. **COOK:** 40 MIN.

My husband and I share a love for all kinds of soup and came up with this delicious recipe together. It really does taste like beef Stroganoff.
—Karen Shiveley
Springfield, Minnesota

> 1/2 **pound boneless beef sirloin steak *or* beef tenderloin, cut into thin strips**
> 1/2 **cup chopped onion**
> 1 **tablespoon butter**
> 2 **cups water**
> 1-1/2 **cups milk**
> 1/4 **cup tomato paste**
> 2 **teaspoons beef bouillon granules**
> 1 **can (8 ounces) mushroom stems and pieces, drained**
> 1 **teaspoon salt**
> 1/8 **teaspoon pepper**
> 1 **can (12 ounces) evaporated milk**
> 1/3 **cup all-purpose flour**
> 2 **cups cooked wide egg noodles**
> 1/2 **cup sour cream**

In a 3-qt. saucepan, cook beef and onion in butter over medium heat, until meat is browned. Stir in the water, milk, tomato paste and bouillon. Add mushrooms, salt and pepper; bring to a boil. Reduce heat; cover and simmer for 20-30 minutes or until meat is tender.

Combine evaporated milk and flour until smooth. Gradually add to soup. Bring to a boil; cook and stir for 2 minutes until thickened. Add noodles; cook until heated through. Remove from the heat; stir in sour cream. Yield: 6 servings.

Beefy Tomato Pasta Soup

If you're a fan of Italian fare, you'll like this chunky combination. I look forward to eating this soup, and it's easier to fix than lasagna.
—Nancy Rollag
Kewaskum, Wisconsin

Beefy Tomato Pasta Soup

PREP: 15 MIN. **COOK:** 45 MIN.

- 1 **pound ground beef**
- 2 **medium green peppers, cut into 1-inch chunks**
- 1 **medium onion, cut into chunks**
- 2 **garlic cloves, minced**
- 5 **to 6 cups water**
- 2 **cans (14-1/2 ounces each) Italian diced tomatoes, undrained**
- 1 **can (6 ounces) tomato paste**
- 1 **tablespoon brown sugar**
- 2 **to 3 teaspoons Italian seasoning**
- 1 **teaspoon salt**
- 1/4 **teaspoon pepper**
- 2 **cups uncooked spiral pasta**

Croutons, optional

In a Dutch oven or soup kettle, cook the beef, green peppers, onion and garlic over medium heat until meat is no longer pink; drain. Add the water, tomatoes, tomato paste, brown sugar, Italian seasoning, salt and pepper. Bring to a boil. Add pasta. Cook for 10-14 minutes or until pasta is tender, stirring occasionally. Serve with croutons if desired. Yield: 10 servings (about 2-1/2 quarts).

Harvest Soup

PREP: 10 MIN. **COOK:** 25 MIN.

- 1 **pound lean ground beef**
- 3/4 **cup chopped onion**
- 2 **garlic cloves, minced**
- 3-1/2 **cups water**
- 2-1/4 **cups chopped peeled sweet potatoes**
- 1 **cup chopped red potatoes**
- 1 **cup chopped peeled acorn squash**
- 2 **teaspoons beef bouillon granules**
- 2 **bay leaves**
- 1/2 **teaspoon chili powder**
- 1/2 **teaspoon pepper**
- 1/8 **teaspoon ground allspice**
- 1/8 **teaspoon ground cloves**
- 1 **can (14-1/2 ounces) diced tomatoes, undrained**

In a large saucepan, cook the beef, onion and garlic over medium heat until meat is no longer pink; drain well. Add the water, potatoes, squash, bouillon, bay leaves, chili powder, pepper, allspice and cloves. Bring to a boil. Reduce heat; cover and simmer for 15-20 minutes or until vegetable are tender.

Add the tomatoes. Cook and stir until heated through. Discard bay leaves. Yield: 6 servings.

Harvest Soup
Loaded with ground beef and veggies, this simple soup makes a great family meal on a busy night. Substitute any of the vegetables with those that better suit your family's tastes.
—Janice Mitchell
Aurora, Colorado

French Onion Soup

I adapted a basic recipe to copy the onion soup served at my favorite restaurant. No matter what my entree, I always ordered the soup. Now I can make it at home. It's a meal in itself or an impressive beginning to a full-course dinner.
—Barbara Brunner, Steelton, Pennsylvania

Beefy Minestrone Soup

PREP: 20 MIN. **COOK:** 3-1/2 HOURS

- 1 boneless beef chuck roast (4 pounds)
- 4 quarts water
- 2 bay leaves
- 2 medium onions, diced
- 2 cups sliced carrots
- 2 cups sliced celery
- 1 can (28 ounces) diced tomatoes, undrained
- 1 can (15 ounces) tomato sauce
- 1/4 cup chopped fresh parsley

Salt and pepper to taste

- 4 teaspoons dried basil
- 1 teaspoon garlic powder
- 2 packages (9 ounces *each*) frozen Italian *or* cut green beans
- 1 package (16 ounces) frozen peas
- 2 cans (16 ounces *each*) kidney beans, rinsed and drained
- 2 packages (7 ounces *each*) shell macaroni, cooked and drained

Grated Parmesan cheese

Place beef roast, water and bay leaves in a large kettle or Dutch oven; bring to a boil. Reduce heat; cover and simmer until meat is tender, about 3 hours. Remove meat from broth; set aside until cool enough to handle cool.

Add the onions, carrots and celery to broth; cook for 20 minutes or until vegetables are tender. Cut meat into bite-size pieces; add to broth. Add the tomatoes, tomato sauce, parsley, seasonings, beans, peas and kidney beans. Cook until vegetables are done, about 10 minutes. Add macaroni and heat through. Discard bay leaves. Serve with Parmesan cheese. Yield: 40 servings (10 quarts).

French Onion Soup

PREP: 55 MIN. **BAKE:** 10 MIN.

- 2 medium onions, chopped
- 1 teaspoon sugar
- 6 tablespoons butter, *divided*
- 1 tablespoon all-purpose flour
- 1/8 teaspoon pepper

Dash ground nutmeg

- 2-1/2 cups beef *or* vegetable broth

Beefy Minestrone Soup

Here's the perfect soup to put fresh garden vegetables to good use. It's great for a light lunch served with a salad and warm bread.
—Lana Rutledge
Shepherdsville, Kentucky

South-of-the-Border Soup

Cooking and creating new recipes is a favorite pastime of mine. As a matter of fact, this is an original recipe, which earned me first place in the Wisconsin Beef Cookoff some years ago.
—*Lynn Ireland*
Lebanon, Wisconsin

2 tablespoons grated Parmesan cheese

2 slices French bread (1 inch thick)

4 slices provolone cheese

In a large saucepan, saute onions with sugar in 3 tablespoons of butter until golden brown. Stir in the flour, pepper and nutmeg until blended. Gradually stir in broth. Bring to a boil; cook and stir for 2 minutes. Reduce heat; cover and simmer for 30 minutes. Stir in the Parmesan cheese.

Meanwhile, in a large skillet, melt remaining butter; add bread. Cook until golden brown on both sides. Ladle soup into two oven-proof bowls. Place a slice of cheese in each bowl; top with bread and remaining cheese. Bake at 375° for 10 minutes or until the cheese is bubbly. Yield: 2 servings.

South-of-the-Border Soup

PREP: 15 MIN. **COOK:** 35 MIN.

1 egg

1/4 cup dry bread crumbs

1/2 teaspoon salt

1/4 teaspoon pepper

1 pound ground beef

1 jar (16 ounces) picante sauce

1 can (15-1/4 ounces) whole kernel corn, drained

1 can (15 ounces) black beans, rinsed and drained

1 can (14-1/2 ounces) diced tomatoes, undrained

1-1/4 cups water

In a large bowl, combine the first four ingredients. Crumble beef over mixture and mix well. Shape into 1-in. balls.

In a large saucepan, brown meatballs; drain. Add the picante sauce, corn, beans, tomatoes and water; bring to a boil. Reduce heat; cover and simmer for 20 minutes or until the meat is no longer pink. Yield: 8 servings (2 quarts).

Old-World Tomato Soup

PREP: 25 MIN.
COOK: 3 HOURS 10 MIN.

- 3 **quarts water**
- 4 **bone-in beef short ribs (2 pounds)**
- 2 **to 3 meaty soup bones (beef shanks *or* short ribs, about 2 pounds)**
- 1 **can (28 ounces) diced tomatoes, undrained**
- 3 **celery ribs, halved**
- 1 **large onion, quartered**
- 1/2 **cup chopped fresh parsley, *divided***
- 1 **tablespoon salt**
- 1-1/2 **teaspoons pepper**
- 4 **carrots, cut into 1-inch pieces**
- 2 **parsnips, peeled and quartered**
- 2 **cups (16 ounces) sour cream**
- 1/2 **cup all-purpose flour**
- 1/2 **teaspoon ground nutmeg, optional**
- 1 **package (8 ounces) egg noodles, cooked and drained**

In a large kettle, combine the water, ribs, soup bones, tomatoes, celery, onion, 1/4 cup parsley, salt and pepper. Slowly bring to a boil, about 30 minues. Cover and simmer for 2 hours. Add carrots and parsnips; cover and simmer for 1 hour or until meat and vegetables are tender.

With a slotted spoon, remove meat, bones and vegetables. Strain broth and skim off fat; return all but 1 cup broth to kettle. Set reserved broth aside. Remove meat from the bones; dice and return to kettle. Discard celery and onion. Cut parsnips, carrots and tomatoes into 1/2-in. pieces and return to kettle. Add remaining parsley.

In a large bowl, combine the sour cream, flour, nutmeg if desired and reserved broth; stir into soup. Add noodles. Cook and stir until thickened and heated through (do not boil). Yield: 16-20 servings (about 4-1/2 quarts).

Homemade Beef Broth

PREP: 10 MIN.
COOK: 5 HOURS 30 MIN. + CHILLING

Roasting soup bones in the oven first gives rich beef flavor to this basic stock. In addition to soups, use the beefy broth to provide extra flavor in stews, gravies, sauces and vegetable dishes.
—*Taste of Home Test Kitchen*

- 4 **pounds meaty beef soup bones (beef shanks *or* short ribs)**
- 3 **medium carrots, cut into chunks**
- 3 **celery ribs, cut into chunks**
- 2 **medium onions, quartered**
- 1/2 **cup warm water**
- 3 **bay leaves**
- 3 **garlic cloves**
- 8 **to 10 whole peppercorns**
- 3 **to 4 sprigs fresh parsley**
- 1 **teaspoon *each* dried thyme, marjoram and oregano**
- 3 **quarts cold water**

Place soup bones in a large roasting pan. Bake, uncovered, at

Old-World Tomato Soup

This traditional soup has been in our family for four generations, and I've never seen another recipe like it. Each spoonful brings back wonderful memories.
—*Linda Pandolfo*
East Haddam, Connecticut

Vegetable Beef Soup

When we come in from playing in the snow, I serve this savory soup.
—Nancy Soderstrom
Roseville, Minnesota

450° for 30 minutes. Add the carrots, celery and onions. Bake 30 minutes longer; drain fat.

Using a slotted spoon, transfer bones and vegetables to a large Dutch oven. Add warm water to the roasting pan; stir to loosen browned bits from pan. Transfer pan juices to kettle. Add seasonings and enough cold water just to cover. Slowly bring to a boil, about 30 minutes. Reduce heat; simmer, uncovered, for 4-5 hours, skimming the surface as foam rises. If necessary, add hot water during the first 2 hours to keep ingredients covered.

Remove beef bones and set aside until cool enough to handle. If desired, remove meat from bones; discard bones and save meat for another use. Strain broth through a cheesecloth-lined colander, discarding vegetables and seasonings. If using immediately, skim fat or refrigerate for 8 hours or overnight; remove fat from surface. Broth can be covered and refrigerated for up to 3 days or frozen for 4 to 6 months. Yield: about 2-1/2 quarts.

Vegetable Beef Soup

PREP: 25 MIN. + COOLING
COOK: 2-1/4 HOURS

- 1 **boneless beef chuck roast (2-1/2 to 3 pounds)**
- 4 **quarts water**
- 1 **cup medium pearl barley**
- 1-1/2 **cups chopped onion**
- 1-1/2 **cups chopped celery**
- 1 **teaspoon salt**
- 1 **teaspoon pepper**
- 1 **can (28 ounces) diced tomatoes, undrained**
- 1-1/2 **cups chopped carrots**
- 1 **package (16 ounces) frozen mixed vegetables**
- 1/4 **cup minced fresh parsley**
- 1/2 **teaspoon dried basil**
- 1/4 **teaspoon dried thyme**
- 1/4 **teaspoon garlic salt**

Place roast in a large Dutch oven or soup kettle. Add the water, barley, onion, celery, salt and pepper; bring to a boil. Reduce heat; cover and simmer for 1 hour and 15 minutes or until meat is tender.

Set beef aside until cool enough to handle. Cut meat into cubes. Skim fat from broth. Add beef and remaining ingredients; bring to a boil. Reduce heat; cover and simmer for 45 minutes or until vegetables are tender. Yield: 15-20 servings (6 quarts).

Pork, Ham & Sausage

Roast Pork Soup

PREP: 15 MIN. **COOK:** 55 MIN.

Chunks of pork, potatoes and navy beans are in this well-seasoned soup. It has been a family favorite for years. Served with corn bread, it's one of our comfort foods in winter.
—Sue Gulledge
Springville, Alabama

- 3 cups cubed cooked pork roast
- 2 medium potatoes, peeled and chopped
- 1 large onion, chopped
- 1 can (15 ounces) navy beans, rinsed and drained
- 1 can (14-1/2 ounces) Italian diced tomatoes, undrained
- 4 cups water
- 1/2 cup unsweetened apple juice
- 1/2 teaspoon salt, optional
- 1/2 teaspoon pepper

Minced fresh basil

In a Dutch oven, combine the first nine ingredients. Bring to a boil. Reduce heat; cover and simmer for 45 minutes or until vegetables are crisp-tender. Sprinkle with basil. Yield: 9 servings (2-1/4 quarts).

Basque Vegetable Soup

PREP: 25 MIN.
COOK: 2-1/4 HOURS + COOLING

- 1 broiler/fryer chicken (2 to 3 pounds)
- 8 cups water
- 2 medium leeks, sliced
- 2 medium carrots, sliced
- 1 large turnip, peeled and cubed
- 1 large onion, chopped
- 1 large potato, peeled and cubed
- 1 garlic clove, minced
- 1-1/2 teaspoons salt
- 1/2 teaspoon pepper
- 1 tablespoon minced fresh parsley
- 1 teaspoon dried thyme
- 3/4 pound fresh Polish sausage links
- 2 cups navy beans, rinsed and drained
- 1 cup shredded cabbage
- 1 can (15 ounces) tomato sauce

In Dutch oven, slowly bring chicken and water to a boil; skim foam. Reduce heat; cover and simmer for 45-60 minutes or until tender. Remove chicken; set aside until cool enough to handle.

Strain broth and skim fat. Return broth to Dutch oven. Add the leeks, carrots, turnip, onion, potato, garlic, salt, pepper, parsley and thyme. Bring to a boil. Reduce heat; cover and simmer for 30 minutes.

In a large skillet, cook sausage over medium heat until no longer pink. Drain on paper towels; set aside.

Meanwhile, remove chicken from bones; discard bones and skin. Cut chicken into bite-size pieces; add to the pan. Add beans, cabbage and cooked sausage. Simmer, uncovered, for 30 minutes or until vegetables are tender. Stir in tomato sauce; heat through. Yield: 10-12 servings (3 quarts).

Basque Vegetable Soup

This is a hearty soup offered here in the many restaurants specializing in Basque cuisine. It's a nice way to use the vegetables that are available in the fall.
—Norman Chegwyn
Richmond, California

Italian Peasant Soup

My father shared this recipe with me, and I use it when I need a healthy meal. It's my sons' favorite. Loaded with sausage, chicken, beans and spinach, the quick soup is nice for special occasions, too.
—Kim Knight, Hamburg, Pennsylvania

Kielbasa Bean Soup

PREP: 10 MIN. **COOK:** 1-1/4 HOURS

- 4-1/2 **cups water**
- 2 **cans (14-1/2 ounces *each*) diced tomatoes, undrained**
- 1 **can (16 ounces) kidney beans, rinsed and drained**
- 1 **can (15-1/2 ounces) great northern beans, rinsed and drained**
- 1 **can (15 ounces) garbanzo beans *or* chickpeas, rinsed and drained**
- 2 **medium green peppers, chopped**
- 2 **medium onions, chopped**
- 2 **celery ribs, chopped**
- 1 **medium zucchini, sliced**
- 2 **teaspoons chicken bouillon granules**
- 2 **garlic cloves, minced**
- 2-1/2 **teaspoons chili powder**
- 2 **teaspoons dried basil**
- 1-1/2 **teaspoons salt**
- 1/2 **teaspoon pepper**
- 2 **bay leaves**
- 3/4 **pound smoked kielbasa *or* smoked Polish sausage, halved lengthwise and sliced**

In a soup kettle or Dutch oven, combine the first 16 ingredients. Bring to a boil. Reduce heat; cover and simmer for 1 hour. Add sausage and heat through. Discard bay leaves. Yield: 12 servings (about 3 quarts).

Italian Peasant Soup

PREP/TOTAL TIME: 25 MIN.

- 1 **pound Italian sausage links, casings removed and cut into 1-inch slices**
- 2 **medium onions, chopped**
- 6 **garlic cloves, chopped**
- 1 **pound boneless skinless chicken breasts, cut into 1-inch cubes**
- 2 **cans (15 ounces *each*) cannellini *or* white kidney beans, rinsed and drained**
- 2 **cans (14-1/2 ounces *each*) chicken broth**
- 2 **cans (14-1/2 ounces *each*) diced tomatoes**
- 1 **teaspoon dried basil**
- 1 **teaspoon dried oregano**
- 6 **cups fresh spinach leaves, chopped**

Shredded Parmesan cheese, optional

Kielbasa Bean Soup

I usually make double batch of this meaty vegetable soup and freeze some in serving-size containers. It makes a nice meal for busy days or unexpected guests.
—Emily Chaney
Penobscot, Maine

and simmer for 45 minutes. Yield: 12 servings (about 3 quarts).

Sausage Bean Soup

Canned beans and quick-cooking sausage make this tasty soup a snap to prepare. It takes just minutes to simmer.
—Marlene Muckenhirn
Delano, Minnesota

In a Dutch oven or soup kettle, cook sausage over medium heat until no longer pink; drain. Add onions and garlic; saute until tender. Add chicken; cook and stir until no longer pink.

Stir in the beans, broth, tomatoes, basil and oregano. Cook, uncovered, for 10 minutes. Add the spinach and heat just until wilted. Serve with Parmesan cheese if desired. Yield: 11 servings (2-3/4 quarts).

Black-Eyed Pea Soup

PREP: 5 MIN. **COOK:** 55 MIN.

Since we raise our own pigs, I like to use ground pork in this zesty soup. But I've used ground beef with equally good results. Green chilies give this dish some Southwestern flair.
—Mary Lou Chernik
Taos, New Mexico

1-1/2   pounds ground pork
1   large onion, chopped
2   garlic cloves, minced
3   cans (15-1/2 ounces *each*) black-eyed peas, rinsed and drained
2   cups water
1   can (14-1/2 ounces) stewed tomatoes
1   can (10 ounces) diced tomatoes and green chilies
1   can (4 ounces) chopped green chilies
1   tablespoon beef bouillon granules
1   tablespoon molasses
1   teaspoon Worcestershire sauce
1/2   teaspoon salt
1/4   teaspoon pepper
1/4   teaspoon ground cumin

In a large soup kettle or Dutch oven, cook the pork, onion and garlic over medium heat until meat is no longer pink; drain. Stir in the remaining ingredients; bring to a boil. Reduce heat; cover

Sausage Bean Soup

PREP/TOTAL TIME: 25 MIN.

3/4   pound bulk Italian sausage
1/2   cup chopped onion
1   garlic clove, minced
1   can (15-1/2 ounces) butter beans, rinsed and drained
1   can (15 ounces) black beans, rinsed and drained
1   can (14-1/2 ounces) diced tomatoes, undrained
1   can (14-1/2 ounces) beef broth
1   tablespoon minced fresh basil *or* 1 teaspoon dried basil
2   tablespoons shredded Parmesan cheese

In a large saucepan, cook sausage, onion and garlic over medium heat until the sausage is no longer pink; drain. Add the beans, tomatoes, broth and basil. Bring to a boil. Reduce heat; cover and simmer for 10 minutes. Sprinkle each serving with Parmesan cheese. Yield: 4-6 servings.

Hearty Minestrone Soup

Packed with sausage and veggies, this soup is not only nutritious, it's also a great way to use up your garden bounty.
—*Donna Smith, Fairport, New York*

Posole

PREP: 15 MIN. + STANDING
COOK: 65 MIN.

Posole

This spicy, stew-like soup is traditionally served in New Mexico at holiday time to celebrate life's blessings, but it's good anytime.
—*Taste of Home Test Kitchen*

4	dried ancho chilies
4	dried guajillo *or* pasilla chilies
2	tablespoons vegetable oil, *divided*
1-1/2	cups boiling water
2	pounds boneless pork, cut into 1-inch cubes
1/2	cup chopped onion
4	garlic cloves, minced
3	cups chicken broth
2	cans (29 ounces *each*) hominy, rinsed and drained
1-1/2	teaspoons dried Mexican oregano
1	teaspoon salt

Lime wedges, sliced radishes, diced avocado and chopped onion, optional

In a Dutch oven, saute chilies in 1 tablespoon oil for 1-2 minutes or until heated through, pressing with a spatula (do not brown). Remove from the pan; remove stems and seeds. Place chilies in a bowl; add boiling water. Soak for 20 minutes or until softened.

Meanwhile, in the Dutch oven, brown pork in remaining oil in batches. Saute onion and garlic with the last batch of pork. Add broth; bring to a boil. Reduce heat; cover and simmer for 30 minutes or until meat is tender.

Transfer chilies and soaking liquid to a blender; cover and process until smooth. Strain through a fine strainer, reserving pulp and discarding skins. Add pulp to pork mixture. Stir in the hominy, oregano and salt. Cover and simmer for 20 minutes or until hominy is heated through and flavors blend. Serve with lime, radishes, avocado and onion if desired. Yield: 8 servings (2-1/2 quarts).

Editor's Note: When handling chilies, use rubber or plastic gloves to protect your hands. Avoid touching your face.

Hearty Minestrone Soup

PREP: 25 MIN. **COOK:** 30 MIN.

1	pound bulk Italian sausage
2	cups sliced celery
1	cup chopped onion
6	cups chopped zucchini
1	can (28 ounces) diced tomatoes, undrained
1-1/2	cups chopped green peppers

Sunday Gumbo

With sausage, chicken and shrimp, plus rice, a medley of vegetables and the heat of cayenne, this warming soup is a spectacular addition to Sunday meals.
—Debbie Burchette
Summitville, Indiana

1-1/2   teaspoons Italian seasoning
1-1/2   teaspoons salt
   1   teaspoon dried oregano
   1   teaspoon sugar
1/2   teaspoon dried basil
1/4   teaspoon garlic powder

In a large saucepan, cook the sausage over medium heat until no longer pink. Using a slotted spoon, remove to paper towel to drain, reserving 1 tablespoon of drippings. Saute celery and onion in drippings for 5 minutes. Add sausage and remaining ingredients; bring to a boil. Reduce heat; cover and simmer for 20-30 minutes or until the vegetables are tender. Yield: 9 servings (2-1/4 quarts).

Sunday Gumbo

PREP: 10 MIN. **COOK:** 50 MIN.

   1   pound Italian sausage links, cut into 1/4-inch pieces
   1   pound boneless skinless chicken breasts, cubed
   3   tablespoons vegetable oil
   1   medium sweet red pepper, chopped
   1   medium onion, chopped
   3   celery ribs, chopped
   1   teaspoon dried marjoram
   1   teaspoon dried thyme
1/2   teaspoon garlic powder
1/2   teaspoon cayenne pepper
   3   cans (14-1/2 ounces *each*) chicken broth
2/3   cup uncooked brown rice

   1   can (14-1/2 ounces) diced tomatoes, undrained
   1   pound uncooked medium shrimp, peeled and deveined
   2   cups frozen sliced okra

In a Dutch oven, brown sausage and chicken in oil. Remove with a slotted spoon and keep warm. In the drippings, saute the red pepper, onion and celery until tender. Stir in the seasonings; cook for 5 minutes. Stir in the broth, rice and sausage mixture; bring to a boil. Reduce heat; cover and simmer for 20-25 minutes or until rice is tender.

Stir in the tomatoes, shrimp and okra; cook for 10 minutes or until shrimp turn pink, stirring occasionally. Yield: 16 servings (about 4 quarts).

Kielbasa Cabbage Soup

Cabbage is plentiful in upstate New York. During winter, I like to keep this hearty soup simmering on the stovetop all day.
—*Patricia Bossee, Darien Center, New York*

Kielbasa Cabbage Soup

PREP: 30 MIN. **COOK:** 1-1/4 HOURS

- 1 small head cabbage, coarsely chopped
- 1 medium onion, chopped
- 4 to 6 garlic cloves, minced
- 2 tablespoons olive oil
- 4 cups water
- 3 tablespoons cider vinegar
- 1 to 2 tablespoons brown sugar
- 1 pound smoked kielbasa *or* Polish sausage, halved, cut into 1/2-inch pieces
- 4 medium potatoes, peeled and cubed
- 3 large carrots, chopped
- 1 teaspoon caraway seeds
- 1/2 teaspoon pepper

In a Dutch oven or soup kettle, saute the cabbage, onion and garlic in oil for 5 minutes or until tender.

Combine the water, vinegar and brown sugar; add to cabbage mixture. Stir in remaining ingredients. Bring to a boil. Reduce heat; cover and simmer for 60-70 minutes or until vegetables are tender. Yield: 8-10 servings (about 2-1/2 quarts).

Italian Sausage Soup

PREP: 10 MIN. **COOK:** 45 MIN.

- 1 can (49-1/2 ounces) chicken broth
- 2 cups cut fresh green beans
- 1 can (15 ounces) cannellini *or* white kidney beans, rinsed and drained
- 1 can (14-1/2 ounces) Italian diced tomatoes
- 1 cup chopped onion
- 1 cup chopped celery
- 1 cup chopped fennel bulb
- 1 can (6 ounces) tomato paste
- 1 teaspoon dried oregano
- 1/2 teaspoon white pepper
- 5 Italian sausage links
- 1 tablespoon olive oil
- 3 cups coarsely chopped fresh spinach

Shredded Parmesan cheese, optional

In a Dutch oven, combine the first 10 ingredients. Bring to a boil. Reduce heat; cover and simmer for 20 minutes.

Meanwhile, in a large skillet, brown sausage in oil over medium heat. Add a small amount of hot water. Cover and cook until sausage is 160°; drain. Cut into 1/4-in. slices and add to soup.

Simmer, uncovered, for 15 minutes.

Add spinach. Simmer, uncovered, for 5 minutes or until spinach is wilted. Garnish with Parmesan cheese if desired. Yield: 8 servings (2 quarts).

Italian Sausage Soup

This full-bodied soup will satisfy every size of appetite.
—*Taste of Home Test Kitchen*

Split Pea Soup With Meatballs

PREP: 20 MIN. **COOK:** 2 HOURS

- 1 pound dried green split peas
- 3 medium carrots, cut into 1/2-inch pieces
- 3/4 cup diced celery
- 1 medium onion, diced
- 8 cups water
- 3 medium potatoes, cut into 1/2-inch cubes
- 2-1/2 teaspoons salt
- 1/4 teaspoon pepper

MEATBALLS:
- 3/4 cup finely chopped celery
- 1 medium onion, finely chopped
- 4 tablespoons vegetable oil, *divided*
- 1 pound ground pork
- 1-1/2 cups soft bread crumbs
- 2 tablespoons water
- 1 teaspoon salt
- 1/2 teaspoon dried sage, crushed
- 1 egg

In a Dutch oven or soup kettle, combine the peas, carrots, celery, onion and water; bring to a boil over medium heat. Reduce heat; cover and simmer for 1 hour.

Add potatoes, salt and pepper; cover and simmer for 30 minutes. Meanwhile, in a large skillet, saute celery and onion in 2 tablespoons oil until tender; transfer to a large bowl. Add pork, bread crumbs, water, salt, sage and egg; mix well. Form into 3/4-in. balls.

In the same skillet, brown meatballs in remaining oil until no longer pink inside. Add to soup; cover and simmer for 15 minutes. Yield: 10-14 servings (3-1/2 quarts).

Hearty Ham Borscht

PREP: 10 MIN.
COOK: 2-1/2 HOURS + COOLING

During busy times on the farm, I like to keep a big pot of this borscht simmering on the stove. That way, folks can dip into the kettle when they have a chance to sit down for a quick meal.
—Joanne Kukurudz
River Hills, Manitoba

- 1 meaty ham bone *or* 2 smoked ham hocks
- 6 cups water
- 2 cups cubed fully cooked ham
- 3 cups chopped cooked beets
- 1 can (14 ounces) pork and beans
- 1 can (10-3/4 ounces) condensed tomato soup, undiluted
- 1 cup frozen peas
- 1 cup chopped carrots
- 1 cup frozen cut green beans
- 1 medium onion, chopped
- 2 to 3 tablespoons snipped fresh dill *or* 1 tablespoon dill weed

Sour cream, optional

Place ham bone and water in a Dutch oven or soup kettle; slowly bring to a boil. Reduce heat; cover and simmer for 1-1/2 hours.

Split Pea Soup with Meatballs

I like to prepare this for our church soup suppers, and I come home with an empty kettle every time. Meatballs put a flavorful spin on ordinary split pea soup.
—Donna Smith
Grey Cliff, Montana

Remove ham bone; set aside until cool enough to handle.

Remove meat from bone; discard bone. Cut meat into bite-size pieces. Return meat to kettle. Add the beets, pork and beans, soup, peas, carrots, beans, onion and dill. Cover and simmer for 45 minutes or until vegetables are tender. Garnish with sour cream if desired. Yield: 12-14 servings (3-1/2 quarts).

Cabbage Sausage Soup

PREP: 10 MIN. **COOK:** 45 MIN.

We grow cabbage and like to use it often in our own recipes. It was a natural choice to add this tomato-based soup.
—Bill Brim, Tiffin, Georgia

- 1 pound bulk Italian sausage
- 1 large onion, chopped
- 2 garlic cloves, minced

- 7 cups chopped cabbage (about 1-1/2 pounds)
- 4 cans (28 ounces *each*) diced tomatoes, undrained
- 2 teaspoons dried basil
- 2 teaspoons brown sugar
- 1 teaspoon dried oregano
- 1 bay leaf
- 3/4 teaspoon minced fresh rosemary *or* 1/4 teaspoon dried rosemary, crushed
- 1/2 teaspoon salt
- 1/8 teaspoon pepper

In a Dutch oven or soup kettle, cook sausage, onion and garlic over medium heat until meat is no longer pink. Add cabbage; cook and stir for 3-5 minutes or until cabbage is crisp-tender.

Stir in remaining ingredients. Bring to a boil. Reduce heat; cover and simmer for 30-35 minutes or until cabbage is tender. Discard bay leaf. Yield: 16 servings (4 quarts).

Sauerkraut Soup

The medley of tomato, sauerkraut and smoked sausage gives this savory soup an old-world flavor. It's simple to make and serve, especially during these cold months. The tangy taste and aroma really warm you up!
—Jean Marie Cornelius
Whitesville, New York

Sauerkraut Soup

PREP: 10 MIN.
COOK: 1 HOUR 10 MIN.

- 1 pound smoked Polish sausage, cut into 1/2-inch pieces
- 5 medium potatoes, peeled and cubed
- 2 medium onions, chopped
- 2 carrots, cut into 1/4-inch slices
- 3 cans (14-1/2 ounces *each*) chicken broth
- 1 can (32 ounces) sauerkraut, rinsed and drained
- 1 can (6 ounces) tomato paste

In a large saucepan or Dutch oven, combine the sausage, potatoes, onions, carrots and chicken broth; bring to a boil. Reduce heat; cover and simmer for 30 minutes or until potatoes are tender.

Add sauerkraut and tomato paste; mix well. Return to a boil. Reduce heat; cover and simmer 30 minutes longer. If a thinner soup is desired, add additional water or chicken broth. Yield: 8-10 servings (2-1/2 quarts).

Whenever I make this soup in the morning, it's gone by evening! Friends and family alike rave about the unbeatable combination of down-home flavors.
—Patricia Batchelder, Fond du Lac, Wisconsin

Cajun Corn Soup

PREP: 20 MIN.
COOK: 1 HOUR 20 MIN.

Cajun Corn Soup

Cajun stewed tomatoes give this recipe a bolder taste than the original version that just used stewed tomatoes. Now I prepare this dish for out-of-state guests who want to taste Cajun food. Everyone who tries it gives it high marks.
—Sue Fontenot
Kinder, Louisiana

- 1 cup chopped onion
- 1 cup chopped green pepper
- 6 green onions, sliced
- 1/2 cup vegetable oil
- 1/2 cup all-purpose flour
- 3 cups water
- 1 can (14-1/2 ounces) Cajun-style stewed tomatoes
- 2 cups chopped peeled tomatoes
- 1 can (16 ounces) tomato paste
- 2 packages (16 ounces *each*) frozen corn
- 3 cups cubed fully cooked ham
- 1-1/2 pounds smoked sausage, cut into 1/4-inch pieces
- 1/8 teaspoon cayenne pepper *or* to taste

Salt to taste

Hot pepper sauce to taste

In a large skillet or Dutch oven, saute the onion, green pepper and green onions in oil for 5-6 minutes or until tender. Gradually stir in flour and cook until bubbly. Stir in water, tomatoes and tomato paste. Stir in the corn, ham, sausage, cayenne pepper, salt and hot pepper sauce. Bring to a boil, stirring frequently. Reduce heat; simmer, uncovered, for 1 hour, stirring occasionally. Yield: 12-14 servings.

Creamy Wild Rice Soup

PREP: 15 MIN.
COOK: 1 HOUR 20 MIN.

- 3/4 cup uncooked wild rice
- 1 tablespoon vegetable oil
- 4 cups water
- 1/2 teaspoon salt
- 1 medium onion, chopped
- 1 celery rib, diced
- 1/2 cup butter, cubed
- 1 medium carrot, diced
- 1/2 cup all-purpose flour
- 3 cups chicken broth
- 2 cups half-and-half cream
- 1 cup diced fully cooked ham
- 1/2 teaspoon dried rosemary
- 1/4 teaspoon pepper

In Dutch oven or soup kettle, saute rice in oil over medium heat, for 5 minutes. Add water and salt; bring to a boil. Reduce heat; cover and simmer for 35 minutes (rice

Zucchini Sausage Soup

I've received numerous 4-H cooking awards over the past few years and often cook for my family...much to my mom's delight.
—Lindsay Gibson
New Springfield, Ohio

Zucchini Sausage Soup

PREP: 10 MIN. **COOK:** 1 HOUR

12	ounces uncooked breakfast sausage links
1	cup chopped celery
1/2	cup chopped onion
1	pound zucchini, sliced
3	cans (14-1/2 ounces *each*) stewed tomatoes
1	can (14-1/2 ounces) chicken broth
2	teaspoons garlic powder
1	teaspoon salt
1/2	teaspoon dried oregano
1/2	teaspoon Italian seasoning
1/2	teaspoon sugar
1/4	teaspoon dried basil
1	medium green pepper, chopped

Cut sausage into 1/4-in. slices; brown in a Dutch oven or soup kettle. Add celery and onion; saute until tender. Drain. Stir in the zucchini, tomatoes, broth and seasonings; bring to a boil. Reduce heat; simmer, uncovered, for 35 minutes. Add green pepper and simmer for 10 minutes. Yield: 6-8 servings (2 quarts).

will not be completely cooked). Drain, reserving 1-1/2 cups cooking liquid; set rice and liquid aside separately.

In the same kettle, saute the onion, celery and carrot in butter until onion is crisp-tender. Reduce heat; stir in flour and cook until bubbly. Gradually add broth and cooking liquid; stirring constantly. Bring to a boil; cook and stir for 2 minutes or until thickened. Add the cream, ham, rosemary, pepper and rice. Reduce heat; cover and simmer for 30-35 minutes or until rice is tender. Yield: 8 servings (2 quarts).

Potato and Cabbage Soup

PREP: 10 MIN. **COOK:** 30 MIN.

This recipe originated with my great-grandmother, whose parents were potato farmers in Ireland.
—Pat Rimmel
Ford City, Pennsylvania

1	large onion, chopped
2	tablespoons butter
10	cups water
6	cups chopped cabbage
4	cups diced peeled potatoes
3	tablespoons chicken bouillon granules
1/2	teaspoon coarsely ground pepper
1/2	teaspoon dried minced garlic
4	cups cubed fully cooked ham

In a large saucepan or Dutch oven, saute onion in butter until tender. Add the water, cabbage, potatoes, bouillon, pepper and garlic. Bring to a boil. Reduce heat; cover and simmer for 20-25 minutes or until potatoes are tender. Stir in ham; heat through. Yield: 12-14 servings (about 3-1/2 quarts).

**Creamy Ham and
Asparagus Soup**

*Like most country cooks, I often
bake a large ham so that I can use
leftovers in tasty dishes like this.
Fresh asparagus is wonderful in
this soup's creamy broth.*
—Maurine Kent
Kilgore, Texas

Creamy Ham and Asparagus Soup

PREP/TOTAL TIME: 30 MIN.

- 1-1/2 cups cut fresh asparagus (1-inch pieces)
- 1 medium carrot, julienned
- 2 tablespoons butter
- 3 small onions, quartered
- 2 tablespoons all-purpose flour
- 1 cup milk
- 1 cup chicken broth
- 1 cup cubed fully cooked ham
- 1 jar (2-1/2 ounces) sliced mushrooms, drained
- 1 cup half-and-half cream

Salt and pepper to taste

Grated Parmesan cheese, optional

Chopped fresh parsley, optional

Place asparagus in a large saucepan with enough water to cover; cook until crisp-tender. Drain and set aside.

In a large heavy saucepan, saute carrot in butter for 3-5 minutes; add onions and saute 2 minutes longer or until tender. Stir in flour; gradually add milk. Bring to a boil; cook and stir for 2 minutes or until thickened. Add the broth, ham, mushrooms and reserved asparagus. Reduce heat; add cream. Heat through but do not boil. Add salt and pepper. Garnish with Parmesan cheese and parsley if desired. Yield: 4 servings.

Sausage Kale Soup

PREP: 10 MIN. **COOK:** 25 MIN.

- 3/4 cup chopped onion
- 2 garlic cloves, minced
- 1 tablespoon olive oil
- 4 cups reduced-sodium chicken broth
- 2 medium potatoes, peeled and cubed
- 1/4 teaspoon salt
- 1/4 teaspoon pepper
- 1 pound fresh kale, trimmed and chopped
- 1 can (15 ounces) white kidney *or* cannellini beans, rinsed and drained
- 1/2 pound reduced-fat smoked Polish sausage *or* turkey kielbasa, sliced

In a large saucepan or Dutch oven, saute onion and garlic in oil until tender. Add the broth, potatoes, salt and pepper. Bring to a boil. Reduce heat; cover and simmer for 10-15 minutes or until potatoes are tender.

Using a potato masher, mash potatoes slightly. Add the kale, beans and sausage; cook over medium-low heat until kale is tender. Yield: 7 servings.

Sausage Kale Soup

*The hearty sausage slices, white
kidney beans and colorful kale in
this soup will have your gang
asking for seconds.*
—Susan Pursell
Fountain Valley, California

French Bread Pizza Soup

PREP: 5 MIN. **COOK:** 40 MIN.

- 2 cans (14-1/2 ounces *each*) diced tomatoes
- 2 cans (10-3/4 ounces *each*) condensed tomato soup, undiluted
- 2-1/2 cups water
- 1 package (3-1/2 ounces) sliced pepperoni, quartered
- 1 medium sweet red pepper, chopped
- 1 medium green pepper, chopped
- 1 cup sliced fresh mushrooms
- 2 garlic cloves, minced
- 1/2 teaspoon rubbed sage
- 1/2 teaspoon dried basil
- 1/2 teaspoon dried oregano

Salt and pepper to taste

- 10 slices French bread, toasted
- 1-1/2 cups (6 ounces) shredded part-skim mozzarella cheese

In a Dutch oven or soup kettle, bring the tomatoes, soup and water to a boil. Reduce heat; cover and simmer for 15 minutes. Mash with a potato masher. Add the pepperoni, red and green peppers, mushrooms, garlic, sage, basil, oregano, salt and pepper. Cover and simmer for 10 minutes or until vegetables are tender.

Ladle into ovenproof bowls. Top each with a slice of bread and sprinkle with cheese. Broil 4 in. from the heat until cheese is melted and bubbly. Yield: 10 servings (about 2-1/2 quarts).

Spicy Zucchini Soup

PREP: 20 MIN. **COOK:** 1-1/2 HOURS

My files are overflowing with recipes I keep meaning to try, so when I encountered a bumper crop of zucchini, I finally had the chance to simmer up this soup. Now, I look forward to it every summer.
—Catherine Johnston
Stafford, New York

- 1 pound bulk Italian sausage
- 3 cans (28 ounces *each*) diced tomatoes, undrained
- 3 cans (14-1/2 ounces *each*) beef broth
- 2 pounds zucchini, diced
- 2 medium green peppers, diced
- 2 cups thinly sliced celery
- 1 cup chopped onion
- 2 teaspoons Italian seasoning
- 1 teaspoon dried basil
- 1 teaspoon dried oregano
- 1 teaspoon salt
- 1/2 teaspoon sugar
- 1/4 teaspoon pepper
- 1/4 teaspoon garlic powder
- 3 cups cooked macaroni

In a Dutch oven or soup kettle, cook sausage over medium heat until no longer pink; drain. Add the tomatoes, broth, zucchini, green peppers, celery, onion and seasonings; bring to a boil. Reduce heat; cover and simmer for 1-1/4 to 1-1/2 hours or until vegetables are tender. Add macaroni; heat through. Yield: 14-16 servings (4 quarts).

French Bread Pizza Soup

This robust soup is a family favorite, and it's a big hit with my canasta group as well. I top each bowl with a slice of toasted bread and cheese, but you can have fun incorporating other pizza toppings such as cooked sausage.
—Jackie Brossard
Kitchener, Ontario

Parmesan Potato Soup
Even my husband, who's not much of a soup eater, likes this. Our two boys do, too. With homemade bread and a salad, it's a complete meal.
—*Tami Walters*
Kingsport, Tennessee

- 1/2 cup all-purpose flour
- 1/2 teaspoon dried basil
- 1/2 teaspoon seasoned salt
- 1/4 teaspoon celery salt
- 1/4 teaspoon garlic powder
- 1/4 teaspoon onion salt
- 1/4 teaspoon pepper
- 1/4 teaspoon rubbed sage
- 1/4 teaspoon dried thyme
- 4-1/2 cups chicken broth
- 6 cups milk
- 3/4 to 1 cup grated Parmesan cheese
- 10 bacon strips, cooked and crumbled

Pierce potatoes with a fork; bake at 375° for 40-60 minutes until tender. Cool, peel and cube; set aside.

In a large Dutch oven or soup kettle, saute onion in butter until tender. Stir in flour and seasonings until blended. Gradually add broth, stirring constantly. Bring to a boil; cook and stir for 2 minutes or until thickened. Add potatoes; return to a boil. Reduce heat; cover and simmer for 10 minutes.

Add milk and cheese; heat through. Stir in bacon. Yield: 10-12 servings (about 3 quarts).

Cauliflower Pork Soup

PREP/TOTAL TIME: 30 MIN.

This recipe was given to me by a friend several years ago.
—*Loretta Wohlenhaus*
Cumberland, Iowa

- 1 pound ground pork
- 1 small head cauliflower, broken into florets
- 2 cups water
- 1/2 cup chopped onion
- 2 cups milk, *divided*
- 1/4 cup all-purpose flour
- 2 cups (8 ounces) shredded sharp cheddar cheese
- 1/2 teaspoon salt
- 1/8 teaspoon pepper

Chopped chives, optional

In a large skillet, cook pork over medium heat until no longer pink; drain and set aside.

In a large kettle or Dutch oven, bring cauliflower and water to a boil. Reduce heat; cook for 10 minutes or until tender. Do not drain. Add the pork, onion and 1-1/4 cups milk to cauliflower.

In a small bowl, combine flour and remaining milk until smooth; stir into cauliflower mixture. Bring to a boil; cook and stir for 2 minutes or until thickened. Remove from the heat; add cheese, salt and pepper, stirring until cheese is melted. Garnish with chives if desired. Yield: 6-8 servings (2 quarts).

Parmesan Potato Soup

PREP: 40 MIN + COOLING
COOK: 20 MIN.

- 4 medium baking potatoes (about 2 pounds)
- 3/4 cup chopped onion
- 1/2 cup butter

Meatless

Vegetarian Split Pea Soup

PREP: 15 MIN. **COOK:** 1-1/2 HOURS

Even the pickiest eater will request this version of split pea soup. Thick and well-seasoned, it packs a nutritional punch, plus plenty of fiber and protein. It's wonderful with a slice of crusty French bread.
—Michele Doucette
Stephenville, Newfoundland and Labrador

- 6 **cups vegetable broth**
- 2 **cups dried green split peas, rinsed**
- 1 **medium onion, chopped**
- 1 **cup chopped carrots**
- 2 **celery ribs with leaves, chopped**
- 2 **garlic cloves, minced**
- 1/2 **teaspoon dried marjoram**
- 1/2 **teaspoon dried basil**
- 1/4 **teaspoon ground cumin**
- 1/2 **teaspoon salt**
- 1/4 **teaspoon pepper**
- 5 **tablespoons shredded carrots**

In a large saucepan, combine the first nine ingredients; bring to a boil. Reduce heat; cover and simmer for 1 hour or until peas are tender, stirring occasionally.

Add salt and pepper; simmer 10 minutes longer. Cool slightly. In small batches, puree soup in a blender; return to the pan. Heat for 5 minutes. Garnish with shredded carrots. **Yield:** 7 servings.

Carrot Zucchini Soup

PREP: 30 MIN. **COOK:** 30 MIN.

- 2 **small onions**
- 2 **cups water**
- 1/2 **pound carrots, cut into 1-inch pieces**
- 1/8 **teaspoon celery salt**
- 1/8 **teaspoon pepper**
- 2 **cups diced zucchini (3 to 4 medium)**
- 1-1/2 **teaspoons olive oil**
- 1-1/2 **teaspoons butter**
- 1/2 **cup chopped seeded tomatoes**
- 2/3 **cup evaporated milk**
- 2 **tablespoons minced fresh parsley**

Chop one onion; set aside. Quarter the other onion and place in a 3-qt. saucepan. Add the water, carrots, celery salt and pepper; bring to a boil. Reduce heat; cover and simmer for 20 minutes or until carrots are tender. Transfer to a blender or food processor; cover and process until pureed. Return to the pan.

In a large skillet, saute the zucchini and chopped onion in oil and butter until tender; add to carrot mixture. Stir in tomatoes. Cover and simmer for 10 minutes or until tomatoes are tender. Stir in milk and parsley; heat through. **Yield:** 2-4 servings.

Carrot Zucchini Soup
Here's an easy way to get kids to eat their vegetables. Carrots were never my family's favorite, but with this delicious soup, they hardly know they're eating them.
—Joanne Novellino
Bayville, New Jersey

This flavorful soup tastes so fresh you'll never know it's been frozen. You can easily double the recipe when tomatoes are plentiful or toss in extra vegetables from your garden. For heartier fare, mix in ground beef, sausage or meatballs.
—*Elizabeth Moore, Frankfort, Kentucky*

Garden Tomato Soup

PREP: 30 MIN. **COOK:** 20 MIN.

- 1 cup chopped celery
- 1 small onion, chopped
- 1 medium carrot, shredded
- 1 small green pepper, chopped
- 1/4 cup butter, cubed
- 4-1/2 cups vegetable *or* chicken broth, *divided*
- 4 cups chopped peeled tomatoes (about 7 medium)
- 2 teaspoons sugar
- 1/2 teaspoon curry powder
- 1/2 teaspoon salt
- 1/4 teaspoon pepper
- 1/4 cup all-purpose flour

In a large saucepan, saute the celery, onion, carrot and green pepper in butter until tender. Add 4 cups broth, tomatoes, sugar, curry, salt and pepper; bring to a boil. Reduce heat; simmer, uncovered, for 20 minutes.

In small bowl, stir flour and remaining broth until smooth. Gradually stir into tomato mixture. Bring to a boil; cook and stir for 2 minutes or until thickened. Yield: 6 servings (1-3/4 quarts).

Garden Tomato Soup
Delicious and filling are the words used to describe this soup whenever I've served it to friends. It makes a tasty lunch alone or with a sandwich.
—*Frances McFarlane*
Winnipeg, Manitoba

Freezer Vegetable Soup

PREP: 1-1/4 HOURS + CHILLING
COOK: 35 MIN.

SOUP BASE:
- 4 cups chopped tomatoes
- 1 cup chopped celery
- 1 cup chopped carrots
- 1 cup chopped onion
- 2 teaspoons sugar
- 1 teaspoon salt, optional
- 1/2 teaspoon pepper
- 1/2 teaspoon dill weed

ADDITIONAL INGREDIENTS
  (for *each* batch):
- 2 cups diced potatoes
- 2 cups water

Combine soup base ingredients in a kettle or Dutch oven; slowly bring to a boil over medium heat. Reduce heat; cover and simmer for 45 minutes. Cool. Place 2 cups each into freezer containers. May be frozen for up to 3 months.

To prepare soup: Thaw soup base in the refrigerator. Transfer to a kettle or Dutch oven. Add potatoes and water. Bring to a

Cold Raspberry Soup

I received this recipe more than 20 years ago and have since improved upon it. I serve my friends this delightful soup for lunch, usually with a large tomato stuffed with chicken or shrimp salad.
—Nola Rice
Miami, Arizona

colander; discard vegetables. If using immediately, skim fat or refrigerate for 8 hours or overnight; remove fat from surface. Broth can be covered and refrigerated for up to 3 days or frozen for up to 4 to 6 months. Yield: 5-1/2 cups.

boil. Reduce heat; cover and simmer for 30-40 minutes. Yield: 2 batches (4 cups each).

Vegetable Broth

PREP: 45 MIN. **COOK:** 1-3/4 HOURS

The flavor of celery and mushrooms comes through in this homemade vegetable broth. It can be used as a substitution for chicken broth, too.
—Taste of Home Test Kitchen

- 2 tablespoons olive oil
- 2 medium onions, cut into wedges
- 2 celery ribs, cut into 1-inch pieces
- 1 whole garlic bulb, separated into cloves and peeled
- 3 medium leeks, white and light green parts only, cleaned and cut into 1-inch pieces
- 3 medium carrots, cut into 1-inch pieces
- 8 cups water
- 1/2 pound fresh mushrooms, quartered
- 1 cup packed fresh parsley sprigs
- 4 sprigs fresh thyme
- 1 teaspoon salt
- 1/2 teaspoon whole peppercorns
- 1 bay leaf

Heat oil in a stockpot over medium heat until hot. Add the onions, celery and garlic. Cook and stir for 5 minutes or until tender. Add leeks and carrots; cook and stir 5 minutes longer. Add the water, mushrooms, parsley, thyme, salt, peppercorns and bay leaf; slowly bring to a boil. Reduce heat; simmer, uncovered, for 1 hour.

Remove from the heat. Strain through a cheesecloth-lined

Cold Raspberry Soup

PREP: 10 MIN. + CHILLING

- 4 cups fresh *or* frozen raspberries, thawed
- 1/4 cup dry red wine *or* white grape juice plus 1 teaspoon dry red wine *or* white grape juice
- 1/2 to 3/4 cup sugar
- 1 cup (8 ounces) sour cream

In a blender or food processor, combine the first three ingredients; cover and process until pureed. Strain seeds if desired. Transfer to a large bowl; whisk in sour cream until blended. Cover and chill for at least 1 hour. Yield: 4-6 servings.

Apricot Squash Soup

This unusual, golden soup combines two of our favorite foods—nutritious butternut squash and apricots. It's thick, rich and simple to make. It will dress up any meal.
—Jean Hennessey Klein, New Berlin, Wisconsin

Creamy Tomato Soup

My husband, who doesn't like tomato soup, really enjoys this creamy version. It's easy, but it tastes like you put a lot of work into it. When I share it with co-workers, everyone loves it.
—Marie Keyes
Cheney, Washington

Creamy Tomato Soup

PREP/TOTAL TIME: 30 MIN.

1	medium onion, chopped
2	tablespoons butter
2	cans (14-1/2 ounces *each*) diced tomatoes, undrained
2	cans (10-3/4 ounces *each*) condensed tomato soup, undiluted
1-1/2	cups milk
1	teaspoon sugar
1/2	to 1 teaspoon dried basil
1/2	to 1 teaspoon paprika
1/8	to 1/4 teaspoon garlic powder
1	package (8 ounces) cream cheese, cubed

In a large saucepan, saute onion in butter until tender. Stir in the tomatoes, soup, milk, sugar, basil, paprika and garlic powder. Bring to a boil. Reduce heat; cover and simmer for 10 minutes. Add cream cheese; stir until melted. Serve immediately. Yield: 8 servings (2 quarts).

Apricot Squash Soup

PREP: 20 MIN. **COOK:** 25 MIN.

1	medium onion, chopped
1	tablespoon olive oil
2	cups cubed peeled butternut squash
1	can (15 ounces) apricot halves in extra light syrup, drained
1	can (14-1/2 ounces) reduced-sodium chicken broth
1/8	teaspoon pepper
1	green onion, thinly sliced

In a saucepan, saute onion in oil until tender. Add squash; cook and stir for 2 minutes. Add the apricots, broth and pepper; bring to a boil. Reduce heat; cover and simmer for 15-20 minutes or until squash is tender. Cool slightly.

Process in small batches in a blender or food processor until smooth. Return to the pan and heat through. Garnish with green onion. Yield: 4 servings.

Cauliflower Soup

Cauliflower and carrots share the stage in this cheesy soup that's sure to warm you up on the chilliest nights. We like it with hot pepper sauce; however, it can be omitted with equally tasty results.
—*Debbie Ohlhausen*
Chilliwack, British Columbia

Tortellini Soup

PREP/TOTAL TIME: 30 MIN.

Fast and flavorful are the two qualities that make this soup a standard in my kitchen. This eye-appealing soup uses fresh vegetables and packaged tortellini.
—*Chris Snyder, Boulder, Colorado*

- 5 **cups vegetable *or* chicken broth**
- 3-1/2 **cups shredded carrots (about 10 ounces)**
- 1 **cup chopped yellow summer squash**
- 3 **cups torn fresh spinach**
- 1 **package (9 ounces) refrigerated cheese tortellini**

In a large saucepan, combine the broth, carrots and squash. Bring to a boil. Reduce heat; simmer, uncovered, for 3 minutes. Stir in spinach and tortellini. Cover and cook for 5 minutes or until tortellini is tender and heated through. Yield: 7 servings.

Cauliflower Soup

PREP/TOTAL TIME: 30 MIN.

- 1 **medium head cauliflower, broken into florets**
- 1 **medium carrot, shredded**
- 1/4 **cup chopped celery**
- 2-1/2 **cups water**
- 2 **teaspoons vegetable *or* chicken bouillon granules**
- 3 **tablespoons butter**
- 3 **tablespoons all-purpose flour**
- 3/4 **teaspoon salt**
- 1/8 **teaspoon pepper**
- 2 **cups milk**
- 1 **cup (4 ounces) shredded cheddar cheese**
- 1/2 **to 1 teaspoon hot pepper sauce, optional**

In a large bowl, combine the cauliflower, carrot, celery, water and bouillon. Bring to a boil. Reduce heat; cover and simmer for 12-15 minutes or until vegetables are tender (do not drain).

In another large saucepan, melt butter. Stir in the flour, salt and pepper until smooth. Gradually add milk. Bring to a boil over medium heat; cook and stir for 2 minutes or until thickened. Reduce heat. Add cheese; stir until melted. Add hot pepper sauce if desired. Stir into the cauliflower mixture. Yield: 8 servings (about 2 quarts).

Summer Vegetable Soup

This vegetable soup is chock-full of garden goodness, from zucchini and green beans to celery and potato, but it's the turmeric that gives it a tasty new twist.
—Edith Ruth Muldoon, Baldwin, New York

Summer Vegetable Soup

PREP/TOTAL TIME: 30 MIN.

- 1 small onion, quartered and thinly sliced
- 1 tablespoon olive oil
- 4 cups vegetable *or* reduced-sodium chicken broth
- 1 cup sliced zucchini
- 1 can (15-1/2 ounces) navy beans, rinsed and drained
- 1/2 cup diced peeled red potato
- 1/2 cup cut fresh green beans (2-inch pieces)
- 1/2 cup chopped peeled tomato
- 1/4 teaspoon pepper
- 1/8 teaspoon ground turmeric
- 1/4 cup chopped celery leaves
- 2 tablespoons tomato paste

In a large saucepan, saute onion in oil until tender. Add the broth, vegetables, pepper and turmeric. Bring to a boil. Reduce heat; cover and simmer for 20-30 minutes or until vegetables are tender.

Stir in celery leaves and tomato paste. Cover and let stand for 5 minutes before serving. Yield: 4 servings.

Fresh Fruit Soup

PREP: 20 MIN. + CHILLING

- 1 can (12 ounces) frozen orange juice concentrate, thawed
- 1-1/2 cups sugar
- 1 cinnamon stick (2 inches)
- 6 whole cloves
- 1/4 cup cornstarch
- 2 tablespoons lemon juice
- 2 cups sliced fresh strawberries
- 2 medium bananas, sliced
- 2 cups halved green grapes

In a large saucepan, mix orange juice with water according to package directions. Remove 1/2 cup of juice; set aside. Add sugar, cinnamon stick and cloves and remaining orange juice to saucepan; bring to a boil. Reduce heat and simmer for 5 minutes.

Combine cornstarch and reserved orange juice until smooth; stir into pan. Bring to a boil; cook and stir until for 2 minutes or until thickened. Remove from the heat and stir in lemon juice.

Pour into a large bowl; cover and chill. Just before serving, remove the spices and stir in fruit. Yield: 8-10 servings (about 2-1/2 quarts).

Fresh Fruit Soup
Entertaining is a big part of a military wife's life—my husband was a career Army man—so my recipe got a lot of use! It's a great cool-down after Mexican food, but I've also served it with butter cookies at a baby shower. We're now retired here in the Utah Rockies.
—Jenny Sampson
Layton, Utah

Broccoli Potato Soup

PREP/TOTAL TIME: 10 MIN.

- 2 cups fresh broccoli florets
- 1 small onion, thinly sliced
- 1 tablespoon butter
- 1 can (10-3/4 ounces) condensed cream of potato soup, undiluted
- 1 cup milk
- 1/2 cup water
- 3/4 teaspoon minced fresh basil or 1/4 teaspoon dried basil
- 1/4 teaspoon pepper
- 1/3 cup shredded cheddar cheese

In a large saucepan, saute broccoli and onion in butter until tender. Stir in the soup, milk, water, basil and pepper; heat through. Add cheese; stir until melted. Yield: 4 servings.

Asparagus Soup

PREP: 15 MIN. **COOK:** 45 MIN.

Each spring, my husband takes our dogs and searches for wild asparagus. He's been so successful that I finally developed this recipe. We look forward to this special soup every year.
—Betty Jones, Kohler, Wisconsin

- 1 cup chopped onion
- 6 green onions, sliced
- 3 tablespoons butter
- 1-1/2 cups sliced fresh mushrooms
- 1 pound fresh asparagus, trimmed and cut into 1/2-inch pieces
- 6 cups vegetable or chicken broth
- 1/2 cup chopped fresh parsley
- 1/2 teaspoon salt
- 1/2 teaspoon dried thyme
- 1/4 teaspoon pepper
- 1/8 teaspoon cayenne pepper
- 2 cups cooked wild rice
- 3 tablespoons cornstarch
- 1/3 cup water

In a 3-qt. saucepan, saute onions in butter for 4 minutes. Add mushrooms and cook until tender. Add the asparagus, broth and seasonings; cover and simmer for 30 minutes.

Add rice. Combine cornstarch and water until smooth; gradually stir into soup. Bring to a boil; cook and stir for 2 minutes or until thickened. Yield: 8-10 servings (2-1/4 quarts).

Pineapple Peach Soup

PREP: 25 MIN. + CHILLING

I like to take this one-of-a-kind, chilled soup to potlucks and other bring-a-dish events. It is usually different than what other people bring, and everyone raves about the flavors.
—Teresa Lynn, Kerrville, Texas

- 6 medium fresh peaches, peeled and sliced
- 1 can (8 ounces) crushed unsweetened pineapple, undrained
- 1/4 cup white grape juice
- 1/4 cup lemon juice
- 2 tablespoons honey

Broccoli Potato Soup

A few handy ingredients can make canned soup taste just like homemade. The creamy mixture that results is brimming with chunks of broccoli and potato.
—Barbara Baker
Valparaiso, Indiana

Vegetable Bean Soup

Ladened with vegetables and beans, this robust soup is sure to satisfy your hungry bunch. It is wonderfully easy to make and very tasty. In summer, use fresh produce from the garden or your local farmers market. In winter, just use frozen or open some cans of veggies—it couldn't be simpler!
—Cathy Seed
Hudson, Ohio

3/4 **teaspoon ground cinnamon**
1/4 **teaspoon ground nutmeg**
1 **medium cantaloupe, peeled, seeded and cubed**
1 **cup orange juice**
Fresh strawberries and whipped cream, optional

In 3-qt. saucepan, combine the peaches, pineapple, grape juice, lemon juice, honey, cinnamon and nutmeg; bring to a boil over medium heat. Reduce heat and simmer, uncovered, for 10 minutes. Remove from the heat; cool to room temperature.

In a blender or food processor, add three-fourths of the cantaloupe and the orange juice in batches; cover and process on high until smooth. Pour into a large bowl. Add remaining cantaloupe. Cover and refrigerate for at least 3 hours. Garnish with strawberries and whipped cream

if desired. Yield: 8-10 servings (2-1/4 quarts).

Vegetable Bean Soup

PREP: 10 MIN. **COOK:** 40 MIN.

1 **cup sliced carrots**
1 **cup thinly sliced zucchini**
3/4 **cup chopped onion**
1/2 **cup chopped sweet red pepper**
1 **tablespoon olive oil**
2 **cans (14-1/2 ounces *each*) vegetable broth**
1 **can (16 ounces) kidney beans, rinsed and drained**
1 **can (16 ounces) chili beans, undrained**
1 **can (15 ounces) garbanzo beans *or* chickpeas, rinsed and drained**

1 **can (14-1/2 ounces) stewed tomatoes, cut up**
1 **cup frozen white *or* frozen shoepeg corn**
4 **teaspoons ground cumin**
1/4 **teaspoon cayenne pepper**
2 **tablespoons minced fresh cilantro**

In a large saucepan or Dutch oven, saute the carrots, zucchini, onion and red pepper in oil until crisp-tender. Add the broth, beans, tomatoes, corn, cumin and cayenne; bring to a boil. Reduce heat; simmer, uncovered, for 30-35 minutes or until vegetables are tender, stirring occasionally. Stir in cilantro. Yield: 6 servings.

Italian Vegetable Soup

PREP/TOTAL TIME: 30 MIN.

- 2 cans (14-1/2 ounces *each*) vegetable *or* chicken broth
- 1 medium potato, peeled and cubed
- 1 medium onion, chopped
- 1 medium carrot, chopped
- 1 celery rib, chopped
- 1/2 cup frozen peas
- 1 bay leaf
- 1 teaspoon Italian seasoning
- 1/8 teaspoon pepper
- 1/2 cup small shell pasta, cooked and drained
- 1 can (14-1/2 ounces) diced tomatoes, undrained

In a large saucepan, combine the first nine ingredients. Bring to a boil. Reduce heat; cover and simmer for 15-20 minutes or until vegetables are crisp-tender.

Add the pasta and tomatoes; heat through. Discard bay leaf. Yield: 6 servings.

Basil Tomato Soup

PREP/TOTAL TIME: 30 MIN.

Corn dresses up this quick and easy tomato soup. My husband and two sons—who don't always care for soup—like this as much as I do. It's a great way to use up end-of-summer tomatoes.
—*Alice Culberson*
Kingsport, Tennessee

- 1/2 cup uncooked small shell pasta
- 3/4 cup chopped red onion
- 3/4 cup diced celery
- 3 garlic cloves, minced
- 4 teaspoons olive oil
- 3/4 cup fresh *or* frozen corn, thawed
- 4-1/2 cups vegetable broth
- 1 to 2 tablespoons minced fresh basil leaves
- 3/4 teaspoon salt
- 1/8 teaspoon pepper
- 6 medium firm tomatoes, peeled, seeded and chopped

Cook pasta according to package directions; drain and set aside.

Meanwhile in a large saucepan, saute the onion, celery and garlic in oil for 8-10 minutes or until tender. Add corn; saute for 2 minutes. Add the broth, basil, salt and pepper. Bring to a boil. Reduce heat; cover and simmer for 15 minutes. Stir in pasta and tomatoes until heated through. Yield: 7 servings.

Knoephla Soup

PREP: 20 MIN. **COOK:** 40 MIN.

While I was growing up, my mom would make this traditional German soup. It tasted so good on chilly fall days. Knoephla (pronounce nip-fla) Soup is still a warm and comforting meal for my family.
—*Lorraine Meyers*
Willow City, North Dakota

- 1/2 cup butter, cubed
- 3 medium potatoes, peeled and cubed
- 1 small onion, grated
- 3 cups milk
- 6 cups water

Italian Vegetable Soup

One night when my husband and I needed a quick supper, I threw together this basic soup using only what we had on hand. It's a family favorite, and it's good for us, too!
—*Margaret Glassic*
Easton, Pennsylvania

Macaroni Minestrone Soup

Brimming with a harvest of garden bounty, this quick-to-fix soup is fresh-tasting and nutritious. The tomato-based broth is chock-full of everything from carrots and zucchini to garbanzo beans and elbow macaroni.
—Heather Ryan
Brown Deer, Wisconsin

6 teaspoons vegetable *or* chicken bouillon granules

KNOEPHLA:

1-1/2 cups all-purpose flour
1 egg, beaten
5 to 6 tablespoons milk
1/2 teaspoon salt

In a large skillet, melt butter; cook potatoes and onion for 20-25 minutes or until tender. Add milk; heat through, but do not boil. Set aside. In a soup kettle or Dutch oven, bring water and bouillon to a boil.

Meanwhile, combine knoephla ingredients to form a stiff dough. Roll into a 1/2-in. rope. Cut into 1/4-in. pieces and drop into boiling broth. Reduce heat; cover and simmer for 10 minutes. Add the potato mixture; heat through. Yield: 8-10 servings (2-1/2 quarts).

Macaroni Minestrone Soup

PREP: 10 MIN. **COOK:** 35 MIN.

4 medium carrots, chopped
1 medium zucchini, sliced
1/4 cup chopped onion
1 garlic clove, minced
1 tablespoon olive oil
2 cans (14-1/2 ounces *each*) vegetable broth
3 cups V8 juice
1 can (15 ounces) garbanzo beans *or* chickpeas, drained
1 can (14-1/2 ounces) diced tomatoes, undrained
1 cup frozen cut green beans
1/2 cup uncooked elbow macaroni
1 teaspoon dried basil
1 tablespoon minced fresh parsley

In a Dutch oven, cook the carrots, zucchini, onion and garlic in oil for 7 minutes or until onion is tender. Add the broth, V8 juice, garbanzo beans, tomatoes, green beans, macaroni and basil. Bring to a boil.

Reduce heat; simmer, uncovered, for 15 minutes. Stir in parsley. Cook 5 minutes longer or until macaroni is tender. Yield: 8 servings (about 2 quarts).

Onion Tomato Soup

Fresh herbs really make the difference in the flavor of this low-fat vegetarian soup. Try it for lunch or savor it for supper.
—Lisa Blackwell
Henderson, North Carolina

Onion Tomato Soup

PREP: 10 MIN. **COOK:** 40 MIN.

- 2 cups thinly sliced onions
- 4 teaspoons olive oil
- 2-2/3 cups tomato juice
- 2 cups water
- 2 tablespoons minced fresh basil
- 2 teaspoons minced fresh oregano
- 1 teaspoon sugar
- 1 teaspoon celery salt
- 2 cups diced seeded plum tomatoes

In a large saucepan, saute onion in oil until tender. Add the tomato juice, water, basil, oregano, sugar and celery salt. Bring to a boil. Reduce heat; simmer, uncovered, for 20 minutes, stirring occasionally. Add the tomatoes; cook 10 minutes longer. Yield: 6 servings.

Taco Twist Soup

PREP/TOTAL TIME: 20 MIN.

- 1 medium onion, chopped
- 2 garlic cloves, minced
- 2 teaspoons olive oil
- 3 cups vegetable broth *or* reduced-sodium beef broth
- 1 can (15 ounces) black beans, rinsed and drained
- 1 can (14-1/2 ounces) diced tomatoes
- 1-1/2 cups picante sauce
- 1 cup uncooked spiral pasta
- 1 small green pepper, chopped
- 2 teaspoons chili powder
- 1 teaspoon ground cumin
- 1/2 cup shredded reduced-fat cheddar cheese
- 3 tablespoons reduced-fat sour cream

In a large saucepan, saute onion and garlic in oil until tender. Add the broth, beans, tomatoes, picante sauce, pasta, green pepper and seasonings. Bring to a boil, stirring frequently. Reduce heat; cover and simmer for 10-12 minutes or until pasta is tender, stirring occasionally. Serve with cheese and sour cream. Yield: 6 servings.

Taco Twist Soup

I lightened up this soup recipe by substituting black beans for the ground beef originally called for, and by topping off bowlfuls with reduced-fat sour cream and cheese. Spiral pasta adds a fun twist.
—Colleen Zertler
Menomonie, Wisconsin

Tomato Green Bean Soup

PREP: 10 MIN. **COOK:** 35 MIN.

- 1 cup chopped onion
- 1 cup chopped carrots
- 2 teaspoons butter
- 6 cups vegetable *or* chicken broth
- 1 pound fresh green beans, cut into 1-inch pieces
- 1 garlic clove, minced
- 3 cups diced fresh tomatoes
- 1/4 cup minced fresh basil *or* 1 tablespoon dried basil
- 1/2 teaspoon salt
- 1/4 teaspoon pepper

In a large saucepan, saute onion and carrots in butter for 5 minutes. Stir in the broth, beans and garlic; bring to a boil. Reduce heat; cover and simmer for 20 minutes or until vegetables are tender.

Stir in the tomatoes, basil, salt and pepper. Cover and simmer 5 minutes longer. Yield: 9 servings.

Winter Vegetable Soup

PREP: 20 MIN.
COOK: 1 HOUR 20 MIN.

Folks always seem to ask for the recipe whenever I make this flavorful filling soup that uses refried beans.
—Gertrude Vinci, Reno, Nevada

- 1 cup chopped celery
- 1/2 cup chopped onion
- 1 garlic clove, minced
- 2 tablespoons olive oil
- 1-1/2 quarts water
- 1 can (14-1/2 ounces) diced tomatoes, undrained
- 3 medium potatoes, peeled and cubed
- 2 medium carrots, diced
- 1 cup chopped cabbage
- 3 tablespoons minced fresh parsley
- 2 teaspoons brown sugar
- 1-1/4 teaspoons salt
- 1 teaspoon dried marjoram
- 1/2 teaspoon dried rosemary, crushed
- 1/4 teaspoon pepper
- 1/8 teaspoon cayenne pepper
- 2 cans (16 ounces *each*) refried beans with green chilies
- 1 can (15 to 16 ounces) kidney beans, rinsed and drained

Hot cooked macaroni

In a Dutch oven, saute the celery, onion and garlic in oil until tender. Add water, vegetables, parsley, sugar, and seasonings; bring to a boil. Reduce heat; cover and simmer for 40 minutes.

Stir in beans. Cover and simmer for 20 minutes or until vegetables are tender. Serve over macaroni. Yield: 12-16 servings (4 quarts).

Southern Garden Soup

PREP/TOTAL TIME: 30 MIN.

Filled with garden-fresh flavors, this soup is a wonderful way to use up summer's produce.
—Leslie Owens
Poplar Bluff, Missouri

Tomato Green Bean Soup

Serve this colorful, delicious soup anytime of year. When I can't get homegrown tomatoes and green beans, frozen beans and canned tomatoes work just fine. Served with warm breadsticks, this soup is a complete meal.
—Bernice Nolan
Granite City, Illinois

Savory Cheese Soup

A friend shared this delectable soup recipe and it instantly became a hit with my husband. Its big cheese flavor blends perfectly with the vegetables. I first served this creamy soup as part of a holiday meal, but now we enjoy it throughout the year.
—Dee Falk
Stromsburg, Nebraska

12-1/4   cups water, *divided*
1/2   cup pearl onions
5   teaspoons vegetable *or* beef bouillon granules
2   cups fresh cauliflowerets
2   pounds fresh asparagus, trimmed and cut into 1/2-inch pieces
1   can (8 ounces) sliced water chestnuts, drained
1   cup chopped fresh spinach
1/2   cup minced chives
1/2   teaspoon dried marjoram
1/2   teaspoon salt
1/8 to 1/4   teaspoon pepper
1/8   teaspoon ground nutmeg
3   tablespoons cornstarch

In a Dutch oven, bring 6 cups water to a boil. Add pearl onions; boil for 3 minutes. Drain and rinse in cold water; peel and set aside.

In another Dutch oven or soup kettle, bring 6 cups water and bouillon to a boil. Add cauliflower and onions; cover and cook for 5 minutes. Add the asparagus, water chestnuts, spinach and seasonings; cover and cook for 5 minutes or until asparagus is tender.

Combine cornstarch and remaining water until smooth; stir into soup. Bring to a boil; cook and stir for 2 minutes or until thickened. Serve immediately. Yield: 9 servings (2-1/4 quarts).

Savory Cheese Soup

PREP/TOTAL TIME: 25 MIN.

1/4   cup chopped onion
3   tablespoons butter
1/4   cup all-purpose flour
1/4   teaspoon salt
1/8   teaspoon pepper
1/8   teaspoon garlic powder
2   cups milk
1   can (14-1/2 ounces) vegetable *or* chicken broth
1/2   cup shredded carrots
1/2   cup finely chopped celery
1-1/2   cups (6 ounces) shredded cheddar cheese
3/4   cup shredded part-skim mozzarella cheese
Minched chives, optional

In a large saucepan, saute onion in butter until tender. Add the flour, salt, pepper and garlic powder; stir until smooth. Gradually add milk; cook and stir over medium heat until thickened and bubbly.

Meanwhile, bring broth to a boil in a saucepan. Add carrot and celery; simmer for 5 minutes or until vegetables are tender. Add to milk mixture and stir until blended. Reduce heat; add cheeses. Cook and stir until melted (do not boil). Garnish with chives if desired. Yield: 4 servings.

Cream Soups & Chowders

Crab Bisque

PREP/TOTAL TIME: 15 MIN.

I love to try new recipes. This down-home chowder has a rich broth that's swimming with tasty chunks of crab and crunchy corn. It also freezes well.
—*Sherrie Manton*
Folsom, Louisiana

- 1 celery rib, thinly sliced
- 1 small onion, chopped
- 1/2 cup chopped green pepper
- 3 tablespoons butter
- 2 cans (14-3/4 ounces *each*) cream-style corn
- 2 cans (10-3/4 ounces *each*) condensed cream of potato soup, undiluted
- 1-1/2 cups milk
- 1-1/2 cups half-and-half cream
- 2 bay leaves
- 1 teaspoon dried thyme
- 1/2 teaspoon garlic powder
- 1/4 teaspoon white pepper
- 1/8 teaspoon hot pepper sauce
- 3 cans (6 ounces *each*) crabmeat, drained, flaked and cartilage removed

In a large saucepan or soup kettle, saute celery, onion and green pepper in butter until tender. Add the corn, soup, milk, cream and seasonings; mix well. Stir in crab; heat through. Discard bay leaves. Yield: 10 servings (2-1/2 quarts).

Bacon Potato Chowder

PREP: 30 MIN. **COOK:** 40 MIN.

- 12 bacon strips, diced
- 2 medium onions, chopped
- 6 celery ribs, sliced
- 12 medium potatoes, peeled and cubed
- 1/3 cup butter
- 1 cup all-purpose flour
- 8 cups milk
- 2 medium carrots, shredded
- 1 tablespoon salt
- 1 teaspoon pepper

In a large skillet, cook bacon over medium heat until crisp. Using a slotted spoon, remove to paper towels. Drain, reserving 3 tablespoons dripping. Saute onions and celery in the reserved drippings until tender; drain.

Meanwhile, place potatoes in a Dutch oven and cover with water. Bring to a boil. Reduce heat; cover and cook for 20 minutes or until tender. Drain; set potatoes aside. In the same pan, melt butter. Stir in flour until smooth; gradually stir in milk. Bring to a boil over medium heat; cook and stir for 2 minutes or until thickened.

Reduce heat; add onion mixture, potatoes, carrots, salt and pepper. Cook for 10 minutes or until heated through. Sprinkle with bacon. Yield: 12-14 servings (about 3-1/2 quarts).

Bacon Potato Chowder
This is a hearty, stick-to-your-ribs potato soup. In place of the bacon, you can substitute cubed cooked ham.
—*Bob Wedemeyer*
Lynnwood, Washington

This is a new twist on an old favorite—pumpkin soup. I add a little ginger and sage to apples and squash to make this home-style soup. My family loves it when autumn rolls around.
—Crystal Ralph-Haughn, Bartlesville, Oklahoma

Mexican Chicken Corn Chowder

PREP/TOTAL TIME: 30 MIN.

Mexican Chicken Corn Chowder

I like to make this smooth, creamy soup when company comes to visit. Its zippy flavor is full of Southwestern flair. My family enjoys dipping slices of homemade bread in this chowder to soak up every bite.
—Susan Garoutte
Georgetown, Texas

1-1/2	pounds boneless skinless chicken breasts, cut into 1-inch pieces
1/2	cup chopped onion
1	to 2 garlic cloves, minced
3	tablespoons butter
2	chicken bouillon cubes
1	cup hot water
1/2	to 1 teaspoon ground cumin
2	cups half-and-half cream
2	cups (8 ounces) shredded Monterey Jack cheese
1	can (14-3/4 ounces) cream-style corn
1	can (4 ounces) chopped green chilies, undrained
1/4	to 1 teaspoon hot pepper sauce
1	medium tomato, chopped

Minced fresh cilantro, optional

In a Dutch oven, brown chicken, onion and garlic in butter until chicken is no longer pink. Dissolve the bouillon in hot water. Add to pan along with cumin; bring to a boil. Reduce heat; cover and simmer for 5 minutes.

Add the cream, cheese, corn, chilies and hot pepper sauce. Cook and stir over low heat until the cheese is melted. Stir in

tomato. Serve immediately; sprinkle with cilantro if desired. Yield: 6-8 servings (2 quarts).

Apple Squash Soup

PREP: 10 MIN.
COOK: 35 MIN. + COOLING

1	large onion, chopped
1/2	teaspoon rubbed sage
2	tablespoons butter
1	can (14-1/2 ounces) chicken broth
3/4	cup water
2	medium Granny Smith *or* other tart apples, peeled and finely chopped
1	package (12 ounces) frozen mashed squash, thawed
1	teaspoon ground ginger
1/2	teaspoon salt
1/2	cup fat-free milk

In a saucepan, saute onion and sage in butter for 3 minutes or until tender. Add the broth, water and apples; bring to a boil. Reduce heat; cover and simmer for 12 minutes. Add the squash, ginger and salt; return to a boil. Reduce

Potato Cheese Soup

My father was Swiss, so cheese has been a basic food in our family as long as I can remember. With its big cheese taste, you'll want to prepare this soup often. A steaming bowl plus a salad and a slice of bread makes a wonderful light meal.
—Carol Smith
New Berlin, Wisconsin

heat; simmer, uncovered, for 10 minutes. Cool until lukewarm.

Process in batches in a blender or food processor until smooth; return to pan. Add milk; heat through. (Do not boil.) Yield: 5 servings.

Potato Cheese Soup

PREP/TOTAL TIME: 30 MIN.

- 3 medium potatoes (about 1 pound), peeled and quartered
- 1 small onion, finely chopped
- 1 cup water
- 1 teaspoon salt
- 3 cups milk
- 3 tablespoons butter, melted
- 2 tablespoons all-purpose flour
- 2 tablespoons minced fresh parsley
- 1/8 teaspoon white pepper
- 1 cup (4 ounces) shredded Swiss cheese

In a large saucepan, bring potatoes, onion, water and salt to a boil. Reduce heat; cover and simmer for 15-20 minutes or until potatoes are tender. Do not drain; mash slightly. Stir in milk.

Meanwhile, in a small bowl, blend the butter, flour, parsley and pepper; stir into the potato mixture. Cook and stir over medium heat until thickened and bubbly. Remove from the heat; add cheese and stir until almost melted. Yield: 6 servings (1-1/2 quarts).

Carrot Leek Soup

PREP: 20 MIN. **COOK:** 15 MIN.

The vegetables in this pretty golden soup are pureed, so you can disguise them from picky eaters!

This is a filling meal in itself.
—Norma Meyers
Huntsville, Arkansas

- 1 medium leek, thinly sliced
- 4 teaspoons reduced-fat margarine
- 6 medium carrots, sliced
- 2 medium potatoes, peeled and cubed
- 3 cans (14-1/2 ounces *each*) reduced-sodium chicken broth
- 2 cups fat-free milk
- 1/8 teaspoon pepper

In a large saucepan, saute leek in margarine until tender. Add the carrots, potatoes and broth; bring to a boil. Reduce heat; cover and simmer until vegetables are tender. Cool to room temperature.

Remove vegetables with a slotted spoon to a blender or food processor. Add enough cooking liquid to cover; blend until smooth. Return to pan. Stir in milk and pepper; heat through. Yield: 10 servings.

Seafood Chowder

My husband, Chad, is an avid fisherman. When a family party was planned and we had to bring something, we created this recipe using fish from our freezer. The chowder got rave reviews from the relatives.
—Heather Saunders, Belchertown, Massachusetts

Seafood Chowder

PREP: 30 MIN. **COOK:** 30 MIN.

- 1/2 **pound sliced bacon, diced**
- 2 **medium onions, chopped**
- 6 **cups cubed peeled potatoes**
- 4 **cups water**
- 1 **pound bay *or* sea scallops, quartered**
- 1 **pound fresh *or* frozen lobster, cut into 1-inch pieces**
- 1 **pound uncooked medium shrimp, peeled and deveined**
- 1 **pound cod, cut into 1-inch pieces**
- 1 **pound haddock, cut into 1-inch pieces**
- 1/2 **cup butter, melted**
- 4 **teaspoons salt**
- 4 **teaspoons minced fresh parsley**
- 1/2 **teaspoon curry powder**
- 2 **quarts milk**
- 1 **can (12 ounces) evaporated milk**

In a large soup kettle or Dutch oven, cook bacon over medium heat until crisp. Using a slotted spoon, remove to paper towels; reserve drippings. Saute onions in drippings until tender. Add potatoes and water; bring to a boil. Cook for 10 minutes.

Add the scallops, lobster, shrimp, cod, haddock. Cook for 10 minutes or until scallops are opaque, shrimp turn pink and fish flakes easily with a fork. Add the butter, salt, parsley and curry powder. Stir in milk and evaporated milk; heat through (do not boil). Garnish with bacon. Yield: 32 servings (8 quarts).

Broccoli Soup

PREP: 5 MIN.
COOK: 30 MIN. + COOLING

- 4 **cups chicken broth**
- 2 **to 2-1/2 pounds fresh broccoli spears, cut into florets**
- 1/2 **cup chopped green onions**
- 1 **tablespoon vegetable oil**
- 1/4 **cup all-purpose flour**
- 1 **teaspoon salt**
- 1/4 **teaspoon ground nutmeg**
- 1/8 **teaspoon pepper**
- 1 **cup half-and-half cream**

In a large saucepan, bring the broth to a boil; add broccoli. Reduce heat; cover and simmer until tender, about 10 minutes.

Meanwhile, in a small skillet, saute onions in oil until tender; stir into broth. Remove from heat; cool 10 to 15 minutes. Puree in small batches in a blender or food processor until smooth. Return all to the saucepan; set aside.

In a small bowl, combine flour, salt, nutmeg and pepper. Slowly add cream, stirring until smooth. Gradually stir in broccoli mixture. Return to the saucepan. Bring to a boil; cook and stir for 2 minutes or until thickened. Yield: 4 servings.

Broccoli Soup
This thick, creamy soup has wonderful broccoli flavor with just a hint of nutmeg. When it comes to broccoli recipes, this is one of my favorites.
—Marion Tipton
Phoenix, Arizona

Asparagus Chicken Chowder

PREP: 20 MIN. **COOK:** 1-3/4 HOURS

- 1 broiler/fryer chicken (3 to 3-1/2 pounds)
- 3-1/2 quarts water
- 2 teaspoons chicken bouillon granules
- 5 bacon strips, diced
- 2 medium carrots, chopped
- 1 medium onion, chopped
- 1/2 pound fresh asparagus, trimmed and cut into 1/2-inch pieces
- 2 cups cubed peeled potatoes
- 1 tablespoon salt
- 1-1/2 teaspoons dried thyme
- 1/2 teaspoon pepper
- 1/2 cup all-purpose flour
- 1-1/2 cups heavy whipping cream
- 2 tablespoons chopped fresh parsley

Place chicken, water and bouillon in a Dutch oven or soup kettle. Cover and slowly bring to a boil; skim foam. Reduce heat; cover and simmer for 45-60 minutes or until chicken is tender. Remove chicken from broth; let stand until cool enough to handle. Remove 1 cup broth and set aside.

In a large skillet, cook bacon over medium heat until crisp. Using a slotted spoon, remove bacon to paper towels. Drain, reserving 2 tablespoons drippings. Saute the carrots, onion and asparagus in drippings over medium heat until crisp-tender. Add to kettle along with the potatoes, salt, thyme and pepper; return to a boil. Reduce heat; cover and simmer for 20 minutes or until potatoes are tender.

Combine flour and reserved broth until smooth; stir into soup. Bring to a boil; cook and stir for 2 minutes. Remove chicken from bones; discard bones and skin. Cut chicken into thin strips; add to soup along with cream and parsley. Heat through (do not boil). Sprinkle with bacon just before serving. Yield: 16-18 servings (4-1/2 quarts).

Editor's Note: If fresh asparagus is unavailable, a 10-ounce box of frozen cut asparagus (thawed), may be used. Add it with the chicken, cream and parsley.

Asparagus Chicken Chowder

It makes me feel great to prepare a delicious soup like this one and set it on the table in my favorite soup tureen. Even my three children love it. The next day, we scramble for the leftovers, if there are any.
—Jona Fell
Appleton, Wisconsin

Curried Pumpkin Soup

PREP/TOTAL TIME: 20 MIN.

I whipped up this satisfying soup last Thanksgiving for my family, and everyone was crazy about it! Even my brother, who is one of the pickiest eaters I know, asked for seconds.
—Kimberly Knepper, Euless, Texas

- 1/2 pound fresh mushrooms, sliced
- 1/2 cup chopped onion
- 2 tablespoons butter
- 2 tablespoons all-purpose flour
- 1/2 to 1 teaspoon curry powder
- 3 cups vegetable broth
- 1 can (15 ounces) solid-pack pumpkin
- 1 can (12 ounces) evaporated milk
- 1 tablespoon honey
- 1/2 teaspoon salt

Spinach Bisque

This creamy, make-in-minutes soup turns an ordinary meal into an extra-special dinner.
—Patricia Tuckwiller
Lewisburg, West Virginia

Spinach Bisque

PREP/TOTAL TIME: 20 MIN.

1/2	cup chopped onion
2	tablespoons butter
1/3	cup all-purpose flour
1/2 to 1	teaspoon salt
1/8	teaspoon ground nutmeg
2-1/2	cups milk
1	cup water
3/4	cup cubed process cheese (Velveeta)
1	package (10 ounces) frozen chopped spinach, thawed and drained

Oyster crackers, optional

In a large saucepan, saute onion in butter until tender. Stir in the flour, salt and nutmeg until smooth. Gradually whisk in milk and water. Bring to a boil; cook and stir for 2 minutes or until thickened. Reduce heat to medium; add cheese and stir until melted. Stir in spinach; heat through. Serve with oyster crackers if desired. Yield: 5-6 servings.

1/4 teaspoon pepper
1/4 teaspoon ground nutmeg
Minced chives

In a large saucepan, saute the mushrooms and onion in butter until tender. Stir in the flour and curry powder until blended. Gradually add the broth. Bring to a boil; cook and stir for 2 minutes or until thickened. Add the pumpkin, milk, honey, salt, pepper and nutmeg; heat through. Garnish with chives if desired. Yield: 7 servings.

Cream of Wild Rice Soup

PREP: 15 MIN. **COOK:** 25 MIN.

I used to make this soup on the evening when we would pick out our Christmas tree. But my husband enjoys it so much, I now make it throughout the year.

—Tammy Bailey
Hastings, Minnesota

1	package (6 ounces) long grain and wild rice mix
1	cup chopped onion
4-1/2	teaspoons butter
4-1/2	teaspoons all-purpose flour
1/2	teaspoon ground mace

Pinch white pepper

3	cans (14-1/2 ounces *each*) chicken broth
2	cups half-and-half cream
1/2	cup white wine *or* additional chicken broth

Prepare rice mix according to package directions.

In a large saucepan, saute onion in butter until tender. Stir in the flour, mace and white pepper until blended. Gradually stir in the broth, cream, wine or additional broth and cooked rice. Bring to a boil, stirring constantly. Yield: 10 servings (2-1/2 quarts).

Canadian Cheese Soup

My family loves Canadian bacon, but I don't run across a lot of dishes that call for this pork product. Everyone was thrilled the first time I offered this succulent soup.
—Jolene Roudebush
Troy, Michigan

Canadian Cheese Soup

PREP: 15 MIN. **COOK:** 30 MIN.

- 3 cups chicken broth
- 4 medium potatoes, peeled and diced
- 2 celery ribs, diced
- 1 medium carrot, diced
- 1 small onion, diced
- 6 ounces Canadian bacon, trimmed and diced
- 2 tablespoons butter
- 2 tablespoons all-purpose flour
- 1 cup milk
- 2 cups (8 ounces) shredded cheddar cheese
- 1/8 teaspoon pepper

In a Dutch oven or soup kettle, combine the first five ingredients; bring to a boil. Reduce heat; cover and simmer for 20 minutes or until vegetables are very tender. With a potato masher, mash vegetables several times. Add bacon; continue to simmer.

Meanwhile, melt butter in a small saucepan; stir in the flour and cook, stirring constantly, for 1 minute. Gradually whisk in milk. Bring to a boil; cook and stir for 2 minutes (mixture will be thick). Add vegetable mixture, stirring constantly. Remove from the heat; add cheese and pepper. Stir just until cheese is melted. Yield: 8 servings (2 quarts).

Chilled Squash And Carrot Soup

PREP: 30 MIN. + CHILLING

- 1-1/2 pounds butternut squash, peeled, seeded and cubed (about 3 cups)
- 1 can (14-1/2 ounces) chicken broth
- 2 medium carrots, sliced
- 1 medium onion, chopped
- 1/4 teaspoon salt
- 1/2 cup fat-free evaporated milk
- 4 tablespoons reduced-fat sour cream

In a large saucepan, combine the squash, broth, carrots, onion and salt. Bring to a boil. Reduce heat; cover and simmer for 15-20 minutes or until vegetables are very tender. Remove from the heat; cool.

In a blender or food processor, puree squash mixture in batches. Transfer to a bowl, stir in milk. Cover and chill until serving. Garnish with sour cream. Yield: 4 servings.

Chilled Squash and Carrot Soup
This smooth soup is colorful as it is nutritious and filling. Served chilled, it makes an elegant first course when entertaining. But it's also good served warm.
—Elaine Sabacky
Litchfield, Minnesota

Creamy Corn Chowder

Corn really stars in this delectable recipe—it hits the spot whenever you crave a rich, hearty soup. I make it each year for a luncheon at our church's flea market, where it's always a big seller.
—*Carol Sundquist, Rochester, New York*

New England Clam Chowder

PREP: 15 MIN. **COOK:** 30 MIN.

- 4 medium potatoes, peeled and cubed
- 2 medium onions, chopped
- 1/2 cup butter
- 3/4 cup all-purpose flour
- 2 quarts milk
- 3 cans (6-1/2 ounces *each*) chopped clams, undrained
- 2 to 3 teaspoons salt
- 1 teaspoon ground sage
- 1 teaspoon ground thyme
- 1/2 teaspoon celery salt
- 1/2 teaspoon pepper

Minced fresh parsley

Place potatoes in a saucepan and cover with water; bring to boil. Cover and cook for 15-20 minutes or until tender.

Meanwhile, in a Dutch oven, saute onions in butter until tender. Add flour; stir until smooth. Gradually stir in milk. Bring to a boil; cook and stir for 2 minutes or until thickened.

Drain potatoes; add to Dutch oven. Add clams and remaining ingredients; heat through. Yield: 10-12 servings (3 quarts).

Creamy Corn Chowder

PREP/TOTAL TIME: 30 MIN.

- 2 chicken bouillon cubes
- 1 cup hot water
- 5 bacon strips
- 1 cup chopped green pepper
- 1/2 cup chopped onion
- 1/4 cup all-purpose flour
- 3 cups milk
- 1-1/2 cups fresh *or* frozen whole kernel corn
- 1 can (14-3/4 ounces) cream-style corn
- 1-1/2 teaspoons seasoned salt
- 1/4 teaspoon salt
- 1/8 teaspoon white pepper
- 1/8 teaspoon dried basil

Dissolve bouillon in water; set aside. In a large Dutch oven, cook bacon over medium heat until crisp. Remove bacon to paper towels to drain; crumble and set aside.

New England Clam Chowder

I wasn't satisfied with other recipes I came across for clam chowder, so I devised this one. Everyone who's tried it raves about it.
—*Rachel Nydam*
Uxbridge, Massachusetts

In a large skillet, saute green pepper and onion in the drippings until tender. Add flour; cook and stir until smooth. Gradually stir in milk and dissolved bouillon. Bring to a boil; cook and stir for 2 minutes or until thickened. Add corn and seasonings. Cook for 10 minutes or until heated through. Sprinkle with bacon. Yield: 6-8 servings (2 quarts).

Curried Zucchini Soup

PREP: 5 MIN.
COOK: 25 MIN. + COOLING

One of my daughters-in-law gave me the recipe for this soup. I freeze it and use it as a special treat on a cold winter's day. It calls to mind memories of the "zucchini summer"

that was—and gives hope of the "zucchini summer" yet to be!
—Ruth McCombie
Etobicoke, Ontario

- 2 pounds zucchini, sliced (about 4 medium)
- 5 green onions, chopped
- 4 cups chicken broth
- 1 to 2 tablespoons butter, optional
- 1-1/2 teaspoons curry powder
- 1 teaspoon salt
- 1/8 teaspoon cayenne pepper

In a large saucepan or Dutch oven, combine all the ingredients; bring to a boil. Reduce heat; cover and simmer until zucchini is soft, about 15 minutes. Cool.

Puree in batches in a blender on low speed; return to pan and heat through. Yield: 6-8 servings (2 quarts).

Cream of Cauliflower Soup
This mildly cheesy cauliflower soup is one of my favorites. I make it often in summer, although it's good anytime.
—Karen Brown
West Lafayette, Ohio

Cream of Cauliflower Soup

PREP/TOTAL TIME: 20 MIN.

- 1/3 cup green onions (tops only)
- 2 tablespoons butter
- 2 tablespoons all-purpose flour
- 1/2 teaspoon salt
- 2 cups chicken broth
- 1 package (10 ounces) frozen cauliflower, thawed and chopped
- 2 cups 1% milk
- 1-1/2 cups (6 ounces) shredded reduced-fat cheddar cheese
- 2 tablespoons dry sherry, optional
- 1 tablespoon minced chives

In a saucepan, saute onions in butter until tender. Stir in flour and salt until blended. Gradually add broth. Bring to a boil; cook and stir for 2 minutes or until thickened. Reduce heat.

Add cauliflower; simmer for 2 minutes. Add the milk and cheese; cook and stir until cheese is melted. Stir in sherry if desired. Garnish with chives. Yield: 6 servings.

Creamy Tomato Bisque

This rich bisque has a wonderful old-fashioned flavor. It makes a nice accompaniment to any meal.
—Cathy Fulton, Hazlet, New Jersey

Creamy Tomato Bisque

PREP: 5 MIN.
COOK: 40 MIN. + COOLING

- 2 cups water
- 4 chicken bouillon cubes
- 1 can (14-1/2 ounces) diced tomatoes
- 1/2 cup chopped celery
- 2 tablespoons chopped onion
- 2 medium fresh tomatoes, peeled and diced
- 1/4 cup butter, cubed
- 3 tablespoons all-purpose flour
- 2 cups half-and-half cream
- 1/3 to 1/2 cup sherry, optional

In a large saucepan, bring first five ingredients to a boil. Reduce heat; cover and simmer for 15-20 minutes or until vegetables are tender. Cool.

Puree mixture in a food processor or blender; set aside. In the same saucepan, saute fresh tomatoes in butter for 5 minutes. Stir in flour to make a smooth paste. Gradually add cream and stir over low heat until thickened. Stir in pureed mixture and sherry if desired; heat through. Yield: about 8 servings (2 quarts).

Panfish Chowder

PREP: 20 MIN. **COOK:** 40 MIN.

- 6 bacon strips, cut into 1-inch pieces
- 2/3 cup chopped onion
- 1/2 cup chopped celery
- 3 medium potatoes, peeled and cubed
- 2 cups water
- 1/2 cup chopped carrots
- 2 tablespoons minced fresh parsley
- 1 tablespoon lemon juice
- 1/2 teaspoon dill weed
- 1/4 teaspoon garlic salt
- 1/8 teaspoon pepper
- 1 pound panfish fillets (perch, sunfish *or* crappie), cut into 1-inch chunks
- 1 cup half-and-half cream

In a large saucepan, cook the bacon over medium heat until crisp. Using a slotted spoon, remove bacon to paper towels; drain, reserving 2 tablespoons drippings. Saute onion and celery in reserved drippings until tender.

Add the potatoes, water, carrots, parsley, lemon juice and seasonings. Bring to a boil. Reduce heat; simmer, uncovered, until vegetables are tender, about 30 minutes. Add fish and bacon; simmer for 5 minutes or just until fish flakes with a fork. Add cream and heat through (do not boil). Yield: 4-6 servings.

Panfish Chowder

With my husband being an avid hunter and fisherman, I can never have enough new fish and wild game recipes. We especially enjoy this chowder. It's a hearty dish with big chunks of fish, potatoes and bacon in a tempting creamy broth.
—Cyndi Fliss
Bevent, Wisconsin

Mushroom and Potato Chowder

My daughter shared this delightful recipe with me. Its rich broth, big mushroom taste and medley of vegetables make this chowder a little different from ordinary mushroom soup.
—Romaine Wetzel, Lancaster, Pennsylvania

Chilled Asparagus Soup

PREP: 10 MIN.
COOK: 1 HOUR + CHILLING

1	pound fresh asparagus, trimmed
5	cups chicken broth
1/2	cup water
1/4	cup butter, cubed
1/4	cup all-purpose flour
3	egg yolks, beaten
3/4	cup heavy whipping cream
1	teaspoon curry powder
1/8	teaspoon pepper

Dash lemon juice

Chilled Asparagus Soup
This is a delicious soup that's perfect for hot weather. The curry seasoning comes through just right.
—Kim Gilliland
Simi Valley, California

Cut asparagus into 1-in. pieces; set tips aside. Place the remaining asparagus in a saucepan; add broth. Bring to a boil; reduce heat. Cover and simmer for 40-45 minutes. Cool slightly.

Process in batches in a blender or food processor until smooth; set aside. In a small saucepan, bring water to a boil. Add the asparagus tips; cook for 2-3 minutes or until tender. Drain and chill until serving.

In a large saucepan, melt butter. Stir in flour until smooth. Gradually add pureed asparagus. Bring to a boil; cook and stir for 2 minutes or until thickened.

Remove from the heat. Stir a small amount of hot soup into egg yolks; return all to the pan, stirring constantly. Cook over low heat for 5 minutes or until mixture is heated through and reaches 160°. Stir in the cream, curry powder, pepper and lemon juice.

Remove from the heat; cool slightly. Cover and chill until serving. Garnish with asparagus tips, gently adding to each bowl. Yield: 8-10 servings.

Mushroom and Potato Chowder

PREP: 20 MIN. **COOK:** 50 MIN.

1/2	cup chopped onion
1/4	cup butter, cubed
2	tablespoons all-purpose flour
1	teaspoon salt
1/2	teaspoon pepper
3	cups water
1	pound fresh mushrooms, sliced
1	cup chopped celery
1	cup diced peeled potatoes
1/2	cup chopped carrots
1	cup half-and-half cream
1/4	cup grated Parmesan cheese

Autumn Chowder

When the weather turns cooler, we enjoy comfort foods like this hearty chowder. It's easy to prepare, and the aroma of it as it simmers makes my mouth water.
—Sheena Hoffman
North Vancouver, British Columbia

Ham 'n' Swiss Soup

PREP/TOTAL TIME: 25 MIN.

Loaded with ham and broccoli, this flavorful soup is sure to warm spirits. Add buttermilk biscuits and a simple spinach salad for a complete dinner.
—*Taste of Home Test Kitchen*

4-1/2 teaspoons butter
4-1/2 teaspoons all-purpose flour
   1 can (14-1/2 ounces) reduced-sodium chicken broth
   1 cup chopped broccoli
   2 tablespoons chopped onion
   1 cup cubed fully cooked ham
1/2 cup heavy whipping cream
1/8 teaspoon dried thyme
3/4 cup shredded Swiss cheese

In a saucepan, melt butter; whisk in flour until smooth. Gradually add broth. Bring to a boil; cook and stir for 2 minutes or until thickened. Add the broccoli and onion; cook and stir until crisp-tender. Add the ham, cream and thyme; heat through. Stir in the cheese until melted. Yield: 2 servings.

In a large saucepan, combine the water, tomato and chilies. Bring to a boil; boil for 5 minutes. Stir in the milk, soups and garlic salt. Cook and stir over medium heat until heated through. Place cheese cubes in serving bowls; ladle hot soup over cheese. Yield: 6 servings.

Autumn Chowder

PREP: 10 MIN. **COOK:** 35 MIN.

   2 bacon strips, diced
1/4 cup chopped onion
   1 medium red potato, cubed
   1 small carrot, halved lengthwise and thinly sliced
1/2 cup water
3/4 teaspoon chicken bouillon granules
   1 cup milk
2/3 cup frozen corn
1/8 teaspoon pepper

2-1/2 teaspoons all-purpose flour
   2 tablespoons cold water
3/4 cup shredded cheddar cheese

In a large saucepan, cook bacon over medium heat until crisp. Using a slotted spoon, remove to paper towels. Drain, reserving 1 teaspoon drippings. In the drippings, saute onion until tender. Add the potato, carrot, water and bouillon. Bring to a boil. Reduce heat; cover and simmer for 15-20 minutes or until the vegetables are almost tender.

Stir in the milk, corn and pepper. Cook 5 minutes longer. Combine the flour and cold water until smooth; gradually whisk into soup. Bring to a boil; cook and stir for 1-2 minutes or until thickened. Remove from the heat; stir in cheese until melted. Sprinkle with bacon. Yield: 2 servings.

Beans & Lentils

Sausage Lentil Soup

PREP: 15 MIN.
COOK: 1-1/4 HOURS

This soup tastes especially good with fresh sourdough bread.
—Catherine Rowe
Berthoud, Colorado

- 1/2   pound bulk Italian sausage
- 1   large onion, chopped
- 1   medium green pepper, chopped
- 1   large carrot, chopped
- 2   cans (10-1/2 ounces *each*) condensed chicken broth
- 1   can (14-1/2 ounces) diced tomatoes, undrained
- 1   cup water
- 1   garlic clove, minced
- 1   teaspoon salt
- 1/2   teaspoon pepper
- 3/4   cup dried lentils, rinsed

In a Dutch oven or soup kettle, crumble sausage. Cook over medium heat until no longer pink; drain. Add the onion, green pepper, carrot, broth, tomatoes, water, garlic, salt and pepper; bring to a boil. Add lentils. Reduce heat; cover and simmer for 60-70 minutes or until the lentils are tender. Yield: 6-8 servings (2 quarts).

Lucky Bean Soup

PREP: 30 MIN. + STANDING
COOK: 2-1/4 HOURS

- 1/4   cup *each* dried yellow split peas, lentils, black beans, great northern beans, pinto beans, baby lima beans and kidney beans
- 1/2   cup *each* dried green split peas, black-eyed peas and navy beans
- 8   cups water
- 1/3   cup dried minced onion
- 1   tablespoon salt
- 1   teaspoon dried thyme
- 1   teaspoon dried rosemary, crushed
- 1   teaspoon garlic powder
- 1/2   teaspoon celery seed
- 1/2   teaspoon dried basil
- 1/4   to 1/2 teaspoon crushed red pepper flakes
- 2   bay leaves
- 1   can (28 ounces) crushed tomatoes

Rinse and sort beans. Place split peas, lentils and beans in a Dutch oven or soup kettle; add water to cover by 2 in. Bring to a boil; boil for 2 minutes. Remove from the heat; cover and let stand for 1 to 4 hours or until beans are softened.

Drain and rinse, discarding liquid. Add water and seasonings; bring to a boil. Reduce heat; cover and simmer for 1-1/2 to 2 hours or until beans are just tender.

Stir in tomatoes; increase heat to medium. Cook, uncovered, for 15-30 minutes. Discard bay leaves. Yield: 14 servings (3-1/2 quarts).

Lucky Bean Soup
I developed this recipe as a bean soup gift pack for a fund-raiser at my church. We provide it along with the beans and a packet containing all the spices. The recipient just adds water and a can of tomatoes for a delicious pot of savory soup.
—Doris Cox
South Orange, New Jersey

Vegetable Black Bean Soup

Black beans and barley take vegetable soup in a tasty new direction. The spinach and tomatoes add extra color!
—Laura Letobar, Livonia, Michigan

White Bean Fennel Soup

PREP: 10 MIN. **COOK:** 45 MIN.

White Bean Fennel Soup

This filling soup is often requested for company dinners. A hint of fennel accents the flavor of this quick-to-fix bean soup, and spinach and tomatoes brighten the pot.
—Donna Quinn
Salem, Wisconsin

- 1 large onion, chopped
- 1 small fennel bulb, thinly sliced
- 1 tablespoon olive oil
- 5 cups reduced-sodium chicken broth *or* vegetable broth
- 1 can (15 ounces) white kidney *or* cannellini beans, rinsed and drained
- 1 can (14-1/2 ounces) diced tomatoes, undrained
- 1 teaspoon dried thyme
- 1/4 teaspoon pepper
- 1 bay leaf
- 3 cups shredded fresh spinach

In a large saucepan, saute onion and fennel in oil until tender. Add the broth, beans, tomatoes, thyme, pepper and bay leaf; bring to a boil. Reduce heat; cover and simmer for 30 minutes or until fennel is tender.

Discard bay leaf. Add spinach; cook 3-4 minutes longer or until spinach is wilted. Yield: 5 servings.

Vegetable Black Bean Soup

PREP: 10 MIN. **COOK:** 30 MIN.

- 2 cups chopped onions
- 1 cup chopped carrots
- 1 cup chopped celery
- 6 cups water
- 3 beef bouillon cubes
- 1 can (28 ounces) diced tomatoes, undrained
- 1 can (15 ounces) black beans, rinsed and drained
- 1 cup quick-cooking barley
- 1 teaspoon garlic powder
- 3/4 teaspoon pepper
- 1 package (10 ounces) frozen chopped spinach, thawed

In a large saucepan or Dutch oven coated with nonstick cooking spray, saute the onions, carrots and celery over medium heat until onions are soft, about 8 minutes. Stir in the water, bouillon, tomatoes, beans, barley, garlic powder and pepper; bring to a boil. Reduce heat; cover and simmer for 10 minutes.

Add spinach; cover and simmer for 10-15 minutes or until the

Chilled Bean Soup
Crunchy fresh veggies are combined with black beans and a splash of hot pepper sauce to create this spicy, chilled soup. I often serve this during the warm summer months, when tomatoes are in season. It tastes best when you let it mellow overnight in the refrigerator.
—Betty Nickels
Tampa, Florida

vegetables are tender. Yield: 14 servings (3-1/2 quarts).

Lemon Lentil Soup

PREP: 10 MIN. **COOK:** 1-1/4 HOURS

Loaded with protein-rich lentils, this hearty soup is rooted in the old-fashioned goodness of leeks, parsnips, celery and carrots. The addition of lemon juice transforms what might otherwise be an everyday soup into something out of the ordinary.
—Jean Rawlings
Saskatoon, Saskatchewan

- 1 cup chopped leeks (white portion only)
- 2 tablespoons vegetable oil
- 1 can (15 ounces) tomato puree
- 1 cup chopped celery
- 1 cup chopped carrots
- 1/4 cup chopped peeled parsnips
- 2 tablespoons dried basil
- 8 cups water
- 1-1/2 cups dried lentils, rinsed
- 2 bay leaves
- 1 tablespoon grated lemon peel
- 1-1/2 teaspoons salt
- 1 teaspoon dill weed
- 1/2 teaspoon pepper
- 2 to 3 tablespoons lemon juice

In a large saucepan, saute leeks in oil until tender. Add the tomato puree, vegetables and basil; saute for 3-4 minutes. Add water; bring to a boil. Add lentils and bay leaves. Reduce heat; cover and simmer for 30 minutes.

Stir in the lemon peel, salt, dill and pepper; simmer 30 minutes longer or until lentils are tender. Discard bay leaves. Stir in lemon juice. Yield: 6 servings.

Chilled Bean Soup

PREP: 15 MIN. + CHILLING

- 4 cups chopped seeded tomatoes
- 2 cups picante V8 juice
- 1 can (15 ounces) black beans, rinsed and drained
- 1 cup chopped cucumber
- 1 cup chopped sweet red *or* yellow pepper
- 1/2 cup chopped red onion
- 2 tablespoons balsamic vinegar
- 1 teaspoon sugar
- 1/4 to 1/2 teaspoon hot pepper sauce
- 1/4 teaspoon ground cumin
- 1/4 teapoon salt
- 1/4 teaspoon pepper
- 7 tablespoons reduced-fat sour cream

Sliced cucumber, optional

In a blender or food processor, combine tomatoes and V8 juice; cover and process just until blended. Transfer to a large bowl. Stir in the beans, chopped cucumber, sweet pepper, onion, vinegar, sugar and seasonings.

Cover and refrigerate for at least 4 hours or overnight. Serve with sour cream. Garnish with sliced cucumber if desired. Yield: 7 servings.

Hearty Lentil Soup

Served with biscuits and a salad, this soup is delicious on a cool autumn weekend. It's one of my all-time favorites.
—*Suzanne Prince, Spokane, Washington*

Hearty Lentil Soup

PREP: 10 MIN. **COOK:** 1 HOUR

- 2 celery ribs, thinly sliced
- 1 medium onion, chopped
- 1 garlic clove, minced
- 2 tablespoons butter
- 6 cups water
- 1 can (28 ounces) diced tomatoes, undrained
- 3/4 cup dried lentils, rinsed
- 3/4 cup medium pearl barley
- 2 tablespoons chicken bouillon granules
- 1/2 teaspoon dried oregano
- 1/2 teaspoon dried rosemary, crushed
- 1/4 teaspoon pepper
- 1 cup thinly sliced carrots
- 1 cup (4 ounces) shredded Swiss cheese, optional

In a Dutch oven or soup kettle, saute the celery, onion and garlic in butter until tender. Add the water, tomatoes, lentils, barley, bouillon, oregano, rosemary and pepper; bring to a boil. Reduce heat; cover and simmer for 40 minutes or until lentils and barley are almost tender.

Add carrots; simmer for 15 minutes or until carrots, lentils and barley are tender. Sprinkle each serving with cheese if desired. Yield: 8-10 servings (about 2-1/2 quarts).

Mexican Bean Soup

PREP: 20 MIN. **COOK:** 45 MIN.

- 2 pounds ground beef
- 1 medium onion, chopped
- 1 quart water
- 3 cans (14-1/2 ounces *each*) diced tomatoes, undrained
- 2 cans (15-1/2 ounces *each*) hominy, drained
- 2 cans (15-1/2 ounces *each*) ranch-style *or* chili beans
- 1 can (16 ounces) kidney beans, rinsed and drained
- 1 can (4 ounces) chopped green chilies
- 2 envelopes taco seasoning mix
- 1 envelope (1 ounce) original ranch dressing mix
- 2 tablespoons brown sugar
- 1/4 teaspoon cayenne pepper

Shredded cheddar cheese and sour cream, optional

In a Dutch oven or soup kettle, cook beef and onion over medium heat until meat is no longer pink; drain. Add the water, tomatoes, hominy, beans, chilies, seasoning mix, ranch dressing mix, sugar and cayenne; bring to a boil. Reduce heat; cover and simmer for 30 minutes. Garnish with cheese and sour cream if desired. Yield: 14-16 servings (4 quarts).

Mexican Bean Soup
For our family's fall birthday bash, I make a big pot of this soup and serve it with plenty of oven-fresh corn bread.
—*Vivian Christian Stephenville, Texas*

Hearty Navy Bean Soup

PREP: 30 MIN. + STANDING
COOK: 1-3/4 HOURS

- 3 cups (1-1/2 pounds) dried navy beans
- 1 can (14-1/2 ounces) diced tomatoes, undrained
- 1 large onion, chopped
- 1 meaty ham hock *or* 1 cup diced cooked ham
- 2 cups chicken broth
- 2-1/2 cups water
- Salt and pepper to taste
- Fresh chopped parsley

Rinse and sort beans. Place beans in a Dutch oven or soup kettle; add water to cover by 2 in. Bring to a boil; boil for 2 minutes. Remove from the heat; cover and let stand for 1 to 4 hours or until beans are softened.

Drain and rinse beans, discarding liquid. Place in a large Dutch oven or soup kettle. Add the tomatoes with juice, onion, ham hock, broth, water, salt and pepper. Bring to a boil. Reduce heat; cover and simmer until beans are tender, about 1-1/2 hours.

Add more water if necessary. Remove ham hock and let stand until cool enough to hand. Remove meat from bone; discard bone. Cut meat into bite-size pieces; set aside. (For a thicker soup, cool slightly, then puree beans in a food processor or blender and return to pan.) Return ham to soup and heat through. Garnish with parsley. Yield: 10 servings (2-1/2 quarts).

Hearty Navy Bean Soup

Beans were a commodity you did not survive without in the '30s. This excellent bean soup is a real family favorite of ours and I make it often.
—Mildred Lewis
Temple, Texas

Wisconsin Split Pea Soup

PREP: 10 MIN. + COOLING
COOK: 3 HOURS + COOLING

Field peas that have been dried (split peas) have been a staple soup ingredient for country cooks for years. Marjoram, garlic, potatoes and carrots blend nicely with peas in this hearty and economical soup.
—Linda Rock
Stratford, Wisconsin

- 1 pound dried green split peas
- 2-1/2 quarts water
- 1 meaty ham bone *or* 2 smoked ham hocks
- 1-1/2 cups chopped onions
- 1 cup *each* diced celery, carrots and potatoes
- 1 teaspoon dried parsley flakes
- 1/2 teaspoon pepper
- 1/4 teaspoon garlic salt
- 1/4 teaspoon dried marjoram
- Salt to taste

In a Dutch oven or soup kettle, add the peas, water and ham bone; bring to a boil. Reduce heat; cover and simmer for 2 hours, stirring occasionally.

Stir in remaining ingredients. Bring to a boil. Reduce heat; cover and simmer for 30 minutes or until vegetables are tender.

Set aside ham bone until cool enough to handle. Remove meat from bone; discard bone. Cut ham into bite-size pieces. Return to the soup and heat through. Yield: 12 servings (3 quarts).

White Bean 'n' Ham Soup

This soup is a winner on all three levels. It's easy on the budget, quick and yummy! While canned beans make this tasty main dish a fast fix, you can save money by soaking and cooking dry beans instead.
—Bissy Crosby
Columbia, Missouri

White Bean 'n' Ham Soup

PREP/TOTAL TIME: 30 MIN.

- 2   cans (15-1/2 ounces *each*) great northern beans, rinsed and drained
- 2   medium carrots, diced
- 1   small onion, chopped
- 2   tablespoons butter
- 2-1/4 cups water
- 1-1/2 cups cubed fully cooked ham
- 1/2 teaspoon salt
- 1/8 to 1/4 teaspoon white pepper
- 1   bay leaf

Mash one can of beans; set aside. In a saucepan, saute the carrots and onion in butter. Stir in the water, ham, seasonings and whole and mashed beans; cook over medium heat until heated through. Discard bay leaf. Yield: 6 servings.

Lentil Vegetable Soup

PREP: 10 MIN. **COOK:** 65 MIN.

Here is one good-for-you dish that our kids really enjoy. Serve this tasty soup as a meatless main dish...or pair it with a favorite sandwich.
—Joy Maynard
St. Ignatius, Montana

- 1/2 cup dried lentils, rinsed
- 3   cans (14-1/2 ounces *each*) vegetable broth
- 1/2 cup uncooked long grain brown rice
- 1   medium onion, chopped
- 1/2 cup tomato juice
- 1   can (5-1/2 ounces) spicy hot V8 juice
- 1   tablespoon reduced-sodium soy sauce
- 1   tablespoon vegetable oil
- 1   medium potato, peeled and cubed
- 1   medium tomato, cubed
- 1   medium carrot, sliced
- 1   celery rib, sliced

In a large saucepan, combine the first eight ingredients. Bring to a boil. Reduce heat; cover and simmer for 30 minutes.

Add the potato, tomato, carrot and celery; simmer 30 minutes longer or until rice and vegetables are tender. Yield: 6 servings.

Provencale Bean Soup

Provencale Bean Soup

We enjoy this soup's homegrown goodness so much I make an extra batch just to freeze it.
—Jan Marto
Algoma, Wisconsin

PREP: 30 MIN. + STANDING
COOK: 2-1/4 HOURS

- 1 **pound dried navy beans**
- 3 **medium leeks (white part only), chopped**
- 1 **medium onion, chopped**
- 2 **garlic cloves, minced**
- 1 **tablespoon vegetable oil**
- 9 **cups water**
- 1 **smoked boneless ham *or* pork shoulder (about 2 pounds), cubed**
- 4 **whole cloves**
- 2 **bay leaves**
- 1 **teaspoon dried thyme**
- 1 **teaspoon salt**
- 1/2 **teaspoon pepper**
- 5 **medium carrots, thinly sliced**
- 2 **medium turnips, peeled and cubed**
- 3 **small potatoes, peeled and cubed**
- 2 **cups shredded kale**
- 1/2 **cup minced fresh parsley**

Rinse and sort beans. Place beans in a Dutch oven or soup kettle; add water to cover by 2 in. Bring to a boil; boil for 2 minutes. Remove from the heat; cover and let stand for 1 to 4 hours or until beans are softened.

Drain and rinse, discarding liquid; set beans aside. In the same pan, saute the leeks, onion and garlic in oil until tender. Add the water, ham, cloves, bay leaves, thyme, salt, pepper and beans; bring to a boil. Reduce heat; cover and simmer for 1-1/4 hours or until the beans are almost tender.

Add carrots, turnips, potatoes, kale and parsley. Cover and simmer 25-35 minutes longer or until the beans and vegetables are tender. Discard bay leaves and cloves before serving. Yield: 16-18 servings (about 4-1/2 quarts).

Editor's Note: 2 cups of shredded cabbage may be substituted for the kale.

Fast Fiesta Soup

PREP/TOTAL TIME: 10 MIN.

- 2 **cans (10 ounces *each*) diced tomatoes and green chilies**
- 1 **can (15-1/4 ounces) whole kernel corn, drained**
- 1 **can (15 ounces) black beans, rinsed and drained**
- **Shredded cheddar cheese and sour cream, optional**

In a saucepan, combine the tomatoes, corn and beans; heat through. Garnish serving with cheese and sour cream if desired. Yield: 4 servings.

Fast Fiesta Soup

This colorful, spicy soup was served at a very elegant lunch, and the hostess was deluged with requests for the recipe.
—Patricia White
Monrovia, California

Black Bean Zucchini Gazpacho

*During the hot summer months, my family enjoys chilled soups.
I came up with this spicy blend when trying to use up our garden zucchini.
It's a hit with friends whenever I serve it, too.*
—*Julie Wilson, Grand Rapids, Ohio*

Campfire Bean 'N' Ham Soup

PREP: 15 MIN. + STANDING
GRILL: 1-1/2 HOURS

1	pound dried navy beans
2	small onions
8	cups water
4	cups cubed fully cooked lean ham (1-1/2 pounds)
2	smoked ham hocks
2	cups chopped celery
1	cup chopped carrots
1/2	teaspoon dried basil
1/2	teaspoon pepper

Campfire Bean 'n' Ham Soup

*These are the best beans and ham
you'll ever taste—bar none!
Friends rave about this classic soup
that I serve hot off the grill.*
—*Tom Greaves*
Carrollton, Illinois

Place beans in an ovenproof Dutch oven; add enough water to cover by 2 in. Bring to a boil; boil for 2 minutes. Remove from the heat; cover and let stand for 1 to 4 hours or until beans are softened. Chop one onion; slice the second onion and separate into rings.

Drain and rinse beans, discarding liquid. Return beans to the pan. Add onions and all the remaining ingredients. Cover pan and place on the grill rack over indirect medium heat. Cover grill; cook for 1 hour or until beans are almost tender.

Uncover the Dutch oven; cover grill and cook 30 minutes longer or until beans are tender. Discard ham hocks. Yield: 12 servings (3 quarts).

Black Bean Zucchini Gazpacho

PREP: 10 MIN. + CHILLING

3	cans (5-1/2 ounces *each*) spicy hot V8 juice
1	can (15 ounces) black beans, rinsed and drained
1	medium onion, chopped
2	large tomatoes, seeded and chopped
2	medium zucchini, chopped
2	tablespoons olive oil
2	tablespoons white wine vinegar
1	garlic clove, minced
1/4	teaspoon salt
1/4	teaspoon pepper
1/4	teaspoon cayenne pepper

In a large bowl, combine all the ingredients. Cover and refrigerate for 8 hours or overnight. Yield: 6 servings.

Mixed Bean Soup

Guests and family alike praise this soup and always ask for seconds. The nicest thing about it is that any variation of dry beans can be used.
—Arlene Hilman
Cawston, British Columbia

Navy Bean Soup

PREP: 10 MIN. + STANDING
COOK: 1 HOUR 10 MIN.

My kids can't resist their grandmother's bean soup. A touch of nutmeg sets it apart from all other kinds.
—Melissa Stuchlik
Lincolnville, Kansas

- 1 pound dried navy beans
- 8 cups water
- 1-1/2 to 2 pounds smoked ham hocks
- 1 cup chopped onion
- 1/4 cup chopped fresh parsley
- 1-1/2 teaspoons salt
- 1 teaspoon dried basil
- 1/2 teaspoon dried oregano
- 1/2 teaspoon pepper
- 1/4 teaspoon ground nutmeg
- 1 bay leaf
- 2 cups thinly sliced carrots
- 1 cup chopped celery
- 3/4 cup mashed potato flakes

Rinse and sort beans. Place beans in a Dutch oven or soup kettle; add water to cover by 2 in. Bring to a boil; boil for 2 minutes. Remove from the heat; cover and let stand for 1 to 4 hours or until beans are softened.

Drain and rinse, discarding liquid. Return beans to Dutch oven; add the water, ham hocks, onion, parsley and seasonings. Bring to a boil. Reduce heat; cover and simmer for 1 hour or until beans are tender.

Add the carrots, celery and potato flakes; mix well. Cover and simmer for 30 minutes or until vegetables are tender. Discard bay leaf. Set side ham hocks until cool enough to handle. Remove meat from bones; discard bones. Cut into bite-size pieces. Return meat to Dutch oven; heat through. Yield: 12-14 servings (3-1/2 quarts).

Mixed Bean Soup

PREP: 30 MIN. + STANDING
COOK: 2-1/2 HOURS

- 1 package (12 ounces) mixed dried beans
- 8 cups water
- 1/2 pound ground beef, cooked and drained
- 1 can (14-1/2 ounces) diced tomatoes, undrained
- 1 cup chopped celery
- 1 tablespoon salt
- 1 teaspoon dried parsley flakes
- 2 garlic cloves, minced
- 1 teaspoon dried thyme
- 2 bay leaves

Pepper to taste

Rinse and sort beans. Place beans in a Dutch oven or soup kettle; add water to cover by 2 in. Bring to a boil; boil for 2 minutes. Remove from the heat; cover and let stand for 1 to 4 hours or until beans are softened.

Drain and rinse, discarding liquid. Add water to the beans; bring to a boil. Cover and simmer for 30 minutes. Add remaining ingredients; bring to a boil. Reduce heat; cover and simmer for 1-1/2 to 2 hours or until beans are tender. Discard bay leaves. Yield: 10 servings (2-1/2 quarts).

Hearty Split Pea Soup

For a different spin on traditional split pea soup, try this recipe. The flavor is peppery rather than smoky, and the corned beef is an unexpected, tasty change of pace.
—Barbara Link, Alta Loma, California

Hearty Split Pea Soup

PREP: 15 MIN. **COOK:** 1-1/2 HOURS

- 1 package (16 ounces) dried split peas
- 8 cups water
- 2 medium potatoes, peeled and cubed
- 2 large onions, chopped
- 2 medium carrots, chopped
- 2 cups cubed cooked corned beef *or* ham
- 1/2 cup chopped celery
- 5 teaspoons chicken bouillon granules
- 1 teaspoon dried marjoram
- 1 teaspoon poultry seasoning
- 1 teaspoon rubbed sage
- 1/2 to 1 teaspoon pepper
- 1/2 teaspoon dried basil
- 1/2 teaspoon salt, optional

In a Dutch oven or soup kettle, combine all the ingredients; bring to a boil. Reduce heat; cover and simmer for 1-1/4 to 1-1/2 hours or until peas and vegetables are tender. Yield: 12 servings (3 quarts).

Mexican Bean Barley Soup

PREP: 10 MIN. **COOK:** 35 MIN.

- 2 medium onions, chopped
- 3 garlic cloves, minced
- 2 tablespoons vegetable oil
- 1 medium turnip, peeled and diced
- 1 medium carrot, diced
- 2 tablespoons finely chopped jalapeno pepper
- 1-1/2 teaspoons ground cumin
- 1/2 teaspoon ground coriander
- 3 cans (14-1/2 ounces *each*) vegetable broth
- 2 cups cooked barley
- 1 can (15 ounces) pinto beans, rinsed and drained
- 2 teaspoons lemon juice

In a large saucepan, saute onions and garlic in oil until tender. Add the turnip, carrot and jalapeno; cook and stir until tender. Add cumin and coriander; cook and stir for 2 minutes. Add broth. Bring to a boil. Reduce heat; cover and simmer for 20 minutes.

Add the barley, beans and lemon juice. Simmer, uncovered, 10-15 minutes longer or until soup thickens slightly. Yield: 7 servings.

Editor's Note: When cutting or seeding hot peppers, use rubber or plastic gloves to protect your hands. Avoid touching your face.

Mexican Bean Barley Soup
Wonderfully warming, this soup is always on the menu for the retreats we host on our woodland farm. Everyone enjoys spooning up its yummy vegetable broth and hearty mix of beans and barley. When I really want to bring smiles, I serve a basketful of my homemade onion-herb bread with it.
—Elizabeth Cole
Mauckport, Indiana

U.S. Senate Bean Soup

Chock-full of ham, beans and celery, this soup makes a wonderful meal any time of year. Freeze the bone from a holiday ham until you're ready to make soup. Plus, once prepared, it freezes well for a great make-ahead supper!
—Rosemarie Forcum, White Stone, Virginia

Hearty Black-Eyed Pea Soup

PREP: 10 MIN. **COOK:** 1 HOUR

- 1 pound bulk pork sausage
- 1 pound ground beef
- 1 large onion, chopped
- 4 cups water
- 3 cans (15-1/2 ounces *each*) black-eyed peas, rinsed and drained
- 1 can (28 ounces) diced tomatoes, undrained
- 1 can (10 ounces) diced tomatoes and green chilies, undrained
- 1 can (4 ounces) chopped green chilies
- 4 beef bouillon cubes
- 4 teaspoons molasses
- 1 teaspoon Worcestershire sauce
- 3/4 teaspoon garlic salt
- 1/2 teaspoon salt
- 1/4 teaspoon pepper
- 1/4 teaspoon ground cumin

In a Dutch oven or soup kettle, cook sausage, beef and onion over medium heat until meat is no longer pink; drain. Add remaining ingredients; bring to a boil. Reduce heat; cover and simmer for 45 minutes. Yield: 12-16 servings (4 quarts).

U.S. Senate Bean Soup

PREP: 30 MIN. + STANDING
COOK: 3-3/4 HOURS + COOLING

- 1 pound dried great northern beans
- 1 meaty ham bone *or* 2 smoked ham hocks
- 3 medium onions, chopped
- 3 garlic cloves, minced
- 3 celery stalks, chopped
- 1/4 cup chopped fresh parsley
- 1 cup mashed potatoes *or* 1/3 cup instant potato flakes

Salt and pepper to taste
Parsley *or* chives

Rinse and sort beans. Place beans in a Dutch oven or soup kettle; add water to cover by 2 in. Bring to a boil; boil for 2 minutes. Remove from the heat; cover and let stand for 1 to 4 hours or until beans are softened.

Drain and rinse, discarding liquid. In a large Dutch oven or soup kettle, place the beans, ham bone or hocks and 3 quarts water. Bring to boil. Reduce heat; cover and simmer for 2 hours.

Hearty Black-Eyed Pea Soup

I had eaten this soup countless times at a small restaurant in our town. When the owner finally retired, he said I deserved the secret recipe and passed it along. Now, my family enjoys it at least once a month!
—Alice Jarrell
Dexter, Missouri

Peasant Soup

Don't let the name fool you! This soup is anything but meager. The hearty vegetable broth really satisfies.
—Bertha McClung
Summersville, West Virginia

Skim fat if necessary. Add the onions, garlic, celery, parsley, potatoes, salt and pepper; simmer 1 hour longer.

Set aside ham bones until cool enough to handle. Remove meat from bones; discard bones. Cut meat into bite-size pieces and return to Dutch oven. Heat through. Sprinkle with parsley or chives. Yield: 8-10 servings (2-1/2 quarts).

Corn and Bean Soup

PREP/TOTAL TIME: 30 MIN.

For lunch or dinner on a chilly day, this fresh-tasting, colorful vegetable soup really hits the spot.
—Betty Andrzejewski
Chino, California

- 1-1/3 cups reduced-sodium chicken broth
- 2 medium carrots, diced
- 2 celery ribs, diced
- 1 small potato, peeled and diced
- 1 small onion, chopped
- 1-1/2 cups frozen corn
- 1 can (15 ounces) white kidney *or* cannellini beans, rinsed and drained
- 1 cup fat-free milk
- 1 teaspoon dried thyme
- 1/4 teaspoon garlic powder
- **Pepper to taste**

In a large saucepan, combine the broth, carrots, celery, potato and onion. Bring to a boil. Reduce heat; cover and simmer for 10-12 minutes or until vegetables are tender. Stir in the remaining ingredients; simmer 5-7 minutes longer or until corn is tender. Yield: 5 servings.

Peasant Soup

PREP: 30 MIN. + STANDING
COOK: 1-3/4 HOURS

- 1 pound dried great northern beans
- 6 cups water
- 3 carrots, sliced
- 3 celery ribs, sliced
- 2 medium onions, chopped
- 2 garlic cloves, minced
- 2 bay leaves
- 1 can (14-1/2 ounces) diced tomatoes, undrained
- 1 teaspoon dried basil
- 1/2 teaspoon pepper
- 2 tablespoons olive oil

Rinse and sort beans. Place beans in a Dutch oven or soup kettle; add water to cover by 2 in. Bring to a boil; boil for 2 minutes. Remove from the heat; cover and let stand for 1 to 4 hours or until beans are softened.

Drain and rinse, discarding liquid. Return to Dutch oven. Add 6 cups water, carrots, celery, onions, garlic, bay leaves, tomatoes, basil and pepper; bring to a boil. Reduce heat; cover and simmer for 1-1/2 hours or until the beans are tender.

Discard bay leaves. Add oil and heat through. Yield: 12 servings (3 quarts).

Chili

Thick Turkey Bean Chili

PREP: 5 MIN. **COOK:** 30 MIN.

When our daughters wouldn't eat the spicy chili beans I prepared, I came up with this milder version, which they love.
—Keri Scofield Lawson
Fullerton, California

- 1 **pound ground turkey**
- 2 **cans (16 ounces *each*) baked beans, undrained**
- 1 **can (16 ounces) kidney beans, rinsed and drained**
- 1 **can (15-1/2 ounces) sloppy joe sauce**
- 1 **can (14-1/2 ounces) diced tomatoes, undrained**
- 1 **tablespoon brown sugar**
- 1/4 **teaspoon *each* garlic powder, salt and pepper**

Shredded cheddar cheese, sour cream and tortilla chips, optional

In a large saucepan, cook turkey over medium heat until no longer pink; drain. Stir in the beans, sloppy joe sauce, tomatoes, brown sugar and seasonings. Simmer, uncovered, for 30 minutes or until heated through. Serve with cheese, sour cream and tortilla chips if desired. Yield: 8-10 servings (about 2-1/2 quarts).

Bulgur Chili

PREP: 10 MIN. + STANDING
COOK: 25 MIN.

- 3/4 **cup bulgur**
- 2 **cups boiling water**
- 1-1/2 **cups finely chopped green peppers**
- 1 **large onion, chopped**
- 2 **teaspoons vegetable oil**
- 2 **cups reduced-sodium tomato juice**
- 1 **can (16 ounces) kidney beans, rinsed and drained**
- 1 **can (15 ounces) ranch-style beans, undrained**
- 1 **can (14-1/2 ounces) diced tomatoes, undrained**
- 1 **can (8 ounces) tomato sauce**
- 1 **cup water**
- 2 **to 3 tablespoons chili powder**
- 2 **garlic cloves, minced**
- 1/2 **teaspoon ground cumin**
- 1/8 **to 1/4 teaspoon cayenne pepper**
- 3/4 **cup shredded reduced-fat cheddar cheese**

Place bulgur in a large bowl; stir in boiling water. Cover and let stand for 30 minutes or until most of the liquid is absorbed. Drain and squeeze dry.

In a large saucepan, saute green peppers and onion in oil until tender. Stir in the bulgur, tomato juice, beans, tomatoes, tomato sauce, water, chili powder, garlic, cumin and cayenne. Bring to a boil. Reduce heat; cover and simmer for 20-25 minutes or until heated through. Garnish with cheese. Yield: 9 servings (2-1/4 quarts).

Editor's Note: Look for bulgur in the cereal, rice or organic food aisle of your grocery store.

Bulgur Chili
This vegetarian chili is zesty, but it also offers a slight hint of sweetness. Because it doesn't have to simmer for hours like other chili recipes, it's ideal for serving to drop-in visitors.
—Jeraldine Hall
Ravenden Springs, Arkansas

You'll need just five ingredients to stir up this quick-and-easy chili. We like to use medium salsa for zippy flavor, but sometimes I use half mild and half medium. Sprinkle hearty servings with shredded cheddar cheese and other tasty toppings.
—*Jane Bone, Cape Coral, Florida*

White Chili with Chicken

PREP/TOTAL TIME: 30 MIN.

White Chili with Chicken

Folks who enjoy a change from traditional tomato-based chili will enjoy this version. The delectable blend has tender chunks of chicken, white beans and just enough zip.
—*Christy Campos*
Richmond, Virginia

- 1 medium onion, chopped
- 1 jalapeno pepper, seeded and chopped, optional
- 2 garlic cloves, minced
- 1 tablespoon vegetable oil
- 4 cups chicken broth
- 2 cans (15-1/2 ounces *each*) great northern beans, rinsed and drained
- 2 tablespoons minced fresh parsley
- 1 tablespoon lime juice
- 1 to 1-1/4 teaspoons ground cumin
- 2 tablespoons cornstarch
- 1/4 cup cold water
- 2 cups cubed cooked chicken

In a large saucepan, cook the onion, jalapeno if desired and garlic in oil until tender. Stir in the broth, beans, parsley, lime juice and cumin; bring to a boil. Reduce heat; cover and simmer for 10 minutes, stirring occasionally.

Combine cornstarch and water until smooth; stir into chili. Add chicken. Bring to a boil; cook and stir for 2 minutes or until thickened. Yield: 6 servings.

Editor's Note: When cutting or seeding hot peppers, use rubber or plastic gloves to protect your hands. Avoid touching your face.

Salsa Chili

PREP/TOTAL TIME: 20 MIN.

- 1 pound ground beef
- 1 medium onion, chopped
- 1 jar (16 ounces) salsa
- 1 can (15 ounces) pinto beans, rinsed and drained
- 1 can (5-1/2 ounces) tomato juice

Shredded cheddar cheese, chopped green peppers, sour cream and thinly sliced green onions, optional

In a saucepan, cook beef and onion over medium heat until meat is no longer pink; drain. Stir in the salsa, beans and tomato juice; bring to a boil. Reduce heat, simmer, uncovered, until heated through. Serve with cheese, peppers, sour cream and onions if desired. Yield: 5 servings.

Roasted Veggie Chili
This spicy entree placed third at a chili contest in Murphy, North Carolina. I wanted to make a good-for-you chili that also used veggies from my garden. My husband and I are chefs, but we also like to have fun and use our imaginations when we cook.
—C.J. Counts
Murphy, North Carolina

Roasted Veggie Chili

PREP: 30 MIN. **COOK:** 40 MIN.

- 2 cups fresh *or* frozen corn
- 2 cups *each* cubed zucchini, yellow summer squash and eggplant
- 2 *each* medium green peppers and sweet red peppers, cut into 1-inch pieces
- 2 large onions, chopped
- 1/2 cup garlic cloves, peeled
- 1/4 cup olive oil
- 4 quarts chicken broth
- 2 cans (14-1/2 ounces *each*) stewed tomatoes
- 2 cans (14-1/2 ounces *each*) tomato puree
- 1/4 cup lime juice
- 4 teaspoons chili powder
- 1-1/4 teaspoons cayenne pepper
- 1 teaspoon ground cumin
- 1/2 cup butter
- 1/2 cup all-purpose flour
- 3 cans (15 ounces *each*) white kidney *or* cannellini beans, rinsed and drained
- 1/2 cup minced fresh cilantro

Sour cream and chopped green onions, optional

Place the vegetables and garlic in a roasting pan. Drizzle with oil; toss to coat. Cover and bake at 400° for 20-30 minutes or until vegetables are tender; cool slightly. Remove and chop garlic cloves.

In a Dutch oven or soup kettle, combine the broth, tomatoes, tomato puree, lime juice, chili powder, cayenne and cumin; bring to a boil. Reduce heat; simmer, uncovered, for 25-35 minutes or until mixture is reduced by a quarter.

In a large saucepan or Dutch oven, melt butter; stir in flour until smooth. Cook and stir until bubbly and starting to brown. Slowly whisk into tomato mixture. Add the roasted vegetables, garlic, beans and cilantro; mix well. Simmer, uncovered, until chili reaches desired thickness. Garnish with sour cream and green onions if desired. **Yield:** 24 servings (6 quarts).

Round Steak Chili

PREP: 15 MIN. **COOK:** 3 HOURS

- 1 pound beef round steak
- 1 large onion, chopped
- 2 garlic cloves, minced
- 1 to 2 tablespoons vegetable oil
- 1 can (46 ounces) V8 juice
- 1 can (28 ounces) crushed tomatoes
- 2 cups sliced celery
- 1 can (16 ounces) crushed tomatoes
- 2 cups sliced celery
- 1 can (16 ounces) kidney beans, rinsed and drained
- 1 medium green pepper, chopped
- 1 bay leaf
- 2 tablespoons chili powder
- 1-1/2 teaspoons salt
- 1 teaspoon dried oregano
- 1 teaspoon brown sugar
- 1/2 teaspoon *each* celery seed, paprika and ground mustard and cumin
- 1/4 teaspoon cayenne pepper
- 1/4 teaspoon dried basil

Cut meat into 1/2-in. cubes. In a large kettle or Dutch oven, brown the meat, onion and garlic in oil. Add remaining ingredients; bring to a boil. Reduce heat; simmer, uncovered, for 3 hours. Discard bay leaf. Yield: 6-8 servings (about 2 quarts).

Green Chili

PREP: 20 MIN. **COOK:** 1-3/4 HOURS

Friends and family never seem to tire of this chili. We like this as a meal in itself but also use it to top our favorite Mexican foods like burritos.
—*Sharon Malleis, Parker, Colorado*

- 1 pork shoulder roast (3-1/2 to 4 pounds)
- 1/2 cup all-purpose flour
- 1/2 teaspoon salt
- 1/4 teaspoon pepper
- 1 tablespoon vegetable oil
- 4 cans (4 ounces *each*) chopped green chilies
- 2 cans (28 ounces *each*) stewed tomatoes
- 2 garlic cloves, minced
- 1 medium onion, chopped
- 1 jalapeno pepper, seeded and chopped
- 1 to 2 teaspoons minced fresh cilantro
- 1/2 teaspoon ground cumin

Warm flour tortillas, optional

Trim pork and cut into 1/2-in. cubes. In a large bowl or resealable plastic bag, combine flour, salt and pepper. Add pork cubes and toss to coat. In a Dutch oven or soup kettle, brown pork in oil; drain.

Add the chilies, tomatoes, garlic, onion, jalapeno, cilantro and cumin; bring to a boil. Reduce heat; cover and simmer for 1-1/2 to 2 hours or until pork is tender. Serve with tortillas if desired. Yield: 10-12 servings (3 quarts).

Editor's Note: When cutting or seeding hot peppers, use rubber or plastic gloves to protect your hands. Avoid touching your face.

Round Steak Chili
The addition of round steak gives this chili recipe a nice change of pace. Everyone in my family just loves it!
—*Linda Goshorn*
Bedford, Virginia

Cowpoke Chili

Many friends and relatives have requested a copy of this dish, which I've been using for around 30 years. It actually won first place in a local contest, chosen from among 10 other entries. It always comes out delicious. Try it and enjoy!
—Ramona Nelson
Fairbanks, Alaska

- 1 can (15 ounces) black beans, rinsed and drained
- 2 tablespoons sugar
- 1 tablespoon butter
- 1 teaspoon chili powder
- 1/4 teaspoon salt
- 1/4 teaspoon dried oregano
- 1/8 teaspoon ground cumin
- 1/8 teaspoon crushed red pepper flakes

Dash cayenne pepper

- 2 cups frozen lima beans, thawed

Cherry tomatoes, fresh oregano and small chili peppers, optional

In a large saucepan, cook the beef, onion and garlic over medium heat until meat is no longer pink; drain. Stir in the broth, tomato sauce and paste until blended. Add the beans, sugar, butter and seasonings; bring to a boil. Reduce heat; cover and simmer for 30 minutes.

Add lima beans; cook 5-10 minutes longer or until beans are heated through. Garnish with the tomatoes, oregano and peppers if desired. Yield: 7 servings.

Corn and Bean Chili

PREP: 10 MIN. **COOK:** 45 MIN.

My favorite things are added to this chili to make it special. Corn gives it extra flavor, texture and color.
—Mary Pitts
Powder Springs, Georgia

- 2 pounds ground beef
- 1 small onion, finely chopped
- 1 envelope chili seasoning mix
- 3 cans (15-1/2 ounces *each*) chili beans, undrained
- 1 can (46 ounces) V8 juice
- 1/2 teaspoon salt
- 1 can (14-3/4 ounces) cream-style corn

Shredded cheddar cheese

In a large Dutch oven or soup kettle, cook beef and onion over medium heat until meat is no longer pink; drain. Stir in the seasoning mix, beans, V8 juice and salt. Bring to a boil. Reduce heat; simmer, uncovered, for 15 minutes. Stir in corn. Cook and stir over low heat for 15 minutes. Sprinkle with cheese. Yield: 14-16 servings (4 quarts).

Cowpoke Chili

PREP: 10 MIN. **BAKE:** 40 MIN.

- 1 pound ground beef
- 1 small onion, chopped
- 1 garlic clove, minced
- 1 can (10-1/2 ounces) condensed beef broth, undiluted
- 1 can (8 ounces) tomato sauce
- 1 can (6 ounces) tomato paste
- 1 can (15-1/2 ounces) hot chili beans

Zippy Pork Chili

In addition to eating this chili the traditional way (with a spoon), my family likes to scoop bites onto tortilla chips. The leftovers are great rolled in tortillas and reheated, too.
—*Michelle Beran, Claflin, Kansas*

Zippy Pork Chili

PREP: 10 MIN. **COOK:** 2-1/4 HOURS

- 1 boneless whole pork loin roast (3 to 4 pounds), cut into 1-inch cubes
- 1 medium onion, chopped
- 1 garlic clove, minced
- 2 tablespoons vegetable oil
- 2 cans (15-1/2 ounces *each*) chili beans, undrained
- 2 cans (10 ounces *each*) diced tomatoes with mild green chilies, undrained
- 1 can (14-1/2 ounces) diced tomatoes, undrained
- 1 cup water
- 1 teaspoon beef bouillon granules

Chili powder, pepper and cayenne pepper to taste

Sour cream, tortilla chips and shredded cheddar cheese, optional

In a Dutch oven or large soup kettle, cook the pork, onion and garlic in oil over medium heat until meat is no longer pink and vegetables are tender.

Add the beans, tomatoes, water, bouillon and seasonings; bring to a boil. Reduce heat; cover and simmer for 2 hours or until meat is tender. Serve with the sour cream, tortilla chips and cheese if desired. Yield: 10 servings.

Heartwarming Chili

PREP/TOTAL TIME: 30 MIN.

- 1 pound ground beef
- 1 pound ground pork
- 1 medium onion, chopped
- 1/2 cup chopped green pepper
- 1-1/2 to 2 cups water
- 1 can (15 ounces) tomato sauce
- 1 can (15 ounces) pinto beans, rinsed and drained
- 1 can (14-1/2 ounces) diced tomatoes, undrained
- 1 envelope chili seasoning
- 1/4 teaspoon garlic salt

Shredded cheddar cheese, sour cream, chopped green onions *and/or* hot pepper slices, optional

In a large saucepan or Dutch oven, cook the beef, pork, onion and green pepper over medium heat until meat is no longer pink and vegetables are tender; drain.

Add the water, tomato sauce, beans, tomatoes, chili seasoning and garlic salt. Bring to a boil. Reduce heat; simmer, uncovered, until heated through. Serve with cheese, sour cream, green onions and/or hot peppers if desired. Yield: 8-10 servings (about 2-1/2 quarts).

Heartwarming Chili
This meaty meal-in-one is very versatile. Sometimes I make it without beans and serve it on hot dogs or over rice as a main dish.
—*Christine Panzarella*
Buena Park, California

White Bean Turkey Chili

Looking for a hearty but healthy chili for your crew? Well, look no further! I serve this robust meal to my gang and they keep coming back for more. Chock-full of ground turkey, white kidney beans and diced tomatoes, it's so full of flavor, your family won't even miss the ground beef!
—Dorothy Muenzner, Perry, New York

Cincinnati Chili

Cinnamon and cocoa give a rich brown color to this regional chili. This appealing dish will warm you up on a cold day.
—Edith Joyce
Parkman, Ohio

Cincinnati Chili

PREP: 20 MIN. **COOK:** 1-1/2 HOURS

- 1 pound ground beef
- 1 pound ground pork
- 4 medium onions, chopped
- 6 garlic cloves, minced
- 2 cans (16 ounces *each*) kidney beans, rinsed and drained
- 1 can (28 ounces) crushed tomatoes, undrained
- 1/4 cup white vinegar
- 1/4 cup baking cocoa
- 2 tablespoons chili powder
- 2 tablespoons Worcestershire sauce
- 4 teaspoons ground cinnamon
- 3 teaspoons dried oregano
- 2 teaspoons ground cumin
- 2 teaspoons ground allspice
- 2 teaspoons hot pepper sauce
- 3 bay leaves
- 1 teaspoon sugar
Salt and pepper to taste
Hot cooked spaghetti
Shredded cheddar cheese, sour cream, chopped tomatoes and green onions

In a Dutch oven, cook the beef, pork, onions and garlic over medium heat until meat is no longer pink; drain. Add the beans, tomatoes, vinegar, cocoa and seasonings; bring to a boil. Reduce heat; cover and simmer for 1-1/2 hours or until heated through.

Discard bay leaves. Serve over spaghetti. Garnish with the cheese, sour cream, tomatoes and onions. Yield: 8 servings (about 2 quarts).

White Bean Turkey Chili

PREP: 10 MIN. **COOK:** 65 MIN.

- 1-1/2 pounds lean ground turkey
- 2 medium onions, chopped
- 1-1/2 teaspoons dried oregano
- 1-1/2 teaspoons ground cumin
- 1 can (28 ounces) diced tomatoes, undrained
- 3 cups beef broth
- 1 can (8 ounces) tomato sauce
- 1 tablespoon chili powder
- 1 tablespoon baking cocoa
- 2 bay leaves
- 1 teaspoon salt

Red, White and Blue Chili

Instead of the usual picnic fare, I surprised family and guests with this mild-flavored dish one Independence Day. They were delighted with the blue tortilla chips and colorful chili.
—Dotty Parker
Christmas Valley, Oregon

1/4 teaspoon ground cinnamon
3 cans (15 ounces *each*) white kidney beans *or* cannellini beans, rinsed and drained

In a Dutch oven or large soup kettle, cook the turkey and onions over medium heat until meat is no longer pink; drain. Add oregano and cumin; cook and stir 1 minute longer.

Stir in the tomatoes, broth, tomato sauce, chili powder, cocoa, bay leaves, salt and cinnamon; bring to a boil. Reduce heat; cover and simmer for 45 minutes. Add beans; heat through. Discard bay leaves. Yield: 12 servings (3 quarts).

Red, White and Blue Chili

PREP: 10 MIN. **COOK:** 55 MIN.

1 medium green pepper, diced
1/4 cup diced onion
2 garlic cloves, minced
1 tablespoon vegetable oil
2 cans (14-1/2 ounces *each*) Mexican diced tomatoes, undrained
2 cans (14-1/2 ounces *each*) chicken broth
2 cups shredded cooked chicken
2 cans (15-1/2 ounces *each*) great northern beans, rinsed and drained

1 can (16 ounces) kidney beans, rinsed and drained
1 envelope chili seasoning
1 tablespoon brown sugar
1 teaspoon salt
1/4 teaspoon pepper
Blue tortilla chips

In a Dutch oven or soup kettle, saute the green pepper, onion and garlic in oil until tender. Stir in the tomatoes, broth, chicken, beans, chili seasoning, brown sugar, salt and pepper; bring to a boil. Reduce heat; cover and simmer for 45 minutes. Serve with tortilla chips. Yield: 8 servings (about 2 quarts).

Zesty Colorado Chili

PREP: 25 MIN. **COOK:** 1-1/2 HOURS

- 1 pound Italian sausage links
- 1 pound pork shoulder
- 2 pounds ground beef
- 2 medium onions, chopped
- 1 large green pepper, chopped
- 1 tablespoon minced garlic
- 1 can (29 ounces) tomato puree
- 1 can (28 ounces) diced tomatoes, undrained
- 1 cup beef broth
- 1 jalapeno pepper, seeded and minced
- 2 tablespoons brown sugar
- 1 tablespoon cider vinegar
- 2 teaspoons chili powder
- 2 teaspoons ground cumin
- 1 to 2 teaspoons crushed red pepper flakes
- 1 teaspoon dried basil
- 1 teaspoon dried oregano
- 1/2 teaspoon hot pepper sauce
- 2 cans (16 ounces *each*) kidney beans, rinsed and drained

Cut sausage into 1/2-in. pieces. Trim pork and cut into 1/2-in. pieces. In a Dutch oven, cook the meat over medium heat, until sausage and beef are no longer pink and the pork juices run clear; drain, reserving 1 tablespoon drippings. Set meat aside.

Saute the onions, green pepper and garlic in reserved drippings until tender. Add the tomato puree, tomatoes, broth, jalapeno, sugar, vinegar and seasonings.

Return meat to the pan; bring to a boil. Reduce heat; cover and simmer for 1 hour. Add the beans and heat through. Yield: 12-14 servings (3-1/2 quarts).

Editor's Note: When cutting or seeding hot peppers, use rubber or plastic gloves to protect your hands. Avoid touching your face.

Hearty Black Bean Chili

PREP: 30 MIN. + STANDING
COOK: 4 HOURS

Featuring beans, ground beef and chicken, this chili is perfect for those with big appetites.
—Colleen Hilliker
Stevens Point, Wisconsin

- 1 pound dried black beans
- 1 pound ground beef
- 2 boneless skinless chicken breast halves, cubed
- 3/4 cup chopped onion
- 3 cups water
- 1 can (15 ounces) tomato sauce
- 1 can (14-1/2 ounces) diced tomatoes, undrained
- 1 tablespoon chili powder
- 2-1/4 teaspoons salt
- 1-1/2 teaspoons ground cumin
- 1/4 teaspoon garlic powder
- 1/4 teaspoon pepper
- Shredded cheddar cheese and thinly sliced green onions, optional

Sort beans and rinse with cold water. Place beans in a Dutch oven; add water to cover by 2 in. Bring to a boil; boil for 2 minutes. Remove from the heat; cover and

Zesty Colorado Chili

Chili, like this meaty version, is a hearty winter staple up here in the mountains—especially for outdoor lovers like the two of us!
—Beverly Bowman
Conifer, Colorado

let stand for 1 to 4 hours or until beans are softened. Drain and rinse beans, discarding liquid.

In a Dutch oven or large soup kettle, cook the beef, chicken and onion over medium heat, until meat is no longer pink; drain. Add the water, tomato sauce, tomatoes and seasonings; mix well.

Add beans; bring to a boil. Reduce heat; cover and simmer for 3-1/2 to 4 hours or until beans are tender. Serve with cheese and green onions if desired. Yield: 6-8 servings (2-1/2 quarts).

Five-Can Chili

PREP/TOTAL TIME: 15 MIN.

Who says a thick, tasty chili has to simmer all day on the stove! With five canned goods and zero prep time, a warm pot of this zesty specialty is a snap to whip up.
—Jo Mann, Westover, Alabama

- 1 can (15 ounces) chili with beans
- 1 can (15 ounces) mixed vegetables, drained
- 1 can (11 ounces) whole kernel corn, drained
- 1 can (10-3/4 ounces) condensed tomato soup, undiluted
- 1 can (10 ounces) diced tomatoes and green chilies

In a large saucepan, combine all ingredients; bring to a boil. Reduce heat; simmer, uncovered, until heat through. Yield: 6 servings.

Vegetarian Chili

PREP: 10 MIN. **COOK:** 40 MIN.

- 4 medium zucchini, chopped
- 2 medium onions, chopped
- 1 medium green pepper, chopped

Vegetarian Chili
This recipe makes a large pot of chili that's loaded with color and flavor. Once the chopping is done, it's quick to cook.
—Marilyn Barilleaux
Bothell, Washington

- 1 medium sweet red pepper, chopped
- 4 garlic cloves, minced
- 1/4 cup olive oil
- 2 cans (28 ounces *each*) Italian stewed tomatoes, cut up
- 1 can (15 ounces) tomato sauce
- 1 can (15 ounces) pinto beans, rinsed and drained
- 1 can (15 ounces) black beans, rinsed and drained
- 1 jalapeno pepper, seeded and chopped
- 1/4 cup *each* minced fresh cilantro and parsley
- 2 tablespoons chili powder
- 1 tablespoon sugar
- 1 teaspoon salt
- 1 teaspoon ground cumin

In a Dutch oven, saute the zucchini, onions, peppers and garlic in oil until tender. Stir in the tomatoes, tomato sauce, beans, jalapeno and seasonings; bring to a boil over medium heat. Reduce heat; cover and simmer for 30 minutes, stirring occasionally. Yield: 16 servings (about 4 quarts).

Editor's Note: When cutting or seeding hot peppers, use rubber or plastic gloves to protect your hands. Avoid touching your face.

30-Minute Chili

PREP/TOTAL TIME: 30 MIN.

- 2 **pounds ground beef**
- 2 **cups chopped onions**
- 2 **cans (16 ounces *each*) chili beans, undrained**
- 2 **cans (10-3/4 ounces *each*) condensed tomato soup, undiluted**
- 4 **teaspoons chili powder**
- 2 **teaspoons paprika**
- 1 **teaspoon pepper**
- 1 **teaspoon salt**
- 1/4 **teaspoon garlic powder**

Chopped green pepper
Shredded cheddar cheese

In a large saucepan, cook beef and onions over medium heat until no longer pink; drain. Add the beans, soup and seasonings; bring to a boil. Reduce heat; cover and simmer for 15 minutes or until thick and bubbly. Garnish with green pepper and cheese. Yield: 6-8 servings (about 2 quarts).

Speedy Chili

PREP/TOTAL TIME: 30 MIN.

- 1 **pound ground beef**
- 1 **large onion, chopped**
- 1 **garlic clove, minced**
- 2 **cans (8 ounces *each*) tomato sauce**
- 1 **tablespoon chili powder**
- 1 **tablespoon red wine vinegar**
- 2 **teaspoons baking cocoa**
- 1/4 **teaspoon ground cinnamon**

Dash ground allspice

- 1 **can (16 ounces) kidney beans, rinsed and drained**

Hot cooked macaroni, shredded cheddar cheese and sliced green onions, optional

In a microwave oven, cook beef, onion and garlic on high for 3 minutes in a covered 2-qt. microwave-safe dish; stir to crumble meat. Cover and cook for 3-minutes; drain. Add the tomato sauce, chili powder, vinegar, cocoa, cinnamon and allspice; cover and cook on high for 6 minutes. Stir in the beans. Cover and cook 4 minutes longer. Let stand for 3-5 minutes. If desired, serve over macaroni and top with cheese and onions. Yield: 4 servings (about 1 quart).

Editor's Note: Recipe was tested using a 700-watt microwave.

Spicy Turkey Chili

*This peppery chili is not for the faint of stomach.
It's saucy and satisfying. According to my daughter, it's the one thing
she can taste when she has a cold. It also freezes very well.*
—*Margaret Shauers, Great Bend, Kansas*

Chili with Potato Dumplings

PREP: 25 MIN. **COOK:** 55 MIN.

Chili with Potato Dumplings
*Now that my husband has retired,
we eat out a lot. If we stay home
though, he asks if we are going to
have this chili! I've been making it,
with a few ingredients added or
changed, most of my married life.*
—*Shirley Marshall
Michigantown, Indiana*

- 1 pound ground beef
- 1 pound ground turkey
- 1/2 cup chopped onion
- 1 can (16 ounces) kidney beans, rinsed and drained
- 1 can (15-1/2 ounces) mild chili beans, undrained
- 1/2 cup chopped green pepper
- 4 teaspoons chili powder
- 1 teaspoon salt
- 1 teaspoon paprika
- 1 teaspoon cumin seeds
- 1/2 teaspoon garlic salt
- 1/2 teaspoon dried oregano
- 1/4 teaspoon crushed red pepper flakes
- 3 cups V8 juice

DUMPLINGS:

- 1 cup mashed potato flakes
- 1 cup all-purpose flour
- 1 tablespoon minced fresh parsley
- 2 teaspoons baking powder
- 1/2 teaspoon salt
- 1 cup milk
- 1 egg, beaten

In a Dutch oven, cook the beef, turkey and onion over medium heat until meat is no longer pink; drain. Add the beans, green pepper, seasonings and V8 juice; bring to a boil. Reduce heat; cover and simmer for 30 minutes, stirring occasionally.

In a large bowl, combine the first five dumpling ingredients. Add milk and egg; stir just until moistened. Let rest for 3 minutes. Drop by tablespoonfuls into simmering chili. Cover and cook for 15 minutes. Yield: 8 servings (2 quarts).

Spicy Turkey Chili

PREP: 5 MIN. **COOK:** 1 HOUR

- 2 pounds ground turkey *or* turkey sausage
- 1 large onion, chopped
- 4 garlic cloves, minced
- 2 cans (15-1/2 ounces *each*) chili beans, undrained
- 2 cans (15 ounces *each*) tomato sauce
- 1 can (28 ounces) crushed tomatoes
- 1-1/2 cups beef broth *or* beer

Barley Chicken Chili

I was looking for a new recipe for chicken when I discovered a dish I thought my husband might like. After making a few minor adjustments to fit our preferences, I had this zesty chili simmering on the stovetop. It was great!
—Kayleen Grew
Essexville, Michigan

2 to 3 tablespoons chili powder
2 teaspoons Italian seasoning
1/4 to 1/2 teaspoon ground cinnamon
1 jalapeno pepper, finely chopped
Dash cayenne pepper

In a Dutch oven or large soup kettle, cook the turkey, onion and garlic over medium heat until no longer pink; drain. Add the remaining ingredients; bring to a boil. Reduce heat; simmer, uncovered, for 45 minutes, stirring occasionally. Yield: 12-14 servings (3-1/2 quarts).

Editor's Note: When cutting or seeding hot peppers, use rubber or plastic gloves to protect your hands. Avoid touching your face.

Barley Chicken Chili

PREP/TOTAL TIME: 25 MIN.

1 cup chopped onion
1/2 cup chopped green pepper
1 teaspoon olive oil
2-1/4 cups water
1 can (15 ounces) tomato sauce
1 can (14-1/2 ounces) chicken broth
1 can (10 ounces) diced tomatoes and green chilies, undrained
1 cup quick-cooking barley
1 tablespoon chili powder
1/2 teaspoon ground cumin
1/4 teaspoon garlic powder
3 cups cubed cooked chicken

In a large saucepan, saute onion and green pepper in oil until tender. Add the water, tomato sauce, broth, tomatoes, barley, chili powder, cumin and garlic powder; bring to a boil. Reduce heat; cover and simmer for 10 minutes.

Add chicken. Cover and simmer 5 minutes longer or until barley is tender. Yield: 9 servings (about 2 quarts).

Chili Verde

Leftover pork adds a meaty quality to this zippy chili. It's great on a cool night with a stack of tortillas. I've taken it to many gatherings and it's always gone when the party's over.
—*Jo Oliverius, Alpine, California*

Chicken Chili With Black Beans

PREP: 10 MIN. **COOK:** 25 MIN.

- 3 whole skinless boneless chicken breasts (1-3/4 pounds), cubed
- 2 medium sweet red peppers, chopped
- 1 large onion, chopped
- 4 garlic cloves, minced
- 3 tablespoons olive oil
- 1 can (4 ounces) chopped green chilies
- 2 tablespoons chili powder
- 2 teaspoons ground cumin
- 1 teaspoon ground coriander
- 2 cans (15 ounces *each*) black beans, rinsed and drained
- 1 can (28 ounces) Italian stewed tomatoes, cut up
- 1 cup chicken broth *or* beer

In a Dutch oven, saute the chicken, red peppers, onion and garlic in oil for 5 minutes or until chicken is no longer pink. Add the green chilies, chili powder, cumin and coriander; cook for 3 minutes. Stir in the beans, tomatoes and broth or beer; bring to a boil. Reduce heat; simmer, uncovered, for 15 minutes, stirring often. Yield: 10 servings (3 quarts).

Chili Verde

PREP/TOTAL TIME: 15 MIN.

- 2 cups cubed cooked pork (about 1 pound)
- 1 can (16 ounces) kidney beans, rinsed and drained
- 1 can (15 ounces) pinto beans, rinsed and drained
- 1 can (15 ounces) chili with beans, undrained
- 1 can (14-1/2 ounces) stewed tomatoes
- 1-1/2 to 2 cups green salsa
- 1 large onion, chopped
- 2 cans (4 ounces *each*) chopped green chilies
- 2 garlic cloves, minced
- 1 tablespoon minced fresh cilantro
- 2 teaspoons ground cumin

In a large saucepan, combine all the ingredients. Bring to a boil. Reduce heat; simmer, uncovered, for 10 minutes or until heated through. Yield: 8 servings (about 2 quarts).

Chicken Chili with Black Beans

Because it looks different than traditional chili, my family was a little hesitant to try this dish at first. But thanks to the full flavor, it's become a real favorite.
—*Jeanette Urbom*
Louisburg, Kansas

Alphabetical Index

A

Acorn Squash Feta Casserole, 123
After-Thanksgiving Turkey Soup, 248
All-American Turkey Potpie, 19
Amish Breakfast Casserole, 101
Angel Hair Shrimp Bake, 73
Apple Chicken Stew, 174
Apple Ham Bake, 48
Apple Pan Goody, 99
Apple Squash Soup, 320
Apple Sweet Potato Bake, 120
Apricot Almond Chicken, 9
Apricot Squash Soup, 306
Artichoke Beef Stew, 201
Asparagus Chicken Chowder, 324
Asparagus Mushroom Casserole, 107
Asparagus Pea Medley, 117
Asparagus Soup, 310
Au Gratin Garlic Potatoes, 240
Au Gratin Spinach 'n' Pork, 56
Autumn Chowder, 337
Autumn Squash, 102

B

Bacon Potato Chowder, 318
Baked Beef Stew, 31
Barbecue Sausage Bites, 133
Barbecued Beef Brisket, 202
Barbecued Chicken Sandwiches, 156
Barbecued Ribs, 224
Barbecued Turkey Chili, 154
Barley Chicken Chili, 369
Barley Peasant Soup, 276
Basil Tomato Soup, 312
Basque Vegetable Soup, 286
Bavarian Pot Roast, 206
Bavarian Wiener Supper, 64
Beef and Barley, 192
Beef 'n' Bean Torta, 205

Beef and Potato Moussaka, 34
Beef Barley Lentil Soup, 144
Beef Barley Soup, 278
Beef Noodle Casserole, 28
Beef Vegetable Soup, 148
Beef Veggie Casserole, 28
Beefy Eggplant Parmigiana, 105
Beefy Minestrone Soup, 282
Beefy Tomato Pasta Soup, 280
Beefy Tortellini Soup, 273
Best-Ever Beans and Sausage, 65
Biscuit-Topped Creamed Ham, 53
Biscuit-Topped Tomato Casserole, 115
Black and Blue Cobbler, 242
Black Bean Lasagna, 87
Black Bean Tortilla Casserole, 84
Black Bean Zucchini Gazpacho, 348
Black-Eyed Pea Soup, 289
Blueberry Brunch Bake, 93
Brats 'n' Kraut Supper, 214
Broccoli Beef Supper, 45
Broccoli Biscuit Squares, 35
Broccoli Casserole, 109
Broccoli Potato Soup, 310
Broccoli Rice Casserole, 123
Broccoli Soup, 323
Broccoli Turkey Supreme, 20
Brown Rice Turkey Soup, 262
Brown Rice Vegetable Casserole, 102
Brunch Lasagna, 92
Brunch Strata, 90
Buffet Meatballs, 128
Bulgur Chili, 354
Burgundy Lamb Shanks, 222
Burgundy Pears, 244
Burrito Bake, 40
Busy-Day Barbecued Ribs, 221
Butternut Squash Bisque, 336
Butterscotch Apple Crisp, 246

C

Cabbage Patch Stew, 198
Cabbage Sausage Soup, 295
Cajun Corn Soup, 296
Calico Squash Casserole, 118
Campfire Bean 'n' Ham Soup, 348
Canadian Cheese Soup, 326
Canadian Meat Pie, 27
Carrot Leek Soup, 321
Carrot Zucchini Soup, 302
Catch-of-the-Day Casserole, 70
Cauliflower Pork Soup, 301
Cauliflower Soup, 307
Cheddar Beef Enchiladas, 37
Cheddar Spirals, 234
Cheesy Ham Macaroni, 56
Cheesy Noodle Casserole, 110
Cheesy O'Brien Egg Scramble, 92
Cheesy Pizza Fondue, 141
Cheesy Potatoes, 232
Cherry Pork Chops, 214
Chicken 'n' Chips, 14
Chicken Chili, 163
Chicken Chili with Black Beans, 370
Chicken Gumbo, 256
Chicken Ham Casserole, 16
Chicken Noodle Soup, 248
Chicken Provencale, 13
Chicken Saltimbocca, 168
Chicken Soup with Beans, 151
Chicken Soup with Spaetzle, 264
Chicken Soup with Stuffed
  Noodles, 259
Chicken Spaghetti Casserole, 18
Chicken Tomato Vegetable Soup, 146
Chicken Tortilla Casserole, 11
Chicken Vegetable Soup, 252
Chickpea-Stuffed Shells, 82
Chili Rellenos, 42

Chili Sandwiches, 150
Chili Verde, 370
Chili with Potato Dumplings, 368
Chilled Asparagus Soup, 332
Chilled Bean Soup, 341
Chilled Squash and Carrot Soup, 326
Chinese Chicken Soup, 256
Chocolate Pecan Fondue, 245
Chunky Chicken Soup, 262
Chunky Potato Soup, 162
Chunky Seafood Chowder, 333
Cider Pork Roast, 220
Cincinnati Chili, 362
Citrus Turkey Roast, 176
Coffee Beef Pot Roast, 200
Cold Raspberry Soup, 305
Colony Mountain Chili, 160
Colorful Chicken and Rice, 22
Colorful Vegetable Casserole, 108
Cordon Bleu Casserole, 10
Corn and Bean Chili, 359
Corn and Bean Soup, 353
Corn Bread Veggie Bake, 80
Corn Spoon Bread, 230
Corned Beef 'n' Cabbage, 192
Corned Beef Dinner, 204
Country Cassoulet, 15
Cowpoke Chili, 359
Crab Bisque, 318
Crab Quiche Bake, 75
Crab Supreme, 72
Crab Thermidor, 66
Cranberry Meatballs, 132
Cranberry Pork Roast, 213
Cream of Cauliflower Soup, 329
Cream of Wild Rice Soup, 325
Creamy Baked Spinach, 112
Creamy Beef and Pasta, 209
Creamy Carrot Soup, 334
Creamy Corn, 240
Creamy Corn Chowder, 328
Creamy Corned Beef Bake, 26
Creamy Ham and Asparagus Soup, 298
Creamy Ham and Potatoes, 210
Creamy Ham 'n' Broccoli, 226
Creamy Monterey Jack Soup, 336
Creamy Red Pepper Soup, 333
Creamy Red Potatoes, 236
Creamy Shrimp Rice Bake, 77
Creamy Swiss Steak, 194
Creamy Tomato Bisque, 331
Creamy Tomato Soup, 306

Creamy Wild Rice Soup, 296
Crescent Beef Casserole, 34
Curried Barley Chicken, 20
Curried Chicken Rice Soup, 250
Curried Pumpkin Soup, 324
Curried Zucchini Soup, 329

D
Deluxe Macaroni 'n' Cheese, 86
Dinner in a Dish, 32

E
Easy Vegetable Soup, 270
Egg Noodle Lasagna, 196
Eggsquisite Breakfast Casserole, 94
Enchilada Casserole, 189
End of Summer Vegetable Bake, 116

F
Fast Fiesta Soup, 346
Festive Cauliflower Casserole, 113
Festive Green Bean Casserole, 124
Fish Stick Supper, 72
Five-Can Chili, 365
Flank Steak Fajitas, 198
Florida Seafood Casserole, 70
Flounder Florentine, 78
Flower Garden Soup, 250
Four-Cheese Chicken Fettuccine, 8
Four-Onion Soup, 271
Four-Pasta Beef Bake, 37
Freezer Vegetable Soup, 304
French Bread Pizza Soup, 300
French Onion Soup, 282
Fresh Fruit Soup, 309

G
Garden Casserole, 109
Garden Tomato Soup, 304
Garlic-Apple Pork Roast, 226
Garlic Beef Stroganoff, 186
Garlic Potato Bake, 110
Golden Pork Chops, 50
Goulash Soup, 277
Grandma's Chicken 'n' Dumpling
   Soup, 264
Granola Apple Crisp, 242
Greek Pasta Bake, 49
Greek Shepherd's Pie, 60
Green Chili, 358
Green Chili Beef Burritos, 197
Green Rice, 120

Ground Beef Vegetable Soup, 268

H
Ham and Asparagus Casserole, 52
Ham and Bean Stew, 213
Ham 'n' Cheese Egg Bake, 96
Ham 'n' Cheese Strata, 99
Ham and Lentil Soup, 158
Ham and Swiss Casserole, 64
Ham 'n' Swiss Soup, 337
Hamburger Garden Soup, 279
Hamburger Hot Dish, 30
Hamburger Supper, 188
Harvest Soup, 280
Harvest Turkey Soup, 258
Hash Brown Pork Bake, 58
Heartwarming Chili, 361
Hearty Baked Beans, 115
Hearty Beef Vegetable Stew, 206
Hearty Black Bean Chili, 364
Hearty Black Bean Soup, 166
Hearty Black-Eyed Pea Soup, 352
Hearty Broccoli Dip, 134
Hearty Chicken Enchiladas, 179
Hearty Chicken Noodle Soup, 162
Hearty Chicken Strata, 22
Hearty Ham Borscht, 294
Hearty Hash Brown Dinner, 192
Hearty Lentil Soup, 343
Hearty Minestrone Soup, 290
Hearty Navy Bean Soup, 344
Hearty Pasta Casserole, 6
Hearty Pork 'n' Beans, 235
Hearty Split Pea Soup, 351
Hearty Wild Rice, 238
Herb Stuffed Chops, 218
Herbed Chicken and Shrimp, 172
Homemade Beef Broth, 284
Homemade Chicken Broth, 263
Hot Chili Cheese Dip, 126
Hot Crab Spread, 138
Hot Fudge Cake, 246
Hot Spiced Lemon Drink, 130
Hungarian Noodle Side Dish, 104

I
Irish Pie, 55
Italian Beef Sandwiches, 167
Italian Bow Tie Bake, 84
Italian Chicken Soup, 255
Italian Meatball Subs, 158
Italian Peasant Soup, 288

Italian Pork Chop Dinner, 220
Italian Sausage Hoagies, 154
Italian Sausage Soup, 293
Italian Shrimp 'n' Pasta, 170
Italian Turkey and Noodles, 13
Italian Vegetable Soup, 312
Italian Wedding Soup, 278
Italian Zucchini Casserole, 121

K

Kapuzta, 224
Kielbasa Bean Soup, 288
Kielbasa Cabbage Soup, 293
Knoephla Soup, 312

L

Leftover-Turkey Bake, 18
Lemon Lentil Soup, 341
Lemonade Chicken, 180
Lemony Turkey Breast, 182
Lemony Turkey Rice Soup, 260
Lentil Vegetable Soup, 345
Linguine with Ham & Swiss Cheese, 62
Lucky Bean Soup, 338

M

Macaroni Minestrone Soup, 313
Marinated Chicken Wings, 136
Marmalade Carrots, 232
Marvelous Mushroom Soup, 334
Meal-in-One Casserole, 208
Meat Lover's Pizza Bake, 26
Meatball Alphabet Soup, 252
Meatball Stew, 209
Meatball Vegetable Soup, 272
Meatballs Sausage Dinner, 24
Meatless Chili Bake, 83
Meaty Cassoulet, 212
Meaty Spinach Manicotti, 62
Melt-in-Your-Mouth Meat Loaf, 193
Mexican Bean Barley Soup, 351
Mexican Bean Soup, 343
Mexican Chicken Corn Chowder, 320
Mexican-Style Pork Chops, 64
Michigan Bean Bake, 240
Minestrone Soup, 146
Mixed Bean Soup, 349
Moist 'n' Tender Wings, 140
Moroccan Braised Beef, 202
Mulled Dr. Pepper, 141
Mulled Pomegranate Sipper, 132
Mushroom and Potato Chowder, 332

Mushroom Barley Soup, 275
Mushroom Chicken Cacciatore, 182
Mushroom Pork Tenderloins, 225
Mushroom Potatoes, 238
Mushroom Round Steak, 204
Mushroom Salsa Chili, 147
Mushroom Wild Rice Bake, 104

N

Nacho Rice Dip, 136
Navy Bean Soup, 349
Navy Bean Vegetable Soup, 151
New England Clam Chowder, 328
New England Lamb Bake, 48
Nostalgic Chicken and Dumplings, 174

O

Old-Fashioned Peach Butter, 133
Old-World Sauerbraten, 188
Old-World Tomato Soup, 284
Ole Polenta Casserole, 43
Onion Tomato Soup, 314
Orange-Flavored Beef and
    Potatoes, 30
Orange Spiced Cider, 138
Oven Beef Hash, 43
Overnight Mushroom Egg
    Casserole, 96
Overnight Sausage and Grits, 90
Overnight Stuffed French Toast, 94

P

Padre Island Shells, 68
Panfish Chowder, 331
Parmesan Fondue, 134
Parmesan Potato Soup, 301
Party Beef Casserole, 42
Party Sausages, 134
Pasta Crab Casserole, 78
Peasant Soup, 353
Pecan Chicken Casserole, 21
Pecan Salmon Casserole, 76
Pecan Sweet Potato Bake, 118
Pennsylvania Pot Roast, 216
Pepper Beef Goulash, 194
Peppered Meatballs, 137
Pineapple Baked Beans, 228
Pineapple Ham Casserole, 55
Pineapple Peach Soup, 310
Pineapple Shrimp Rice Bake, 66
Pineapple Sweet Potatoes, 234
Pinto Beans and Rice, 89

Pizza Casserole, 201
Pizza Rigatoni, 216
Polish Kraut and Apples, 222
Pork and Beef Barbecue, 144
Pork and Corn Casserole, 53
Pork and Pinto Beans, 225
Pork Chop Dinner, 218
Pork Chops with Apple Stuffing, 46
Pork Chops with Sauerkraut, 221
Pork Spanish Rice, 57
Posole, 290
Potato and Cabbage Soup, 297
Potato Cheese Soup, 321
Potato Egg Supper, 100
Potato Puff Casserole, 120
Potato Salmon Casserole, 69
Provencale Bean Soup, 346
Puffy Chile Rellenos Casserole, 89

R

Raisin Bread Pudding, 245
Raspberry Fondue Dip, 142
Red, White and Blue Chili, 363
Reuben Casserole, 30
Reuben Spread, 140
Rich Spinach Casserole, 239
Roast Pork Soup, 286
Roasted Red Pepper Sauce, 234
Roasted Veggie Chili, 357
Rosemary Cashew Chicken, 178
Round Steak Chili, 358

S

Salmon Loaf, 184
Salsa Chili, 356
Santa Fe Cheese Soup, 251
Saucy Green Bean Bake, 113
Sauerkraut Hot Dish, 60
Sauerkraut Soup, 295
Sausage and Broccoli Bake, 58
Sausage Bean Soup, 289
Sausage Dressing, 238
Sausage Kale Soup, 298
Sausage Lentil Soup, 338
Sausage Macaroni Bake, 50
Sausage Spanish Rice, 239
Savory Cheese Soup, 317
Savory Winter Soup, 156
Scalloped Carrots, 108
Scalloped Chicken Supper, 10
Scalloped Potatoes, 107
Scalloped Taters, 230

Scotch Broth Soup, 270
Seafood Chowder, 323
Seafood Lasagna, 68
Seafood Rice Casserole, 77
Seasoned Short Ribs, 208
Shredded Beef Sandwiches, 147
Shredded Steak Sandwiches, 150
Shrimp Chowder, 159
Simmered Smoked Links, 141
Six-Veggie Bake, 100
Slow-Cooked Cabbage Rolls, 190
Slow-Cooked Chili, 166
Slow-Cooked Ham, 216
Slow-Cooked Italian Chicken, 184
Slow-Cooked Lamb Chops, 212
Slow-Cooked Pork Barbecue, 160
Slow-Cooked Sage Dressing, 230
Slow-Cooked Salsa, 128
Slow-Cooked Stew, 186
Slow-Cooked Swiss Steak, 204
Slow-Cooked Vegetables, 228
Slow-Cooked White Chili, 155
Slow-Cooker Barbecue Beef, 152
Slow-Cooker Berry Cobbler, 244
Slow-Cooker Cheese Dip, 132
Smoked Sausage Potato Bake, 57
South-of-the-Border Soup, 283
Southern Barbecue Spaghetti
   Sauce, 183
Southern Chicken Rice Soup, 257
Southern Garden Soup, 316
Southwest Turkey Stew, 178
Southwest Vegetarian Bake, 80
Southwestern Chicken Soup, 263
Southwestern Egg Bake, 97
Southwestern Spaghetti, 24
Southwestern Stew, 224
Southwestern Turkey Dumpling
   Soup, 251
Spaghetti Casserole, 86
Special Scalloped Corn, 124
Speedy Chili, 366
Spice It Up Soup, 272
Spiced Acorn Squash, 236
Spiced Coffee, 128
Spiced Lemon Chicken, 171
Spicy Beefy Chili, 152
Spicy French Dip, 155
Spicy Seafood Stew, 168
Spicy Turkey Chili, 368
Spicy Zucchini Soup, 300
Spinach Bisque, 325

Split Pea 'n' Ham Soup, 154
Split Pea Soup with Meatballs, 294
Spring-Ahead Brunch Bake, 97
Squash Stuffing Casserole, 231
Steak Potpie, 45
Stroganoff Soup, 279
Stuffed Flank Steak, 200
Stuffed Pasta Shells, 20
Stuffed Roast Pepper Soup, 273
Summer Squash Bake, 112
Summer Vegetable Soup, 309
Sunday Chicken Supper, 176
Sunday Gumbo, 291
Sweet-and-Sour Chicken, 170
Sweet 'n' Sour Ribs, 210
Sweet-and-Sour Smokies, 142
Sweet-and-Sour Supper, 40
Sweet 'n' Spicy Meatballs, 140
Sweet 'n' Tangy Chicken, 180
Sweet 'n' Tangy Pot Roast, 190
Sweet Onion Corn Bake, 116
Sweet Pepper Chicken, 175
Swiss Macaroni, 82
Swiss Steak Dinner, 32
Swiss Steak with Dumplings, 38

T

Taco Casserole, 39
Taco Twist Soup, 314
Tangy Barbecue Wings, 130
Tangy Bean Soup, 164
Tender Beef 'n' Bean Stew, 189
Teriyaki Pork Roast, 217
Teriyaki Pulled Pork Sandwiches, 148
Tex-Mex Chicken Soup, 267
Texas-Style Lasagna, 38
Thick Turkey Bean Chili, 354
30-Minute Chili, 366
Three's-a-Charm Shamrock Soup, 277
Toffee Apple French Toast, 101
Tomato Green Bean Soup, 316
Tortellini Soup, 307
Tortellini Vegetable Soup, 268
Tropical Tea, 142
Tuna in the Straw Casserole, 69
Tuna Mushroom Casserole, 75
Tuna Spaghetti Pie, 76
Turkey 'n' Stuffing Pie, 14
Turkey Barley Soup, 265
Turkey Chili, 159
Turkey in Cream Sauce, 178
Turkey Manicotti, 8

Turkey Meatball Soup, 267
Turkey Noodle Soup, 258
Turkey Potpie, 16
Turkey Shepherd's Pie, 6
Turkey Sloppy Joes, 164
Turkey Soup with Slickers, 256
Turkey Tetrazzini, 11
Turkey Thigh Supper, 172
Turkey Tomato Soup, 255
Two-Bean Vegetable Soup, 166

U

Unstuffed Pepper Soup, 275
U.S. Senate Bean Soup, 352

V

Vegetable Bean Soup, 311
Vegetable Beef Soup, 285
Vegetable Beef Stew, 196
Vegetable Black Bean Soup, 340
Vegetable Broth, 305
Vegetable Chicken Noodle Soup, 260
Vegetable Medley, 235
Vegetarian Chili, 365
Vegetarian Split Pea Soup, 302
Veggie Meatball Soup, 163
Veggie Noodle Ham Casserole, 46

W

Warm Broccoli Cheese Dip, 129
Warm Christmas Punch, 137
Warm Spiced Cider Punch, 126
White Bean 'n' Ham Soup, 345
White Bean Fennel Soup, 340
White Bean Turkey Chili, 362
White Chili with Chicken, 356
Wild Rice Soup, 271
Wild Rice Turkey Dinner, 182
Winter Vegetable Soup, 316
Wisconsin Split Pea Soup, 344

Z

Zesty Chicken Soup, 253
Zesty Colorado Chili, 364
Zesty Vegetable Beef Soup, 276
Zippy Bean Stew, 231
Zippy Pork Chili, 361
Zucchini Pork Chop Supper, 61
Zucchini Ricotta Bake, 83
Zucchini Sausage Soup, 297

General Index

APPETIZERS
Barbecue Sausage Bites, 133
Buffet Meatballs, 128
Cheesy Pizza Fondue, 141
Cranberry Meatballs, 132
Hearty Broccoli Dip, 134
Hot Chili Cheese Dip, 126
Hot Crab Spread, 138
Marinated Chicken Wings, 136
Moist 'n' Tender Wings, 140
Nacho Rice Dip, 136
Old-Fashioned Peach Butter, 133
Parmesan Fondue, 134
Party Sausages, 134
Peppered Meatballs, 137
Raspberry Fondue Dip, 142
Reuben Spread, 140
Simmered Smoked Links, 141
Slow-Cooked Salsa, 128
Slow-Cooker Cheese Dip, 132
Sweet-and-Sour Smokies, 142
Sweet 'n' Spicy Meatballs, 140
Tangy Barbecue Wings, 130
Warm Broccoli Cheese Dip, 129

APPLES
Apple Chicken Stew, 174
Apple Ham Bake, 48
Apple Pan Goody, 99
Apple Squash Soup, 320
Apple Sweet Potato Bake, 120
Butterscotch Apple Crisp, 246
Cider Pork Roast, 220
Granola Apple Crisp, 242
Orange Spiced Cider, 138
Polish Kraut and Apples, 222
Pork Chops with Apple Stuffing, 46
Toffee Apple French Toast, 101
Warm Spiced Cider Punch, 126

APRICOTS
Apricot Almond Chicken, 9
Apricot Squash Soup, 306

ASPARAGUS
Asparagus Chicken Chowder, 324
Asparagus Mushroom Casserole, 107
Asparagus Pea Medley, 117
Asparagus Soup, 310
Chilled Asparagus Soup, 332
Creamy Ham and Asparagus Soup, 298
Ham and Asparagus Casserole, 52

BACON
Amish Breakfast Casserole, 101
Bacon Potato Chowder, 318
Canadian Cheese Soup, 326
Cheesy O'Brien Egg Scramble, 92
Eggsquisite Breakfast Casserole, 94
Hearty Baked Beans, 115
Overnight Mushroom Egg
  Casserole, 96
Parmesan Potato Soup, 301
Potato Egg Supper, 100
Southwestern Egg Bake, 97

BARLEY
Barley Chicken Chili, 369
Barley Peasant Soup, 276
Beef and Barley, 192
Beef Barley Lentil Soup, 144
Beef Barley Soup, 278
Curried Barley Chicken, 20
Mexican Bean Barley Soup, 351
Mushroom Barley Soup, 275
Turkey Barley Soup, 265

BEANS
Casseroles
  Best-Ever Beans and Sausage, 65
Black Bean Lasagna, 87
Black Bean Tortilla Casserole, 84
Chicken Provencale, 13
Country Cassoulet, 15
Festive Green Bean Casserole, 124
Hearty Baked Beans, 115
Meatless Chili Bake, 83
Pinto Beans and Rice, 89
Saucy Green Bean Bake, 113
Slow Cooker
Barbecued Turkey Chili, 154
Beef 'n' Bean Torta, 205
Chicken Chili, 163
Chicken Soup with Beans, 151
Chili Sandwiches, 150
Colony Mountain Chili, 160
Ham and Bean Stew, 213
Hearty Black Bean Soup, 166
Hearty Pork 'n' Beans, 235
Meaty Cassoulet, 212
Michigan Bean Bake, 240
Minestrone Soup, 146
Mushroom Salsa Chili, 147
Navy Bean Vegetable Soup, 151
Pineapple Baked Beans, 228
Pork and Pinto Beans, 225
Slow-Cooked Chili, 166
Slow-Cooked White Chili, 155
Spicy Beefy Chili, 152
Tangy Bean Soup, 164
Tender Beef 'n' Bean Stew, 189
Turkey Chili, 159
Two-Bean Vegetable Soup, 166
Zippy Bean Stew, 231
Soups
Beefy Minestrone Soup, 282
Black Bean Zucchini Gazpacho, 348
Bulgur Chili, 354
Campfire Bean 'n' Ham Soup, 348
Chicken Chili with Black Beans, 370

Chili Verde, 370
Chili with Potato Dumplings, 368
Chilled Bean Soup, 341
Cincinnati Chili, 362
Corn and Bean Chili, 359
Corn and Bean Soup, 353
Cowpoke Chili, 359
Fast Fiesta Soup, 346
Five-Can Chili, 365
Heartwarming Chili, 361
Hearty Black Bean Chili, 364
Hearty Navy Bean Soup, 344
Italian Peasant Soup, 288
Kielbasa Bean Soup, 288
Lucky Bean Soup, 338
Macaroni Minestrone Soup, 313
Mexican Bean Barley Soup, 351
Mexican Bean Soup, 343
Mixed Bean Soup, 349
Navy Bean Soup, 349
Peasant Soup, 353
Provencale Bean Soup, 346
Red, White and Blue Chili, 363
Roasted Veggie Chili, 357
Round Steak Chili, 358
Salsa Chili, 356
Sausage Bean Soup, 289
Speedy Chili, 366
Spicy Turkey Chili, 368
Thick Turkey Bean Chili, 354
30-Minute Chili, 366
Tomato Green Bean Soup, 316
U.S. Senate Bean Soup, 352
Vegetable Bean Soup, 311
Vegetable Black Bean Soup, 340
Vegetarian Chili, 365
White Bean 'n' Ham Soup, 345
White Bean Fennel Soup, 340
White Bean Turkey Chili, 362
White Chili with Chicken, 356
Zesty Colorado Chili, 364
Zippy Pork Chili, 361

BEEF (also see Corned Beef;
Ground Beef)
Casseroles
Baked Beef Stew, 31
Beef Veggie Casserole, 28
Eggsquisite Breakfast Casserole, 94
Orange-Flavored Beef and
   Potatoes, 30
Oven Beef Hash, 43

Party Beef Casserole, 42
Steak Potpie, 45
Swiss Steak Dinner, 32
Swiss Steak with Dumplings, 38
Slow Cooker
Artichoke Beef Stew, 201
Barbecued Beef Brisket, 202
Bavarian Pot Roast, 206
Chili Sandwiches, 150
Coffee Beef Pot Roast, 200
Colony Mountain Chili, 160
Creamy Swiss Steak, 194
Flank Steak Fajitas, 198
Garlic Beef Stroganoff, 186
Green Chili Beef Burritos, 197
Hearty Beef Vegetable Stew, 206
Italian Beef Sandwiches, 167
Moroccan Braised Beef, 202
Mushroom Round Steak, 204
Old-World Sauerbraten, 188
Pepper Beef Goulash, 194
Pork and Beef Barbecue, 144
Seasoned Short Ribs, 208
Shredded Beef Sandwiches, 147
Shredded Steak Sandwiches, 150
Slow-Cooked Stew, 186
Slow-Cooked Swiss Steak, 204
Slow-Cooker Barbecue Beef, 152
Spicy French Dip, 155
Stuffed Flank Steak, 200
Sweet 'n' Tangy Pot Roast, 190
Tender Beef 'n' Bean Stew, 189
Vegetable Beef Stew, 196
Soups
Barley Peasant Soup, 276
Beef Barley Soup, 278
Beefy Minestrone Soup, 282
Goulash Soup, 277
Homemade Beef Broth, 284
Mushroom Barley Soup, 275
Old-World Tomato Soup, 284
Round Steak Chili, 358
Scotch Broth Soup, 270
Stroganoff Soup, 279
Vegetable Beef Soup, 285
Zesty Vegetable Beef Soup, 276

BERRIES (also see Cranberries)
Black and Blue Cobbler, 242
Blueberry Brunch Bake, 93
Cold Raspberry Soup, 305
Fresh Fruit Soup, 309

Overnight Stuffed French Toast, 94
Raspberry Fondue Dip, 142
Slow-Cooker Berry Cobbler, 244

BEVERAGES
Hot Spiced Lemon Drink, 130
Mulled Dr. Pepper, 141
Mulled Pomegranate Sipper, 132
Orange Spiced Cider, 138
Spiced Coffee, 128
Tropical Tea, 142
Warm Christmas Punch, 137
Warm Spiced Cider Punch, 126

BREAKFAST & BRUNCH
Amish Breakfast Casserole, 101
Apple Pan Goody, 99
Blueberry Brunch Bake, 93
Brunch Lasagna, 92
Brunch Strata, 90
Cheesy O'Brien Egg Scramble, 92
Crab Quiche Bake, 75
Eggsquisite Breakfast Casserole, 94
Ham 'n' Cheese Egg Bake, 96
Ham 'n' Cheese Strata, 99
Hearty Chicken Strata, 22
Overnight Mushroom Egg
   Casserole, 96
Overnight Sausage and Grits, 90
Overnight Stuffed French Toast, 94
Potato Egg Supper, 100
Six-Veggie Bake, 100
Southwestern Egg Bake, 97
Spring-Ahead Brunch Bake, 97
Toffee Apple French Toast, 101

BROCCOLI
Broccoli Beef Supper, 45
Broccoli Biscuit Squares, 35
Broccoli Casserole, 109
Broccoli Potato Soup, 310
Broccoli Rice Casserole, 123
Broccoli Soup, 323
Broccoli Turkey Supreme, 20
Hearty Broccoli Dip, 134
Sausage and Broccoli Bake, 58
Warm Broccoli Cheese Dip, 129

CABBAGE & SAUERKRAUT
Bavarian Wiener Supper, 64
Brats 'n' Kraut Supper, 214
Cabbage Patch Stew, 198

Cabbage Sausage Soup, 295
Corned Beef 'n' Cabbage, 192
Kapuzta, 224
Kielbasa Cabbage Soup, 293
Polish Kraut and Apples, 222
Pork Chops with Sauerkraut, 221
Potato and Cabbage Soup, 297
Reuben Casserole, 30
Reuben Spread, 140
Sauerkraut Hot Dish, 60
Sauerkraut Soup, 295
Sausage Kale Soup, 298
Slow-Cooked Cabbage Rolls, 190
Three's-a-Charm Shamrock Soup, 277

CARROTS
Carrot Leek Soup, 321
Carrot Zucchini Soup, 302
Chilled Squash and Carrot Soup, 326
Creamy Carrot Soup, 334
Marmalade Carrots, 232
Scalloped Carrots, 108

CAULIFLOWER
Cauliflower Pork Soup, 301
Cauliflower Soup, 307
Cream of Cauliflower Soup, 329
Festive Cauliflower Casserole, 113

CHEESE
Acorn Squash Feta Casserole, 123
Au Gratin Garlic Potatoes, 240
Au Gratin Spinach 'n' Pork, 56
Beefy Eggplant Parmigiana, 105
Black Bean Lasagna, 87
Brunch Lasagna, 92
Canadian Cheese Soup, 326
Cheddar Beef Enchiladas, 37
Cheddar Spirals, 234
Cheesy Ham Macaroni, 56
Cheesy Noodle Casserole, 110
Cheesy O'Brien Egg Scramble, 92
Cheesy Pizza Fondue, 141
Cheesy Potatoes, 232
Cordon Bleu Casserole, 10
Creamy Monterey Jack Soup, 336
Deluxe Macaroni 'n' Cheese, 86
Egg Noodle Lasagna, 196
Four-Cheese Chicken Fettuccine, 8
Ham 'n' Cheese Egg Bake, 96
Ham 'n' Cheese Strata, 99
Ham and Swiss Casserole, 64

Ham 'n' Swiss Soup, 337
Hot Chili Cheese Dip, 126
Linguine with Ham & Swiss Cheese, 62
Nacho Rice Dip, 136
Parmesan Fondue, 134
Parmesan Potato Soup, 301
Potato Cheese Soup, 321
Santa Fe Cheese Soup, 251
Savory Cheese Soup, 317
Scalloped Carrots, 108
Scalloped Potatoes, 107
Scalloped Taters, 230
Seafood Lasagna, 68
Slow-Cooker Cheese Dip, 132
Special Scalloped Corn, 124
Swiss Macaroni, 82
Texas-Style Lasagna, 38
Warm Broccoli Cheese Dip, 129
Zucchini Ricotta Bake, 83

CHICKEN (also see Turkey)
Casseroles
Apricot Almond Chicken, 9
Chicken 'n' Chips, 14
Chicken Ham Casserole, 16
Chicken Provencale, 13
Chicken Spaghetti Casserole, 18
Chicken Tortilla Casserole, 11
Colorful Chicken and Rice, 22
Country Cassoulet, 15
Curried Barley Chicken, 20
Four-Cheese Chicken Fettuccine, 8
Hearty Chicken Strata, 22
Irish Pie, 55
Meaty Spinach Manicotti, 62
Pecan Chicken Casserole, 21
Scalloped Chicken Supper, 10
Stuffed Pasta Shells, 20
Slow Cooker
Apple Chicken Stew, 174
Barbecued Chicken Sandwiches, 156
Chicken Chili, 163
Chicken Saltimbocca, 168
Chicken Soup with Beans, 151
Chicken Tomato Vegetable Soup, 146
Hearty Chicken Enchiladas, 179
Hearty Chicken Noodle Soup, 162
Herbed Chicken and Shrimp, 172
Italian Shrimp 'n' Pasta, 170
Lemonade Chicken, 180
Marinated Chicken Wings, 136
Moist 'n' Tender Wings, 140

Mushroom Chicken Cacciatore, 182
Nostalgic Chicken and
  Dumplings, 174
Rosemary Cashew Chicken, 178
Slow-Cooked Italian Chicken, 184
Slow-Cooked White Chili, 155
Spiced Lemon Chicken, 171
Sunday Chicken Supper, 176
Sweet-and-Sour Chicken, 170
Sweet 'n' Tangy Chicken, 180
Sweet Pepper Chicken, 175
Tangy Barbecue Wings, 130
Soups
Asparagus Chicken Chowder, 324
Barley Chicken Chili, 369
Basque Vegetable Soup, 286
Chicken Chili with Black Beans, 370
Chicken Gumbo, 256
Chicken Noodle Soup, 248
Chicken Soup with Spaetzle, 264
Chicken Soup with Stuffed
  Noodles, 259
Chicken Vegetable Soup, 252
Chinese Chicken Soup, 256
Chunky Chicken Soup, 262
Curried Chicken Rice Soup, 250
Flower Garden Soup, 250
Grandma's Chicken 'n' Dumpling
  Soup, 264
Hearty Black Bean Chili, 364
Homemade Chicken Broth, 263
Italian Chicken Soup, 255
Italian Peasant Soup, 288
Mexican Chicken Corn Chowder, 320
Red, White and Blue Chili, 363
Santa Fe Cheese Soup, 251
Southern Chicken Rice Soup, 257
Southwestern Chicken Soup, 263
Sunday Gumbo, 291
Tex-Mex Chicken Soup, 267
Vegetable Chicken Noodle Soup, 260
White Chili with Chicken, 356
Zesty Chicken Soup, 253

CORN
Cajun Corn Soup, 296
Corn and Bean Chili, 359
Corn and Bean Soup, 353
Corn Bread Veggie Bake, 80
Corn Spoon Bread, 230
Creamy Corn, 240
Creamy Corn Chowder, 328

Golden Pork Chops, 50
Mexican Chicken Corn Chowder, 320
Mexican-Style Pork Chops, 64
Ole Polenta Casserole, 43
Pork and Corn Casserole, 53
Santa Fe Cheese Soup, 251
South-of-the-Border Soup, 283
Southwest Vegetarian Bake, 80
Southwestern Turkey Dumpling
   Soup, 251
Special Scalloped Corn, 124
Sweet Onion Corn Bake, 116

CORNED BEEF
Corned Beef 'n' Cabbage, 192
Corned Beef Dinner, 204
Creamy Corned Beef Bake, 26
Hearty Split Pea Soup, 351
Reuben Casserole, 30
Reuben Spread, 141
Three's-a-Charm Shamrock Soup, 277

CRABMEAT (see Seafood)

CRANBERRIES
Apple Pan Goody, 99
Cranberry Meatballs, 132
Cranberry Pork Roast, 213
Leftover-Turkey Bake, 18
Warm Christmas Punch, 137
Wild Rice Turkey Dinner, 182

DESSERTS
Black and Blue Cobbler, 242
Burgundy Pears, 244
Butterscotch Apple Crisp, 246
Chocolate Pecan Fondue, 245
Granola Apple Crisp, 242
Hot Fudge Cake, 246
Raisin Bread Pudding, 245
Slow-Cooker Berry Cobbler, 244

FISH (see Seafood)

GROUND BEEF
Casseroles
Beef and Potato Moussaka, 34
Beef Noodle Casserole, 28
Beefy Eggplant Parmigiana, 105
Broccoli Beef Supper, 45
Broccoli Biscuit Squares, 35
Burrito Bake, 40
Canadian Meat Pie, 27

Cheddar Beef Enchiladas, 37
Chili Rellenos, 42
Crescent Beef Casserole, 34
Dinner in a Dish, 32
Four-Pasta Beef Bake, 37
Greek Pasta Bake, 49
Hamburger Hot Dish, 30
Hearty Baked Beans, 115
Meat Lover's Pizza Bake, 26
Meatballs Sausage Dinner, 24
Ole Polenta Casserole, 43
Southwestern Spaghetti, 24
Sweet-and-Sour Supper, 40
Taco Casserole, 39
Texas-Style Lasagna, 38
Slow Cooker
Beef and Barley, 192
Beef 'n' Bean Torta, 205
Beef Barley Lentil Soup, 144
Beef Vegetable Soup, 148
Buffet Meatballs, 128
Cabbage Patch Stew, 198
Cranberry Meatballs, 132
Creamy Beef and Pasta, 209
Egg Noodle Lasagna, 196
Enchilada Casserole, 189
Hamburger Supper, 188
Hearty Broccoli Dip, 134
Hearty Hash Brown Dinner, 192
Hearty Pork 'n' Beans, 235
Hearty Wild Rice, 238
Italian Meatball Subs, 158
Meal-in-One Casserole, 208
Meatball Stew, 209
Melt-in-Your-Mouth Meat Loaf, 193
Mushroom Salsa Chili, 147
Nacho Rice Dip, 136
Peppered Meatballs, 137
Pineapple Baked Beans, 228
Pizza Casserole, 201
Savory Winter Soup, 156
Slow-Cooked Cabbage Rolls, 190
Slow-Cooked Chili, 166
Slow-Cooker Cheese Dip, 132
Spicy Beefy Chili, 152
Veggie Meatball Soup, 163
Soups
Beefy Tomato Pasta Soup, 280
Beefy Tortellini Soup, 273
Chili with Potato Dumplings, 368
Cincinnati Chili, 362
Corn and Bean Chili, 359

Cowpoke Chili, 359
Easy Vegetable Soup, 270
Ground Beef Vegetable Soup, 268
Hamburger Garden Soup, 279
Harvest Soup, 280
Heartwarming Chili, 361
Hearty Black Bean Chili, 364
Hearty Black-Eyed Pea Soup, 352
Italian Wedding Soup, 278
Meatball Vegetable Soup, 272
Mexican Bean Soup, 343
Mixed Bean Soup, 349
Salsa Chili, 356
South-of-the-Border Soup, 283
Speedy Chili, 366
Spice It Up Soup, 272
Stuffed Roast Pepper Soup, 273
30-Minute Chili, 366
Tortellini Vegetable Soup, 268
Unstuffed Pepper Soup, 275
Wild Rice Soup, 271
Zesty Colorado Chili, 364

HAM
Casseroles
Apple Ham Bake, 48
Biscuit-Topped Creamed Ham, 53
Brunch Lasagna, 92
Brunch Strata, 90
Cheesy Ham Macaroni, 56
Chicken Ham Casserole, 16
Cordon Bleu Casserole, 10
Ham and Asparagus Casserole, 52
Ham 'n' Cheese Egg Bake, 96
Ham 'n' Cheese Strata, 99
Ham and Swiss Casserole, 64
Linguine with Ham & Swiss
   Cheese, 62
Pineapple Ham Casserole, 55
Pineapple Shrimp Rice Bake, 66
Spring-Ahead Brunch Bake, 97
Veggie Noodle Ham Casserole, 46
Slow Cooker
Chicken Saltimbocca, 168
Chunky Potato Soup, 162
Creamy Ham and Potatoes, 210
Ham and Bean Stew, 213
Ham and Lentil Soup, 158
Minestrone Soup, 146
Navy Bean Vegetable Soup, 151
Slow-Cooked Ham, 216
Split Pea 'n' Ham Soup, 154

Soups
Cajun Corn Soup, 296
Campfire Bean 'n' Ham Soup, 348
Chicken Gumbo, 256
Creamy Ham and Asparagus
   Soup, 298
Creamy Wild Rice Soup, 296
Ham 'n' Swiss Soup, 337
Hearty Ham Borscht, 294
Hearty Navy Bean Soup, 344
Navy Bean Soup, 349
Potato and Cabbage Soup, 297
U.S. Senate Bean Soup, 352
White Bean 'n' Ham Soup, 345
Wisconsin Split Pea Soup, 344

LAMB
Burgundy Lamb Shanks, 222
Greek Pasta Bake, 49
Greek Shepherd's Pie, 60
Meaty Cassoulet, 212
New England Lamb Bake, 48
Slow-Cooked Lamb Chops, 212

LEMON
Citrus Turkey Roast, 176
Hot Spiced Lemon Drink, 130
Lemon Lentil Soup, 341
Lemonade Chicken, 180
Lemony Turkey Breast, 182
Lemony Turkey Rice Soup, 260
Spiced Lemon Chicken, 171

LENTILS
Beef Barley Lentil Soup, 144
Ham and Lentil Soup, 158
Hearty Lentil Soup, 343
Lemon Lentil Soup, 341
Lentil Vegetable Soup, 345
Sausage Lentil Soup, 338

MUSHROOMS
Asparagus Mushroom Casserole, 107
Brunch Strata, 90
Creamy Swiss Steak, 194
Eggsquisite Breakfast Casserole, 94
Garlic Beef Stroganoff, 186
Marvelous Mushroom Soup, 334
Mushroom and Potato Chowder, 332
Mushroom Barley Soup, 275
Mushroom Chicken Cacciatore, 182
Mushroom Pork Tenderloins, 225

Mushroom Potatoes, 238
Mushroom Round Steak, 204
Mushroom Salsa Chili, 147
Mushroom Wild Rice Bake, 104
Overnight Mushroom Egg
   Casserole, 96
Stroganoff Soup, 279
Tuna Mushroom Casserole, 75
Turkey Tetrazzini, 11

NUTS
Apricot Almond Chicken, 9
Chocolate Pecan Fondue, 245
Pecan Chicken Casserole, 21
Pecan Salmon Casserole, 76
Pecan Sweet Potato Bake, 118
Rosemary Cashew Chicken, 178

ONIONS
Carrot Leek Soup, 321
Four-Onion Soup, 271
French Onion Soup, 282
Onion Tomato Soup, 314
Sweet Onion Corn Bake, 116

ORANGE
Citrus Turkey Roast, 176
Fresh Fruit Soup, 309
Marmalade Carrots, 232
Orange-Flavored Beef and
   Potatoes, 30
Orange Spiced Cider, 138
Tropical Tea, 142

PASTA
Casseroles
Angel Hair Shrimp Bake, 73
Beef Noodle Casserole, 28
Brunch Lasagna, 92
Catch-of-the-Day Casserole, 70
Cheesy Ham Macaroni, 56
Cheesy Noodle Casserole, 110
Chicken Spaghetti Casserole, 18
Chickpea-Stuffed Shells, 82
Deluxe Macaroni 'n' Cheese, 86
Four-Cheese Chicken Fettuccine, 8
Four-Pasta Beef Bake, 37
Greek Pasta Bake, 49
Hearty Pasta Casserole, 6
Hungarian Noodle Side Dish, 104
Italian Bow Tie Bake, 84
Italian Turkey and Noodles, 13

Linguine with Ham & Swiss
   Cheese, 62
Meatless Chili Bake, 83
Meaty Spinach Manicotti, 62
Padre Island Shells, 68
Pasta Crab Casserole, 78
Sausage Macaroni Bake, 50
Seafood Lasagna, 68
Southwestern Spaghetti, 24
Spaghetti Casserole, 86
Stuffed Pasta Shells, 20
Swiss Macaroni, 82
Tuna Mushroom Casserole, 75
Tuna Spaghetti Pie, 76
Turkey Manicotti, 8
Turkey Tetrazzini, 11
Veggie Noodle Ham Casserole, 46
Slow Cooker
Cheddar Spirals, 234
Creamy Beef and Pasta, 209
Egg Noodle Lasagna, 196
Garlic Beef Stroganoff, 186
Hearty Chicken Noodle Soup, 162
Italian Shrimp 'n' Pasta, 170
Meal-in-One Casserole, 208
Minestrone Soup, 146
Pizza Casserole, 201
Pizza Rigatoni, 216
Southern Barbecue Spaghetti
   Sauce, 183
Soups
Beefy Minestrone Soup, 282
Beefy Tomato Pasta Soup, 280
Beefy Tortellini Soup, 273
Chicken Noodle Soup, 248
Chicken Soup with Stuffed
   Noodles, 259
Macaroni Minestrone Soup, 313
Stroganoff Soup, 278
Taco Twist Soup, 314
Tortellini Soup, 307
Tortellini Vegetable Soup, 268
Turkey Noodle Soup, 258
Vegetable Chicken Noodle Soup, 260

PEACHES
Old-Fashioned Peach Butter, 133
Pineapple Peach Soup, 310

PEAS
Asparagus Pea Medley, 117
Black-Eyed Pea Soup, 289

General Index **379**

Chickpea-Stuffed Shells, 82
Hearty Black-Eyed Pea Soup, 352
Hearty Split Pea Soup, 351
Split Pea 'n' Ham Soup, 154
Split Pea Soup with Meatballs, 294
Vegetarian Split Pea Soup, 302
Wisconsin Split Pea Soup, 344

PEPPERS & CHILIES

Chili Rellenos, 42
Chili Verde, 370
Creamy Red Pepper Soup, 333
Flank Steak Fajitas, 198
Green Chili, 358
Green Chili Beef Burritos, 197
Green Rice, 120
Italian Beef Sandwiches, 167
Pepper Beef Goulash, 194
Posole, 290
Puffy Chile Rellenos Casserole, 89
Roasted Red Pepper Sauce, 234
Spice It Up Soup, 272
Stuffed Roast Pepper Soup, 273
Sweet Pepper Chicken, 175
Unstuffed Pepper Soup, 275

PINEAPPLE

Barbecue Sausage Bites, 133
Pineapple Baked Beans, 228
Pineapple Ham Casserole, 55
Pineapple Peach Soup, 310
Pineapple Shrimp Rice Bake, 66
Pineapple Sweet Potatoes, 234
Sweet-and-Sour Chicken, 170
Sweet 'n' Sour Ribs, 210
Sweet-and-Sour Smokies, 142
Teriyaki Pulled Pork Sandwiches, 148
Tropical Tea, 142

PORK (also see Bacon; Ham; Sausage)
Casseroles
Au Gratin Spinach 'n' Pork, 56
Canadian Meat Pie, 27
Golden Pork Chops, 50
Hash Brown Pork Bake, 58
Mexican-Style Pork Chops, 64
Pork and Corn Casserole, 53
Pork Chops with Apple Stuffing, 46
Pork Spanish Rice, 57
Sauerkraut Hot Dish, 60
Zucchini Pork Chop Supper, 61

Slow Cooker
Barbecued Ribs, 224
Busy-Day Barbecued Ribs, 221
Cherry Pork Chops, 214
Cider Pork Roast, 220
Cranberry Pork Roast, 213
Herb Stuffed Chops, 218
Italian Pork Chop Dinner, 220
Kapuzta, 224
Meaty Cassoulet, 212
Michigan Bean Bake, 240
Mushroom Pork Tenderloins, 225
Pennsylvania Pot Roast, 216
Pork and Beef Barbecue, 144
Pork and Pinto Beans, 225
Pork Chop Dinner, 218
Pork Chops with Sauerkraut, 221
Slow-Cooked Pork Barbecue, 160
Southwestern Stew, 224
Sweet 'n' Sour Ribs, 210
Teriyaki Pork Roast, 217
Teriyaki Pulled Pork Sandwiches, 148

Soups
Black-Eyed Pea Soup, 289
Cauliflower Pork Soup, 301
Chili Verde, 370
Cincinnati Chili, 362
Green Chili, 358
Heartwarming Chili, 361
Posole, 290
Provencale Bean Soup, 346
Roast Pork Soup, 286
Split Pea Soup with Meatballs, 294
Zesty Colorado Chili, 364
Zippy Pork Chili, 361

POTATOES (also see Sweet Potatoes)
Amish Breakfast Casserole, 101
Au Gratin Garlic Potatoes, 240
Autumn Chowder, 337
Bacon Potato Chowder, 318
Beef and Potato Moussaka, 34
Broccoli Potato Soup, 310
Cheesy O'Brien Egg Scramble, 92
Cheesy Potatoes, 232
Chili with Potato Dumplings, 368
Chunky Potato Soup, 162
Creamy Ham and Potatoes, 210
Creamy Red Potatoes, 236
Garlic Potato Bake, 110
Greek Shepherd's Pie, 60

Hash Brown Pork Bake, 58
Hearty Hash Brown Dinner, 192
Irish Pie, 55
Knoephla Soup, 312
Mushroom and Potato Chowder, 332
Mushroom Potatoes, 238
Orange-Flavored Beef and Potatoes, 30
Oven Beef Hash, 43
Parmesan Potato Soup, 301
Potato and Cabbage Soup, 297
Potato Cheese Soup, 321
Potato Egg Supper, 100
Potato Puff Casserole, 120
Potato Salmon Casserole, 69
Scalloped Chicken Supper, 10
Scalloped Potatoes, 107
Scalloped Taters, 230
Smoked Sausage Potato Bake, 57
Three's-a-Charm Shamrock Soup, 277
Tuna in the Straw Casserole, 69
Turkey Shepherd's Pie, 6

RICE

Broccoli Rice Casserole, 123
Brown Rice Turkey Soup, 262
Brown Rice Vegetable Casserole, 102
Chicken Gumbo, 256
Colorful Chicken and Rice, 22
Cream of Wild Rice Soup, 325
Creamy Shrimp Rice Bake, 77
Creamy Wild Rice Soup, 296
Curried Chicken Rice Soup, 250
Green Rice, 120
Hearty Wild Rice, 238
Lemony Turkey Rice Soup, 260
Mushroom Wild Rice Bake, 104
Nacho Rice Dip, 136
Pineapple Shrimp Rice Bake, 66
Pinto Beans and Rice, 89
Pork Spanish Rice, 57
Sausage Spanish Rice, 239
Seafood Rice Casserole, 77
Slow-Cooked Cabbage Rolls, 190
Southern Chicken Rice Soup, 257
Stuffed Roast Pepper Soup, 273
Sunday Gumbo, 291
Unstuffed Pepper Soup, 275
Wild Rice Soup, 271
Wild Rice Turkey Dinner, 182

SALMON (see Seafood)

SANDWICHES
Barbecued Chicken Sandwiches, 156
Chili Sandwiches, 150
Italian Beef Sandwiches, 167
Italian Meatball Subs, 158
Italian Sausage Hoagies, 154
Pork and Beef Barbecue, 144
Shredded Beef Sandwiches, 147
Shredded Steak Sandwiches, 150
Slow-Cooked Pork Barbecue, 160
Slow-Cooker Barbecue Beef, 152
Spicy French Dip, 155
Teriyaki Pulled Pork Sandwiches, 148
Turkey Sloppy Joes, 164

SAUSAGE
Casseroles
Bavarian Wiener Supper, 64
Best-Ever Beans and Sausage, 65
Country Cassoulet, 15
Irish Pie, 55
Meat Lover's Pizza Bake, 26
Meatballs Sausage Dinner, 24
Meaty Spinach Manicotti, 62
Overnight Sausage and Grits, 90
Sausage and Broccoli Bake, 58
Sausage Macaroni Bake, 50
Smoked Sausage Potato Bake, 57
Slow Cooker
Barbecue Sausage Bites, 133
Brats 'n' Kraut Supper, 214
Colony Mountain Chili, 160
Hearty Pork 'n' Beans, 235
Hearty Wild Rice, 238
Italian Meatball Subs, 158
Italian Sausage Hoagies, 154
Kapuzta, 224
Meaty Cassoulet, 212
Mushroom Salsa Chili, 147
Party Sausages, 134
Pizza Casserole, 201
Pizza Rigatoni, 216
Polish Kraut and Apples, 222
Sausage Dressing, 238
Sausage Spanish Rice, 239
Simmered Smoked Links, 141
Slow-Cooker Cheese Dip, 132
Sweet-and-Sour Smokies, 142
Sweet 'n' Spicy Meatballs, 140

Soups
Basque Vegetable Soup, 286
Cabbage Sausage Soup, 295
Cajun Corn Soup, 296
French Bread Pizza Soup, 300
Hearty Black-Eyed Pea Soup, 352
Hearty Minestrone Soup, 290
Italian Peasant Soup, 288
Italian Sausage Soup, 293
Kielbasa Bean Soup, 288
Kielbasa Cabbage Soup, 293
Sauerkraut Soup, 295
Sausage Bean Soup, 289
Sausage Kale Soup, 298
Sausage Lentil Soup, 338
Spicy Zucchini Soup, 300
Sunday Gumbo, 291
Zesty Colorado Chili, 364
Zucchini Sausage Soup, 297

SEAFOOD
Casseroles
Angel Hair Shrimp Bake, 73
Catch-of-the-Day Casserole, 70
Crab Quiche Bake, 75
Crab Supreme, 72
Crab Thermidor, 66
Creamy Shrimp Rice Bake, 77
Fish Stick Supper, 72
Florida Seafood Casserole, 70
Flounder Florentine, 78
Padre Island Shells, 68
Pasta Crab Casserole, 78
Pecan Salmon Casserole, 76
Pineapple Shrimp Rice Bake, 66
Potato Salmon Casserole, 69
Seafood Lasagna, 68
Seafood Rice Casserole, 77
Tuna in the Straw Casserole, 69
Tuna Mushroom Casserole, 75
Tuna Spaghetti Pie, 76
Slow Cooker
Herbed Chicken and Shrimp, 172
Hot Crab Spread, 138
Italian Shrimp 'n' Pasta, 170
Salmon Loaf, 184
Shrimp Chowder, 159
Spicy Seafood Stew, 168
Soups
Chicken Gumbo, 256
Chunky Seafood Chowder, 333
Crab Bisque, 318

New England Clam Chowder, 328
Panfish Chowder, 331
Seafood Chowder, 323
Sunday Gumbo, 291

SHRIMP (see Seafood)

SIDE DISHES
Casseroles
Acorn Squash Feta Casserole, 123
Apple Sweet Potato Bake, 120
Asparagus Mushroom Casserole, 107
Asparagus Pea Medley, 117
Autumn Squash, 102
Beefy Eggplant Parmigiana, 105
Biscuit-Topped Tomato Casserole, 115
Broccoli Casserole, 109
Broccoli Rice Casserole, 123
Brown Rice Vegetable Casserole, 102
Calico Squash Casserole, 118
Cheesy Noodle Casserole, 110
Colorful Vegetable Casserole, 108
Creamy Baked Spinach, 112
End of Summer Vegetable Bake, 116
Festive Cauliflower Casserole, 113
Festive Green Bean Casserole, 124
Garden Casserole, 109
Garlic Potato Bake, 110
Green Rice, 120
Hearty Baked Beans, 115
Hungarian Noodle Side Dish, 104
Italian Zucchini Casserole, 121
Mushroom Wild Rice Bake, 104
Pecan Sweet Potato Bake, 118
Potato Puff Casserole, 120
Saucy Green Bean Bake, 113
Scalloped Carrots, 108
Scalloped Potatoes, 107
Special Scalloped Corn, 124
Summer Squash Bake, 112
Sweet Onion Corn Bake, 116
Slow Cooker
Au Gratin Garlic Potatoes, 240
Cheddar Spirals, 234
Cheesy Potatoes, 232
Corn Spoon Bread, 230
Creamy Corn, 240
Creamy Red Potatoes, 236
Hearty Pork 'n' Beans, 235
Hearty Wild Rice, 238
Marmalade Carrots, 232

Michigan Bean Bake, 240
Mushroom Potatoes, 238
Pineapple Baked Beans, 228
Pineapple Sweet Potatoes, 234
Rich Spinach Casserole, 239
Roasted Red Pepper Sauce, 234
Sausage Dressing, 238
Sausage Spanish Rice, 239
Scalloped Taters, 230
Slow-Cooked Sage Dressing, 230
Slow-Cooked Vegetables, 228
Spiced Acorn Squash, 236
Squash Stuffing Casserole, 231
Vegetable Medley, 235
Zippy Bean Stew, 231

SOUPS

Beans & Lentils
Black Bean Zucchini Gazpacho, 348
Campfire Bean 'n' Ham Soup, 348
Chilled Bean Soup, 341
Corn and Bean Soup, 353
Fast Fiesta Soup, 346
Hearty Black Bean Soup, 166
Hearty Black-Eyed Pea Soup, 352
Hearty Lentil Soup, 343
Hearty Navy Bean Soup, 344
Hearty Split Pea Soup, 351
Lemon Lentil Soup, 341
Lentil Vegetable Soup, 345
Lucky Bean Soup, 338
Mexican Bean Barley Soup, 351
Mexican Bean Soup, 343
Mixed Bean Soup, 349
Navy Bean Soup, 349
Navy Bean Vegetable Soup, 151
Peasant Soup, 353
Provencale Bean Soup, 346
Sausage Lentil Soup, 338
Tangy Bean Soup, 164
Two-Bean Vegetable Soup, 166
U.S. Senate Bean Soup, 352
Vegetable Black Bean Soup, 340
White Bean 'n' Ham Soup, 345
White Bean Fennel Soup, 340
Wisconsin Split Pea Soup, 344

Beef & Ground Beef
Barley Peasant Soup, 276
Beef Barley Lentil Soup, 144
Beef Barley Soup, 278
Beef Vegetable Soup, 148
Beefy Minestrone Soup, 282

Beefy Tomato Pasta Soup, 280
Beefy Tortellini Soup, 273
Easy Vegetable Soup, 270
Four-Onion Soup, 271
French Onion Soup, 282
Goulash Soup, 277
Ground Beef Vegetable Soup, 268
Hamburger Garden Soup, 279
Harvest Soup, 280
Homemade Beef Broth, 284
Italian Wedding Soup, 278
Meatball Vegetable Soup, 272
Mushroom Barley Soup, 275
Old-World Tomato Soup, 284
Savory Winter Soup, 156
Scotch Broth Soup, 270
South-of-the-Border Soup, 283
Spice It Up Soup, 272
Stroganoff Soup, 279
Stuffed Roast Pepper Soup, 273
Three's-a-Charm Shamrock Soup, 277
Tortellini Vegetable Soup, 268
Unstuffed Pepper Soup, 275
Vegetable Beef Soup, 285
Veggie Meatball Soup, 163
Wild Rice Soup, 271
Zesty Vegetable Beef Soup, 276

Chicken & Turkey
After-Thanksgiving Turkey Soup, 248
Brown Rice Turkey Soup, 262
Chicken Gumbo, 256
Chicken Noodle Soup, 248
Chicken Soup with Beans, 151
Chicken Soup with Spaetzle, 264
Chicken Soup with Stuffed
   Noodles, 259
Chicken Tomato Vegetable Soup, 146
Chicken Vegetable Soup, 252
Chinese Chicken Soup, 256
Chunky Chicken Soup, 262
Curried Chicken Rice Soup, 250
Flower Garden Soup, 250
Grandma's Chicken 'n' Dumpling
   Soup, 264
Harvest Turkey Soup, 258
Hearty Chicken Noodle Soup, 162
Homemade Chicken Broth, 263
Italian Chicken Soup, 255
Lemony Turkey Rice Soup, 260
Meatball Alphabet Soup, 252
Santa Fe Cheese Soup, 251
Southern Chicken Rice Soup, 257

Southwestern Chicken Soup, 263
Southwestern Turkey Dumpling
   Soup, 251
Tex-Mex Chicken Soup, 267
Turkey Barley Soup, 265
Turkey Meatball Soup, 267
Turkey Noodle Soup, 258
Turkey Soup with Slickers, 256
Turkey Tomato Soup, 255
Vegetable Chicken Noodle Soup, 260
Zesty Chicken Soup, 253

Chili
Barbecued Turkey Chili, 154
Barley Chicken Chili, 369
Bulgur Chili, 354
Chicken Chili, 163
Chicken Chili with Black Beans, 370
Chili Verde, 370
Chili with Potato Dumplings, 368
Cincinnati Chili, 362
Colony Mountain Chili, 160
Corn and Bean Chili, 359
Cowpoke Chili, 359
Five-Can Chili, 365
Green Chili, 358
Heartwarming Chili, 361
Hearty Black Bean Chili, 364
Mushroom Salsa Chili, 147
Red, White and Blue Chili, 363
Roasted Veggie Chili, 357
Round Steak Chili, 358
Salsa Chili, 356
Slow-Cooked Chili, 166
Slow-Cooked White Chili, 155
Speedy Chili, 366
Spicy Beefy Chili, 152
Spicy Turkey Chili, 368
Thick Turkey Bean Chili, 354
30-Minute Chili, 366
Turkey Chili, 159
Vegetarian Chili, 365
White Bean Turkey Chili, 362
White Chili with Chicken, 356
Zesty Colorado Chili, 364
Zippy Pork Chili, 361

Cream Soups & Chowders
Apple Squash Soup, 320
Asparagus Chicken Chowder, 324
Autumn Chowder, 337
Bacon Potato Chowder, 318
Broccoli Soup, 323
Butternut Squash Bisque, 336

Canadian Cheese Soup, 326
Carrot Leek Soup, 321
Chilled Asparagus Soup, 332
Chilled Squash and Carrot Soup, 326
Chunky Seafood Chowder, 333
Crab Bisque, 318
Cream of Cauliflower Soup, 329
Cream of Wild Rice Soup, 325
Creamy Carrot Soup, 334
Creamy Corn Chowder, 328
Creamy Monterey Jack Soup, 336
Creamy Red Pepper Soup, 333
Creamy Tomato Bisque, 331
Curried Pumpkin Soup, 324
Curried Zucchini Soup, 329
Ham 'n' Swiss Soup, 337
Marvelous Mushroom Soup, 334
Mexican Chicken Corn Chowder, 320
Mushroom and Potato Chowder, 332
New England Clam Chowder, 328
Panfish Chowder, 331
Potato Cheese Soup, 321
Seafood Chowder, 323
Shrimp Chowder, 159
Spinach Bisque, 325

Meatless
Apricot Squash Soup, 306
Asparagus Soup, 310
Basil Tomato Soup, 312
Broccoli Potato Soup, 310
Carrot Zucchini Soup, 302
Cauliflower Soup, 307
Cold Raspberry Soup, 305
Creamy Tomato Soup, 306
Freezer Vegetable Soup, 304
Fresh Fruit Soup, 309
Garden Tomato Soup, 304
Itallan Vegetable Soup, 312
Knoephla Soup, 312
Macaroni Minestrone Soup, 313
Onion Tomato Soup, 314
Pineapple Peach Soup, 310
Savory Cheese Soup, 317
Southern Garden Soup, 316
Summer Vegetable Soup, 309
Taco Twist Soup, 314
Tomato Green Bean Soup, 316
Tortellini Soup, 307
Vegetable Bean Soup, 311
Vegetable Broth, 305
Vegetarian Split Pea Soup, 302
Winter Vegetable Soup, 316

PORK, HAM & SAUSAGE
Basque Vegetable Soup, 286
Black-Eyed Pea Soup, 289
Cabbage Sausage Soup, 295
Cajun Corn Soup, 296
Cauliflower Pork Soup, 301
Chunky Potato Soup, 162
Creamy Ham and Asparagus Soup, 298
Creamy Wild Rice Soup, 296
French Bread Pizza Soup, 300
Ham and Lentil Soup, 158
Hearty Ham Borscht, 294
Hearty Minestrone Soup, 290
Italian Peasant Soup, 288
Italian Sausage Soup, 293
Kielbasa Bean Soup, 288
Kielbasa Cabbage Soup, 293
Minestrone Soup, 146
Parmesan Potato Soup, 301
Posole, 290
Potato and Cabbage Soup, 297
Roast Pork Soup, 286
Sauerkraut Soup, 295
Sausage Bean Soup, 289
Sausage Kale Soup, 298
Spicy Zucchini Soup, 300
Split Pea 'n' Ham Soup, 154
Split Pea Soup with Meatballs, 294
Sunday Gumbo, 291
Zucchini Sausage Soup, 297

SPINACH
Au Gratin Spinach 'n' Pork, 56
Creamy Baked Spinach, 112
Flounder Florentine, 78
Italian Wedding Soup, 278
Meaty Spinach Manicotti, 62
Rich Spinach Casserole, 239
Spinach Bisque, 325

SQUASH & ZUCCHINI
Acorn Squash Feta Casserole, 123
Apple Squash Soup, 320
Apricot Squash Soup, 306
Autumn Squash, 102
Black Bean Zucchini Gazpacho, 348
Brunch Strata, 90
Butternut Squash Bisque, 336
Calico Squash Casserole, 118
Carrot Zucchini Soup, 302
Chilled Squash and Carrot Soup, 326
Curried Pumpkin Soup, 324

Curried Zucchini Soup, 329
Hearty Pasta Casserole, 6
Italian Zucchini Casserole, 121
Spiced Acorn Squash, 236
Spicy Zucchini Soup, 300
Squash Stuffing Casserole, 231
Summer Squash Bake, 112
Wild Rice Turkey Dinner, 182
Zucchini Pork Chop Supper, 61
Zucchini Ricotta Bake, 83
Zucchini Sausage Soup, 297

SWEET POTATOES
Apple Ham Bake, 48
Apple Sweet Potato Bake, 120
Pecan Sweet Potato Bake, 118
Pineapple Sweet Potatoes, 234

TOMATOES
Basil Tomato Soup, 312
Beefy Tomato Pasta Soup, 280
Biscuit-Topped Tomato Casserole, 115
Creamy Tomato Bisque, 331
Creamy Tomato Soup, 306
Garden Tomato Soup, 304
Mushroom Salsa Chili, 147
Old-World Tomato Soup, 284
Onion Tomato Soup, 314
Roasted Red Pepper Sauce, 234
Salsa Chili, 356
Slow-Cooked Salsa, 128
Southern Barbecue Spaghetti
    Sauce, 183
Tomato Green Bean Soup, 316
Turkey Tomato Soup, 255

TUNA (see Seafood)

TURKEY (also see Chicken)
Casseroles
All-American Turkey Potpie, 19
Broccoli Turkey Supreme, 20
Cordon Bleu Casserole, 10
Greek Shepherd's Pie, 60
Hearty Pasta Casserole, 6
Italian Turkey and Noodles, 13
Leftover-Turkey Bake, 18
Turkey 'n' Stuffing Pie, 14
Turkey Manicotti, 8
Turkey Potpie, 16
Turkey Shepherd's Pie, 6
Turkey Tetrazzini, 11

Slow Cooker
Barbecued Turkey Chili, 154
Citrus Turkey Roast, 176
Lemony Turkey Breast, 182
Southern Barbecue Spaghetti
Sauce, 183
Southwest Turkey Stew, 178
Turkey Chili, 159
Turkey in Cream Sauce, 178
Turkey Sloppy Joes, 164
Turkey Thigh Supper, 172
Wild Rice Turkey Dinner, 182

Soups
After-Thanksgiving Turkey Soup, 248
Brown Rice Turkey Soup, 262
Chili with Potato Dumplings, 368
Harvest Turkey Soup, 258
Lemony Turkey Rice Soup, 260
Meatball Alphabet Soup, 252
Southwestern Turkey Dumpling
Soup, 251
Spice It Up Soup, 272
Spicy Turkey Chili, 368
Thick Turkey Bean Chili, 354
Turkey Barley Soup, 265
Turkey Meatball Soup, 267
Turkey Noodle Soup, 258

Turkey Soup with Slickers, 256
Turkey Tomato Soup, 255
White Bean Turkey Chili, 362

VEGETABLES (also see specific kinds)
Basque Vegetable Soup, 286
Beef Vegetable Soup, 148
Beef Veggie Casserole, 28
Beefy Minestrone Soup, 282
Brown Rice Vegetable Casserole, 102
Chicken Tomato Vegetable Soup, 146
Chicken Vegetable Soup, 252
Colorful Vegetable Casserole, 108
Corn Bread Veggie Bake, 80
Easy Vegetable Soup, 270
End of Summer Vegetable Bake, 116
Flower Garden Soup, 250
Freezer Vegetable Soup, 304
Garden Casserole, 109
Ground Beef Vegetable Soup, 268
Hamburger Garden Soup, 279
Harvest Soup, 280
Harvest Turkey Soup, 258
Hearty Beef Vegetable Stew, 206
Hearty Minestrone Soup, 290
Italian Vegetable Soup, 312

Lentil Vegetable Soup, 345
Macaroni Minestrone Soup, 313
Meatball Vegetable Soup, 272
Minestrone Soup, 146
Navy Bean Vegetable Soup, 151
Roasted Veggie Chili, 357
Six-Veggie Bake, 100
Slow-Cooked Vegetables, 228
Southern Garden Soup, 316
Summer Vegetable Soup, 309
Tortellini Vegetable Soup, 268
Two-Bean Vegetable Soup, 166
Vegetable Bean Soup, 311
Vegetable Beef Soup, 285
Vegetable Beef Stew, 196
Vegetable Black Bean Soup, 340
Vegetable Broth, 305
Vegetable Chicken Noodle Soup, 260
Vegetable Medley, 235
Vegetarian Chili, 365
Veggie Meatball Soup, 163
Veggie Noodle Ham Casserole, 46
Winter Vegetable Soup, 316
Zesty Vegetable Beef Soup, 276